PSYCHOLOGY LIBRARY EDITIONS:
NEUROPSYCHOLOGY

Volume 11

COGNITIVE APPROACHES IN NEUROPSYCHOLOGICAL REHABILITATION

COGNITIVE APPROACHES IN NEUROPSYCHOLOGICAL REHABILITATION

Edited by
XAVIER SERON AND GÉRARD DELOCHE

LONDON AND NEW YORK

First published in 1989 by Lawrence Erlbaum Associates, Inc.

This edition first published in 2019
by Routledge
2 Park Square, Milton Park, Abingdon, Oxon OX14 4RN

and by Routledge
711 Third Avenue, New York, NY 10017

Routledge is an imprint of the Taylor & Francis Group, an informa business

© 1989 by Lawrence Erlbaum Associates, Inc.

All rights reserved. No part of this book may be reprinted or reproduced or utilised in any form or by any electronic, mechanical, or other means, now known or hereafter invented, including photocopying and recording, or in any information storage or retrieval system, without permission in writing from the publishers.

Trademark notice: Product or corporate names may be trademarks or registered trademarks, and are used only for identification and explanation without intent to infringe.

British Library Cataloguing in Publication Data
A catalogue record for this book is available from the British Library

ISBN: 978-1-138-48894-6 (Set)
ISBN: 978-0-429-45935-1 (Set) (ebk)
ISBN: 978-1-138-59494-4 (Volume 11) (hbk)
ISBN: 978-0-429-48851-1 (Volume 11) (ebk)

Publisher's Note
The publisher has gone to great lengths to ensure the quality of this reprint but points out that some imperfections in the original copies may be apparent.

Disclaimer
The publisher has made every effort to trace copyright holders and would welcome correspondence from those they have been unable to trace.

COGNITIVE APPROACHES IN
NEUROPSYCHOLOGICAL
REHABILITATION

Edited by

Xavier Seron

*Unité de Neuropsychologie Expérimentale
de L'Adulte, Belgium*

Gérard Deloche

*Institut National de la Santé et de la
Recherche Médicale, Paris*

LEA LAWRENCE ERLBAUM ASSOCIATES, PUBLISHERS
1989 Hillsdale, New Jersey   Hove and London

Copyright © 1989 by Lawrence Erlbaum Associates, Inc.
All rights reserved. No part of this book may be reproduced in
any form, by photostat, microfilm, retrieval system, or any other
means, without the prior written permission of the publisher.

Lawrence Erlbaum Associates, Inc., Publishers
365 Broadway
Hillsdale, New Jersey 07642

Library of Congress Cataloging-in-Publication Data

Cognitive approaches in neuropsychological rehabilitation.

(Neuropsychology and neurolinguistics)
Includes bibliographies and indexes.
1. Cognitive therapy.   2. Clinical neuropsychology.
I. Seron, Xavier.   II. Deloche, Gérard.   III. Series.
[DNLM: 1. Cognition Disorders — rehabilitation.   2.Com-
municative Disorders — rehabilitation.   3. Neuropsychology
— methods.   WL 340 C676]
RC489.C63C625   1989   616.89'14   89-1236
ISBN 0-89859-615-7

Printed in the United States of America
10 9 8 7 6 5 4 3 2 1

Contents

INTRODUCTION
Xavier Seron and Gérard Deloche

1

1. SPONTANEOUS RECOVERY AND LANGUAGE REHABILITATION
Anna Basso

17

Spontaneous Recovery   *17*
Aphasia Rehabilitation   *22*
Cognitive Rehabilitation   *27*
Recovery of Function   *28*
Right Hemisphere   *31*
Concluding Remarks   *33*
References   *34*

2. MODELS FOR THERAPY
David Howard and Karalyn Patterson

39

Why Use Processing Models?   *40*
Different Approaches to Treatment   *45*
Evaluating the Effects of Treatment   *54*
Concluding Comments   *59*
References   *61*

v

vi CONTENTS

3. SOME ISSUES IN THE NEUROPSYCHOLOGICAL
   REHABILITATION OF ANOMIA   65
   Ruth Lesser

   Visual Naming Versus Naming in Conversation: Same or
   Different? *66*
   A Component Model of Visual Naming *69*
   Application of the Model to Naming Disorders *72*
   Dynamics of Naming Not Captured by the Model *84*
   Implications for Intervention *87*
   Conclusion *98*
   References *99*

4. REORGANIZATION THERAPY FOR MEMORY
   IMPAIRMENTS   105
   Martial Van der Linden and Marie-Anne Van der Kaa

   A Cognitive Approach to Memory *106*
   The Neuropsychology of Memory *112*
   Reeducational Strategies for Memory Disorders *119*
   Conclusion *146*
   Acknowledgments *150*
   References *150*

5. A TREATMENT FOR SURFACE DYSLEXIA   159
   Max Coltheart and Sally Byng

   Rehabilitation *161*
   Case Report *161*
   Postscript: Visual Word Recognition and Distributed
   Processing *170*
   References *173*

6. WRITING REHABILITATION IN BRAIN-DAMAGED
   ADULT PATIENTS: A COGNITIVE APPROACH   175
   Sergio Carlomagno and Vincenzo Parlato

   Writing Rehabilitation: A Survey of the Literature *176*
   The Reorganizational Rationale: A Single Case Study *182*
   General Discussion *200*
   Acknowledgments *203*
   References *204*

CONTENTS vii

7. COORDINATION OF TWO REORGANIZATION THERAPIES IN A DEEP DYSLEXIC PATIENT WITH ORAL NAMING DISORDERS 211

Noëlle Bachy-Langedock and Marie-Pierre de Partz

Clinical Case *214*
Conclusions *244*
References *245*
Appendix *247*

8. REEDUCATION OF NUMBER TRANSCODING MECHANISMS: A PROCEDURAL APPROACH 249

Gérard Deloche, Xavier Seron, and Isabelle Ferrand

Testing Batteries for the Investigation of the Patient's Numerical Skills *253*
First Therapy Program: From Numbers to Numerals *256*
Second Therapy Program: From Numeral to Number *276*
Conclusion *282*
References *286*

9. A RETROSPECTIVE ANALYSIS OF A SINGLE CASE NEGLECT THERAPY: A POINT OF THEORY 289

Xavier Seron, Gérard Deloche, and Francoise Coyette

Neglect Recovery *289*
Neglect Reeducation *291*
Critical Appraisal *296*
Case Description *299*
Therapy *303*
Discussion *309*
References *314*

10. PRAGMATICS AND COGNITION IN TREATMENT OF LANGUAGE DISORDERS 317

G. Albyn Davis

Cognition and Pragmatics *317*
A Disorder of Pragmatic Skills *323*
General Implications for Rehabilitation of Aphasia *326*
Pragmatic Treatment *333*
Epilogue: Coordinating Responsibilities *347*
References *348*

viii   CONTENTS

11. THE EMERGENCE OF MICROCOMPUTER
     TECHNOLOGY IN NEUROPSYCHOLOGICAL THERAPIES   *355*
     Larry Fisher

     What Is Computer Assisted Cognitive Rehabilitation?   *357*
     Why Use a Computer?   *359*
     How Did It Begin?   *361*
     What Is Available?   *365*
     What Does the Future Hold?   *368*
     References   *373*
     Appendix 11.1   *377*
     Appendix 11.2   *377*
     Appendix 11.3   *380*

12. COGNITIVE NEUROPSYCHOLOGY AND
     REHABILITATION: AN UNFULFILLED PROMISE?   *383*
     Alfonso Caramazza

     Cognitive Neuropsychology   *384*
     Conclusion   *395*
     Acknowledgment   *397*
     References   *398*

AUTHOR INDEX   *399*

SUBJECT INDEX   *409*

ACKNOWLEDGMENTS

This publication has been supported by the grant from the "Loterie Nationale de Belgique."

The editors are deeply grateful to Marie-Rose Peeters for her careful typing of many chapters and for her painstaking and invaluable assistance during the production of the book.

Introduction

Xavier Seron
Gérard Deloche

This book presents some recent attempts to reconsider neuropsychological rehabilitation in the light of the theoretical approach formulated by cognitive psychology. This perspective in reeducation is radically new, even though Luria's work in the 1960s constituted the first coherent attempt to link a specified psychological framework of neuropsychological disorders to the elaboration of rehabilitation strategies (Luria, 1963).

The term "cognitive" is a label used so widely in neuropsychology that it requires clarification. In a very general sense, all treatment in neuropsychology can be called cognitive merely because the disorders with which they are concerned are cognitive in nature. In such a broad sense, the word "cognitive" offers no precise theoretical denotation of the treatment. The perspective adopted here is quite different: We call "cognitive" those therapeutic approaches that are explicitly based on a model describing the organization of the cognitive apparatus viewed as a complex architecture of at least partially autonomous functional units. This therapeutic approach presumes that neuropsychological disorders reflect the total cognitive apparatus minus specific altered components. In such a perspective a therapy must be designed on the basis of hypotheses on the locus of the defective and intact processing components. Such an approach can only be elaborated on a single-case basis.

In this introduction, we will stress the conditions of the emergence of cognitive-oriented therapies in standard clinical practice and the consequence for the therapists' work. Such an emphasis on everyday practice is necessary because, even apart from the concrete modifications that may necessarily result from a change in theoretical perspective, the development of truly cognitivist therapies would otherwise be impossible or would risk being limited to rare and exceptional single case reports. Interesting though they may be on a theoretical level, they are without benefit to patients on a much larger scale. We will thus consider in succession the usual practical steps present in all therapeutic approaches—diagnosis, treatment, and evaluation—to determine at each level the specific and concrete consequences of a cognitive approach. Of course, cognitive rehabilitation may in turn give rise to modifications in the theoretical considerations on which they were based.

In this introduction, we will not discuss in detail the critical differences between cognitive versus stimulation therapies or between cognitive versus behavioral therapies. It suffices to stress that the main characteristic of a cognitive reeducative approach is that it is elaborated with reference to a model that depicts the processing of information subjacent to the different psychological activities and this in function of hypotheses about the location in such a cognitive architecture of the impaired components responsible for the apparent surface disorders. Facilitation and stimulation approaches like those formulated by Schuell (1974); Wepman (1951) and Ducarne (1986) (in the French literature) are largely dependent on the classic syndromic classification of the disorders and on the grossly associationist interpretation that is linked to the anatomoclinical approaches. As for behavioral approaches, the contrast is easier to describe: Behavioral therapies are almost by definition neutral as regards the structure and the organization of the mental processes underlying behavior (normal or defective), and, as a matter of fact, their impact in neuropsychological therapy has been mainly methodological (Seron, 1987).

PRETHERAPEUTIC EVALUATION BEYOND DIAGNOSIS

A usual step preceding any therapy is establishing the diagnosis. This step has been considered a necessary prerequisite because treatments were generally framed according to the classical anatomoclinical syndromes. For example, in the language area different reeducative methods have been proposed according to the main aphasia types or to semiological profiles defined in reference to gross language functions, such as repetition, oral comprehension, verbal production, naming, writing, reading, and so on. Much criticism has been leveled at these

INTRODUCTION 3

syndromic or semiological approaches in therapy. They have emerged from two very different theoretical considerations: On the one hand, it has been argued that semiological/syndromic approaches are not sufficiently precise or justified on a psychological processing level; on the other, it has been argued that they lack ecological utility. We will consider later on the problem of the ecological value of the therapy (see also Davis' contribution to this book), but we will first discuss the limits of the classic approaches from a cognitive perspective.

There is strong evidence that the syndromic approach has consisted in grouping together patients who present highly heterogeneous deficits at the psychological and anatomical levels and that the behavioral categorization, as well as the neuroanatomical implementation, of these classifications, was suspect (Caramazza, 1984; Marshall, 1986). Whatever their historical interest, the classic syndromes were not established according to present-day hypotheses describing the locus of disturbed treatment of information resulting from a cerebral lesion. Being unable to capture the nature of the subjacent disorders responsible for the impaired and preserved processing, they can no longer inspire therapeutic strategies based on a psychological interpretation of the disorders. There is thus no longer any impelling necessity to diagnose an anatomopathological clinical condition in order to devise a course of therapy.

The first temptation is for the clinician to replace the old taxonomy by a new cognitive one and then to generate specific and more appropriate reeducative methods in function of it. However, there are several reasons why we doubt that such a change in the categorization of the patient's condition would constitute a suitable heuristic course for the evolution of therapy or that such a syndrome reorganization based on information processing models is presently feasible.

First, such taxonomy changes are only conceivable in very restricted areas of neuropsychological disorders, the putative candidates being reading, writing, anomia, and perhaps memory disorders.

Second, even if the initial descriptions of reading disorders could give the appearance of the emergence of a new taxonomy, the main interest of the cognitive approach has not been to isolate specific disorders in order to establish new pathological categories but to relate the observed disorders to models of the cognitive operations implied in normal reading. Further, by a kind of dialogue between the analysis of single-case behavior and the predictions of the various models, the object is to specify and reframe the functioning components and the general architecture of the models. If, for example, so many discussions have concentrated on such reading disorders as deep, surface, and phonological alexia (Coltheart, Patterson and Marshall, 1980; Patterson, Marshall and Coltheart, 1985), it has not been to establish their existence as frequent and well isolated syndromes, but it is because of the arguments they furnish in favor of the dual route reading models (Coltheart et al., 1980). At present, it does seem that most of these entity disorders are the result of different subjacent processing deficits. They could thus be divided into several subtypes, and some of them (i.e., deep dyslexia) are in fact the results of simultaneous but different processing deficits (Patterson, 1981; Coltheart et al., 1980).

Third, all we know and do not know of the organization of the cognitive processes converge to underline the subtlety and the complexity of their organization. The unavoidable consequence of such evidence is, if one considers that the problem of taxonomy is still relevant, that we shall be rapidly confronted with a massive multiplication of qualitatively different disorders. A taxonomic point of view thus risks being very uneconomical. Of course, given the existence of independent regularities in the pathological conditions linked to etiological, genetic, and biological factors, some processing deficits would appear more frequently than others, and some logically predictible deficits would never or very rarely appear. Nevertheless, and whatever its utility could be, at present any predictions about what such a new taxonomy would be are premature and implicitly assume that there is a one-to-one correspondence between the nature and the location of the cerebral dysfunction and the resulting processing deficits, which is, of course a controversial issue (Mehler, Morton, and Jusczyk, 1984).

Consequently, the clinician is in a very uncomfortable position: First we propose that he or she abandon the classical taxonomy, and second, that he or she not try to find security in a new one. In our view, what the clinician has to do is operate as researchers and try to interpret the patient's disorders by reference to one or more hypothetical models of what is presently known about the normal processing systems. Such an approach is clearly presented in the chapter of this book by Howard and Patterson. Here, we will discuss only its feasibility in everyday clinical practice.

A major objection to the cognitive perspective is that an approach requiring an interpretation of the disorder that has to be reinitialized with each single case is time-consuming and unrealistic. Classic approaches that apply ready-made exercises or training modules according to semiological or severity level criteria issuing from a standardized pretherapeutic evaluation protocol seem to offer a more pragmatic value for routine practice. Nevertheless, one must avoid confounding the rapidity of an intervention with its efficacy. First of all, the efficacy of neuropsychological interventions is presently not at all well established, and some studies (even if they themselves are liable to criticism) have questioned the utility of the intervention of therapists (Meikle et al., 1979; David, Enderby and Bainton, 1982; Lincoln et al., 1984; see also Basso, Chapter 1, this volume). Second, the presence in the cognitive approach of a long pretherapeutic evaluation period is less dramatic if one considers that the patient is at least regularly stimulated during these evaluation sessions. He thus receives a kind of stimulation therapy that is, in fact, the core of many traditional therapeutic approaches (Wepman, 1951; Schuell, 1974). Thus, the best solution (if one agrees that therapy has to be framed according to some hypothesis in function of the nature of the processing deficits) is to take enough time to be able to generate sufficiently precise hypotheses. As a matter of fact, the main obstacle is psychoaffective: Clinicians must learn to work without anxiety because they do not have at the outset of their assessment an appropriate, ready-made solution. The counterargument "the sooner a therapy begins, the better it is" thus need not be considered too seriously, and if, during the spontaneous recovery period, what is important is that the patient be stimulated, then the cognitive approach certainly does this before the "official" therapy begins.

The cognitive approach we recommend consists of searching, for each individual case, the nature of the underlying deficit by reference to the normal multicomponent information processing system and the subject's previous preferred strategies. Yet, such an approach is constrained by different factors including:

1. The progress made in psychology in the elaboration of sufficiently precise cognitive models in relation to various cognitive domains
2. The actual penetration into neuropsychology of the cognitive approaches developed for normal behavior
3. The single or multiple processing deficits presented by the patient
4. The different specific strategies the subjects can use in particular tasks

The first two constraints mean that it is not possible to elaborate detailed cognitive therapies if there is no model of the normal information processing system or if no relationship has been established between models elaborated for normal behavior and neuropsychological disorders. It is thus not mere chance that the best illustrations of cognitive therapies in neuropsychology are in the areas of writing and reading disorders (Hatfield, 1982; Beauvois and Derouesné, 1982; de Partz, 1986; and, in the present work Howard and Patterson, Chapter 2; Carlomagno and Parlato, Chapter 6; Bachy-Langedock and de Partz, Chapter 7; Coltheart and Byng, Chapter 5) and number transcoding disorders (see Deloche, Seron and Ferrand, Chapter 8). Nevertheless, clinicians do not generally have the opportunity to choose what disorders to reeducate, and it does not seem to be legitimate, at least for deontological reason, to limit the therapy to those deficits areas for which there are detailed information processing models.

Another problem is that there is no a priori definition of what would be a sufficiently detailed information processing model usable for reeducation. Little has been done in some deficit areas, and there certainly is no organized theoretical framework. In such cases, the clinician can only test partial hypotheses (see Seron, Deloche and Coyette later, on hemineglect therapy and the very interesting and detailed work on syntax of Byng and Coltheart (in press) and Byng (1985)). Finally, in cases where no advances have been made in the theoretical interpretation of the disorder, the clinician can always have recourse to traditional approaches.

Another general limitation of research in neuropsychology (cognitive or whatever) that has a clear influence on therapy is the lack of studies focusing on the evolution of the disorders. For reasons of simplicity, researchers have preferred to analyze stable pathological conditions that permit reliable analyses over sufficiently long periods of time. However, clinicians are generally confronted with the disorders near the lesion onset, that is, in a period where the pathological condition is susceptible to evolution. Such a lack of longitudinal analyses hampers not only clinicians but also scientific progress in neuropsychology in general. One may hope that this state of affairs will soon change. The major consequence for clinical evaluation is that, in case of rapid evolution of the disorders, the condition of the patient must be regularly reassessed and, in some cases, it could be more economical to wait until some stabilization occurs before attempting a detailed cognitive assessment.

In summary, pretherapeutic assessment is viewed not as a taxonomic categorization but as a theoretically oriented testing of hypotheses conducted with an individual patient. Viewed in such a way, clinical practice is profoundly modified.

INTRODUCTION   7

1. The clinician in the line of his or her own objectives (i.e., therapy) must approach each patient like a researcher by considering the disorder to be a true theoretical question to be solved.
2. The clinician's activity is centered around the analysis of the single case, which clearly constitutes another resemblance to the in-depth analysis of single cases favored by the cognitive approach in research.
3. If theoretically motivated, the treatment becomes a means of checking the theoretical hypothesis, even if falsification is clearly more difficult to establish in therapy than in experimental work.
4. More important, the results of such theoretically motivated single-case therapies can be cumulative; that is, the reasons for success or failure can be interpreted and thus generate new strategies for future therapy.

TREATMENT

The connection between the treatment and the pretherapeutic evaluation is not at all simple. The evaluation offers hypotheses on the locus of the processing components that are defective and on those that are intact. Yet the degree of disturbance of a processing component may vary, and there probably is a continuum between a total alteration of a processing component and intermediate situations in which, under some facilitation conditions or contexts, a component could still operate partially or correctly. Another and perhaps similar distinction is regularly proposed between degradation of the structure of stored information and a disturbance of access to still preserved information. Shallice (1987) has offered criteria for semantic processing for distinguishing a loss of stored information from an access difficulty. He argues that consistency of item errors across several test sessions and across modality, as well as inefficacy of facilitation procedures, may characterize a degraded memory store. However, because one may equally suggest that a structural description of stored information can always be interpreted in procedural steps, the distinction is not so important theoretically. Nevertheless, from a therapeutic point of view, the distinction may be heuristic: In cases of loss of stored information or radical alteration of a processing component, a reestablishment rationale or a detour strategy may be used, whereas in cases of access difficulty or partial alteration of a processing component, a facilitation rationale may be more effective.

We will not discuss here what kind of reestablishment, reorganization, or facilitation procedures have been developed in cognitive rehabilitation neuropsychology. This book contains detailed illustrations of such procedures for writing (Carlomagno and Parlato, Chapter 6), reading and anomia (Bachy-Langedock and de Partz, Chapter 7; Coltheart and Byng, Chapter 5) number transcoding (Deloche, Seron, and Ferrand, Chapter 8), as well as extended evaluation of cognitive therapies in the field of memory disorders (Van Der Linden and Van Der Kaa, Chapter 4) anomia (Lesser, Chapter 3) and language at large (Howard and Patterson, Chapter 2). We will only comment on some aspects of the therapeutic intervention not considered in most chapters of this book, that is, therapies of disorders that result from the alteration of less specific subjacent components, such as attentional deficits. Indeed, there is evidence that the main difficulties the patient encounters in some pathological conditions (for example, severe head trauma) are not restricted to specific activities, such as language production, reasoning, object recognition, gestures, and the like, but result from attention problems. As suggested by Posner and Boies (1971), at least three main aspects of attentional processing must be considered: alertness or arousal, selective attention, and vigilance or conscious attention. Some rehabilitation programs, like those developed by Ben-Yishay, Piasetsky, and Rattock (1987), propose exercises structured more or less according to such a partition of attentional processes. Whatever the present difficulties in determining for each patient what component of the attentional system is altered, the problem of the allocation of attentional resources may be a central issue in any kind of therapy, regardless of its specificity. It is, for example, clearly not sufficient to teach a patient to encode new information by an imagery strategy in case of memory disorders or to teach an alexic patient to use a letter-name code to restructure the nonlexical route. It is also necessary to automate these strategies so that they require the allocation of progressively fewer attentional resources to reestablish efficacious behavior. Of course, no a priori criteria can determine how intensive a treatment would have to be to guarantee the automation of the new restructured, reestablished, or facilitated processing. Nevertheless, behavioral modification techniques, such as the determination during therapy of various criteria of response to be attained, could be useful. Moreover, the level of efficiency required should take into consideration progressive diminution of the attentional resources needed to execute the exercises. This problem of progressive automation of the new processing, which has been discussed in detail by Luria (Luria, 1963) under the label of internaliza-

INTRODUCTION 9

tion, is presently being given too little attention by cognitive therapists. For example, the level of automation of a new strategy may be able to be evaluated by measuring the degree of interference caused by the execution in parallel of concurrent tasks requiring more or less similar processing components.

POSTTHERAPEUTIC EVALUATION

All the chapters of this book discuss the evaluation problem in depth. Two main points are regularly stressed.

First, the efficacy of a therapy must be demonstrated. It must be clearly distinguished from spontaneous recovery or the results of general stimulation, the requirement being the ability to demonstrate that progress is present and that it is the result of therapy.

Second, efficacy must be evaluated on a large behavioral scale ranging from the stimuli that have been used in therapy to other stimuli or tasks not trained but sharing processing components with the therapy tasks (the transfer problem). However, it should be stressed that the effect of a therapy must also be evaluated in daily life situations (as clearly shown in the chapters by Davis; Van Der Linden and Van Der Kaa).

For the first point, several authors have indicated the kind of methodology—multiple baseline measurement and crossover treatment design—that has to be developed to be able to establish a causal relation between the treatment and the progress (Lapointe, 1977; Seron, 1987; Coltheart, 1983; and Howard and Patterson, Chapter 2). Apart from these methodological requirements, there are other ways to demonstrate the specific influence of a therapy. One way for therapies that consist of teaching the patient new processing strategies may be to evaluate the performance in contexts or conditions in which the new learned strategy could not be used or is not efficacious. Beauvois and Derouesné (1982), for example, have presented a reeducation of a bilateral tactile anomia. The treatment consisted of teaching the patient to name objects he palpated by elaborating an intermediate covert visual representation of the shape and then by naming that visual representation. The results these authors obtained with this visual relay therapy were not only good but were in themselves indicative of the specificity of the effects they obtained in that the difficulties the patient still presented after therapy were restricted to objects such as pieces of cloth for which mental visualization could offer no shape discriminating information. Another control method is to prevent the use of the new learned strategy to demonstrate that the strategy is the cause of progress. For example, one may ask the patient to apply the new strategy in a situation for which the strategy would be difficult or impossible to realize. If one wants to demonstrate that the progress observed in memory therapy is due to the patient's use of a mental visual imagery strategy during information encoding, one may ask the patient to encode or retrieve information in situations in which he is required to master another task demanding visual processing. To be sure that the interference effect is specific and not simply due to a complexity factor, one could also confront the patient with another divided attentional task not related to visual imagery, in which case no bottleneck of attentional resources in visual processing is present and the learned visual encoding strategy could thus still operate.

Another important point in the causal analysis of a treatment is related to the technique of intermediate evaluation of progress at each pertinent step during the therapy. If the progress evaluated at intermediate steps concerns specific structural dimensions of stimuli or tasks that have been trained, one may conclude that this progress resulted from the therapy, at least if the progression expected in therapy does not mimic progression expected from spontaneous recovery.

The second evaluation problem (very evident for any expert clinician) raises the question of the ecological validity of very pointillistic cognitive approaches, such as those presented or discussed in this book. The problem of the patient's adaptation to daily life situations cannot be limited to compensation strategies, that is, to those treatments whereby one tries either to modify the environmental variables that cause problems for the patients or to enhance alternative adaptive behavior (e.g., by replacing verbal by gestural communication or memory encoding by a diary). The question of the ecological validity of a therapy concerns all kinds of therapy, whatever their specific theoretical background.

The difficulty is obvious here: Cognitive psychologists usually limit themselves to carrying out experiments in very simplified and well-controlled laboratory situations. Their model of the architecture of the mind has been elaborated to understand and integrate only experimental data, so the question of the generality of their findings and theoretical background is still largely open. Nevertheless, there is presently in cognitive psychology a tendency to move out of the laboratory, and such an enlargement of the field of psychological analysis has proved to be interesting for practical as well as theoretical reasons. In memory research, for example, concepts such as absent mindedness and planning of actions (Reason, 1979, 1984), as well as the distinction between retrospective and prospective memory, have clearly emerged from observation of everyday memory functioning. In language, the appearance of the pragmatic orientation has generated a great amount of theoretical research and studies that focus on the everyday functioning of language processing in natural communication situations such as conversation and dialogue (see Davis, Chapter 10). The problem, as noted by Baddeley (1984), Baddeley and Wilkins (1984), and Van Der Linden and Van Der Kaa (Chapter 4) is not to oppose laboratory work to natural observation but to develop a unitary theoretical framework for both kinds of data.

A first step in this direction would be to use the existing theories that have issued from classic laboratory paradigms as the relevant theoretical background and to confront them with natural situations. Another and complementary step would be to take pertinent and unexplored data observed in everyday situations and to try to clarify and identify their processing components by creating new laboratory paradigms to deal with them. The solution will have to derive from constant interaction between laboratory study and natural observation. There is no reason to think that the same integrative work could not be done in neuropsychological therapies. The problem is not to eliminate pointillistic cognitive therapies (for example, by stressing their artificial character) in favor of more pragmatic approaches, but to try to clarify their ecological relevance and to examine what kind of everyday difficulties encountered by patients are being neglected in specific processing-oriented cognitive therapies. Whatever the enormous complexity of the problem and the complex chain of assumptions between a cognitive analysis of neuropsychological impairments in the laboratory and the disabilities as they appear in daily life activities, we think that the cognitive perspective is better able to deal with these questions than the classical taxonomist or biologically oriented neuropsychology. Variables, such as allocation of attentional resources, time pressure, and the influence of context in the triggering of top-down versus bottom-up processing, may well constitute some exploratory ways for dealing with differences between the laboratory and daily life.

A MICROCOMPUTER REVOLUTION?

Even though this book is not devoted to the introduction of the microcomputer technology in practice and research in neuropsychology, we think it appropriate to devote a chapter to this topic because the emergence of microcomputers will necessarily cause practical modifications and theoretical reconsiderations in neuropsychological re-education. Beyond technical considerations, the main advantage of computers probably resides in the clear specifications that pro-gramers need. These constraints offer an opportunity to neuropsy-chologists to clarify and reformulate the body of their knowledge and theoretical frameworks. But it also involves the danger of taking for granted computerized analyses without considering the precise the-oretical issues underlying the logical structure of the individual pro-grams.

Of course, microcomputer-administered testing and training exer-cises ensure consistency of presentation conditions, measure subtle processing time variations, and allow subjects to work independently, provided that real-time control procedures are implemented. More important, adaptative programs may automatically adjust the diffi-culty levels of rehabilitation exercises and select the set of assessment tests in function of the subject's performance. However, the classic paper and pencil exercises cannot be simply transferred to microcom-puters without careful reassessment (Beaumont, 1982) and there is often the danger that patients would be persuaded that improving scores in a computer setting reflects a general recovery, although it is only a task-dependent effect. Due to the intersubject variability of impaired profiles, it seems quite unrealistic and theoretically un-justified to try to construct training programs where neither the struc-ture of the exercises nor the item lists can be tailored to the particular patient's case. In this respect, more sophisticated programing lan-guages should be developed together with easily accessible databases to feed special purpose testing and rehabilitation batteries (Coltheart, 1981). The availability of new input/output microcomputer devices, such as touch sensitive screens, speech synthesizers, or analyzers, will expand their areas of application, which were initially restricted to visual/auditory stimulation and manual responses (Seron, Deloche, Moulard & Rousselle, 1980; Katz, 1986). Computer simulation of normal functioning should lead to fine-grained information process-ing analyses and precise classification of cognitive mechanisms that may have practical implications in the design of training programs, such as the kind of mental prosthesis for lexical retrieval that has benefited anomic patients (Colby, Christinaz, Parkinson, Graham & Krapf, 1981). This rehabilitation procedure was a successful attempt to effect a cognitive transfer from the search algorithm implemented on a microcomputer to the patient's spontaneous processing. The scope of human-machine interactions has recently been widened by the demonstration that patients might be taught programing lan-guages (Glisky, Schacter, & Tulving, 1986).

Some of these issues are reviewed in Fisher's chapter. A retrospective and prospective historical account of microcomputer-based therapies is presented with detailed practical information on the available software and a discussion of the implications of the involvement of microcomputers in neuropsychological rehabilitation practice.

CONCLUSION

One of the main practical consequence of the emergence of a cognitive point of view in therapy has been the stress on the intrinsic complexity of any neuropsychological therapy that must move from a taxonomic classification as a key to addressing a specific therapy to a hypothetical-deductive approach, which, in the context of an information processing model, produces hypotheses on the nature of the deficits.

However, is it reasonable to ask clinicians to read regularly all the scientific literature in neuropsychology in order to elaborate adequate therapies? Moreover, because it is common for a clinician in the same day to treat in succession an alexic patient, an anomic patient, a dysarthric patient, a patient with an attentional problem, and a patient with a memory deficit, is it reasonable to think that the therapist could sufficiently master the theoretically relevant information in all these areas? We hardly think so. The emergence of cognitive therapies, therefore, requires professional and institutional modification. First, therapists must specialize. Such a situation occurs in every discipline as the scientific database expands. In medicine, there are several specialities; why not specialties in cognitive rehabilitation? Second, and as a consequence, cognitive therapy must develop in centers where there are a sufficient number of therapists capable of working together. Third, a new profession may be created, that of research therapist, whose main job would be to develop new ideas in therapy by linking together research in neuropsychology and clinical intervention. Without such institutional and professional modifications, cognitive therapies risk remaining an atypical and very rare professional activity.

ACKNOWLEDGMENTS

The editors are deeply grateful to Marie-Rose Peeters for her careful typing of many chapters and for her painstaking and invaluable assistance during the production of the book.

14 SERON AND DELOCHE

This publication has been supported by a grant from the "Loterie Nationale de Belgique."

REFERENCES

Baddeley, A. (1984). Memory theory and memory therapy. In B. A. Wilson & N. Moffat (Eds.), *Clinical Management of memory problems* (pp. 5–27). London: Croom Helm.

Baddeley, A., & Wilkins, A. (1984). Taking memory out of the laboratory. In J. E. Harris & P. E. Morris (Eds.), *Everyday memory, actions and absent-mindedness* (pp. 1–17). London: Academic Press.

Beaumont, J. G. (1982). System requirements for interactive testing. *International Journal of Man-Machine Studies, 17*, 311–320.

Beauvois, M. F., & Derouesné, J. (1982). Recherche en neuropsychologie et rééducation: quels rapports? [Research in Neuropsychology and Reeducation: What Relationships?] In X. Seron & C. Laterre (Eds.), *Rééduquer le cerveau.* (pp. 163–189). Bruxelles: Mardaga.

Ben-Yishay, Y., Piasetsky, E. B., & J. Rattock (1987). A systematic method for ameliorating disorders in basic attention. In M. J. Meiler, A. L. Benton, & L. Diller (Eds.), *Neuropsychological rehabilitation* (pp. 165–181). Edinburgh: Churchill Livingstone.

Byng, S. (1985). Sentence comprehension deficit: theoretical analysis and remediation. *Paper presented at the Venice Meeting on Cognitive Neuropsychology.*

Byng, S., & Coltheart, M. (in press). Aphasia therapy research: Methodological requirements and illustrative results. In E. Hjelmquist & L. B. Nilson (Eds.), *Communication and Handicap.*

Caramazza, A. (1984). The logic of neuropsychological research and the problem of patient classification in aphasia. *Brain and Language, 21*, 9–20.

Colby, K. M., Christinaz, D., Parkinson, R. C., Graham, S., & Karpf, C. (1981). A word-finding computer program with a dynamic lexical-semantic memory for patients with anomia using an intelligent speech prosthesis. *Brain and Language, 14*, 272–281.

Coltheart, M. (1981). The MRC psycholinguistic database. *Quarterly Journal of Experimental Psychology, 33A*, 497–505.

Coltheart, M. (1983). Aphasia therapy research: A single case study approach. In C. Code & D. J. Muller (Eds.), *Aphasia therapy* (pp. 193–202). London: Arnold.

Coltheart, M., Patterson, K. E., & Marshall, J. C. (Eds.) (1980). *Deep dyslexia.* London: Routledge and Kegan Paul.

David, R., Enderby, P., & Bainton, D. (1982). Treatment of acquired aphasia: speech therapists and volunteers compared. *Journal of Neurology, Neurosurgery, and Psychiatry, 45*, 957–961.

de Partz, M. P. (1986). Reeducation of a deep dyslexic patient: rationale of the method and results. *Cognitive Neuropsychology, 3*, 149–178.

Ducarne, B. (1986). *Rééducation sémiologique de l'aphasie* [Semiological rehabilitation for Aphasia]. Paris: Masson.

Glisky, E. L., Schacter, D. L., & Tulving, E. (1986). Computer learning by memory-impaired patients: Acquisition and retention of complex knowledge. *Neuropsychologia, 24*, (3), 313–328.

Hatfield, F. M. (1982). Diverses formes de désintégration du langage écrit et implication pour la rééducation. In X. Seron & C. Laterre (Eds.), *Rééduquer le cerveau* (pp. 135–156). Bruxelles: Mardaga.

Katz, R. C. (1986). *Aphasia treatment and microcomputers.* London: Taylor and Francis.

Lapointe, L. L. (1977). Base-10 programmed stimulation: task specification, scoring and plotting performance in aphasia therapy. *Journal of Speech and Hearing Disorders, 42,* 90–105.

Lincoln, N. B., Mulley, G. P., Jones, A. L., McGuirk, E., Lendrem, W., & Mitchell, J. R. A. (1984). Effectiveness of speech therapy for aphasic stroke patients. A randomised controlled trial. *The Lancet, 8388,* 1197–1200.

Luria, A. R. (1963). *Restoration of function after brain injury.* New York: McMillan.

Marshall, J. (1986). The description and interpretation of aphasic language disorder. *Neuropsychologia, 24,* 5–24.

Mehler, J., Morton, J., & Jusczyk, P. (1984). On reducing language to biology. *Cognitive Neuropsychology, 1,* 83–116.

Meikle, M., Wechsler, E., Tupper, A., Benenson, M., Buttler, J., Mulhall, D., & Stern, G. (1979). Comparative trial of volunteer and professional treatments of dysphasia after stroke. *British Medical Journal, 2,* 87–89.

Patterson, K. E. (1981). Neuropsychological approaches to the study of reading. *British Journal of Psychology, 72,* 151–174.

Patterson, K. E., Marshall, J. C., & Coltheart, M. (Eds.) (1985). *Surface dyslexia.* London: Lawrence Erlbaum Associates.

Posner, M. I., & Boies, S. W. (1971). Components of attention. *Psychological Review, 78,* 391–408.

Reason, J. T. (1979). Actions not as planned: the price of automation. In G. Underwood & R. Stevens (Eds.), *Aspects of consciousness, vol. 1* (pp. 67–89). London: Academic Press.

Reason, J. T. (1984). Absent-mindedness and cognitive control. In J. E. Harris & P. E. Morris (Eds.), *Everyday memory, actions and absent-mindedness* (pp. 113–132). London: Academic Press.

Schuell, H. M. (1974). *Aphasia theory and therapy, selected lectures and papers of Hildred Schuell.* Baltimore: University Park Press.

Seron, X. (1987). Operant procedures and neuropsychological rehabilitation. In M. J. Meier, A. L. Benton, & L. Diller, *Neuropsychological rehabilitation* (pp. 132–161). Edinburgh: Churchill Livingstone.

Seron, X., Deloche, G., Moulard, G., & Rousselle, M. (1980). A computer-based therapy for the treatment of aphasic subjects with writing disorders. *Journal of Speech and Hearing Disorders, 45,* 45–58.

Shallice, T. (1987). Impairments of semantic processing: multiple dissociations. In M. Coltheart, G. Sartori, & R. Job (Eds.), *The Cognitive neuropsychology of language* (pp. 111–127). London: Lawrence Erlbaum Associates.

Wepman, J. M. (1951). *Recovery from aphasia.* New York: The Ronald Press Company.

1 Spontaneous Recovery and Language Rehabilitation

Anna Basso
Istituto di Clinica Neurologica, Milan University

This chapter briefly reviews the natural course of aphasia and considers the factors that have a prognostic value, among them rehabilitation. However, what occurs under the heading of aphasia rehabilitation in one place may have nothing in common with what occurs in a different place, except for the fact that a speech therapist and a patient interact with each other. Nevertheless, there are some main approaches to aphasia therapy.

Today, emphasis is given to a relatively new label in the field of neuropsychological rehabilitation: cognitive rehabilitation. As was true of the base term rehabilitation, cognitive rehabilitation has come to mean different things to different persons. I shall try to clarify my understanding of cognitive rehabilitation and its possible advantages or drawbacks.

Also important for rehabilitation are the neurological bases for recovery. These are considered in the next section of the chapter. Those retraining techniques founded on a specific hypothesis of how recovery occurs will then be described.

SPONTANEOUS RECOVERY

Aphasia is a complex process that, with time, generally evolves toward partial remission of the language dysfunction. Even though not much is known about the natural course of aphasia, some of the factors that have prognostic value have been identified and we have some knowledge about the temporal limits of spontaneous recovery and about how language modalities change over time.

Results of studies of spontaneous recovery of language impairment in aphasics agree that improvement occurs, albeit to different degrees, and not in all of the patients. Improvement is most evident in the first 2 to 3 months postonset and then decelerates. However, it has sometimes been reported to occur for longer periods (Luria, 1963; Hagen, 1973).

By "spontaneous" recovery, I only mean recovery without any specific retraining, but patients do not live in a vacuum and are always exposed to language. Although it is well known that very severely aphasic patients do not improve if not rehabilitated, it would be interesting to see whether a necessary condition to prolong recovery is the ability to use some language or whether, once the most impaired have been excluded, all aphasics will recover "spontaneously" over longer periods of time, not only those patients that have already attained a functional level of language.

Pattern of Recovery

Some patients display a general improvement in all the various modalities, but this is not always the case. A higher percentage of patients improve in comprehension than in expression, and likewise more improve in the oral modalities than in the written ones (Kenin & Swisher, 1972; Hanson & Cicciarelli, 1978; Lomas & Kertesz, 1978; Prins, Snow, & Wagenaar, 1978). The pattern of changes in the individual aphasic patient is less well known. In a recent study (Basso, Capitani, & Zanobio, 1982b), we found that in the individual nonrehabilitated patient improvement of oral production, written comprehension, and spontaneous writing are always significantly associated. On the contrary, improvement of auditory language comprehension is not significantly linked to improvement of any other modality, probably because many nonrehabilitated patients improve exclusively in oral comprehension without any corresponding improvement in the other language functions. Nevertheless, even for the nonrehabilitated patients, recovery seems to be a relatively consistent improvement of all language modalities, the only exception being that auditory comprehension tends to recover better.

As the modality performances change, so obviously does the overall pattern of performance (i.e., the aphasic syndrome). A global aphasic for instance, can become a Broca aphasic, or a Wernicke aphasic can become an anomic aphasic. However, the type of aphasia—considered along the fluency/nonfluency dimension—tends to be stable, a fluent aphasic being only very rarely reclassified as nonfluent or vice versa. This is true only if one reserves the label of anomic aphasia for the full blown form of fluent anomic aphasia. In fact, many moderate patients have a chance of recovering to a stage where they only present some rare anomias (Kertesz & McCabe, 1977; Basso et al., 1982b).

Psychological Factors

The question of the relationship between intelligence and improvement of the aphasic disorder is a very delicate one and data are scanty. Messerli, Tissot, and Rodriguez (1976) found that among the prognostic factors they studied, the "operational" level of intelligence, determined at first examination through the Piaget Conservation of Physical Quantities test, had the greatest prognostic value in a group of 53 reeducated patients. The same results were obtained in a later study by Bailey, Powell, and Clark (1981). Fifty-three patients underwent a second assessment approximately 5 months after the first. It is not stated whether the patients had undergone rehabilitation between the first and second examinations. Results on the Coloured Progressive Matrices (PM) test were unchanged, but there was a substantial gain in the Schuell test and the scores on PM on first examination correlated positively with the number of points of improvement on the Schuell test. This is, in fact, what is generally taught to speech therapists: "Intelligent" patients improve more than "unintelligent" ones. In a retrospective study, we (Basso, 1987) investigated 101 patients to determine whether the improvement in the Token Test score can be predicted from the level of performance in the PM on first examination. The correlation coefficient turned out to be $-.17$ for the whole group, but moderately aphasic patients with higher Token Test scores have a limited scope for improvement, which could explain this result. In very severely affected patients, scoring 0 to 5 in the Token Test on first examination, the correlation coefficent was $-.06$. Lack of positive correlation between the initial PM scores and improvement on the Token Test, therefore, cannot be traced back to a sampling bias. Our results do not agree with previous data indicating a negative influence of a low intelligence score on language recovery. David and Skilbeck (1984), too, did not find any evidence of a relationship between initial Raven scores and subsequent language recovery.

20 BASSO

Neurological Factors

As for the neurological variables, the size of the lesion has been related to the outcome of aphasia. Yarnell, Monroe, & Sobel (1976) concluded from their study of 14 patients whose CT scans had been systematically analyzed that size and number of lesions are highly correlated with the outcome. Patients with larger lesions or more than one lesion fare poorly. Kertesz, Harlock, and Coates (1979) also report on the correlations between CT scan and aphasic outcome in 52 patients at 1-year follow-up examinations. Negative correlations were found between the recovery rates of fluency, repetition, naming and lesion size, though these correlations were not statistically significant. However, the only positive correlation found, between recovery of comprehension and lesion size, was statistically significant. The authors suggest that in large lesions the comprehension deficit is severe, and the more severe the initial deficit the more room there is for recovery. An alternative explanation would be that recovery of comprehension relies on right hemisphere resources more than other language parameters, and this could also explain why the comprehension deficit recovers more than other language modalities.

It is not only the extent of the lesion that plays a role in aphasia outcome; the site of the lesion is also considered important by some authors. Only transient Broca aphasia has been reported to occur with lesions in Broca's area (Mohr et al., 1978; Brunner, Kornhuber, Seemueller, Suger, and Wallesch, 1982) that do not involve the underlying basal ganglia. Superficial lesions involving Wernicke's area, however, have been reported to cause long-lasting aphasia (Brunner et al., 1982). In the same direction are the results of a study on lesion volume in fluent and nonfluent aphasics (Basso, Capitani, Laiacona, & Luzzatti, 1980). Lesion volumes were calculated for 169 left-hemisphere-brain-damaged patients, counting the number of pixels (a pixel corresponding approximately to 15.5 mm^3) comprised in each pathological cut of the CT scan and adding them up to obtain the volume of the lesion. Patients were subdivided according to type (fluent/nonfluent) and severity of aphasia (patients scoring more or less than the mean Token Test score obtained by a group of 200 aphasic patients (De Renzi & Faglioni, 1978). Nonfluent patients (moderate and severe) had much larger lesion volumes than corresponding fluent patients: severe fluent (N=40): 1966; moderate fluent (N=35): 1114; severe nonfluent (N=69): 3440; moderate nonfluent (N=25): 1983. Although this study did not deal with recovery, it backs up the statement that anterior lesions have a better prognosis than similar posterior lesions, as they need to be much larger to show the same degree of impairment on the Token Test. Brunner et al. (1982) advance the hypothesis that "Broca's area, the supplementary motor area, and the basal ganglia can compensate for the functional effect of destruction of one by action of the remaining two, thus explaining the transient character of the aphasic syndromes resulting from lesions in one of these areas." (p. 286–287). The same would not apply to Wernicke's area, which is functionally unique.

Severity of the language disorder is strictly interconnected with site and size of lesion and has a significant negative effect on improvement (Basso, Capitani, & Vignolo, 1979).

Data on the influence of etiology on recovery are clear cut. Traumatic aphasia has a better prognosis than vascular aphasia (Alajouanine, Castaigne, Lhermitte, Escourolle, & De Ribaucourt, 1957; Kertesz & McCabe, 1977; Basso et al., 1980). Among the vascular etiologies, hemorrhages appear to have the worst prognosis (Anderson, Bourestom, & Greenberg, 1970). Not much is known about the prognosis of aphasia following such other etiologies as, for example, infections; however, these forms of aphasia are rather rare. Aphasia following a neoplasm obviously follows the course of the neoplasm itself.

Anagraphic Factors

Age at onset of aphasia is reported to have been an important factor in recovery (younger patients fared better than older ones) in groups of posttraumatic patients rendered aphasic in war time (Eisenson, 1949; Wepman, 1951). Nevertheless, the effects of age on recovery in generally older vascular patients are not consistent, age at onset having been reported to be an important factor (Sands, Sarno, & Shankweiler, 1969; Marshall, Tompkins, & Phillips, 1982) and also as having no effect on improvement of communication (Basso, Capitani, & Vignolo, 1979). All in all, age does not appear to be an important drawback for or facilitator of recovery.

Kertesz and McCabe (1977) compared the initial 3-month recovery rates of groups of 23 male and 23 female aphasic patients and did not find any statistically significant difference. The influence of sex on recovery from aphasia was studied in two subsequent investigations for auditory comprehension and oral expression. Basso, Capitani, and Moraschini (1982a) report a significantly better recovery in oral expression in women than in men but not in auditory verbal comprehension. The results in the study by Pizzamiglio, Mammucari, and Razzano (1985) are partly different: Women recovered significantly better than men in three auditory comprehension tests but not in the Token Test. There was no difference between men and women in recovery of oral expression. One possible explanation of the better recovery of female patients is the proposed differential anatomical organization in men and women (McGlone, 1980), which presupposes that recovery is due to the intervention of the right hemisphere. An alternative explanation is that there might have been a lesser initial neurological severity (aphasia severity was controlled) in the women than in the men.

Both Subirana (1969) and Gloning, Trappl, Heiss, and Quatember (1976) report a better prognosis for left-handed and ambidextrous patients than for right-handed patients. Only 6% of 65 right-handed patients recovered as opposed to 100% of 6 left-handed aphasics (Subirana, 1969). It is interesting to note that right-handers with family history of left-handedness also recover better than right-handers without left-handedness in their family (Luria, 1970).

I have briefly sketched what is known today about the most important factors that influence spontaneous recovery, with the exception of treatment, which will be considered separately. It must be remembered that these factors are not independent and often interact when they are not strictly dependent on each other, as is the case with severity of aphasia and site and extent of lesion. This makes it more difficult, although theoretically not impossible, to study their specific effects on recovery. Another problem in evaluating improvement is that we do not as yet have available enough reliable and detailed scales for the different neuropsychological behaviors, as, for example, language. Notwithstanding all the difficulties encountered in the study of recovery, we now know a great deal about it, and we can predict with a reasonable degree of accuracy the outcomes for a group of aphasic patients. Unfortunately, this does not apply to the individual patient, our knowledge being only of a statistical nature and individual variability being very large. Only when many or even most of the positive or negative prognostic factors are found in a single patient can we predict good or poor recovery.

APHASIA REHABILITATION

An important factor for recovery that I have not yet considered is rehabilitation. Despite the fact that aphasia rehabilitation is now normally undertaken in many different countries, it is very difficult to know exactly what is meant by "aphasia therapy." I will briefly delineate what is included under this heading.

The most debated question is whether rehabilitation really helps in recovering language skills. Many recent English papers compare patients reeducated by speech therapists with patients reeducated by volunteers (Meikle et al., 1979; David, Enderby, & Bainton, 1982) or compare reeducated and nonreeducated patients (Lincoln, Pickersgill, Hankey, & Hilton, 1982; Lincoln et al., 1984). The outcome is always the same. After variable periods (never very long) of aphasia therapy, there was no significant difference among the groups. They all recovered, or did not recover, to the same extent. Generally the authors' conclusion is that aphasia therapy has no specific effect.

These papers, however, have been criticized on the grounds that they are not methodologically correct and, more important, because different conclusions could be drawn (Cubelli, 1985). In some previous papers results had been different, namely aphasia rehabilitation had been found to have a significant effect on recovery of specific language skills (Hagen, 1973; Basso, Faglioni, & Vignolo, 1975; Basso, et al., 1979; Marshall, et al., 1982). The difference in the results can be due to the fact that in these studies there was no control group for the type of treatment. Results of the English papers, however, could also mean that the aphasia therapy had not been well conducted. Even a cursory reading of the literature in fact reveals the differences and inhomogeneity of rehabilitation texts. I will give some examples from the field of aphasia rehabilitation and I will regroup aphasia rehabilitation techniques into three categories according to how detailed the analysis (explicit or implicit) of the nature of the disorder to be reeducated is. There is, in fact, no general agreement about exactly what aphasia is. To justify specific intervention, it would seem sensible to state one's own opinions, but this is rarely done, and the various methods proposed are justified by their reported efficacy, which is (as everybody concerned with the problem knows) very difficult to prove.

In the first category, the exercises proposed have very little relation to the disorder, in the second the relationship is very general, and in the third it is highly specified. As examples of the first category, we can list the treatment of global aphasia proposed by Collins (1983) or that for transcortical motor aphasia described by Johnson (1983). Having stated that in global aphasia "yes" and "no" responses are often equivocal, Collins (1983) chose as his first objective to establish unequivocal "yes" and "no" responses, following the procedure illustrated here.

24   BASSO

Shaping the Yes and No Response

1. Physically assist the patient with five repetitions of yes (head nod), then no (side to side head movements) while clinician says the word.
2. Alternate gestured yes, then no, with physical assistance while clinician says the word. Pause approximately 5 seconds between responses.
3. Request gestured responses to simple unambiguous questions while clinician assists with gestures and says the word. The therapist is then invited to stabilize the responses approximately by the same means.

Treatment of transcortical motor aphasia by Johnson (1983) has as its primary goal improvement of motor processing, on the assumption that there are motor processing problems in transcortical motor aphasia interrelated functionally with language problems. The patient is first requested to imitate gross conventional movements ("wave good-bye"), to pantomime ("show me how you throw a ball") and finally to verbalize what he is doing while doing the required movements. For rehabilitation in clinical neuropsychology other than aphasia, a good example of the first category is the text of Golden (1981). The nature and the rehabilitation of "mathematical disorders," for instance, are described in 10 lines (p. 256), and rehabilitation of memory functions, being more complex, requires 26 lines, the basic strategy being "building upon the abilities of the brain as a whole to take over memory functions" (p. 254). The crudeness of this approach is equalled only by the oversimplification of the theory of brain function presented. Discussing the neuropsychological significance of the WAIS, Golden (1981) states

> As noted earlier, Digit Span may be used to lateralize brain injury. If both digits forward and digits backward are down (normal for an average adult is remembering six numbers in a row forward, five backward), this indicates a left hemisphere injury. Generally, digits forward must be at least three digits longer than digits backward to strongly indicate a right brain disfunction. (Golden, 1981, p. 99)

However, the situation is not so bad as would appear from what I have just said. Most of the different language intervention strategies that have been elaborated can tentatively be grouped under what is generally called the classic or stimulation approach (Schuell, Jenkins, & Jimenez-Pabon, 1964; Wepman, 1951; Chapey, 1981, etc.) and fall into the second category. This approach is based on two general assumptions that should influence aphasia rehabilitation. The first is that aphasia is a central or nuclear language disorder, which thus affects all language modalities (e.g., comprehension, production) somewhat differently, but always within the limits of a certain overall pattern. The second assumption is that aphasia is characterized by reduced efficiency in accessing language knowledge. Aphasia is approached, therefore, from the viewpoint of levels of language availability. Selective loss of the levels of highest intention is highly significant for rehabilitation treatment. From this point of view, aphasia would consist of a restriction of language availability and not of an actual loss of language itself. The speech therapist should not teach specific responses to particular stimuli, but should stimulate the patient to improve his accessing strategies.

Equally important for the rehabilitation techniques are the consequences of the first assumption: If aphasia is due to the breakdown of one central mechanism, in rehabilitation one should seek the best means of reaching this particular mechanism. Improvement, like the deficit, will manifest itself simultaneously in all the behaviors. Schuell's (Schuell et al., 1964) reeducation techniques for example, basically consist of intense auditory stimulation, quantitatively controlled by the therapist so that different aphasic patients are required to process different amounts of information.

Another group of rehabilitation techniques, which pays attention not so much to the nature of the disorder as to the methodology for application of a rehabilitation program, is based on the principles of operant conditioning. The remediation plan is systematically designed and specifies a priori the teaching and the learning behaviors required. Application of these principles to aphasia therapy can be found in Brookshire (1969), Holland (1970), Holland and Sonderman (1974), and Goldfarb (1981).

Finally the relationship between the disorder and the intervention strategies proposed is highly specified in some recent papers in which rehabilitation is viewed as strictly tied up with research (Hatfield, 1982, 1983; Beauvois and Derouesne', 1982). Only after the processes underlying a specific disorder have been precisely identified is it possible to program the rehabilitation of the disorder. Unlike the preceding strategies, these intervention strategies are highly individualized and cannot easily be generalized to groups of patients.

The field of neuropsychological rehabilitation, and particularly of aphasia therapy, as emerges from this rapid review, is very uneven, the differences among the various approaches being large in both accuracy of description and in content. This state of affairs, however, cannot be entirely blamed on the speech pathologists. Speech thera-

26 BASSO

pists have always been requested to rehabilitate Wernicke, Broca, conduction, or other types of aphasics, without clear understanding of the meaning of these labels.

The classical Wernicke-Lichtheim classification is not appropriate for the task of disclosing linguistic generalizations. It is useful for indicating the locus of a lesion or what the associated deficits are, but it does not indicate an invariant linguistic pattern shared by all members of the group. Moreover, any given symptom can be present in more than one aphasic syndrome. One reason for this could well be that aphasia has traditionally been a neurologist's preserve, and neurologists were obviously more interested in knowing the consequences of the presence of a lesion in a given part of the brain than in studying cognitive processes per se.

The study of brain damaged populations, however, has provided much information on the relationship between the brain and cognitive processes; cognitive psychologists have become interested in aphasia on the assumption that it is possible to use data from pathological populations to construct models of normal cognition. A complex psychological function (such as language comprehension) is thought to be constructed of more basic components of processing, and the pathological performance of brain damaged patients is thought to provide a basis from which to draw inferences about normal processes. Aphasia should represent a fractionation of the normal language processing system along psycholinguistically significant lines, the working of the normal cognitive system without the impaired linguistic process. Such an approach requires that the hypotheses concerning the computation system underlying normal performance be explicitly formulated; on this basis, one should be able to predict all the possible types of deficits that can occur.

Because of the many difficulties in drawing inferences about the functional systems from group studies, cognitive psychologists rely more on information from single case studies. Within the domain of a theory, dissociations found in individual cases lend support for particular fractionations of the general function.

The advantages for aphasia therapy of such an approach are quite obvious. If a patient arriving at the rehabilitation center were to be accompanied by such a detailed analysis of his impairment, the therapist would know exactly what the deficit is and how the impaired function normally works. The therapist could then plan a very accurate, specific and rational therapeutic program. If by cognitive rehabilitation we mean that the patient's deficit must be adequately studied, especially with reference to psycholinguistics models, and that rehabilitation must not ignore how the normal function is supposed to work, then it goes without saying that cognitive rehabilitation is exactly what everybody concerned with rehabilitation is supposed to address. If, however, by cognitive rehabilitation we mean a reeducation strategy detailed in a way that is directly proportional to the degree of explicitness of the normal model that has served as a basis for the individuation of the deficit, some further considerations seem necessary.

COGNITIVE REHABILITATION

Before considering whether cognitive rehabilitation is beneficial or even possible, we should try to understand better what cognitive rehabilitation means. It is now a fashionable label used to describe many different things, whereas at other times it is simply used to mean rehabilitation of cognitive disturbances without further qualifying what is meant by rehabilitation.

The assumptions on which cognitive neuropsychology is based are the modularity assumption, the fractionability assumption, and the transparency assumption (Caramazza, 1984). The principle of modularity states that any cognitive system is composed of several modules, interrelated but functionally independent. According to the second assumption, the brain lesion destroys one or more modules of a specific cognitive system leaving others unharmed. Finally, the transparency assumption states that the pathological behavior is the result of the functioning of the system with the exclusion of the impaired modules. Although it is reasonably clear what is meant by cognitive neuropsychology and how a patient should be approached to qualify an impairment (i.e., exactly which modules are rendered nonfunctional by the brain damage), it is much more difficult to understand what is meant by cognitive rehabilitation. The cognitive approach undoubtedly helps in elaborating a model-motivated rationale for aphasia therapy, but it does not say what rehabilitation should do. It represents a step forward in aphasiology in that it clarifies better the starting point. But even if one considers that the contribution of cognitive neuropsychology is confined to the examination of the patients, things are not completely straightforward. Let us first consider objections to the construction of cognitive models of the widely heterogeneous aphasic disruptions, that is, to the examination of the aphasic patients from the standpoint of cognitive neuropsychology, and then those directly involving the conduction of the rehabilitation.

28   BASSO

The first group generally comprise only practical objections that we can hope will be overcome in the future. For example, at the moment there is no sufficiently well-developed theory of language processing that can predict all (or even many) aphasic behaviors. A further consideration is that, at least up to now, many models based on the information processing approach consider separately reading, writing, syntactic production, etc. and identify the locus of impairment for one behavior without considering impairments in other verbal behaviors. Rehabilitation based on such an analysis would focus on one disorder alone. This would make sense only if it had been demonstrated that impairments of different verbal behaviors were independent. Moreover, human beings are not computers; they do not only process information. There is always some noise. The uttered form of the sentence, for instance, the prosody, the syntax, and lexicon, are all affected by the emotional states, social status, and beliefs of speakers. Language use in real time must take account of this and exactly the same detailed rehabilitation program cannot be used for different patients even with the same deficits. Finally, many patients have such severe degrees of impairment, as in global aphasics, that it is difficult to understand how a cognitive approach would help in identifying the loci of impairment.

As for the rehabilitation techniques themselves, it is not clear how a better understanding of the deficit can help in deciding what has to be done next. It is a necessary but not a sufficient step. Shall we just drill the impaired subsystem? Or find a way to bypass it? The behavioral level of aphasia therapy and the more basic level of the anatomical correlates thought to subserve restitution of function after damage are not in a biunivocal correspondence. Nevertheless, it seems to me that if rehabilitation has to be so meticulous, detailed, and individualized as presupposed by the necessity of such a careful investigation of the disorder, we also need to know how recovery occurs.

RECOVERY OF FUNCTION

Many different explanations of recovery, which are not necessarily mutually exclusive, have been given; this makes evaluation of individual theories difficult, since evidence in favor of one does not make the others less plausible. According to a first group of theories, there are two components in the observed impairment after brain damage: In addition to the primary deficit, the injury produces temporary disturbances in the functioning of other parts of the brain not involved in the primary deficit. These secondary deficits are due to inactivation rather than to loss. Edema is one currently used explanation; diaschisis is another. These phenomena are not disputed and are certainly of great interest, but they are transient and do not explain recovery that takes place over longer periods of time (months or years). In fact, recovery due to resolution of edema or diaschisis is only apparent recovery because the function had actually only been inhibited and not lost.

Of more interest are theories of anatomical substitution, which are based on the assumption that when there is a lesion in one part of the brain, recovery can take place because other intact parts of the brain assume the impaired function. Anatomical substitution is a commonly accepted explanation for recovery, and I believe that in young children, even with very extensive lesions, anatomical substitution can occur to some extent. Things are not so definite for adults. Probably the explanation of recovery from aphasia offered most often that fits into this category is the assumption that the right hemisphere takes over language functions. There is in fact some experimental evidence in favor of the right hemisphere taking over. Pettit and Noll (1979) found that 25 aphasic subjects examined on two occasions in tests of dichotic listening became relatively more able to detect and report dichotic stimuli presented to the left ear. However, paying greater attention to stimuli presented to the left ear is another possible explanation for the results. A statistically significant left ear preference has been reported in a group of 30 aphasic patients using bilateral tachistoscopic presentation of words (Moore and Weidner, 1974). Czopf (1972) studied 22 aphasic patients, injecting amytal sodium in the right carotid artery. He found that the inactivation of the right hemisphere had the most devastating effects on language production of those patients who had been aphasic for a long time and the least effects on acute patients. Czopf (1972) considers these results to support the hypothesis that the right hemisphere takes over the language functions and that this process requires time. We have had the chance to observe a young lady with conduction aphasia following a left hemisphere disease. Eventually she recovered nearly normal language, but a few years later she had a right hemisphere infarct. After that, she was severely aphasic: She had fluent paraphasic speech and comprehension, especially auditory comprehension, was severely affected.

Functional adaptation is a third possible mechanism of improvement and is aimed at the subject's recovery of functions as goals in themselves and not with recovery of some particular means for achieving the goals, as in anatomical reorganization. The general idea is that it is possible to achieve a certain goal by means other than those originally employed and impaired as a consequence of the lesion. Functional adaptation probably plays the major role in recovery but it is unfortunately only a vague and general concept and the detailed mechanisms involved or the factors that determine adaptation are unknown. In neuropsychological rehabilitation, this type of strategy has been proposed for a long time by Luria (1963, 1966, 1970; Luria, Naydin, Tsvetkova, Vinarskaya, 1969), and it exists in numerous traditional therapeutic approaches. All the reeducational procedures directed toward the use of some sensory-motor biofeedback that is different from that normally used in verbal activity are in fact functional adaptation strategies. More recent and well documented studies are those by Beauvois and Derouesne' (1982), referring to rehabilitation of different syndromes and by Hatfield (1982, 1983) for the rehabilitation of deep and surface dysgraphias.

To conclude, our knowledge of recovery is limited. Three different theories of recovery have been briefly sketched. According to the first, the neural bases of the function to be recovered (i.e., the hardware of the whole process of recovering) are not impaired but simply inhibited; when they start working again they use the same algorithms as before to perform exactly the same goals as before. Theories of anatomical substitution and functional reorganization, on the contrary, consider that the original hardware has been destroyed by the lesion and a new hardware must be substituted to the old one. The two theories differ at the level of the algorithms that these new hardware utilize. In the case of anatomical substitution, the same algorithms will be used, and the goals to be attained have not changed; for aphasia therapy, the therapist strives to attain a normal language. Functional reorganization presupposes that the algorithms change, too. These new algorithms can lead to the same goals as before (a normal language, for instance) or to new goals. The rehabilitation of the severe agrammatic patient as suggested by Hatfield and Shewell (1983) presupposes that the patient will not be able to correctly use the grammatical rules and suggests to retrain the patient to use a semantically based grammar: "soon I go," for instance, instead of "I'll go." The patient succeeds in conveying the idea that the action will take place in a near future, but language differs from the normal language.

We thus have three levels at which recovery can be studied: the hardware, the algorithms and the more abstract level of the language itself. Intervention strategies should be different when the objective is to reestablish the impaired behavior in its initial form by means of the same algorithms as before, or to attain the same goals but by different means. In the first case, the impaired behavior probably must be rebuilt step by step and the therapist's job is to establish a hierarchy of difficulty for the proposed exercises. If, on the contrary, one supposes that recovery is based on functional compensation, one must reorganize the processes that are intact and use them differently to compensate for the existing impairment. The therapist's behavior is thus in opposition to that required to rebuild an impaired function.

Unfortunately, as is apparent from what I have just said, there is considerable disagreement over the nature of the reasons for recovery and consequently rehabilitation strategies cannot as yet be based on the nature of recovery. Although this does not seem to me a very serious drawback for those rehabilitation strategies general enough to be applicable to groups of similar but not identical patients, it does seem a more serious obstacle to the application of very specific, detailed techniques based on the individuation of the unique disorder presented by a given aphasic. Should we try to circumvent the deficit or to drill the impaired subsystem? Moreover, who knows whether drilling really helps in rebuilding the impaired function, and which hierarchies of difficulty work best?

RIGHT HEMISPHERE

Some relatively new techniques explicitly take mechanisms of recovery into account. I refer to those techniques that attempt to involve the right hemisphere in the recovery of language. They are not very numerous and can be subdivided into two groups according to whether they simply use some known capacity of the right hemisphere or specifically drill language processing in the right hemisphere. A good example of the first group is Melodic Intonation Therapy (Sparks, Helm, & Albert, 1974), for which it is suggested that both dominance for music and existence of less developed language areas in the right hemisphere are being used to support the damaged left hemisphere, which, however, continues to be language dominant. Blissymbolics is a visuographic communication system that uses logically based symbols and has recently been used in aphasia therapy (Bailey, 1983). This system has also been suggested to rely on the right hemisphere's capacity to acquire an artificial language. Those rare attempts to directly enhance right hemisphere language capacity are interesting.

Buffery and Burton (1982) stimulate the right hemisphere of their patient, presenting words through three different input channels: the left visual field, the left ear, and the left hand. Masking of the left hemisphere is obtained by presentation of neutral stimuli in all three modalities. Code (1983) presents a similar case. With the tachistoscope and the dichotic listening apparatus he selectively stimulates his patient's right hemisphere to take over linguistic processing. Significant improvement in general communication capacity and a modest change in the Token Test were recorded. However, many questions remain unanswered. Two recent studies performed in Milan, one on recovery from aphasia and one from acalculia, although testifying that improvement occurred, pose some additional general problems on why and how it occurred.

In a recent study (Basso et al., 1982b), we addressed the question of whether improvement in one language modality is associated with a higher probability of improvement in another. In 250 reeducated and 138 nonreeducated aphasics, we studied the relationships in individual patients between improvement in oral and written expression and comprehension. Aphasia therapy most emphasized oral language, and within oral language, comprehension more than production. Improvements of all pairs of modalities were found to be significantly associated in rehabilitated patients. The main result of this study is that it showed that language therapy centered most on oral comprehension brought about uniform improvement in both written and oral verbal behavior. Improvement was not confined to the treated verbal behavior, but in this study only verbal behaviors were considered.

In a further study we investigated in aphasic subjects whether improvement of acalculia was associated with language improvement. We considered only right-handed patients without familial history of left handedness, with a left hemisphere disease, and at least 5 years of schooling who had pathological scores in the Token Test, a test of acalculia (Basso and Capitani, 1979), and the Raven Coloured Progressive Matrices at first examination. These patients were reeducated and given a second test 6 months later. In a series of 780 aphasics, we found 41 such patients, 28 with a nonfluent aphasia and 13 with a fluent aphasia. Improvement in the acalculia test at the second examination was not significantly influenced by the initial scores on the Token Test, Progressive Matrices, or acalculia test. In both fluent and nonfluent aphasics, improvement in the acalculia test was significantly associated with improvement in the Token Test, though oral comprehension had been specifically reeducated in all patients and acalculia in none. Improvement in the acalculia test cannot be considered a general aspecific improvement because, at least in nonfluent patients, improvement in the Raven Progressive Matrices was not significantly associated with improvement in the acalculia test. These studies are two instances of improvement in rehabilitated patients that are neither an aspecific improvement of the general behavior of the patients nor restricted to the modality retrained.

CONCLUDING REMARKS

I am convinced that aphasia therapy must take advantage of advances in cognitive psychology. However, at this time there are so many things that are not known, such as why and how recovery occurs, that we must be cautious about very detailed and individualized treatments that consider only the linguistic disorder.

Cognitive rehabilitation has been undertaken only in individual patients more to validate a model than for the sake of rehabilitation itself. Moreover, cognitive rehabilitation is legitimate and well grounded only if the cognitive underlying model is correct. Our data on recovery are not in agreement with the basic assumption of the cognitive approach. The recovery pattern of our patients showed a certain degree of coherence but was not modular. Patients can be treated with a highly detailed rehabilitation strategy if the impairment has been precisely qualified, that is, only in case the impairment is limited to one or few modules. These patients are rare. Many more patients present such severe impairments in all language behaviors that it would be impossible to identify the corresponding impaired modules and retrain them separately. The cognitive approach is thus a very stimulating approach, but at the moment it can not be the only approach used in a clinical setting. There is, however, a field where it already seems possible to transfer cognitive research into aphasia rehabilitation. Experiments within the frame of cognitive psychology and investigating the ability of aphasic patients to name pictures have shown that a phonemic cuing has an immediate effect on the patients' ability to produce the target word, but this effect is very short-lasting (Patterson, Purell and Morton, 1983). On the contrary, facilitations that require the patients to access the semantic representation of the word can last for up to 24 hours (Howard, Patterson, Franklin, Orchard-Lisle and Morton, 1985). Word finding difficulties are always present in aphasia, and the findings of more effective treatment techniques for such a general disorder must have an immediate and important effect on rehabilitation.

REFERENCES

Alajouanine, T., Castaigne, P., Lhermitte, E., Escourolle R., & Ducarne, B. (1957). Etude de 43 cas d'aphasie post-traumatique. *Encephale, 46*, 1–45.
Anderson, T. P., Bourestom, N., & Greenberg, F. R. (1970). *Rehabilitation predictors in completed stroke: final report*. Minneapolis: American Rehabilitation Foundation.
Bailey, S. (1983). Blissymbolics and aphasia therapy: a case study. In C. Code and D. J. Mueller (Eds.), *Aphasia Therapy* (pp. 178–186). London: Arnold.
Bailey, S., Powell, G., & Clark, E. (1981). A note on intelligence and recovery from aphasia: the relationship between Raven's Matrices scores and change on the Schuell aphasia test. *British Journal of Disorders of Communication, 16*, 193–203.
Basso, A. (1987). Approaches to neuropsychological rehabilitation. Language disorders. In M. Meier, A. Benton, & L. Diller (Eds.), *Neuropsychological rehabilitation* (pp. 234–319). London: Churchill Livingstone.
Basso, A., & Capitani, E. (1979). Un test standardizzato per la diagnosi di acalculia. *AP Rivista di applicazioni psicologiche, 1*, 551–568.
Basso, A., Capitani, E., Laiacona, M., & Luzzatti, C. (1980). Factors influencing type and severity of aphasia. *Cortex, 16*, 631–636.
Basso, A., Capitani, E., & Moraschini, S. (1982a). Sex differences in recovery from aphasia. *Cortex, 18*, 469–475.
Basso, A., Capitani, E., & Vignolo, L. A. (1979). Influence of rehabilitation on language skills in aphasic patients. A controlled study. *Archives of Neurology, 36*, 190–196.
Basso, A., Capitani, E., & Zanobio, M. E. (1982b). Pattern of recovery of oral and written expression and comprehension in aphasic patients. *Behavioral Brain Research, 6*, 115–128.
Basso, A., Faglioni, P., & Vignolo, L. A. (1975). Etude controlee de la reeducation du language dans l'aphasie: comparaison entre aphasiques traites et non-traites. *Revue Neurologique, 131*, 607–614.
Beauvois, M. F., & Derouesne', J. (1982). Recherche en neuropsychologie cognitive et reeducation: quels rapports? In X. Seron, & C. Laterre (Eds.), *Reeduquer le cerveau* (pp. 163–189). Bruxelles: Pierre Mardaga.
Brookshire, R. (1969). Probability learning by aphasic subjects. *Journal of Speech and Hearing Research, 12*, 857–864.
Brunner, R. J., Kornhuber, H. H., Seemueller, E., Suger, G. & Wallesch, C. W. (1982). Basal ganglia participation in language pathology. *Brain and Language, 16*, 281–299.
Buffery, A., & Burton, A. (1982). Information-processing and redevelopment: towards a science of neuropsychological rehabilitation. In A. Burton (Ed.), *The pathology and psychology of cognition* (pp. 253–292). London: Methuen.
Caramazza, A. (1984). The logic of neuropsychological research and the problem of patient classification in aphasia. *Brain and Language, 21*, 9–20.
Chapey, R. (1981). Language intervention strategies in adult aphasia. Baltimore: Williams & Wilkins.
Code, C. (1983). Hemispheric specialization retraining in aphasia: possibilities and

1. SPONTANEOUS RECOVERY 35

problems. In C. Code, & D. J. Mueller (Eds.), *Aphasia therapy* (pp. 42–59). London: Arnold.

Collins, M. (1983). Treatment of global aphasia. In W. H. Perkins (Ed.), *Language handicaps in adults* (pp. 25–33). New York: Thieme Stratton.

Cubelli, R. (1985). Sull'impiego dei volontari nella rieducazione degli afasici. *Logopedia Contemporanea, 1*, 21–26.

Czopf, G. (1972). Ueber die Rolle der nicht dominanten Hemisphaere in der Restitution der Sprache der Aphasischen. *Archives Psychiatrie Nervenkrankheiten, 216*, 162–171.

David, R., Enderby, P., & Bainton, D. (1982). Treatment of acquired aphasia speech therapists and volunteers compared. *Journal of Neurology Neurosurgery and Psychiatry, 45*, 957–961.

David, R., & Skilbeck, C. E. (1984). Raven IQ and language recovery following stroke. *Journal of Clinical Neuropsychology, 6*, 302–308.

De Renzi, E., & Faglioni, P. (1978). Normative data and screening power of a shortened version of the Token Test. *Cortex, 14*, 41–49.

Eisenson, J. (1949). Prognostic factors related to language rehabilitation in aphasic patients. *Journal of Speech and Hearing Disorders, 14*, 262–264.

Gloning, K., Trappl, R., Heiss, W. D., & Quatember, R. (1976). Prognosis and speech therapy in aphasia. In Y. Lebrun and R. Hoops (Eds.), *Recovery in aphasics* (pp. 57–64). Amsterdam: Swets and Zeitlinger.

Golden, A. M. (1981). *Diagnosis and rehabilitation in clinical neuropsychology* (2nd ed.). Springfield: Charles Thomas.

Goldfarb, R. (1981). Operant conditioning and programmed instruction in aphasia rehabilitation. In R. Chapey (Ed.), *Language intervention strategies in adult aphasia* (pp. 249–263). Baltimore: Williams & Wilkins.

Hagen, C. (1973). Communications abilities in hemiplegia: effect of speech therapy. *Archives of Physical Medicine and Rehabilitation, 54*, 454–463.

Hanson, W. R., & Cicciarelli, A. W. (1978). The time, amount and pattern of language improvement in adult aphasics. *British Journal of Disorders of Communication, 13*, 59–63.

Hatfield, F. M. (1982). Diverses formes de desintegration du langage ecrit et implications pour la reeducation. In X. Seron, & C. Laterre (Eds.), *Reeduquer le cerveau* (pp. 135–160). Bruxelles: Pierre Mardaga.

Hatfield, F. M. (1983). Aspects of acquired dysgraphia and implication for re-education. In C. Code, & D. J. Mueller (Eds.), *Aphasia therapy* (pp. 157–169). London: Arnold.

Hatfield, F. M., & Shewell, C. (1983). Some applications of linguistics to aphasia therapy. In C. Code, & D. J. Mueller (Eds.), *Aphasia therapy* (pp. 61–75). London: Arnold.

Holland, A. (1970). Case studies in aphasia rehabilitation using programmed instruction. *Journal of Speech and Hearing Research, 35*, 377–390.

Holland, A., & Sonderman, J. (1974). Effect of a program based on the Token Test for teaching comprehension skills to aphasics. *Journal of Speech and Hearing Research, 17*, 589–598.

Howard, D., Patterson, K., Franklin, S., Orchard-Lisle V., & Morton, J. (1985). The facilitation of picture naming in aphasia. *Cognitive Neuropsychology, 2*, 49–80.

Johnson, M. G. (1983). Treatment of transcortical motor aphasia. In W. H. Perkins (Ed.), *Language handicaps in adults* (pp. 87–95). New York: Thieme Stratton.

Kenin, M., & Swisher, L. P. (1972). A study of pattern of recovery in aphasia. *Cortex, 8*, 56–68.

36 BASSO

Kertesz, A., & McCabe, P. (1977). Recovery patterns and prognosis in aphasia. *Brain, 100*, 1–18.

Kertesz, A., Harlock, W., & Coates, R. (1979). Computer tomographic localization, lesion size and prognosis in aphasia and non verbal impairment. *Brain and Language, 8*, 34–50.

Lincoln, N. B., McGuirk, E., Mulley, G. P., Lendrem, W., Jones, A. C., & Mitchell, J. R. A. (1984). Effectiveness of speech therapy for aphasic stroke patients. *The Lancet, 1*, 1197–1200.

Lincoln, N. B., Pickersgill, M. J., Hankey, A. I., & Hilton, C. R. (1982). An evaluation of operant training and speech therapy in the language rehabilitation of moderate aphasics. *Behavioral Psychotherapy, 10*, 162–178.

Lomas, J., & Kertesz, A. (1978). Patterns of spontaneous recovery in aphasic groups: a study of adult stroke patients. *Brain and Language, 5*, 388–401.

Luria, A. R. (1963). *Recovery of function after brain injury.* New York: Macmillan.

Luria, A. R. (1966). *Higher cortical functions in man.* London: Tavistock.

Luria, A. R. (1970). *Traumatic aphasia.* Le Hague: Mouton.

Luria, A. R., Naydin, V. L., Tsvetkova, L. S., & Vinarskaya, E. N. (1969). Restoration of higher cortical function following local brain damage. In P. J. Vinken, & G. W. Bruyn (Eds.), *Handbook of clinical neurology.* (Vol. III, pp. 368–433). Amsterdam: North Holland Publishing Company.

Marshall, R. C., Tompkins, C. A., & Phillips, D. S. (1982). Improvement in treated aphasia: examination of selected prognostic factors. *Folia Phoniatrica, 34*, 305–315.

McGlone, J. (1980). Sex differences in human brain asymmetry: a critical review. *The Behavioral and Brain Sciences, 3*, 215–263.

Meikle, M., Wechsler, E., Tupper, A. M., Benenson, M., Butler, J., Mulhall, & D., Stern, G. (1979). Comparative trial of volunteer and profesional treatments of dysphasia after stroke. *British Medical Journal, 2*, 87–89.

Messerli, P., Tissot, A., & Rodriguez, R. (1976). Recovery from aphasia: some factors for prognosis. In Y. Lebrun, & R. Hoops (Eds.), *Recovery in aphasics* (pp. 124–135). Amsterdam: Swets and Zeitlinger.

Mohr, J. P., Pessin, M. S., Finkelstein, S., Funkestein, H. H., Duncan, G. W., & Davies, K. R. (1978). Broca aphasia: pathology and clinical. *Neurology, 28*, 311–324.

Moore, W. H., & Weidner, W. E. (1974). Bilateral tachistoscopic word perception in aphasic and normal subjects. *Perceptual and Motor Skills, 39*, 1003–1011.

Patterson, K. E., Purell, C., & Morton, J. (1983). Facilitation of word retrieval in aphasia. In C. Code, & D. J. Mueller (Eds.), *Aphasia therapy* (pp. 76–87). London: Arnold.

Pettit, J. M., & Noll, J. D. (1979). Cerebral dominance in aphasia recovery. *Brain and Language, 7*, 191–200.

Pizzamiglio, L., Mammucari, A., & Razzano, C. (1985). Evidence for sex differences in brain organization from recovery in aphasia. *Brain and Language, 25*, 213–223.

Prins, R. S., Snow, C. E., & Wagenaar, E. (1978). Recovery from aphasia: spontaneous speech versus language comprehension. *Brain and Language, 6*, 192–211.

Sands, E., Sarno, M. T., & Shankweiler, D. (1969). Long-term assessment of language function in aphasia due to stroke. *Archives of Physical Medicine and Rehabilitation, 52*, 175–179.

Schuell, H., Jenkins, J., & Jimenez-Pabon, E. (1964). *Aphasia in adults.* New York: Harper.

Sparks, R., Helm, N., & Albert, M. (1974). Aphasia rehabilitation resulting from melodic intonation therapy. *Cortex, 10*, 303–316.

Subirana, A. (1969). Handedness and cerebral dominance. In P. J. Vinken, & G. W.

Bruyn (Eds.), *Handbook of clinical neurology* (Vol. 4, pp. 248–272). Amsterdam: North Holland.

Yarnell, P., Monroe, P., & Sobel, L. (1976). Aphasia outcome in stroke: a clinical neuroradiological correlation. *Stroke, 7,* 516–522.

Wepman, J. (1951). *Recovery from aphasia.* New York: Ronald Press.

2 Models for Therapy

David Howard
Department of Psychology, University College, London
Department of Speech Therapy, Homerton Hospital, London

Karalyn Patterson
MRC Applied Psychology Unit, Cambridge

In the last 10 years, a greater proportion of psychologists and linguists have been devoting a greater proportion of their time and attention to the behavior of neurological patients. There is no doubt that this attention has proved beneficial. Contrary to what a lay person might expect and hope, however, this benefit has been almost all for the scientist rather than the patient. We know considerably more than we did even a decade ago about the organization of cognitive processes, especially language, and how these can be disrupted by brain injury. It is from our patients that we have learned these things. In return, we have said very little other than "thank you."

Admittedly, this lack of reciprocation does not necessarily reflect meanness on the part of the researcher. Problem solving may be what researchers are (supposed to be) able to do, but some problems are harder to solve than others. Analyzing impaired cognitive processes, though complicated enough, is still easier than deducing how to rehabilitate them. Furthermore, there is a widespread (though, one could argue, unsubstantiated) belief that the development of treatment methods depends on, or at least will be facilitated by, analysis of underlying impairments. The claim is made (often, as Saffran (1986) noted, in the last line of applications for research grants) that better understanding of both the surface and deep structure of neuropsychological deficits will enable design of more rational and coherent treatment techniques.

Is the claim true? We know the answer no better than anyone else and can only say that we (are trying to) behave as if it were true. This

39

chapter represents one instance of that behavior. In other words, we shall argue here that rehabilitation can be informed by, as well as inform, models of cognitive processes, and indeed that this is beginning to occur. It is still a rare event, and even more rarely is it a properly designed and executed event; but there are grounds for cautious optimism.

Our discussion will derive entirely from the area of language deficits and, within language, mostly disorders of reading because language (particularly reading) currently is, as argued by Coltheart (1985), probably the best developed sphere of cognitive neuropsychology. Any general principles regarding the relationship between theory and therapy, however, should be just as germane to other domains, such as memory or perception. To readers more intrigued by these other topics, we apologize for the rather narrow net with which we cast. Furthermore, we acknowledge the artificial nature of the boundaries that differentiate such traditional domains within cognitive processes. It is clear, for example, that no model of language processing will accomplish its task unless it (eventually) incorporates various memory mechanisms (see Barnard, 1985, for one of the few attempts to deal with language and memory phenomena in the same framework).

The organization of our chapter will take the following form. The first section argues that analysis of neuropsychological deficits in terms of processing models allows us to identify specific target functions for therapy. The next section deals with the implications of this model-based deficit analysis for the design of therapy. The last section discusses the need for, and some guidelines for, properly designed experiments or trials to evaluate the effects of therapy.

WHY USE PROCESSING MODELS?

Most of the models currently popular in cognitive neuropsychology, although differing from one another in various ways, share certain common features. The major similarity is the assumption of modularity, namely that within a domain like language processing, there are a number of separable subcomponents responsible for different aspects of processing. The assumption is not, or at least need not be, that these individual components operate with complete independence when the system is functioning normally. Rather, it is that the manner in which the system is organized will allow one component to be disrupted without complete dissolution of processing within the domain.

This assumption of modularity may seem sensible on logical and/or biological grounds (Fodor, 1983; Shallice, 1979), but it is by no means a necessary or proven assumption. Furthermore, although we claim that most current approaches entail this assumption, they do so to varying degrees. Within the set of models for recognition, comprehension, and production of spoken and written words, for instance, some propose a separate module (or 'box') for virtually every potentially discrete process (see for example Ellis, 1982); others, based more on notions of parallel distributed processing (see for example McClelland, & Rumelhart, 1985), may only assume modularity at the level of rather gross domains of language processing. Thus, Allport (1986) acknowledges that we must distinguish a phonological domain from an orthographic one, but he suggests that complex and inevitable interactions among all aspects within one domain make it inappropriate to think in terms of highly discrete, separable components.

Each of these approaches (which are not, we emphasise, sharply conceptually distinct but rather lie on a continuum) has its strengths and weaknesses. A high degree of modularity holds special appeal for many neuropsychologists and neurolinguists because it seems compatible with the observed variety of distinct patterns of impaired and retained abilities. But it is far too early to judge whether this position will, in the long run, provide the best account of language behavior.

What are the reasons for preceding therapy with (and indeed basing therapy on) a deficit analysis in terms of a well articulated process model? First and foremost are the following pair of assumptions: (a) that deficits tend to be highly selective, and (b) that treatment for these deficits will be maximally effective only when the direction of treatment is determined by precise knowledge of the patients' processing capacities and incapacities. We acknowledge and emphasise that both of these are assumptions, and that the credibility of the former may be stressed or stretched by aphasic patients with a severe and wide-ranging disruption of language. Nevertheless, this assumption is by no means incompatible with any known evidence or case. Furthermore, it seems to us the only sensible working assumption until and unless we are persuasively challenged by an alternative hypothesis.

Before embarking on a treatment regimen with an aphasic patient, then, the goal is to determine which components of the patient's language system are impaired and which are operating with at least partial efficiency. Even with a processing model, this goal is not always easy to achieve; with some patients it may involve a lengthy and sophisticated assessment. Without a model, however, we claim that it will be all but impossible to determine what is (and what is not) impaired.

The basis for this claim is the fact that the same symptom can arise for a number of different reasons. To take a trivial but obvious example, a patient who can recognize printed words but cannot speak and a patient who can speak but cannot recognize printed words will both fail the oral reading section of any standard aphasia battery. No one would be likely to assume that these two patients should be accorded the same therapeutic treatment. Yet other instances of the same phenomenon (perhaps less blatant but, in the long run, no less misguided) may well result in identical treatment in the speech therapy clinic. That most ubiquitous of aphasic symptoms, word finding difficulty, can doubtless be caused by a number of different underlying impairments. The most common therapeutic technique for this symptom is probably phonemic cueing, despite the fact that such cueing will benefit only patients whose impairment is at a certain level (Howard, Patterson, Franklin, Orchard-Lisle, & Morton, 1985a). The most effective therapy will consist of treatment directed at the underlying procedure or knowledge base that is impaired. Analysis limited to the surface symptoms will not enable one to construct effective treatments because such symptoms can arise in various ways.

We have said that selection of an effective treatment depends crucially on knowledge of intact, as well as impaired, processing components. This will be more apparent in some approaches to treatment than others (e.g., reconstitution of function; see "Different Approaches to Treatment"). But even in approaches that do not attempt to substitute intact but unusual procedures for the impaired ones that would normally be used to accomplish the task, treatment must take account of the patient's remaining abilities. In fact, since it is always the pattern of retained and lost skills that is revealing, our claim is that one cannot really know what is wrong without also knowing what is right.

By no means do we intend to imply that a model-based deficit analysis solves all problems. For one thing, it is only the first stage. For another thing, there are no guarantees that the answer obtained will be the right one. The likelihood of getting it wrong, however, should be inversely related to the thoroughness and sophistication of the analysis. If one has the time, energy, and knowledge to assess all relevant aspects of function and furthermore to use converging sources of information, one should be able to make a well-informed decision as to the nature of the underlying deficit. By converging sources of information, we mean a number of different tests, all of which putatively require the same processing component. Thus, for example, an analysis of a patient's phonological output skills must assess spontaneous speech, naming, repetition, and oral reading; the tests of repetition and oral reading should evaluate sensitivity to a variety of factors, such as semantic variables (e.g., comparing concrete and abstract words), syntactic variables (e.g., comparing open and closed class words or nouns and verbs, and looking at sentence-level as well as word-level production), psychological variables (e.g., using words from a range of frequencies of usage), lexicality (comparing familiar words with pronounceable nonwords), and so on.

Another aspect of processing models important for the design of treatment is that the models offer hypotheses not just about the components of the system but also about the ways in which these components communicate with one another (i.e., the arrows as well as the boxes). Boxes in a process model correspond to representations of knowledge and/or procedures; arrows depict access from one representation or procedure to another. Therefore, impairments to (a) boxes and (b) arrows map directly on to classical notions, from the diagram makers of the 19th century (e.g., Lichtheim, 1885), of (a) lost centers of knowledge and (b) disconnection between (relatively) intact centers. The same basic distinction became popular in information processing approaches to the study of normal human memory and forgetting in the 1960s; in the terms used by Tulving and Pearlstone (1966), the question was whether a person failed to retrieve previously learned information because it was not available (meaning that the information had actually been lost) or because it was not accessible (meaning that the information was intact but, for some reason, difficult or impossible to retrieve). One of the main purposes of a model-based neuropsychological analysis is to determine whether a particular patient's deficit reflects problems in availability or in accessibility. This is one of the reasons underlying the need, previously expressed, for using a number of different tests that converge on a particular component. If, for example, a patient has lost actual representations in a phonological output lexicon used in many different tasks (naming, repetition, oral reading), then of course one expects failure in all of these tasks. If, on the other hand, the problem is one of access (say from a central conceptual/semantic system to phonological output representations, which are themselves intact), then one expects a different pattern of performance: possibly impaired naming but intact repetition and oral reading.

Shallice (1987) lists a number of criteria diagnostic of these two basic varieties of deficit. Apart from the procedure of testing various access routes to a particular component, there is for example the criterion of consistency. If a patient is asked to name the same object five times and fails five times, this is at least compatible with (though by no means does it conclusively prove) a deficit in the representation for phonological output. On the other hand, if the patient succeeds on two out of five occasions, then the phonological representation may be 'weak' but it is not lost. Another criterion involves cues or prompts. If a phonemic cue enables a patient to produce an object name that cannot be retrieved without the cue, then once again, the phonological form of the word cannot be *missing* from an output lexicon, although access processes are clearly impaired.

There is one final point to be made in this first section. A thorough, detailed deficit analysis in the context of a processing model must be applied to individual patients rather than to syndromes. Anyone who has tried to use standard aphasia classifications knows that syndromes are hypothetical constructs, useful for shorthand communication with other colleagues but for little else. Such classifications operate at a different level of specificity from that of well articulated process models. Even in the best standard reference works available (e.g., Goodglass & Kaplan, 1972, or Sarno, 1981), the typical level of a syndrome description is to suggest that auditory comprehension is impaired in syndrome *x*, or reading is impaired in syndrome *y*. There are two problems with such a description. First, it does not specify the way in which auditory comprehension or reading is impaired. Second, it fails to capture the very large and meaningful differences that are often found between two patients both of whom would be assigned the same syndrome classification. The level of an information processing model is better suited to a precise deficit analysis. First, it specifies a number of different potential reasons for an impairment in auditory comprehension or reading or whatever. Second, by focusing on all of the various components of the system and each individual's pattern of performance, it allows one to account for differences between two patients who are, in many respects, similar.

In all things related to rehabilitation, however, one must stay in touch with the pragmatics and constraints of the real world. It is all very well to suggest that every patient should be subjected to the most thorough possible assessment and, further, to imply that the range of available treatment techniques is so broad and rich that every distinct pattern of deficit could be accorded a uniquely designed therapy program. In practice, one does as much assessment as is feasible and, if patient *A* shows a pattern rather similar to that of patient *B* for whom treatment *x* seemed appropriate, one probably tries treatment *x*. Knowing that there are practical limitations on one's methods of operation, however, is not an argument against specifying potentially better ways to operate.

2. MODELS FOR THERAPY   45

DIFFERENT APPROACHES TO TREATMENT

Proper analysis of an aphasic patient's difficulties in terms of an information processing model should allow the therapist to decide the underlying cause(s) of a patient's problem. Many patients will have multiple problems, requiring a decision as to which problem should be the focus of treatment. There are two dimensions of this issue, and a deficit analysis is germane to only one. If the patient has two impairments of roughly equal significance in his or her everyday life, then it is possible that the analysis resulting in the treatment plan will dictate or at least suggest an order of attack. For example, Bachy-Langedock and de Partz (Chapter 7) treated their patient's reading disorder before his naming impairment because the therapy for naming could make use of skills developed in the treatment of reading. As for the other dimension, however, strategic decisions involving the importance of various impairments cannot be determined by a deficit analysis, but should instead reflect an assessment of a patient's needs and wishes in communication. Put crudely, there is little point in working to improve the reading of an aphasic patient who is not interested in reading.

Not only is an information processing deficit analysis mute on the topic of the patient's needs in therapy, it also has little or nothing to say about actual techniques for therapy. Two aspects of the deficit analysis, however, are important in this regard: whether the treatment target is knowledge of specific items, rules, or procedures and whether the problem is one of *loss* of stored information or of *defective access* to intact information structures.

There are three general approaches to specific treatment for specific problems: (a) reteaching of the missing information, rules or procedures; (b) teaching a different way to do the same task; and (c) facilitating the use of defective access routines. We shall consider each of these in turn with some examples of their use in well-designed studies of aphasia treatment. We shall exclude approaches that do not attempt to improve a patient's language, but aim simply to enable the patient to use his or her remaining language abilities as efficiently as possible (e.g., Davis & Wilcox, 1985).

Restoration Therapies

E.E. fell from a ladder when painting and suffered a severe head injury. His residual problems, 9 months after the accident, included surface dyslexia: He misread words with an irregular spelling-to-sound correspondence (e.g., SEW, PINT), pronouncing them as if they were nonwords ('/sju/,' '/pɪnt/'). This problem affects reading comprehension as well as oral reading: In general, E.E. understands printed words as he reads them (e.g., BUSY → "buzzy—that's making noises;" see Howard and Franklin, 1987). E.E. seems to have retained procedures for deriving predictable phonology from print, but has lost word-specific knowledge that would allow him to pronounce the irregular words of English.

Byng and Coltheart (1986) confronted this problem head on. First they took a set of 24 English words ending in OUGH (DOUGH, THROUGH, TOUGH, THOROUGH, BOUGH, COUGH, etc.), which represent one of the most notorious examples of inconsistency in English pronunciation. Before treatment, E.E. read 5 of 24 of these OUGH words correctly. The 24 words were divided into two balanced sets; for 3 weeks one set was the focus of treatment, which consisted of a simple mnemonic technique emphasizing the word meaning. For example, E.E. would have a card with a picture of the bough of a tree and the written word BOUGH. Each day, at home, he spent 15 minutes practicing the pronunciation of the 12 words in the treatment set.

At the beginning of each weekly session, E. E. was given all 24 words to read; over the 3 weeks he averaged 68% correct on reading the treated words compared to 31% for the untreated set. Although performance was significantly better with treated than with control items, there also seemed to be some improvement on the untreated items. Byng and Coltheart suggest that it is unlikely that this can be attributed to spontaneous recovery because, in the two months before treatment, repeated testing of the patient's oral reading of irregular words showed unchanged performance. It seems most likely that the improvement in the untreated set represented genuine generalization of treatment effects. In the next 2 weeks the focus of treatment was changed to the second set of words, which, up to that point, had been tested but not treated. At the end of these two sessions, E.E. made no errors on any of the OUGH words.

In treating a deep dyslexic patient, de Partz (1986) directly taught him a set of rules for relating spelling to sound (which she, in common with many other authors, calls "grapheme-to-phoneme conversion rules"). Like other deep dyslexics, S.P. was unable to read nonwords aloud; with real words he made a variety of errors including semantic errors (e.g., CERCLE → "rond;" CÈDRE → "olivier"), and he had particular difficulty with reading abstract words and function words (cf. Coltheart, Patterson, & Marshall, 1980). De Partz argued that if his nonlexical reading routine could be improved, S.P. would be able to use information from this routine to assist lexical routes to reading.

After 9 months of intensive therapy, S.P. had learned all the simple grapheme-to-phoneme correspondence rules in French, and his read-

2. MODELS FOR THERAPY   47

ing was reassessed. Nonword reading had improved from 2/30 before treatment to 27/30, and real word reading from 73/238 to 204/238. He used grapheme-phoneme rules with real words as well as nonwords, so that the majority of his errors in word reading were due to use of the simple, learned rules; these can of course give inappropriate results in a language like French. For example he had not been taught the context-sensitive rule for the pronunciation of C and G (C → /s/ when followed by E or I, otherwise C → /k/); therefore, he pronounced CESSE as "/kes/" and CELLE as "/kel/." This indicates that the patient's reading performance had changed as a result of his specific treatment rather than any nonspecific factors(s), such as spontaneous recovery. In fact, over a 9-month period, de Partz had turned S.P. from a deep dyslexic into a surface dyslexic! After a further period of treatment, during which S.P. was taught more complex grapheme-phoneme rules, his reading was even more substantially improved (98% correct overall).

Two recent papers present the results of treatment aimed at teaching information processing *procedures* to aphasic patients. Byng (1986) and Byng and Coltheart (1986) describe treatment of B.R.B., and Jones (1986) describes the treatment of B.B. Both studies deal with patients who were classically agrammatic in speech production: They omitted closed class words and inflectional suffixes, and main verbs were conspicuously lacking. In comprehension both patients showed difficulties with matching grammatically-complex sentences to pictures (e.g., in the TROG test; Bishop, 1982). Each investigator, however, claims that her patient's problem was not primarily syntactic, but concerned the mapping of meaning relations onto syntactic structures (knowledge of thematic roles; see Jackendoff, 1972; Linebarger, Schwartz, & Saffran, 1983; Schwartz, Saffran, & Marin, 1980). In Jones' (1984) test of verb comprehension, both patients showed the same pattern of performance. The test assesses sentence-to-picture matching with simple active reversible subject-verb-object (SVO) sentences involving three types of verb: nonmotion verbs (e.g., THE VICAR SHOOTS THE DOCTOR), nondirectional verbs of motion (e.g., THE TRAMP KICKS THE AIRMAN), and directional verbs of motion (e.g., THE MINER PASSES THE BUTLER). The three sentence types are identical in their syntactic structure (NP-V-NP) and differ only in the complexity of the thematic relations determining the semantic roles of subject and object. Both patients performed especially poorly with directional verbs of motion (e.g., PUSH, PULL, CHASE), where the meaning critically depends on knowledge of the thematic roles of the subject and object. Prepositions, particularly spatial ones, constitute another domain where thematic roles are vital: ON and UNDER describe

48 HOWARD AND PATTERSON

an identical spatial relation, differing only in the specification of their thematic roles.

The two patients were treated in complementary ways: Byng and Coltheart treated B.R.B. by teaching him about thematic roles in prepositional phrases. They used only written material for him to work with at home. He had to choose a picture to match a sentence involving a locational preposition (e.g., match THE PAN IS IN THE JUG to either a picture of a pan in a jug or a picture of a jug in a pan); he would then check to see if he was right. To start with, the words in the sentence and the objects in the picture were color coded, and B.R.B. had a mnemonic card to remind him of the relationship represented by the preposition and the roles of the noun phrases relative to it. The mnemonic card would have written on it "1 is in 2", and a picture of a "1" inside a "2;" the "1" was written in red and the "2" in blue in both the sentence and the picture. On the test cards, PAN was written in red and JUG in blue, and the objects were drawn in the same colors in the target picture. In the reverse role distractor, the colors in the picture were reversed. The color coding thus provided a backup; where B.R.B. was unsure he could use the colors to work out the answer. As he learned to perform this task, he had to test himself using sentences that were not color coded, which forced him to rely on the meaning relations expressed by the preposition. Therapy was based around five sentences for each of four prepositions. After 1 week of working at home, B.R.B. scored 17/20 on the practice sentences (tested without the color-coded cards); he asked to have another week to work on this. When he was retested at the end of the second week, B.R.B. was fast and made no errors on the treatment sentences.

Working with the patient B.B., Jones concentrated on tasks that required him to identify constituents that played different thematic roles. Treatment did not directly involve either sentence comprehension or sentence production; speech production was specifically *discouraged*. First, B.B. was given simple, written sentences, and taught to identify and label the verb. Then he was taught to identify the 'actor' and the verb in simple intransitive subject-verb sentences; he would label the 'actor' with the written term "who" (if it was animate) or "what" (if inanimate). The next stage was to identify verb, actor, and theme in transitive SVO sentences; this started with sentences where the actor was animate and the theme was inanimate. As B.B. gained confidence, he was given sentences where both actor and theme were animate and then reversible sentences. In the next stage, B.B. had to identify settings in sentences that involved locational prepositional phrases, labeling them with the written term "where."

2. MODELS FOR THERAPY   49

Further thematic roles were then introduced; B.B. learned to label constituents with "why," "when," and "how." In the next stage, more complex sentence structures were used, including passives, relative clauses, and other kinds of subordinate relations. Throughout, B.B. was not required to produce any spoken responses; all he learned was to identify the thematic roles played by different syntactic constituents.

According to both Byng and Coltheart and Jones, the difficulty in assignment of thematic roles was at least partly responsible for deficits in both sentence comprehension and sentence production. This theoretical account, therefore, predicts that treatment, although aimed exclusively at comprehension, should also result in improvement in sentence production (especially in producing all the arguments for a verb in the appropriate syntactic structure).

Both B.R.B. and B.B. improved in treatment. In both cases comprehension of grammatically-complex senences improved, as did comprehension of directional verbs in Jones' test. With B.R.B., Byng (1986) tested performance with both written sentences and spoken sentences; although treatment had involved only written sentences, B.R.B. had improved in comprehension in both modalities. Although treatment had involved only prepositions, his comprehension of both prepositional phrases and the argument structure around verbs had improved. Furthermore, his sentence production had improved as well; specifically, not only did he produce more correct sentences but verbs were used with more arguments. In other words, although treatment was confined to comprehension with one modality of input, its effects generalized across both task and modality. Byng (1986) was able to reject any suggestion that the improvement could be attributed to some nonspecific cause (spontaneous recovery and/or the interest of the therapist). Other functions, which had not been the focus of treatment, such as comprehension and oral reading of abstract words, were unchanged. There was not even a general improvement in all aspects of sentence processing: The patient's impaired ability to decide whether sentences violated strict subcategorisation conditions (e.g., SHE CARES FOR HER HAMSTER VS. SHE CARES UP HER HAMSTER) was unchanged. With B.R.B., then, specific therapy aimed at a specific procedure resulted in specific improvement in that process alone, which cannot be attributed to spontaneous recovery or to any nonspecific effects of treatment.

Both these studies support the theoretical claim that grammatical difficulties may reflect an impairment in relating semantic roles to syntactic structure. The outcome of the therapy studies provides strong evidence that impairments in sentence comprehension and

50 HOWARD AND PATTERSON

production were functionally, and not just accidentally, associated in these two patients. As Jones emphasizes, however, the appropriate treatment will be different for different agrammatic patients. Patients with types of agrammatic impairment at levels other than that shown by B.R.B. and B.B. (cf. Howard, 1985) may need to be treated in other ways.

Reconstitution of Function

The success of the restoration therapies just discussed may depend on the patient's ability to relearn procedures that normally underlie the performance in question. A different option is to use the patient's remaining processing abilities to achieve the same functional result in another (abnormal/unusual) way. This technique was popularized by Luria (1947, 1948, 1962) who invented the term "reconstitution of function," although the approach has roots that stretch back much further. Perhaps the most common example of this technique is teaching lip reading to a person with acquired deafness; if a person who can no longer perceive speech sounds auditorily learns to identify words from the speaker's visible articulatory gestures, then the same result is achieved but in a different way. A number of recent studies have applied such approaches with individual aphasic patients. The underlying assumption—that the defective processing system cannot be reacquired—is in a sense pessimistic. Nevertheless its implications, that human information processing systems are sufficiently elaborated to allow the same task to be achieved in multiple ways, are optimistic.

Hatfield (1982, 1983) used an approach based on item-specific reconstitution of function in the treatment of two deep dysgraphic patients (D.E. and B.B.). Initially both patients had great difficulty in writing function words to dictation (D.E., 49%; B.B., 34%). However, in parallel with the observations of Gardner and Zurif (1975) and of Morton and Patterson (1980) for reading, Hatfield noticed that her patients could often write content words homophonic with (or at least similar in sound to) the unavailable function words. Thus, a patient might be able to write INN but not IN, BEAN but not BEEN and OVER with reference to cricket but not to a spatial relationship. Hatfield used a set of content word homophones and near homophones as associated relay words in treating the function word disorder. When the patient heard each function word involved in therapy, he was to write the relay word; presented with "in," the patients learned to write INN; presented with "on," they learned to write RON. They were then taught necessary changes for each relay word to convert it into the corre-

2. MODELS FOR THERAPY   51

sponding function word; for RON, remove the first letter, and for INN remove the last. As the patients gained practice, they no longer needed to produce the relay word overtly but could internalize its use. At the end of the treatment phase, B.B. was substantially improved (64%), whereas for D.E. the improvement was less marked (67%).

A variety of examples of reorganization of function are described by Beauvois and Derouesne (1982). For four different patients, they provide an analysis of the patients' problems and detail the rationale for the treatment approach that they adopted. We shall summarize only one here. R.G. was a phonological dyslexic patient (indeed, the first patient to be described in the literature with this pattern of reading performance: Beauvois and Derouesne, 1979). He performed very badly in oral reading of unfamiliar words (simple, orthographically regular nonwords) but, apart from a mild deficit with function words and inflected words, R.G. correctly read all classes of real words presented as single items. His reading performance, however, was very much worse given text, and function words that would have been read correctly in isolation were often replaced by other contextually appropriate function words. Indeed, if asked to read aloud sentences with contextually inappropriate prepositions (e.g., The river flows over the old bridge), R.G. never read the sentences exactly as presented but always substituted semantically appropriate words.

Beauvois and Derouesne argued that R.G. was, as normal people do, using contextual information to generate expectations about words in sentences. Unlike normal readers, however, R.G. was apparently unable to override his expectations in order to read the words actually present. To improve his sentence reading, the authors adopted the somewhat paradoxical procedure of instructing R.G. to read sentences as if they were sets of isolated words. After a rehabilitation program lasting 1 month, R.G. showed considerable improvement in reading words (from 63% to 85% correct) and particularly function words (from 50% to 82%) in sentences; in contrast, reading of isolated words was unchanged. An alteration in R.G.s strategy for sentence reading, therefore, had caused an improvement specific to the target task.

Bruce and Howard (1987) describe a different approach to reconstitution of function. They were interested in enabling aphasic patients with word retrieval problems to use self-generated phonemic cues to aid word finding. Bruce and Howard argued that suitable patients will be those who (a) benefit from therapist-given phonemic cues, (b) are able to indicate the initial letter of the names of pictures they cannot name orally, and (c) are able to sound single written letters. As Behrman and Peelle (1967) suggest, such patients should be able to write down the first letter of a word they cannot produce orally and then sound out that letter, thereby producing a phonemic cue to help their word finding. In a study of 20 Broca's aphasics, Bruce and Howard (1988) failed to find any patients who were capable of all of these essential component tasks. With five patients who could both make effective use of phonemic cues and select appropriate letters, they used a microcomputer that produced auditory letter sounds when letter keys were pressed. Thus, an external prosthetic device was substituted for the patients' impaired ability to sound written letters aloud. After five sessions of practice, four of the five patients were very much better at naming with assistance from the microcomputer than at unaided naming. In Bruce and Howard's treatment, an external physical aid is used to provide the missing element for the successful use of a compensatory word retrieval strategy.

Facilitation Treatments

Two famous figures of aphasia therapy of the postwar period in the United States, Joseph Wepman and Hildred Schuell, developed treatment approaches (the 'stimulation school' of therapy) based on the assumption that aphasia usually involves defective access to intact linguistic knowledge. It is our belief that impaired access cannot be assumed but must be demonstrated, since aphasia may instead reflect loss of stored information. Earlier, we mentioned several different criteria germane to this distinction (Shallice, 1987). Where access routines can be shown to be defective, treatment approaches based on facilitation of those routines will be appropriate.

One aphasic symptom that often reflects impaired access is anomia. For example, in a study with 12 aphasic patients, we (Howard, Patterson, Franklin, Morton, & Orchard-Lisle, 1984) observed considerable day-to-day variability in the names that they were able to produce (although the overall naming score remained remarkably constant). Furthermore, most of the patients were significantly better at reading printed names aloud than at naming the corresponding pictures. Finally, with appropriate prompts (most notably phonemic cues), these patients could access names that they otherwise could not produce (Patterson, Purell, & Morton, 1983). All of these features suggest disruption of access to phonological word forms rather than a loss of the stored word forms themselves.

How might such impaired access be facilitated? The traditional approach has been to provide the patient with a 'mixed cocktail' of prompts, associates, and other kinds of additional information to enable production of the sought-for words; the assumption is simply that the more often a patient produces the appropriate word, the more accessible it will subsequently be, even without assistance from the therapist (see e.g., Schuell, Jenkins, & Jimenez-Pabon, 1964). Treatment studies demonstrate that these traditional combined approaches can indeed be effective in improving patients' word retrieval (Seron, Deloche, Bastard, Chassin, & Hermand, 1979; Wiegel-Crump & Koenigsknecht, 1973).

An unsophisticated drinker, wanting to reproduce the pleasant effects of drinking a mixed cocktail, would not know whether the entire mixture was essential or whether the effects were attributable to a particular ingredient. The same is true with mixed treatment regimens. Therefore, we attempted to assess the differential effects of specific techniques of the kinds often blended together. The design of our study, involving individual applications of each technique, enabled us to attribute any observed improvement to a single event. In different experiments we probed the effects of treatment after intervals varying from minutes to weeks. Using this approach, which is a development from Weigl's (1961) de-blocking technique, we were able to assess the long-term effects of single treatment events.

Two different classes of treatment techniques could be distinguished. Where the patients were provided with phonological information about the form of the wanted word (by word repetition, phonemic cueing, or rhyme judgments), there were large immediate effects on naming that disappeared after delays as short as 2 or 3 minutes. For example, in one experiment (Patterson et al., 1983), 58% of previously failed picture names were produced immediately with a phonemic cue; but when performance was probed 30 minutes later, the patients were no more likely to name the treated pictures correctly than comparable control pictures whose names had not been prompted. Such phonological treatments could be distinguished from techniques requiring patients to access the meanings of words that they could not retrieve as picture names; these semantic treatments included spoken word-to-picture matching (e.g., match the word "cat" to one of four pictures: a CAT, a DOG, a RABBIT or a PIG), written word-to-picture matching, and auditorily presented semantic judgments (e.g., answer the yes/no question "Is a cat an animal?"). All three semantic treatments produced significant facilitation of subsequent name retrieval, effects that were still substantial when probed 20 minutes or even 24 hours later (Howard et al., 1985a).

We followed these individual-event facilitation studies with a therapy experiment, contrasting both day-by-day and longer-term effects of phonological techniques with those of semantic techniques when each class was used repeatedly in daily therapy sessions (Howard, Patterson, Franklin, Orchard-Lisle, & Morton, 1985b). Performance on the treated items was compared with both naming control items (pictures presented for naming exactly as often as the treated pictures but for which assistance was never provided) and baseline control items (pictures never seen during therapy). Both classes of treatment produced steady improvement day by day. Because the treated items improved at a greater rate than the naming controls, we can be sure that these were specific effects of the treatments. After 2 weeks of therapy, patients were on average approximately 80% correct in producing the names of treated items, which they had failed to name on both of two presentations in pretests. Posttests at 1 and 6 weeks after cessation of treatment showed an advantage for the semantic class of techniques, primarily due to greater generalization from the semantic treatments to naming controls. Both classes of facilitation techniques caused item-specific improvements in access to phonological word forms.

EVALUATING THE EFFECTS OF TREATMENT

Selecting Experimental Designs

If specific treatment routines are to be applied to a patient's specific deficit, we would expect specific improvement. Improvement during the course of treatment will, of itself, be insufficient to establish that the treatment was effective. There are at least three possible sources of improvement, and treatment studies must adopt methodologies that allow these to be distinguished. First, there is improvement that would have happened independently of treatment, that is, spontaneous recovery. Second, there are nonspecific effects of treatment that can be attributed to the therapist's interest, encouragement, involvement, and help, but that are independent of the precise treatment routines involved. Third, there are specific effects of the particular treatment routines employed; this third variety is, of course, the kind of improvement most evaluations of treatment hope to detect.

Benefit from each of these three sources has, in principle, at least some unique characteristics. Two features of spontaneous recovery should help to make it identifiable as a source of improvement. First, it is generally accepted that spontaneous recovery is most pronounced in the first few months postonset (Culton, 1969) but may continue for periods of at least 1 year (Kertesz & McCabe, 1977; Sarno & Levita 1981). It seems likely that spontaneous recovery may continue beyond 1 year, but at an ever-decreasing rate, so that its effects may finally become undetectable (cf. Marshall, Holmes, & Newcombe, 1975). Treatment studies, therefore, may minimize (though not entirely preclude) the effects of spontaneous improvement by considering only patients who are at least 1 year postonset. The second point is this: Most aphasic patients have deficits in more than one aspect of language processing. Although there is no good reason to suppose that spontaneous recovery will benefit all of these aspects equally and simultaneously, it is rather implausible that spontaneous recovery should single out just the function that is the focus of therapy, at just the appropriate time. Therefore, as long as single case studies of treatment incorporate appropriate control conditions, they should be capable of discriminating between spontaneous recovery and treatment as the sources of significant change.

Effects of treatment can be distinguished in terms of the following (decreasing) levels of generalizability:

1. improvement that applies to all (or at least a number of) modalities and tasks in language performance
2. improvement specific to the modality or task that has been the focus of treatment
3. improvement specific to the actual items that have been treated and that does not generalize to other items within the same modality or task.

From the patient's point of view, improvement that applies to multiple modalities and tasks is of course that most desirable outcome. The experimental therapist, however, will find global improvement as a result of treatment hard to differentiate from general effects due to therapist involvement or spontaneous recovery. The only experimental method that can be usefully applied is the weakest available: the so-called time series design (for discussion of this design see McReynolds, & Kearns, 1983; Pring, 1986; and for an example of its use in aphasia see Weniger, Huber, Stachowiak, & Poeck, 1980). Here, the experimenter has to measure the rate of improvement during a period of treatment and also subsequently in a period when treatment is withdrawn or, preferably, when interest and support are provided without any specific treatment. In more sophisticated versions of the design, a series of treatment phases of the two types can be alternated; the treatment phases need last only as long as a single day (cf. Helmick & Wipplinger, 1975). This approach is not restricted to comparisons between treatment and no treatment (or therapist support); the effects of two different approaches to treatment can be compared in a time series design (e.g., Howard et al.,

1985b). If the rate of improvement during the one treatment phase is greater than during the other, we may conclude that the first treatment is having specific effects.

Although this approach is clear and straightforward in principle, it has some practical limitations. Where improvement happens during both types of treatment, it may be difficult to show that there is a real and significant difference in the rate of improvement. For this practical reason, it might be best to delay treatment until after the period of likely spontaneous improvement. However, as Schuell et al. (1964) claim, it may be that generalized improvement, even in response to treatment, is most likely in the period soon after injury, and so delaying treatment may reduce the probability that real effects of therapy occur.

It will be methodologically easier to establish the effects of treatment where they are specific rather than general. The basic approach is simple: If the treatment is directed at modality A (or task A), we would expect improvement to be confined to A, or possibly extend to other tasks that use (some of) the same information processing systems. We need to select a second task, B, which is, as far as possible, independent of A (in terms of the processing systems involved). Treatment should cause improvement in A and not in B; spontaneous recovery or therapist interest and support should result in improvement in both A and B.

This simple multiple baseline design has one important limitation. Because tasks A and B have to be tested using different task-specific tests, one could argue that B failed to improve simply because the tests of B were not sensitive to improvement (if, for example, there were not enough items, or if all the items were either very easy or very difficult, with none to detect improvement over a middle range), whereas A improved because the test for A was sensitive to improvement. Moreover, because the tests involve different modalities or tasks, there is no simple means of establishing that the two test routines are of equal sensitivity to improvement.

Coltheart (1983) suggests that the solution to this potential snag is a crossover design (which is otherwise called multiple baseline across behaviors; cf. McReynolds & Kearns, 1983); this adds a second phase to the experiment. After a period of treatment directed at task A, improvement is measured; then, there is a phase of treatment directed at task B, followed once again by measurement of performance. If A but not B improves when A is the focus of treatment, and B but not A improves when B is the focus of treatment, then we have very strong experimental grounds for claiming that each treatment has had specific effects. These results could not be explained away as any artifact of differential test sensitivity. The outcome of this kind of treatment experiment can be rather more difficult to interpret if *A* shows *some* improvement when *B* is the focus of treatment. Then it is not clear whether effects of treatment are generalizing (perhaps due to a shared processing component between tasks) or whether both tasks are improving from spontaneous recovery. To reduce the risk of generalization, the two tasks involved should be as independent as possible. Just as a time series design can be extended by further alternations of treatment, a crossover design may be extended by comparing three (or more) different treatments directed at three (or more) tasks.

Where improvement as a result of therapy is item-specific, all the problems of test sensitivity can be avoided. Individual items can be randomly allocated to either a treatment condition or a control condition, which should ensure that items in the two conditions will be directly comparable. If there is significantly greater improvement with the treated items than the controls, we can be confident that there are real effects of treatment. Only a single phase of treatment is necessary to establish treatment effects in a study of this kind (cf. Byng & Coltheart, 1986; Howard et al., 1985b).

Thus, three distinguishable classes of experimental design can be used to study the effects of treatment while avoiding the problems, for such studies, of comparisons *among* different aphasic subjects (see Howard, 1986). In practice, it may be possible (and wisest) to combine elements of more than one type of design. In our study of treatment of naming disorders, for example, we included both a comparison of two different therapy methods applied at different times (a time series design), and, for each therapy method, a comparison between treated items and untreated controls. By adopting a mixed design of this kind, we were able to examine both (a) whether effects within one treatment method were mainly item-specific or could be generalized to the procedure of word retrieval, and (b) whether the benefit, be it item-specific or item-independent, was specific to (or at least more substantial with) one of the two types of therapy. Ultimately, the choice of experimental design will depend on predictions that the therapist can make regarding the kind of improvement to be expected in treatment; this in turn will depend on the relationship, at a theoretical level, between the treatment used and the underlying information-processing deficit at which it is directed.

Practical Considerations

If one obtains significant and specific effects of a treatment directed at a specific target function in well-designed study, we can be confident that the treatment was appropriate for that problem in that patient. For other aphasia therapists to benefit from the information, both the treatment and the patient have to be described in considerable detail. The description of the patient needs to be sufficiently precise (a) to demonstrate the basis for identification of the underlying disorder, and (b) to allow another therapist to determine the ways in which a new patient resembles (and differs from) the original patient. Description of the treatment involved must be in sufficient depth that another therapist could use exactly the same treatment routines with his or her patient; in other words, it needs to be in 'cookbook' detail (cf. Coltheart, 1983).

Clearly described studies of treatment are easy to interpret where the outcome was success. Interpretation of null results, that is, where no significant treatment effects were found despite a properly designed study, are fraught with difficulty. The failure to find treatment effects could be due to any of the following four reasons:

1. The treatment was not appropriate for the patient involved.
2. Although the treatment was appropriate, the patient failed to improve because of additional impairments (e.g., frailty, ill health, lack of concentration, dementia, lack of motivation, etc.).
3. Although the treatment was appropriate, the patient failed to benefit because either treatment was not applied intensively enough, or was not continued for long enough.
4. There was real improvement in the target skill as a result of treatment, but this was not detected because the tests were not sensitive to improvement.

Although there is no way to guarantee in *advance* that a particular patient will be suitable or that a particular amount of treatment will be sufficient, etc., one can at least minimize the probability of obtaining a null result for any of the three final reasons by exercising common sense and making plausible choices on these matters. If, despite sensible design and planning, treatment is ineffective, then it may be reasonable to conclude that the first reason was responsible. We know, however, of no study of aphasia treatment that, in reporting a null result, has convincingly excluded the latter three reasons (see Howard, 1986).

Traditional approaches to the study of treatment efficacy, which depend on comparison between *groups* of patients, have naturally been concerned with questions of patient selection; this is because they have to ensure that the comparison groups are initially com-

2. MODELS FOR THERAPY   59

parable. In adopting experimental designs that compare the effects of treatment *within-subjects*, we need no longer worry whether patients are typical of the aphasic population as a whole or even of any subgroup within this population. Decisions about therapy for a given patient (whether to treat, how to treat, how much to treat), therefore, will depend on the specifics of the case, not its similarity to other cases.

In the best of all possible worlds, every aphasic patient would receive as much therapy as possible. In the real world of limited resources, however, attention will be preferentially devoted to those patients considered most likely to benefit. Such priorities seem especially defensible in decisions about whom to include in a controlled trial of efficacy of therapy. Thus, in order to give treatment its fairest chance, patients in therapy trials should in so far as possible be fit, motivated, and lacking in additional disabilities that might interfere with capacity to benefit from treatment.

The treatment needs to be sufficiently intensive and prolonged to give the therapy a reasonable chance of working. In a retrospective study, Vignolo (1964) found that global improvement in language was only likely after at least 72 hours of formal treatment over at least 6 months. By comparison, some more recent studies provide therapy that appears grossly inadequate; some of the patients reported by Sarno, Silverman, and Sands (1970) were treated for as little as two hours, and in Lincoln et al. (1984), almost 40% of patients had less than 12 hours of treatment. Under such circumstances, a null result can scarcely be surprising.

One must also be concerned about the sensitivity of pre-treatment and post-treatment assessments. Given that patients do not, generally, show remarkable consistency, item-by-item (Head, 1926; Howard et al., 1984), tests need to have a sizeable number of items if they are to serve as measures of change. Standardized aphasia tests rarely allow for this; the BDAE, for example, has only ten items in each of a number of its subtests. Lapointe (1977) suggests that improvement can be measured using a test with as few as 10 items; but this will only be possible where patients start off with very low performance levels and show great item-by-item consistency. Few patients are so frail as to necessitate assessments of this brevity; a minimum of 50 items seems reasonable. We (Howard et al., 1985b) used a naming test with 300 items and provoked no protest. Furthermore, the variety, as well as the number of items comprising a test, may be vital. In the BDAE assessment of oral reading for single words, none of the 10 words has an irregular spelling-to-sound correspondence. The rather dramatic improvement in irregular word reading that Byng and Col-

60 HOWARD AND PATTERSON

theart (1986) report for patient E.E. would not have altered his BDAE score at all. Ideally, our full range of assessment tests should capture all of the variables (that we know of) to which language performance is sensitive (though of course no individual patient's performance will be influenced by all of these). Finally, patients must still have room for improvement; there is no point in assessing performance on a test where the patient is near perfect.

CONCLUDING COMMENTS

If rehabilitation proves to be more effective when guided by processing models, then we will have both models for therapy and therapy for models. Theory will benefit therapy and benefit from it. This may occur in several ways.

First, it is often claimed that studies of normal and of impaired performance should provide converging sources of information for our understanding of cognitive processes (e.g., Shallice, McLeod, & Lewis, 1985). We endorse this claim and wish to extend it by arguing that a further potential source of confirmatory (or contradictory! but in any case pertinent) evidence is available from studies of treatment. For example, as noted in the report of our study on phonological treatments for anomia (Patterson et al., 1983), we already had reason to suspect that activation of a phonological code for output might produce more short-lived effects than activation at other levels in the processing system (e.g., components for recognizing and/or comprehending words). The results of the treatment study were compatible with our intuitions derived from experiments with normal subjects.

Second, studies of treatment may even address some theoretical issues that cannot (so easily) be illuminated by more typical neuropsychological case studies. For example, associated deficits in a single patient are always theoretically suspect. Does a patient show grammatical problems in both comprehension and production because these language functions share one or more processing components, or is the association attributable to impairments of separable (but anatomically 'close') modules? Valid theoretical conclusions, therefore, are thought to derive only from cases showing dissociations (Shallice, 1979). Treatment studies, on the other hand, may be a source of evidence (or at least hypotheses) regarding meaningful associations. As noted earlier in this chapter, only comprehension tasks were used in therapy for the agrammatic patients studied by Byng (Byng, 1986; Byng & Coltheart, 1986) and Jones (1986), but the patients' performance improved in sentence production, as well as comprehension. This suggests that the component of the processing system influenced by the treatment (according to the authors, mapping relations between semantic and syntactic structures) is one shared by language comprehension and production.

We make these points only to emphasize that, just as careful analysis of neuropsychological deficits provides a rich source of ideas and evidence concerning cognitive processes, proper studies of the way in which these deficits respond to treatment may also be informative. The main focus of our chapter, however, is the design of such treatments. We have argued that, to give therapy the best possible chance of succeeding, one must

1. Assess each patient's specific pattern of relevant performance
2. Analyze this assessment with reference to a detailed processing model
3. Direct treatment at the underlying deficit(s) identified by the analysis
4. Design the treatment in such a way as to enable evaluation of its efficacy.

Although these requirements will not always be easy to fulfill, the examples presented earlier 'convince us that they can often be achieved.

REFERENCES

Allport, D. A. (1986). Separable components? *Paper presented at the Cognitive Neuropsychology Workshop*, Johns Hopkins University, Baltimore.

Barnard, P. (1985). Interacting cognitive subsystems: a psycholinguistic approach to short-term memory. In A. W. Ellis (Ed.), *Progress in Psychology Language* (Vol. 2) (pp. 197–258). London: Lawrence Erlbaum Associates.

Beauvois, M. F., & Derouesné, J. (1979). Phonological alexia: three dissociations. *Journal of Neurology, Neurosurgery and Psychiatry, 42*, 1115–1124.

Beauvois, M. F., & Derouesné, J. (1982). Recherche en neuropsychologie et rééducation: quels rapports? In X. Seron and C. Laterre (Eds.), *Rééduquer le cerveau*, Brussels: Mardaga.

Behrman, M., & Peelle, L. M. (1967). Self-generated cues: a method for aiding aphasic and apraxic patients. *Journal of Speech and Hearing Disorders, 32*, 372–376.

Bishop, D. V. M. (1982). *Test for reception of grammar*. The Medical Research Council. Abingdon, Oxon, England: Thomas Leach Ltd.

Bruce, C., & Howard, D. (1987). Computer-generated phonemic cues: an effective aid for naming in aphasia. *British Journal of Disorders of Communication, 22*, 191–201.

Bruce, C., & Howard, D. (1988). Why don't Brocas's aphasics cue themselves? An investigation of phonemic cueing and tip of the tongue information. *Neuropsychologia, 26*, 253–264.

62   HOWARD AND PATTERSON

Byng, S. (1986). *Sentence processing deficits in aphasia: investigation and remediation.* Unpublished doctoral dissertation, University of London.

Byng, S., & Coltheart, M. (1986). Aphasia therapy research: methodological requirements and illustrative results. In E. Hjelmquist, & L. B. Nilsson (Eds.), *Communication and handicap* (pp. 191–213). Amsterdam: North Holland, Elsevier.

Coltheart, M. (1983). Aphasia therapy research: a single case study approach. In C. Code, & D. J. Muller (Eds.), *Aphasia therapy* (pp. 194–202). London: Arnold.

Coltheart, M. (1985). Cognitive neuropsychology and the study of reading. In M. I. Posner, & O. S. M. Marin (Eds.), *Attention and performance XI* (pp. 3–37). Hillsdale, NJ: Lawrence Erlbaum Associates.

Coltheart, M., Patterson, K. E., & Marshall, J. C. (Eds.). (1980). *Deep dyslexia.* London: Routledge and Kegan Paul.

Culton, G. L. (1969). Spontaneous recovery from aphasia. *Journal of Speech and Hearing Research, 12,* 825–832.

Davis, G. A., & Wilcox, M. J. (1985). *Adult aphasia rehabilitation; applied pragmatics.* Windsor: NFER-Nelson.

de Partz, M. P. (1986). Reeducation of a deep dyslexia patient: rationale of the method and results. *Cognitive Neuropsychology, 3,* 149–177.

Ellis, A. W. (1982). Spelling and writing (and reading and speaking). In A. W. Ellis (Ed.), *Normality and pathology in cognitive functions* (pp. 113–146). London: Academic Press.

Fodor, J. A. (1983). *The modularity of mind.* Cambridge, MA: MIT Press.

Gardner, H., & Zurif, E. B. (1975). Bee but not be: oral reading of single words in aphasia and alexia. *Neuropsychologia, 13,* 170–181.

Goodglass, H., & Kaplan, E. (1972). *The assessment of aphasia and related disorders.* Philadelphia: Lea & Febiger.

Hatfield, F. M. (1982). Diverses formes de desintégration du langage écrit et implications pour la rééducation. In X. Seron, & C. Laterre (Eds.), *Rééduquer le cerveau* (pp. 135–156). Brussels: Mardaga.

Hatfield, F. M. (1983). Aspects of acquired dysgraphia and implications for reeducation. In C. Code, & D. J. Muller (Eds.), *Aphasia therapy* (pp. 157–169). London: Arnold.

Helmick, J. W., & Wipplinger, M. (1975). Effects of stimulus repetition on the naming behaviour of an aphasic adult: a clinical report. *Journal of Communication Disorders, 8,* 23–29.

Head, H. (1926). *Aphasia and kindred disorders of speech.* Cambridge: Cambridge University Press.

Howard, D. (1985). Agrammatism. In S. K. Newman, & R. Epstein (Eds.), *Current perspectives in dysphasia* (pp. 1–31). Edinburgh: Churchill Livingstone.

Howard, D. (1986). Beyond randomised controlled trials; the case for effective case studies of the effects of treatment in aphasia. *British Journal of Disorders of Communication, 21,* 89–102.

Howard, D. and Franklin, S. (1987). Three ways for understanding written words and their use in two contrasting cases of surface dyslexia. In D. A. Allport, D. G. McKay, W. Prinz, & E. Scheerer (Eds.), *Language perception and production: shared mechanisms in listening, speaking, reading and writing* (pp. 340–366). New York: Academic Press.

Howard, D., Patterson, K. E., Franklin, S., Morton, J., & Orchard-Lisle, V. M. (1984). Variability and consistency in picture naming by aphasic patients. In F. C. Rose (Ed.), *Advances in neurology: Vol. 42. Progress in aphasiology* (pp. 263–276). New York: Raven.

2. MODELS FOR THERAPY 63

Howard, D., Patterson, K. E., Franklin, S., Orchard-Lisle, V. M., & Morton, J. (1985a). The facilitation of picture naming in aphasia. *Cognitive Neuropsychology, 2,* 41–80.

Howard, D., Patterson, K. E., Franklin, S., Orchard-Lisle, V. M., & Morton, J. (1985b). Treatment of word retrieval deficits in aphasia; a comparison of two therapy methods. *Brain, 108,* 817–829.

Jackendoff, R. S. (1972). *Semantic interpretation in generative grammar.* Cambridge, MA: MIT Press.

Jones, E. V. (1984). Word order processing in aphasia: effect of verb semantics. In F. C. Rose (Ed.), *Advances in neurology: Vol. 42. Progress in aphasiology* (pp. 159–181). New York: Raven.

Jones, E. V. (1986). Building the foundations for sentence production in a non-fluent aphasic. *British Journal of Disorders of Communication, 21,* 63–82.

Kertesz, A., & McCabe, P. (1977). Recovery patterns and prognosis in aphasia. *Brain, 100,* 1–18.

Lapointe, L. L. (1977). Base 10 programmed stimulation: task specification, scoring and plotting performance in aphasia therapy. *Journal of Speech and Hearing Disorders, 42,* 92–105.

Lichtheim, L. (1985). Ueber Aphasie. *Deutsches Archiv für klinische Medizin, 36,* 204–268. English translation, 1885: On aphasia. *Brain, 7,* 433–485.

Linebarger, M. C., Schwartz, M. F., & Saffran, E. M. (1983). Sensitivity to grammatical structure in so-called agrammatic aphasics. *Cognition, 13,* 361–392.

Lincoln, N. B., McGuirk, E., Mulley, G. P., Lendrem, W., Jones, A. C., & Mitchell, J. R. A. (1984). Effectiveness of speech therapy for aphasic stroke patients; a randomised controlled trial. *Lancet, 1,* 1197–1200.

Luria, A. R. (1947). *Travmaticheskaya afazia.* Moscow: Izd Akad Ped Nauk RSFSR. Translated by D. Bowden, 1970. *Traumatic aphasia.* The Hague: Mouton.

Luria, A. R. (1948). *Vosstanovlenie funktsii mozga posle traumy.* Moscow: Medgiz. Translated by B. Haigh, 1963. *Restoration of function after brain injury.* Oxford: Pergamom.

Luria, A. R. (1962). *Vysshie korkovye funktsii cheloveka.* Moscow: Moscow University Press. Translated by B. Haigh, 1966. *Higher cortical functions in man.* London: Tavistock.

Marshall, J. C., Holmes, J. M., & Newcombe, F. (1975). Fact and theory in recovery from the aphasias. In CIBA symposium 34; *Outcome of severe damage to the nervous system.* Amsterdam: Elsevier.

McClelland, J. L., & Rumelhart, D. E. (1985). Distributed memory and the representation of general and specific information. *Journal of Experimental Psychology: General, 114,* 159–188.

McReynolds, L. V., & Kearns, K. P. (1983). *Single subject experimental designs in communicative disorders.* Baltimore, MD: University Park Press.

Morton, J., & Patterson, K. E. (1980). Little words—no! In M. Coltheart, K. E. Patterson, & J. C. Marshall (Eds.), *Deep dyslexia* (pp. 270–285). London: Routledge and Kegan Paul.

Patterson, K. E., Purell, C., & Morton, J. (1983). The facilitation of word retrieval an aphasia. In C. Code, & D. J. Muller (Eds.), *Aphasia therapy* (pp. 76–87). London: Arnold.

Pring, T. R. (1986). Evaluating the effects of speech therapy for aphasics: developing the single case methodology. *British Journal of Disorders of Communication, 21,* 103–115.

Saffran, E. M. (1986). Reflecting on cognitive neuropsychology. Talk presented to the Cognitive Neuropsychology Workshop, Johns Hopkins University, Baltimore.

64 HOWARD AND PATTERSON

Sarno, M. T. (Ed.). (1981). *Acquired aphasia.* New York: Academic Press.

Sarno, M. T., & Levita, E. (1981). Natural course of recovery in severe aphasia. *Archives of Physical Medicine and Rehabilitation, 52,* 175–189.

Sarno, M. T., Silverman, M., & Sands, E. (1970). Speech therapy and language recovery in severe aphasia. *Journal of Speech and Hearing Research, 13,* 607–623.

Schuell, H. M., Jenkins, J. J., & Jimenez-Pabon, E. (1964). *Aphasia in adults: diagnosis, prognosis and treatment.* New York: Harper and Row.

Schwartz, M. F., Saffran, E., & Marin, O. S. M. (1980). The word order problem in agrammatism I: comprehension. *Brain and Language, 10,* 249–262.

Seron, X., Deloche, G., Bastard, V., Chassin, G., & Hermand, N. (1979). Word finding difficulties and learning transfer in aphasic patients. *Cortex, 15,* 149–155.

Shallice, T. (1979). The case study approach in neuropsychological research. *Journal of Clinical Neuropsychology, 1,* 183–211.

Shallice, T. (1987). Impairments of semantic processing; multiple dissociations. In M. Coltheart, R. Job, & G. Sartori (Eds.), *The Cognitive neuropsychology of language* (pp. 111–127). London: Lawrence Erlbaum Associates.

Shallice, T., McLeod, P., & Lewis, K. (1985). Isolating cognitive modules with the dual-task paradigm: Are speech perception and production separate processes? *Quarterly Journal of Experimental Psychology, 37A,* 507–532.

Tulving, E., & Pearlstone, Z. (1966). Availability versus accessibility of information in memory for words. *Journal of Verbal Learning and Verbal Behaviour, 5,* 381–391.

Vignolo, L. A. (1964). Evaluation of aphasia and language rehabilitation: a retrospective exploratory study. *Cortex, 1,* 344–367.

Weigl, E. (1961). The phenomenon of temporary de-blocking in aphasia. *Zeitschrift für phonetisches Sprachwissenschaft und Kommunikationsforschung, 14,* 337–361.

Weniger, D., Huber, W., Stachowiak, F. J., & Poeck, K. (1980). Treatment of aphasia on a linguistic basis. In M. T. Sarno, & O. Höök (Eds.), *Aphasia assessment and treatment* (pp. 149–157). Stockholm: Almquist and Wiksell.

Wiegel-Crump, C. A., & Koenigsknecht, R. A. (1973). Tapping the lexical store of the adult aphasic: analysis of the improvement made in word-retrieval skills. *Cortex, 9,* 410–417.

3 Some Issues in the Neuropsychological Rehabilitation of Anomia

Ruth Lesser
Department of Speech,
University of Newcastle upon Tyne, England

The starting point for neuropsychological rehabilitation should be a secure model of the cognitive function to be restored. Such a model should have built into it the possibilities of dysfunctions of components that correspond to observed behaviors in neuropathological conditions. Given such a desirable situation, the rehabilitator then has to consider what theory of recovery is most plausible for the formulated dysfunction (reactivation, reorganization or compensatory strategies, see Seron, 1982 and Lesser, 1985, and later discussion). The third step is to design and implement activities that might have some expectation of succeeding in initiating or fostering this recovery. Finally, the success or not of the activities in achieving this aim should be evaluated, feeding back, perhaps, necessary revisions to the rehabilitator's hypotheses about the nature of the disorder in this particular patient and to the original model of cognitive functioning proposed.

To what extent has the cognitive rehabilitation of anomia achieved these desirable aims? Most work has addressed the formulation of models of naming, with progressively less thought devoted to the other stages noted earlier. Before this work is reviewed, however, we ought to consider what activities are to be included in anomia, and what general therapeutic issues arise in the practice of persuading patients to produce names. Although mention will be made of modality-specific anomias, the following discussion will relate primarily to the multimodal naming disorder in aphasia, which Geschwind (1967) labeled "classical anomia," the main theme being an attempt to break

65

66   LESSER

down this condition into a number of disorders, each attributable to a different stage of dysfunctioning in the process of producing names. If these stages are confirmed, the extent to which different rehabilitative strategies are indicated will be discussed.

VISUAL NAMING VERSUS NAMING IN CONVERSATION: SAME OR DIFFERENT?

Naming activities can occur as part of natural language, that is, as the retrieval of content words in connected speech, or as referential naming (linking a word with the object to which it refers) as an isolated activity. The referential naming of objects or activities is a speech act that predominantly occurs in restricted situations, such as a mother looking at picture books with a toddler, or a therapist eliciting names in a clinic. Naming as an everyday activity is more likely to be concerned with expressing choice ("The minestrone"; "Day return to London") and, therefore, more likely to include qualification. It is noticeable, indeed, that some fluent patients in the clinic, when asked to go through a naming task, find it hard to restrict themselves to the production of only the name ("Well, that's a little bird"). It is inherent in the naming situation with the mother and toddler, or the therapist and aphasic patient, that the information which the production of the name conveys to the listener is not that inherent in the sense of the word, but is rather the metalinguistic information that the speaker can (or cannot) utter that name appropriately. The presumption is made in therapy that exercises in naming will be useful because they will help the patient to retrieve words when they are needed in sentences as part of natural discourse. It is a working hypothesis, but it ignores the fact that the processes used in confrontation naming must be, at a peripheral level at the very least, different from those involved in retrieving content words in the contexts of syntactic frameworks. Metalinguistic naming is stimulated by an object in the outside world, seen, felt, heard or associated with a definition, whereas retrieval of names in natural discourse is a more complex activity undertaken with a communicative and social purpose. Indeed, Brown (1972) has suggested from clinical observations that subtypes within his categories of semantic and nominal aphasias can be distinguished according to whether the predominant deficit is in referential or expositional naming. Some tentative evidence supports this clinical intuition. Williams and Canter (1982) found that confrontation naming abilities in anomia did not correlate well with the retrieval of lexical items in sentences describing activities in a picture. Wernicke's aphasics produced more names successfully for the composite picture, which encouraged use of sentences, whereas Broca's aphasics produced more names for simple pictures seen in isolation. More recently, Nicholas, Obler, Albert, and Helm-Estabrooks (1985) have reported that naming deficits, as measured by confrontation naming, did not correlate with the production of empty discourse (discourse with few content words) in their two kinds of aphasic patients (anomic and Wernicke's aphasics), as well as in patients with Alzheimer's dementia. Hadar, Jones, and Mate-Kole (1987) quantified a significant discrepancy in their head-injured case, P.B., between adequate word-finding in spontaneous speech and poor naming on formal tasks.

Such discrepancies cannot simply be a matter of having to process external stimuli in one condition and not in another because Nicholas et al.'s study used pictures in both conditions. Parisi (1985), advocating a careful analysis of the procedures involved in any language activity, notes that the load on working memory of a task needs to be taken into consideration. Load on working memory, he points out, may be less in describing pictures than in spontaneously generating an utterance because the visual stimulus remains in front of the patient as an aide-memoire. Explanations simply in terms of processing load, however, come across the incompatible situation that many anomic patients are able to contribute extended utterances giving partial information about a single word they are attempting to achieve when they cannot perform the apparently simpler task of producing the name itself. Thus, when the phonological form of a word is not available, anomic patients may overtly display that they can retrieve either partial phonological information or partial semantic information (functions, attributes, locations, personal reactions) or both. Indeed, some patients may produce in their circumlocutions the actual word they are seeking, while still continuing to search for it. We shall discuss shortly the extent to which a separation of semantic information from the phonological information in lexical items is justified by the evidence, but the anomic's behavior in retrieving partial semantic information also raises the question of the extent to which the semantic information in words has itself to·be reassembled. If a phonological pattern is available, reassembly does not seem to be required, and this is likely to be the case with words of high frequency. When this pattern is not immediately available, as in the tip-of-the-tongue condition, the assembly of semantic information seems to be achieved interactively with partial assembly of phonological information.

This possibility that semantic information has to be actively reas-

68   LESSER

sembled for infrequent word concepts has received little discussion in the psycholinguistic literature. In aphasia, with the shift of frequency often noted, high frequency words become treated as low frequency words. One case study has tentatively suggested that success in achieving associations in a word association task is related to the size of the potential pool from which those associations are drawn in such a way as to suggest that reassembly is easier when the components are not diffusely distributed (Lesser, 1973). Restriction of response choice aided response production in this patient.

For the proposed reassembly of grammatical (as opposed to semantic) features, there has been more extensive discussion in the literature, crystallizing around the claim that affixed words are stored in the lexicon in a form in which the base word is separate from the grammatical or derivational affix. Much of the evidence for and against this claim is drawn from the analysis of speech errors in normal speakers. Stemberger (1985a), for example, reviewing his corpus of 6,300 speech errors, found a general problem in accessing forms containing bound morphemes, detected when the base form was produced in error instead. Henderson (1985) has a comprehensive review of the evidence from normal subjects (including that obtained from priming experiments and lexical decision tasks) concerning the style in which affixed words may be stored in the lexicon. The neuropsychological literature provides some support for the claim that base forms of words are stored in the lexicon separately from affixes. Caramazza, Miceli, Silveri, and Laudanna (1985), from an analysis of the reading difficulties of two patients with phonological dyslexia, proposed that this applied both to inflectional affixes, which function grammatically, and to derivational affixes, which change meaning and grammatical class. Although known words may be read in their entirety by these patients, words unfamiliar to them may be processed by a morphological parsing device. Martin and Caramazza (1986) have also proposed that in deep and phonological dyslexia "it is the level of morphological decomposition and not the whole word recognition system that is disrupted" (p. 381). Lexical decision tasks in these patients may not show the influence of morphological decomposition because they only require the accessing of an address in the lexicon; in contrast, the requirement to read a word aloud does reveal the use of morphologically decomposed entries in the orthographic lexicon that must be accessed to obtain the phonological forms needed for speech.

At the level of morphological reassembly, then, and possibly at the level of semantic reassembly of unfamiliar words, there is some suggestion of an overlapping of cognitive activity between lexical retrieval and the syntactic formulation of sentences. It is also assumed that lexical selection and insertion into syntactic frames is a distinguishable stage in the microgenesis of an utterance. On this somewhat tenuous basis, there is some justification for using naming exercises in aphasia therapy as a step towards facilitating the more functional use of language in communication.

Naming difficulties are common in aphasia, occurring in all types, although they are the dominating feature in anomic aphasia, where they are not overshadowed by problems of comprehension or articulation. The origin of the naming difficulty, however, is likely to be located at different stages of the lexicalization process in different types of aphasia. Types of aphasic patients typically show different behaviors in picture naming (Kohn & Goodglass, 1985). Although semantic paraphasias are ubiquitous, according to this study, Broca's aphasics give more refusals to name or make more partial attempts, whereas anomic patients make fewest phonemic errors and most multiword circumlocutions. Wernicke's aphasics are the least helped by phonemic cuing with the initial sound of the target word. Kohn and Goodglass have distinguished two subgroups within the category of anomic aphasia, frontal and posterior. The frontal aphasics differed significantly from other groups in making most errors that consisted of naming a whole rather than the part which was indicated, for example by naming "hose" instead of "nozzle". The diagnostic potential for identifying types of aphasia through naming behavior alone, therefore, is limited. More important for the purpose of rehabilitation, however, is locating the probable source of the deficit for an individual, whether or not it coincides with that typical for the syndrome to which he or she approximates.

A COMPONENT MODEL OF VISUAL NAMING

A model of stages in the oral naming of stimuli in one modality, vision, is presented in Figure 3.1. It includes both the naming of objects (or pictures) and of written words. No distinction is made between the naming of objects and the naming of pictures because there is no evidence for any distinction in difficulty between them in "classical anomia." There is, however, very clear evidence that the naming of objects differs from the naming of written words in the many studies of patients who show marked discrepancies of ability between the two activities, and this will be discussed later with its implications for therapy. Figure 3.2 shows how some researchers have attempted to map types of object naming disorders on to a

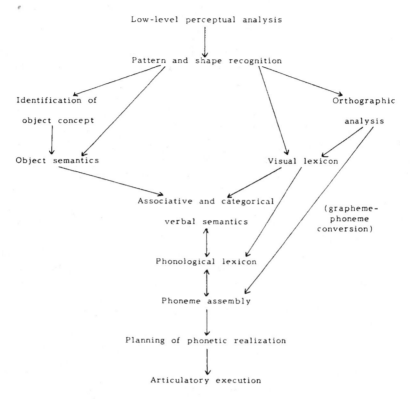

FIGURE 3.1. A simplified model of some stages in the visual naming of objects and words.

model of stages of naming such as that shown in Figure 3.1. Reading disorders have been omitted from Figure 3.2 because a plethora of models that attempt to map reading disorders on to cognitive models is available (see, for example, Coltheart, Patterson, & Marshall, 1980; Patterson, Marshall, & Coltheart, 1985). We shall first describe what the model in Figure 3.1 is attempting to capture and then try to justify the distinctions it makes.

In Figure 3.1, the first two stages are conceived of in terms of Marr's analysis of the first stages of perception into a "primal sketch" and "2½-D analysis", as interpreted by Ratcliffe and Newcombe (1982). The third stage in the naming of objects, of identification of the object concept, incorporates both Marr's creation of a 3-D model and the categorization of objects into what Morton (1985) has called "pictogens". The figure does not attempt to capture all the processes of translating visual perception into object recognition, for instance the achievement of object constancy. Morton (1985) makes a distinction between this and an object-semantics system that can be directly accessed, bypassing object pictogens. Beauvois and Saillant (1985) have also distinguished a visual-semantics system, leaving open the question of at what stage tactile information about objects should be incorporated. McCarthy and Warrington's (1988) patient, T.O.B., provides further support for the claim that there are separate visual and verbal semantic systems. This man had a selective and consistent

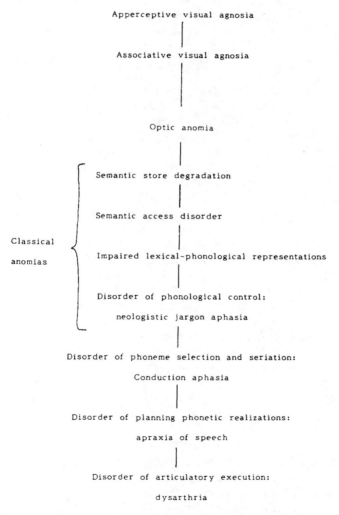

FIGURE 3.2. Conditions of impairment of object naming.

72 LESSER

impairment in understanding and defining heard names of living things (animals and plants) in contrast to objects, although able to name and supply information about pictured living things. Stage five, verbal semantics, is indeterminately described as associative or categorical in its organization because both forms may apply to different aspects of the system. Verbal semantics has been described as a pool of semantic features, related associatively or in categories with a hierarchic structure, or, alternatively, as the semantic lexicon, a somewhat misleading label if it is interpreted as a stage before lexical formulation. The phonological lexicon refers to the whole word forms to which semantic items are attached, before their realization, and corresponds to the system of output logogens in Morton's model. The realization of the lexical phonology into speech begins, it is assumed, with an assembly that comprises a selection of the appropriate phonemes (or perhaps syllables) and their seriation into the correct order. Following Stemberger (1985b), the model takes these central stages to be activated partially concurrently through parallel processing or cascading activity in which there is constant referral from the developing word. Phoneme selection and seriation is followed by preparations for the translation of the phoneme assembly into its phonetic realization. Finally, the phonetically organized instructions are transmitted to the articulators. The routes for the naming of written words, as shown in Figure 3.1, follow Morton's (1980) model. From visual orthographic analysis a direct route to phoneme assembly (or the "response buffer" in Morton's terminology) is possible through "grapheme-phoneme" conversion and is the means whereby nonwords are read. (We do not need to discuss the size of the units here, but see Coltheart, 1985.) More usually reading is achieved through a visual lexicon (or visual input logogens), which has direct access to the phonological lexicon (for reading whole words in an automatic way without accessing their meaning) and to the semantics systems.

APPLICATION OF THE MODEL
TO NAMING DISORDERS

The validity of the model presented in Figure 3.1, and its neuropsychological analogy in Figure 3.2, is crucial in planning the thrust of therapy for anomia. Therefore, we shall now attempt to justify the model, particularly in its central supramodal stages. Disorders of planning phonetic realizations (apraxia of speech) and of articulatory execution (dysarthria) are unimodal difficulties that are generally more easily diagnosed and will not be further discussed here (see Lesser, 1978, however, for discussions of the possible interactions between apraxia of speech and higher levels of language organization). In trying to validate the model we shall use the supporting evidence of neuropathological conditions, beginning with the stage of pattern and shape recognition.

Apperceptive visual agnosia, a failure to name objects due to lack of recognition of them, is empirically distinguished from aphasic anomia in that the patient cannot match objects or copy drawings. Ratcliffe and Newcombe (1982) have questioned its independence from low level perceptual analysis, although it is generally aligned with a failure in pattern and shape recognition (the second stage in Figure 3.1). Larrabee, Levin, Huff, Kay, and Guinto (1985) have described a case of apperceptive visual agnosia, which they contrast with visuoverbal disconnection. A particular form of apperceptive visual agnosia has been described by Humphreys and Riddoch (1984): this is a failure to achieve object constancy after right brain damage, which shows in an inability to recognize photographs of objects taken from unconventional angles. Humphreys and Riddoch have singled out two subprocesses in the achievement of object constancy that can be selectively impaired. These are, first, through processing of an object's local distinctive features and, second, through describing the object's structure relative to the frame of its principal axis.

Another form of visual agnosia has been described as "associative" rather than apperceptive because the patient can match and copy but cannot demonstrate the use of seen objects by gesture. Humphreys and Riddoch (1986) have presented a detailed case study of an individual with this disorder. Ratcliffe and Newcombe note that naming of three-dimensional moving objects is superior to the naming of line drawings by these patients. Both forms are considered to be visual disturbances rather than verbal disturbances and to parallel other modality-specific agnosias, such as tactile agnosia.

More detailed examination, however, has revealed that some cases of apparent visual agnosia are more appropriately interpreted as visual or "optic" anomias. That this is not a disturbance of perception or of higher order visual recognition is demonstrated by the patient's ability to identify objects visually by a description of their use or by their name (Poeck, 1984). Because these patients have signs of a left occipital lesion and callosal damage, the disorder is said to result from a physical disconnection between the registration of visual information by the right hemisphere and verbal semantics in the central zone of the left hemisphere. The naming difficulty occurs most

74   LESSER

conspicuously in the reading aloud of written materials, but silent reading is also compromised if the right hemisphere does not support the visual lexicon. Just as associative visual agnosia implies not knowing what the object means, this pure alexia implies not knowing what the written word means (although in some patients some limited comprehension of written words has been shown, e.g., Landis, Regard, & Serrat [1980]). The spontaneous production of speech and writing is unaffected in this condition, and the optic anomia may be restricted to colors. This visual-orthographic disconnection, called by Beauvois and Derouesné (1982) "agnosic alexia", can be bypassed by tracing over the letters in words to read them because writing is not disconnected from orthography. Overt tracing movements can gradually become internalized. Over time, such patients can learn to read sufficiently quickly by this tracing method to derive meaning and pleasure from the activity.

Some patients with this reading disorder of alexia without agraphia, however, do not respond to such a strategy, and Beauvois and her colleagues (Beauvois and Derouesné, 1982; Beauvois and Saillant, 1985) have demonstrated that the disorder in such patients can be profitably reinterpreted, not just as a failure of orthographic route to meaning and the phonological lexicon, but as an interference between visual semantics and verbal semantics at a more central level or visuoverbal alexia. The inspiration for such a reinterpretation came from a study of patients described as having a color agnosia whose behavior suggested that the disorder was in fact optic anomia (Beauvois uses the term "optic aphasia") for colors. A detailed case is described by Beauvois and Saillant (1985). Patient M.P. was given tests in which the cognitive processing required was purely verbal (describing a color association), purely visual (matching colors) or visuoverbal (with a visual stimulus and a spoken response or vice versa). The deficit occurred only on visuoverbal tasks, and, significantly, was maintained even when the visual element had to be imagined rather than being a visual stimulus. For example, although the patient was able to say what color people associate with snow (a verbal task), she failed when asked to imagine a snow scene and to say what color the snow was ("It is winter. Imagine a beautiful snowy landscape. There are mountains and you can see skiers going down the slopes. . . . now tell me what color snow is"). If M.P. inhibited speech on a visual task, such as categorizing colors, her performance was almost normal. Beauvois and Saillant locate the patient's difficulty as between "some high-level central visual processes (involved in visual identification as well as visual imagery) and some central linguistic processes" (Beauvois & Saillant, 1985, p. 35).

Beauvois and Derouesné (1982) provide an excellent example of how such an interpretation can be applied in remediation. M.P.'s alexia had failed to be remedied by the tactile tracing method because it was felt that, although the gestural perception so achieved might be able to access the visual lexicon, it was impossible to transfer this to reading aloud due to the visuoverbal interference. Some reading by a direct semantic route, without speech, was possible. M.P. was asked to look for several days at words written in poor handwriting (to discourage analysis through letter identification) and to think of what meaning they aroused for her without attempting any verbalization. She was then able to select an appropriate word from a set of three to match the picture. This task was performed without error on 35 words, showing a link between the visual lexicon and verbal semantics, provided that all verbalization, even implicit, was inhibited (i.e., if phonology was not involved). To extend her reading further to include reliable letter naming, a relay route using gesture was devised that bypassed the visuoverbal malfunction. The patient was taught to associate an arbitrary gesture with an arbitrary verbal code and then to associate the arbitrary verbal code with a letter name. This strategy was effective in eventually enabling M.P. to read for pleasure again.

An extension of this interpretation of alexia in terms of a high level visuoverbal malfunction has been proposed by Peña-Casanova, Roig-Rovira, Bermudez, and Tolosa-Sarro (1985). They describe a patient A.R. who could not use gesture to demonstrate the use of seen objects he could not name. The authors excluded (apperceptive) visual agnosia on the basis of A.R.'s good copying and discrimination of drawings and his WAIS Performance Scale results. Like Warrington's (1981) patient A.B., A.R. experienced more difficulty in understanding concrete words (with their strong visual and tactile associations) than abstract words. He also reported a loss of mental imagery and dreaming. The researchers suggest that the dysfunction in this case was not only between verbal semantics and visual semantics but was a form of visuogestural disconnection because the memory image of the object in use was not available.

The disorders so far described are typically not accompanied by a frank aphasia because spontaneous speech and writing are unaffected and auditory comprehension is unimpaired (hence Poeck's [1984] recommendation that the term optic anomia rather than optic aphasia should be used). At the next stage in the model we come to the question of naming disorders that are truly supramodal (i.e., those naming disorders which show themselves in errors in naming pictures because they are a reflection of a central problem affecting the use of names in any medium of language). In particular, some

76 LESSER

naming disorders are accompanied by a failure to understand the full meaning of words. This central anomia occurs not only in patients described as Wernicke's aphasics or anomic, but is also reported in unselected groups of aphasics (Butterworth, Howard, & McLaughlin, 1985), although the nature of the deficit is different in degree and may be different in kind in anterior and posterior patients. Two possibilities have been suggested as explanations. One is that the semantic representations of words have become degraded, and only partial information about word meaning is retained; another is that the information is potentially intact, but access to it is faulty, partial and intermittent (Shallice, 1986). As Ellis (1985) has pointed out, a model of name retrieval like the logogen model, which envisages words as achieving thresholds of activation before they can be passed on to output systems, does not account for the availability of partial information about word meaning, a behavior common not only in the target-related paraphasias of neologistic jargon described by Ellis but also in the circumlocutions of anomic speakers.

Semantic degradation has been described in a number of ways. Grober, Perecman, Kellar, and Brown (1980) interpreted it in terms of the defining and characteristic attributes of categories. They concluded that posterior aphasics base their decisions about category membership on characteristic features rather than defining ones. They might, for example, accept "chair" and "window" as members of the category of furniture, but not "rug" or "balloon", taking the characteristic feature of furniture as being made out of wood as their guideline. The semantic lexicons of these posterior patients appeared to be organized around personal situations and experiences (e.g., one patient rejected "airplane" as a vehicle, saying "I can't drive it, so it's not a vehicle").

Allport (1983) concluded that the anomic patient he studied could assign words to a broad semantic field but had difficulty in making more precise differentiation of word meanings (e.g., between a nail and a screw). Allport suggested that, because the patient was well aware of the different uses of such fixings in his Do-It-Yourself activities, "his disability must be located in the processes that translate between the word-forms and their underlying conceptual representations" (Allport, 1983, p. 77). Ellis (1985) observes that such findings endorse the distinction between a conceptual system and a lexical-semantic system (as is reflected in Figure 3.1), but postulates that the latter system comprises "a set of units, each of which corresponds to a word in the language, and each of which incorporates the definition of a word" (Ellis, 1985, p. 116). It is questionable whether such a tidy proposal takes sufficient consideration of the fuzzy and shifting nature of word meanings and of the difficulty normal speakers have in giving definitions of what even high-frequency words mean. The semantic paraphasias produced by aphasic patients during the course of attempting to name share many semantic features with the target word. Howard and Orchard-Lisle (1984) suggest that such semantic paraphasias, in a patient they studied with severe aphasia, show that the semantic representations of the potential words were incomplete. This patient was willing to accept associates to a picture as satisfactory names for it. Warrington (1981) and Warrington and McCarthy (1984) have also described aphasic patients in whom precise representations of word meanings appear to be unavailable, although broad category information (such as whether the word refers to a plant or animal) is retained.

The semantic degradation has also been described in terms of selective impairment to specific classes of words. The disorder can be interpreted according to one of three ways of classifying words (i.e., by degree of abstraction, by grammatical class or by semantic categories). Although most aphasic patients are expected to have more difficulty in retrieving abstract words (which are generally of lower frequency) than concrete words, Warrington (1981) describes a patient A.B. who was significantly worse in defining concrete words (e.g., "carrot") than abstract (e.g., "supplication"). She draws the implication that the neuropsychological organization for each must be different, concrete words being organized categorically and abstract words on bipolar dimensions. Warrington also describes differential impairment of semantic categories within the class of concrete words. A double dissociation was found in two patients between the names of living things and the names of objects. Selective semantic degradation of some categories compared with relative preservation of others in global aphasia has been used by Warrington and McCarthy (1987) in support of a theory that knowledge is organized categorically according to the relative importance of its perceptual and motor associations. Visual information may be important in categorizing plants, for example, but somatosensory information is important in categorizing small man-made objects. Operativity (the ease with which an object can be acted upon or with) has been reported to be influential on naming in aphasia (Gardner, 1973), although age-of-acquisition and picture familiarity were found to be better predictors of aphasic naming than operativity in Feyereisen, Van Der Borght and Seron's (1988) replication of this study. Another implication from a specific categorical naming difficulty has been drawn by Hart, Berndt, and Caramazza (1985). Patient M.D. showed considerable difficulty in naming fruits and vegetables, although he was not clinically aphasic and could name easily a large range of other pictures and objects. He was also impaired in sorting pictures of fruits and vegetables into their appropriate categories, and on tactile naming of them; he was able, however, to sort written names accurately and to point to pictures when he heard the name. Hart et al. (1985) adduce this as evidence that lexical categorization can be achieved through lexical information only (i.e., the phonological lexicon and orthography) without drawing on the semantic system. These claims are not incompatible with the degraded store hypothesis. The difficulties do not represent an absolute loss of words in one or other category. Warrington's (1981) patient, for example, who had an impairment in naming of living things achieved a range of success in giving definitions of them of 18% to 25% compared with 76% to 83% with objects. Neither failure nor success, therefore, was absolute.

The same applies to the other categorical disorder proposed by a number of researchers, that of problems with verb forms compared to noun forms; however, this has been explicitly linked with type of aphasia. Miceli, Silveri, Villa, and Caramazza (1984) reported that Broca's aphasics had more difficulty naming pictures of actions (i.e., producing single verbs) than naming pictures of objects, although anomic aphasics like normal subjects named more verbs correctly than nouns. The agrammatic Broca's aphasics' difficulty was apparently not in constructing the correct semantic representation for the action to be named but in retrieving a word of the correct grammatical form. Miceli et al. (1984) point out that retrieval of a verb in such a situation does not necessarily implicate syntactic processing and argue that the disability is at a lexical rather than a syntactic level. This implies that one dimension along which the lexicon is organized is that of grammatical form, and this study would suggest that this is at the level of lexical phonology rather than semantics. McCarthy and Warrington (1985) offer corroborating evidence from a case study. When a 42-year-old agrammatic patient with a progressively degenerating disease attempted to name actions, he frequently omitted the main verb (e.g., saying "The woman is a cup of tea") or used a noun as a verb (e.g., "The daughter was chairing").

The alternative to the semantic degradation hypothesis, the semantic access hypothesis, also has its advocates. The technique of priming with a related word in a lexical decision task has been used by Milberg and Blumstein (1981) and Blumstein, Milberg, and Schrier (1982) to investigate whether Wernicke's aphasics have a loss of semantic information or impaired access to lexical semantics. These studies report a priming effect, both in respect of fewer errors and faster reaction times. The researchers concluded that the semantic impairment in Wernicke's aphasia is not in lexical semantics itself but in voluntary access to such information. The distinction between voluntary and automatic processing is an important one in aphasiology, and we shall return to this later. Meanwhile Shallice (1986) has questioned Milberg and Blumstein's interpretation of their results as showing that lexical semantics as such may not be impaired in Wernicke's aphasia. He points out that the decrease in error rate they reported, from 40% with unrelated primes to 33% with related primes, shows that the error rate remains high despite facilitation through priming. As Shallice comments, such group studies conceal the possibility that individual patients may suffer different impairments. Shallice argues that an access problem in an individual would be revealed by inconsistency of performance and improved success when given more time. A degradation of the semantic store, in contrast, would show in consistency and in particular sensitivity to the effects of word frequency. (It should be noted, however, that word frequency effects could be interpreted as operating particularly at the stage of lexical phonology rather than semantics because frequency calculations have been based on word forms.)

These two hypotheses have different entailments for rehabilitation. An access problem would be expected to respond to assisted practice in retrieval under optimum conditions, supported by strategies for obtaining the desirable delay to allow processing time. A degraded store hypothesis has more implication that the patient and his listeners should adopt compensatory rather than reactivational strategies. Allport (1985), however, has questioned the division of semantics into store and access. The model of parallel distributed memory he applies to aphasia implies that a store does not exist independently of access to it because continuous processing and activation are inherent in the nature of the "store." Retrieval "is not a matter of fetching information from some storage location" but consists of "the reactivation of a specific activity pattern in a specific (that is, code-specific or content-specific) subset of elements" (p. 48). Content-specific subelements for "telephone," for example, might be the properties of shape, surface texture, size, manipulation, talk, and complex action routines. Unless the damage is extensive, loss of entire concepts would not be the consequence, some partial reconstruction always being possible. John (1982) proposes a similar theory of multipotentiality in neurophysiological terms.

Figure 3.1 implies that verbal (or "lexical") semantics is processed at a different stage from lexical phonology, and this is reflected in the different disorders distinguished in Figure 3.2. This claim, the "double-lookup lexicalization hypothesis," has been made by Butterworth

80   LESSER

(1980) and a number of other psycholinguists in respect to sentence generation. Kempen and Huijbers (1983) have also applied this hypothesis to the naming and describing of pictures. They describe two stages in naming, the first (L1) yielding abstract prephonological items and the second (L2) adding their phonological shapes. In connected speech, they propose several L1 items may be selected simultaneously in preparation for the utterance; retrieval of the L2 item, which corresponds to a given L1 item, waits until it has been checked by a monitoring process and all other L1 items needed for the utterance under construction have become available.

A distinction between lexical-semantic disability and lexical phonological disability is supported by two recent case studies. Hadar et al. (1987) describe an anomic woman, P.B., with good comprehension of word names and good retrieval in spontaneous narrative, but poor naming of objects and animals, though she made very few semantic paraphasias and benefited dramatically from phonemic cueing. They interpret this as a disconnection between semantics and the phonological lexicon. Kay and Ellis' (1987) patient, E.S.T., experienced severe word finding difficulties, characterized by circumlocutions rather than semantic paraphasias, both in reading aloud and in naming pictures, as well as in spontaneous speech (his reading behavior was in fact interpreted as surface dyslexia, see Kay and Patterson [1986]). His searching behavior while trying to find a name suggested that both semantic information and phonological information could be available (e.g., for stool: "[stɒp], [stɛp] . . seat, small seat, round seat, sit on the . . . sit on the. . . . [stə] . . . aye, there's five in it. . . . seat, that can't be . . . [stə], [stip], [stoʊn] it's [stoʊl] . . [stei] [stit]). Unlike Howard and Orchard-Lisle's (1984) patient J.C.U., E.S.T. was able to reject phonemic cuing of an associate of a target word as being inappropriate. Although giving him a correct phonemic cue often did not help him to retrieve the word, in about half of the occasions it assisted him to retrieve some partial information. The partial information he obtained, with or without this cuing, generally included the initial consonant cluster or syllable and maintained the syllable structure of the target word. Forty-two percent of his paraphasic responses corresponded to real words. Kay and Ellis propose that this patient's "word-finding difficulty should be understood in terms of a deficit in activating spoken word forms in a phonological (output) lexicon" (p. 625). They suggest that the strong influence of word frequency on success in E.S.T.'s naming can be used to corroborate this theory.

Kay and Ellis claim, moreover, that a deficit in the same process can result in neologistic jargon where the patient does not circumlocute or pause because of his word finding difficulties, but litters his speech with paraphasias and neologisms due to his problems in self-monitoring. This would be compatible with Butterworth's (1985) interpretation of jargon aphasia as a difficulty in addressing the phonological forms of words. In contrast to anomic patients like E.S.T., who does not produce jargon, patients with neologistic jargon aphasia appear to allow a "random phoneme generator" to fill word finding gaps in speech. In Figure 3.2 we have referred to this as a disorder of phonological control. Although neologistic jargonaphasics seem to have difficulty monitoring their own speech, their comprehension of other speakers is not necessarily impaired.

The "tip-of-the-tongue" state characteristic of E.S.T.'s naming behavior is different from that of the naming difficulties associated with conduction aphasia, a behavior characterized as "conduite d'approche." The phonemic paraphasias typical of this syndrome suggest that the phonological form of the word has been retrieved, but that the assembly of phonemes for its realization cannot be satisfactorily achieved. A key distinction between this behavior and E.S.T.'s is that these phonemic paraphasias are present (and indeed are even more marked) in echoic repetition in conduction aphasia, whereas E.S.T. had no difficulty in repeating target words and phrases. For the disorder of phonemic assembly in conduction aphasia, a remediation technique is to present the patient with the written form of the word (or to ask him to visualize it) and to show how its components can be broken down into shorter, more manageable units.

The phonological misproductions of conduction aphasics have been contrasted with those of Broca's aphasics by Monoi, Fukusako, Itoh, and Sasanuma (1983), corroborating the distinction proposed in Figure 3.2 between disorders of phoneme selection and seriation and those of planning phonetic realizations. Three patients with conduction aphasia (defined as having fluent, grammatical, well-articulated spontaneous speech but marked difficulty in repetition, increasing with polysyllabic words and unfamiliar phrases) were contrasted in a naming and repetition task with Broca's aphasics (who had non-fluent, effortful, short-phrased speech with awkward articulation). An analysis of the misnamings showed qualitative differences. Conduction aphasics made errors on both consonants and vowels, whereas Broca's aphasics made errors predominantly on consonants, which demand closer control of the articulators. Substitution errors counted for two thirds of the consonant errors in Broca's aphasics, but less than half in the conduction aphasics, for whom transposition errors were equally common. Substitution errors were closer to their targets in Broca's aphasia, most being deviant by only one distinctive

82   LESSER

feature. Monoi et al. (1983) proposed that the deficit in conduction aphasia is in phonological processing including the proper sequencing of phonemes, whereas in Broca's aphasia it extends to the articulatory planning of speech.

Comparing conduction aphasics with both Broca's aphasics and anomic aphasics on picture naming, Kohn (1984) found that all the conduction aphasics produced proportionately more phonologically-oriented series of searches (i.e., those sequences that contain only attempts with a phonological resemblance to the target word). Kohn discusses the possibility that the unit of planning for the utterance at this stage is the syllable rather than the phoneme and points out the tendency for these sequences to maintain a consonant-vowel structure and to be influenced by the frequency of syllables in making substitutions (e.g., in incorporating "ing" in naming "igloo" as in [ɪŋglu].

We have attempted to justify all the components of the model in Figure 3.1, except the disorder of reading, to which we shall return shortly, together with some comments on naming disorders expressed in writing rather than speech. The model, however, does not capture some aspects of naming behavior that are important in considering remediation (i.e., its dynamics and the coping strategies that patients employ). Moerman, Saerens, and Guleac (1985) have attempted to include these aspects in their analysis of a large corpus of misnamings. They examined 4,612 errors made by 61 nonselected aphasics in a visual naming task that required each person to name 40 colored slides five times, producing a total of 12,200 responses. Moerman and his colleagues identified six factors. The first factor was primarily linked with semantic paraphasias, perseverations, and delayed responses (the latter being distinguished operationally in terms of number of intervening items). This appeared to be a purely semantic factor, with no sign of a phonemic component, but signaling a defect in "conceptual background," according to the researchers' interpretation. Factor 2 was almost exclusively identified with phonemic paraphasia. Factor 3 was associated with circumlocutions, and was identified with all "escape mechanisms" except saying "don't know;" this factor appears to relate to preservation of the underlying concept but difficulty in retrieving lexical phonology. Adequate circumlocutions (i.e., target aimed, rather than tangential) showed no sign of phonemic disorder as such, corroborating the distinction made in Figure 3.1 between the phonological lexicon and phoneme assembly. Factor 4 was related to the few (40) portmanteau words that were produced, nearly 70% of which included a correct component linked with a paraphasic, perseverated or delayed response; this appears to reflect a difficulty in inhibiting additional semantic arousals at the earlier stage of isolating the required lexical phonological representation. Factor 5 was less well defined but was linked with aborted words (false starts), repeated sounds, and verbal paraphasias that share phonemic features with the target word; the researchers guessed that this was associated with a mechanism responsible for omissions, but do not interpret this further. Factor 6, loaded almost entirely on semantic paraphasias, might show incomplete disruption of a "guide-line linking concept and word" (Moerman et al., 1985, p. 118). This study, using factor analysis of group data, may therefore be taken as generally corroborative of the neuropsychological model that has been largely derived from single case studies.

The distinctiveness of the processes in naming pictures from those in naming written words has been discussed by Morton (1985). On the basis of absence of facilitation of word reading by priming from naming a picture (although the reverse occurred), Morton concluded that there is a fast direct route to the cognitive-semantic systems from pictures that is separate from the visual system used in reading. Object recognition can be achieved from partial information, whereas written word recognition requires processing of the entire word. Objects, Morton considers, can be recognized by direct processing in an objects-semantics system that can bypass the object categorization (pictogen) system.

One way in which the naming of written words has been proposed to differ from the naming of objects is in the specification of two routes that bypass the semantic system (Coltheart, 1985). One is a route that directly converts graphemes (and other subword units) into phonemes; it is claimed that the behavior of those patients who read irregular words as if they are regular (surface dyslexics) is evidence for this route. A second route is a direct route to the phonological lexicon (but not to lexical semantics) from the visual lexicon that allows whole words to be read aloud without comprehension of meaning, a phenomenon documented in hyperlexic children. In the reading route that does not bypass the semantic system, the naming of objects and written words meets a common semantic system (although Marshall (1988) raises the question of whether written and auditory input may access different semantic information). The semantic paralexias reported in deep dyslexia, therefore, are usually similar to the semantic paraphasias of aphasia.

Anomia occurs in writing as well as speech. The partial independence of these two modalities is evident in the common clinical observation of patients who, when unable to retrieve a spoken name,

84   LESSER

write it or parts of it or spell it aloud or by gestures in the air. That this is not due to any peripheral difficulty in articulating the words is evident when these patients follow these attempts by a fluent pronunciation of the word thus retrieved. Margolin (1984), therefore, infers that writing does not follow the phonological route used in oral naming, but may be generated through a direct route from a semantic input to orthography. This independence of the semantic route from phonology, however, has only been documented for one class of words, high frequency concrete words; the written naming of lower frequency words and of abstract words may require the mediation of phonology. Bub and Kertesz (1982) describe a patient whose spoken description of pictures was anomic with preserved syntax, whereas her written responses to pictures were agrammatic but with good use of nouns. They suggest that the direct lexical-semantic route the patient was using in writing only functions well with single words but cannot independently generate syntactically correct structures. The dissociation of disorders in speech and writing can be used to advantage in therapy. Fortunately, the combination of fluent retrieval of syntax in speech and of names in writing (or of sufficient graphic information for a reader to interpret the writer's intention) is not uncommon in aphasia and offers a functionally effective means of communication that the patient and family may learn to find acceptable.

When the disorder is in the semantic system itself, the prediction is that any task requiring creative lexical mediation will be disturbed. Nolan and Caramazza (1983), in accordance with this hypothesis, have described a patient V.S. with deep dyslexia who made similar errors in the oral reading of words and writing. These were semantic, visual, and derivational errors and showed significant effects of grammatical class and concreteness. V.S. was able to repeat spoken words and evidently had an intact auditory-phonological processing system that could bypass semantics.

DYNAMIC ASPECTS OF NAMING NOT CAPTURED BY THE MODEL

We have already referred to the ways in which a model, such as that in Figure 3.1 does not do justice to the dynamics of naming. One important aspect of these dynamics, which is particularly relevant to rehabilitation, is the discrepancy between volitional and automatic production. This phenomenon in neuropsychological syndromes has been described in amnesia, blindsight, neglect and prosopagnosia as well as in dyslexia and aphasia (Schacter, McAndrews and Mosco-vitch, 1988). In aphasia the phenomenon has been most discussed in respect of the stage of planning of phonetic realization in the behav-ior of apraxia of speech, but it also occurs at earlier stages of name retrieval. Willed searching for a presently unavailable word may not be successful, although the word may come to mind automatically in another context later. This has been reported as frequent in normal subjects (Reason and Lucas, 1984) as well as in aphasia. Whether the later successful retrieval is achieved simply as a function of delay or whether an interval of relaxation is facilitative is a moot point. Some evidence concerning this will be given later. There is also speculation regarding the extent to which volition may also draw on the same cognitive operations as underlie verbal semantics. Reason (1984) has proposed a three-component model of cognitive control. This first comprises schemata of preprogramed sequences, including speech, second an intention system, and third an attentional control re-source. The last is a superordinate selective agency, closely related to consciousness. Reason, discussing the application of this model to a theory of absent mindedness, draws the analogy of a blob of limited volume that skids from point to point over the schemata with their associated intention potentials. The blob, being of constant volume but not shape, can be focused on one point or more loosely dis-tributed, giving either focal or diffuse awareness of an activity. Rea-son argues that the cognitive strategies for coping with stress (in which one might include the stress of word finding in anomia) make heavy demands on the limited attentional resource, hence the in-crease in cognitive failures and the presence of recurrent thought patterns, a diminution of flexibility in the processing of information. On the basis of evidence from diaries kept by volunteers about their "tip-of-the-tongue" states, Reason and Lucas (1984) comment that particular sections of the word-store are "stirred up remotely by our intention, causing partial or complete items to be propelled into con-sciousness. By some means of which we are largely unaware these intermediates are matched against the "gap" unique to the tar-get. . . . This process may be repeated many times over several hours or even days of intermittent searching" (p. 54). Approximately 30% of all tip-of-the-tongue states resolved themselves spontaneously by the word eventually coming to mind. In about another 48% the word was brought to mind by the searcher applying a conscious strategy, such as alphabetic research, recall of contextual information or (most suc-cessfully) by generating "similar items" (the authors unfortunately do not specify the nature of the similarity, whether semantic or phonemic). Fifty-nine percent of tip-of-the-tongue states became

86   LESSER

"blocked", that is, an error word kept coming to mind, and sometimes these had to be resolved by seeking external help, asking friends, or looking in a reference book. These blocking error words were generally of a higher frequency/familiarity than the target. Where such blocks occur Reason and Lucas suggest that the best strategy is to abandon active searching, as this tends to establish the blocking word, and there is a reasonable chance that the target word will appear spontaneously without voluntary effort.

Neumann (1984) has also discussed the difference between automatic and voluntary processing. He proposes that mental operations function in two modes: one is an automatic passive consequence of stimulation, the second being controlled by the person's volitional though not necessarily conscious intentions. Both are subject to capacity limits and to control, but automatic processing is controlled at levels below conscious awareness. Discussing semantic priming effects, Neumann makes a distinction between the unconscious achieving of a state of readiness through priming by a related word and the interference caused by priming with an unrelated word. The latter, he proposes, becomes involved (and therefore conflicts) with the processing of the target word rather than assisting with the state of readiness for it. It is useful, therefore, he claims, to distinguish a state of readiness (involuntary) from processing itself, which is under voluntary control, although not necessarily open to conscious analysis. Priming offers some insights into the mental processes underlying language. Priming by category name is less effective than priming by an associate, but greater facilitation is achieved by a sentence context than by a single word. Even one or two intervening words abolish the priming effect when lists of single words are used, whereas priming can occur over a distance of more than 10 words in a sentence context. Moreover pictures can be used to prime words successfully even though the pictures are presented below the threshold for conscious identification. On the other hand, having to pronounce the word rather than simply to decide whether it is a real word can abolish the effect of priming; as Neumann points out, and as we have already discussed, an oral naming response can be derived from a phonological code without involving semantic access.

Neumann's analysis makes a distinction between voluntary processing and conscious awareness. Kuhlenbeck (1982) makes distinctions within consciousness. He considers that consciousness is used as "a generalization referring to an integrated manifold of modalities" (p. 106) (i.e., there is optic consciousness, acoustic consciousness, thought consciousness, emotional consciousness etc.). Although the neural basis for consciousness is cortical, subcortical structures seem to be essential for directing attention. Emotional consciousness in particular "represents a highly complex pattern of feelings or sensations superimposed or interwoven with other conscious modalities, and its neural substrate involves not only cortical but thalamic, hypothalamic and interlinking circuits" (p. 139).

Emotion has been linked with the right hemisphere by a number of researchers (e.g., Cicone, Wapner, & Gardner, 1980) as well as with limbic subcortical structures. In semantics connotative, or emotional, meaning would seem to be differently organized from denotive, or referential and sense meaning. Patients with right hemisphere damage are influenced by denotation and not by connotation in their decisions about which pair out of three words are best matched, whereas patients with left hemisphere damage show the opposite result (Brownell, Potter, Michelow, & Gardner, 1984). When aphasic patients have impaired access to some aspects of denotative linguistic knowledge or have a degraded semantic store, they may fall back on connotative elements of word meaning that rest on more general conceptual or interpretive cognitive abilities, perhaps partly mediated by the right hemisphere. The implication has been drawn from this for aphasia therapy that more success will be achieved, in naming and in other tasks, when items are used that are emotionally relevant to the patient. Wallace and Canter (1985) have reported significantly better performance by severely aphasic patients on naming and other tasks when personally relevant rather than nonpersonal items were used.

IMPLICATIONS FOR INTERVENTION

We have reviewed some of the issues involved in the analysis of the complex disorders that underlie anomia and the planning of model-related therapy. Before we turn to a survey of how therapists have in fact attempted to help patients with anomia, we will give a brief account of the theories of recovery from aphasia that have been proposed and their implications for principles of active intervention in rehabilitation.

Kertesz (1984) has briefly reviewed the neurobiology of recovery from brain damage. It is noteworthy that slow growing lesions do not result in the same deficit as lesions of sudden onset. The evidence for this comes not only from studies of animals given small serial lesions, but from observations of patients with neoplasms that do not result in aphasia until at an advanced state. Some adjustment of function in compensation for damage is therefore the norm, and it is the suddenness of the insult, from stroke, head injury, or other cause, that typically provokes the symptoms of aphasia. The initial damage from a sudden insult is compounded by diaschisis or malfunctioning of areas around the zone of major damage where the nerve cells have died. Studies of metabolic changes, using Positron Emission Tomography, have confirmed this depression of activity in the surrounding areas. There is an inhibitory effect of catecholamines after a stroke that gradually disappears after a few months. Some biologically based functional recovery, therefore, may be achieved through involvement of these recovering peripheral areas in the activity formerly performed by the dead tissue.

It has also been proposed that the homologous areas in the right cerebral hemisphere also participate in the transfer of function. There have been several suggestions that the residual language of aphasic patients is in fact being mediated by the right hemisphere; this has been proposed not only for globally aphasic patients with extensive left hemisphere damage, but for patients with a milder disorder, in that the restricted lexical-semantic abilities of the right hemisphere have been credited with the semantic paraphasias that occur in deep dyslexia (Coltheart, 1980). Regard and Landis (1984) have extended this claim to include the experimentally induced semantic paraphasias of normal subjects. The implications for therapy will be discussed briefly later.

Maximum potential recovery, however, may not be achieved spontaneously through this biological recovery and interhemispheric reorganization. John (1982), even in the context of Lashley's multipotentiality theory of recovery of function, notes that recovery need not occur spontaneously but "depends on the quality and quantity of postoperative stimulation" (p. 251) in lesioned animals. Seron (1982, 1984) has analyzed the issues for aphasia therapists in deciding which rehabilitative strategy to adopt: to reactivate, to reorganize, or to accommodate to the patients' difficulties by improving their environment. Rehabilitative neuropsychology can encompass four main kinds of strategy. First the aim can be to reestablish the function exactly as it was before the lesion. Stimulation therapy falls into this category and inherently involves decisions about hierarchies of difficulty in language, so that therapy can begin with what is considered to be the easiest level. Such hierarchies may be derived from linguistic notions, from norms of language acquisition, or from observations of the performance of groups of patients on aphasia tests; but, as Seron points out, none of these hierarchies has been reliably established.

A second strategy is to support the deficient activity by using another modality, for example gestures, pictures of mouth shapes, or kinesthetic feedback to assist speech production in apraxia of speech. The new modality may act as a temporary aid to improve the damaged function toward its original state, or it may substitute for the defective one, laying down, for example, new patterns of mouth movements controlled by different neural schema from the original.

A third strategy is aimed at this last possibility, that of reorganizing the central processes themselves by using different processes to achieve the same surface behavior. Underlying this approach is the belief that the original competence has been lost and that alternative means must be found to achieve the same ends. This form of recovery is referred to by Miller (1984) as "functional adaptation" and is emphasized by him as a particularly important means of recovery. Although the approach used is often pragmatic, this strategy should be based on a clear model of what processes are dysfunctioning and what alternative systems might be available to the patient.

The fourth strategy identified by Seron is the use of external prostheses. Seron cites the example of a patient with left visual field neglect who failed to generalize from training of awareness of this field in clinical exercises. The therapists supplied him with a little box, the size of a packet of cigarettes, which he was asked to carry in his left pocket; this emitted a sound at irregular intervals, which the patient had to turn off, thus drawing his attention to his left field. An application of this strategy to anomia is the keeping of a reference book in which the names with which the patient often has difficulty can be written down and read when needed. The increasing availability of microcomputers is making it practical to consider drawing on such resources to help patients with word finding difficulties. Colby, Christinaz, Parkinson, Graham, and Karpf (1981) have described the development of a word finding computer program that can assist a patient with an anomic difficulty if some information about the word can be supplied (i.e., at least three pieces of information concerning, first, the topic area; second to fourth, the initial, final, or a middle letter; and, last, an associate of the word). The program is capable of adjusting the word search according to the frequency with which the patient shows the need to retrieve a word. At least one less sophisticated version of such a package is now commercially available. In this program, a word prediction facility offers a choice of words from a dictionary, the five most likely words being shown on the display according to the letter selected; the dictionary adapts itself to the individual patient.

In discussing the rehabilitation of patients with anomia, we should remind ourselves that the aim of rehabilitation is not to restore the ability to name pictures or single written words. It is the restoration of the ability to use words in communication, almost invariably within sentence and discourse constraints. Although, as we reported earlier, the ability to name pictures does not necessarily correspond to the ability to use nouns in connected speech, the assumption is made that therapy for anomia will have a carry-over effect on the functional use of language in communication. The assumption that anomia should be considered as a distinctive problem is one expression of the currently powerful claim that the mind is organized in interacting but essentially separable modules. In language one multifaceted module has been assumed to be a lexicon, another the syntactic organization of sentences, and another phonological processing. That this is an oversimplification is evident from the fact that the lexicon includes phonological and grammatical components, the latter not only in respect of grammatical inflections and derivational inflections that mark grammatical class but also in respect of the grammatical arguments that are entailed in predicative words. Nonetheless, the observation that there are patients who seem to have more problems in lexical retrieval than in constructing sentences and others who seem to have more problems in constructing sentences than in lexical retrieval has been used as justification for treating anomia as a distinct problem.

In discussing rehabilitation strategies for anomia, we shall adopt Howard, Patterson, Franklin, Orchard-Lisle, and Morton's (1985a) distinction between facilitation (achieving a temporary performance) and therapy (achieving a longer lasting benefit that may generalize to other performances).

Techniques used to facilitate naming include phonemic cuing (with initial sound or rhyme), sentence cuing, cuing with semantic associates (deblocking), repetition of the whole word, introducing a delay (perhaps with relaxation), cuing with a written word and picture, and requiring both a gesture or a written rehearsal and an oral one. Techniques used in therapy for anomia fall broadly into two classes: the first includes stimulation and drilling, the second the use of bypass strategies ranging from mental devices to the use of external (low technology or computerized) aids.

A few studies have compared and evaluated the use of some of the facilitation techniques listed. Pease and Goodglass (1978) compared the relative effectiveness of six kinds of clues: initial phoneme, rhyme, open-ended sentence, superordinate word, location, and function. The most effective facilitator was the phonemic cue, the second being the sentence, and all types of aphasics (anomic, Broca's and Wernicke's) had the same rank order. If the model presented in Figure 3.1 is correct, it seems that the most common difficulty was access to the phonological lexicon from verbal semantics. Facilitation by sentence cuing could support word retrieval in two ways: first it includes an associate word ("She bought a saddle for her. . . ."), and second, it activates another aspect of the language system, syntax.

Patterson, Purell, and Morton (1983) compared the effects of repetition and phonemic cuing. In repetition, they varied the number of repetitions and the time gap before retesting. There was a short-term beneficial effect of repetition (an increase of success from 30% to 70%), but it did not increase significantly according to the number of repetitions, and after a filled delay of about 5 minutes, naming was only slightly better after repetition than without it. Phonemic cuing was confirmed as facilitating, especially if up to three of the initial phonemes were progressively given. With such help, 87% of the words that the patients had previously failed to name were successfully named after 20 seconds, compared with a success rate of 58% after 20 seconds when only the initial phoneme of the word had been given as a prompt. However, even when no help at all had been provided, 20% of words that had not been retrieved initially were successfully retrieved after 20 seconds, and, 30 minutes later, both cued and uncued words were named with an equal success rate of 25%. Such brief help over a short session, therefore, achieved some short-lived facilitation, but, within this span, no longer-term effect was detected. Had such an effect occurred, anomia therapy would have been very much easier to apply than generations of aphasia therapists have experienced.

This study also shows that some improvement in naming occurs simply as a function of delay. Two studies have examined whether relaxation training enhances the retrieval of words during this delay. Marshall and Watts (1976) compared 16 aphasic subjects' ability to name 15 common objects, supply the names as sentence completions, repeat the names, and give the functions of the objects. The patients were tested both after a 30-minute relaxation schedule and in a control condition where they spent the same amount of time in a quiet room. Mean scores for the naming task (but not for the other tasks taken singly) were significantly higher in the relaxation condition than in the control condition. PICA-type scoring (as developed in the Porch Index of Communicative Abilities) was used, however, which includes the dimensions of efficiency, delay, responsiveness and completeness besides correctness. Nonetheless this parallels the experiences of normal speakers referred to earlier who can retrieve names better when they are not actively searching for them, a situation that

92   LESSER

can create blocking error words. The psychophysiological basis for an improvement in anomia with delay and relaxation remains an intriguing area for exploration. A second study gives some corroboration to these findings (Honeygosky, 1979). This study used "creative imagination" exercises in relaxing the patients, such as are used in hypnosis. Ten patients showed improved naming when results on two sets of 50 pictures were compared after 18 minutes spent on the 10 creative imagination exercises. The improvement was an average of 15.6 more words named out of the 50, greater than would be expected simply as a function of delay.

Weigl (1961) has outlined two case studies showing facilitation of picture naming through the "phenomenon of temporary deblocking." In patient P.I. this was achieved through repetition, with a reported improvement from 60% to 100%; in the other patient, L.D., naming improved from 30% to 100% when the patient was given a set of four words to read, one of which was the name of one of three pictures that he saw. Weigl considered that deblocking was effective because it was the summation of two subliminal processes. These two examples use processes drawn from different modalities to provoke this summation.

Another application of this notion of cross-modal summation is the use of gesture cuing, with Amerind signs. Drummond and Rentschler (1979) have compared this type of cuing with phonemic cuing and with sentence completion cuing. Eight patients were given daily treatment sessions lasting up to 30 minutes for a period of 2 weeks. No significant differences were found between cuing conditions at the end of the period, however.

In another paper, Weigl (1970) recommends deblocking by prestimulation of semantic fields, including not only the target word itself, but a superordinate, a synonym, a semantically related word, an antonym etc. He notes that this can be counterproductive on some occasions because the patient uses one of the incorrect words that has been supplied. This was the experience reported by Howard and Orchard-Lisle (1984) with their patient J.C.U. who, when given a phonemic cue for an associate word, accepted it as the target word. It appears, in fact, to be a blocking technique rather than a deblocking technique. Podraza and Darley (1977) have confirmed this theory. They investigated in five patients the effect of supplying semantic associates for a target word. Their study compared unprompted picture naming with naming after four types of auditory cues, using, in addition to sets of three semantic associates, the first phoneme, an open-ended sentence, or hearing of a list of three words that included the target word. The last three conditions all facilitated naming, but providing the three semantic associates produced a significant deterioration in naming success. Four of the five patients made an increased number of semantic paraphasias in this condition. In terms of our earlier discussion of the location of central anomias, this implies a degradation of the semantic store because, in an access problem or a disorder of the phonological lexicon, one would expect the incorrect word to be rejected for a picture presented to the patient.

The type of open-ended sentence provided also has an influence on the amount of facilitation of naming achieved. Cohen, Engel, Kelter, and List (1979) compared sentences where there was a degree of choice for the final word ("Around the garden there was a high . . . ") with sentences where the final word was absolutely constrained, as in nursery rhymes and clichés. After an interval of 24 hours, naming that had been assisted through the use of the first type of sentence was more successful (77%) than that cued by the second type (68%), which in turn was more successful than naming that had been unassisted (14%). The researchers suggest that the better facilitation was due to the patients' need to undertake a semantic search when choices for open-ended sentences were available.

Howard et al. (1985a, 1985b) have further explored this notion of a semantic search being important in facilitating naming. Techniques that required the patient to process meaning were compared with techniques that required processing only of the phonological form of the word. In one experiment (1985a) the semantic condition involved pointing to one of four pictures to match a heard word, with or without naming of the picture after six intervening events (i.e., work on other words); in the control condition no semantic decisions had to be made. The facilitation of naming by the semantic condition lasted at least 20 minutes. In a second experiment, it was found that this facilitation applied only if the semantic search involved the target word itself rather than an associate (such as "lion" if the target word was "tiger"). There was no facilitation if an associate word had to be sought; facilitation only occurred when the meaning of the target word itself was processed, but this effect lasted at least 24 hours. In a third experiment, selecting pictures for a written word as a treatment was compared with making semantic judgments (e.g., "Is a roof part of a house?") without pictures. Both conditions improved naming when this was tested about 20 minutes later. The only activity common to all these facilitations was that they were all comprehension tasks requiring the patients to access semantic representations for the name. A fourth experiment investigated the effects of repeating a name, judging whether the target name rhymed with another, or being given a rhyming cue; none of these activities necessarily drew

94 LESSER

on semantics. These conditions all tended to have a short-lived facilitating effect, but this was substantially less than the strong facilitating effect of having to perform a semantic search.

In Howard et al. (1985b) the effects of "semantic therapy" and "phonological therapy" were compared directly, with all the semantic techniques and all the phonological techniques applied respectively as packages. Each patient was given eight treatment sessions. Semantic therapy proved to be more effective than phonological therapy on retesting after 1 week, although both resulted in significant improvement. The improvement was no longer observed by 6 weeks, however.

These are all small-group studies, and interpretation in terms of the model given in Figure 3.1, and its pathological analogies in Figure 3.2 would require more information about individuals than is given in the published reports of the studies. In general it seems that most aphasic patients respond better to semantic facilitation, and this suggests that a semantic difficulty may be the prevalent one in anomia or that there are more interactive links between semantics and the phonological lexicon than the model implies. Ogrezeanu and Voinescu (1984) consider that naming requires a two-stage semantic operation, first in the selection of the semantic field and secondly in the selection of the individual word from that semantic field. The facilitation they suggest is the use of semantic divergent techniques, such as naming unusual uses for objects, discussing what other objects share similar shape, color, material features with the target etc.

The prevalent form of therapy for anomia used in clinics is probably still that recommended by Wepman (1951) and Schuell, Jenkins, and Jiménez-Pabón (1964), as stimulation therapy. These recommendations, in particular those of Schuell, rely heavily on repetitive auditory stimulation rather than aiming to elicit a specific response. In terms of the model proposed in Figure 3.1, this kind of technique may only be appropriate if the difficulty is in mapping the verbal semantics on to the phonological lexicon. Howard et al.'s group studies suggest that improvement in naming does not indeed depend on requiring the patient to produce that name in speech, but that activity at a central semantic level is likely to be the important component in most aphasics in an unselected group. The implication is that intensive auditory stimulation (i.e., hearing the word repeated several times) is not the most effective technique. Auditory lexical analysis, like graphemic analysis, does not necessarily require access to the lexical semantic system.

Some success has been reported with the multimodal versions of stimulation therapy (for which many kits and workbooks exist, e.g.,

Keith, 1980). Wiegel-Crump and Koenigsknecht (1973) reported success with four anomic patients trained with a multimodal approach over 18 therapy sessions. There was an improvement in naming on words in categories that had been drilled and also some generalization to words that had not been drilled. Seron, Deloche, Bastard, Chassin, and Hermand's (1979) study used a similar multimodality approach to therapy in 20 sessions over 2 months with eight patients. Four received therapy aimed at 10 words from each of four categories (clothes, houses, tools, action verbs), whereas four received "classical" therapy aimed at a large number of items. The first group showed more improvement than the second, and there was transfer of learning to words in undrilled categories (food and animals).

All these studies of facilitation and therapy have been undertaken within a frame of reference in which reactivation is seen as the dominant role of intervention. Techniques that draw on what are claimed to be right hemisphere abilities are assuming a theory of reorganization underlying recovery rather than reactivation. Three main rehabilitative strategies for involving the right hemisphere have been proposed: using its resources in prosody, drawing on its capacity for imagery, and strengthening its involvement in lexical comprehension.

Using the right hemisphere's participation in music and the intonational aspects of prosody provides the rationale for Melodic Intonation Therapy as described by Helm-Estabrooks (1983). Essentially, however, its main application is in the facilitation of the production of short phrases that may be of communicative use, rather than in naming as a way of fostering lexical retrieval. In terms of our model in Figure 3.1, Melodic Intonation Therapy aims at helping a relatively peripheral aspect of word production, that of planning phonetic realizations. It is, therefore, likely to be most helpful to patients with apraxia of speech and intact semantics.

Visual imagery would be predicted to operate at the central level of verbal semantics and to be of assistance if the problem is one of access to a semantic store. Its use has been advocated by Maly and Wikus (1979) and Fitch-West (1983). Maly and Wikus studied 10 anomic patients, comparing their ability to retrieve nouns in a sentence completion format with that using an imagery technique. This consisted of pairing a name that the patient had not been able to retrieve with one successfully retrieved, using imagery to show how the two concepts could be linked in a joint action. A naming test 7 days later showed a significantly superior performance on the words to which the imagery technique had been applied. Fitch-West summarizes two unpublished Masters' theses showing that verbal descriptions heightening visual imagery enhanced recognition memory for written words in 16 aphasic patients, and that paired-associate learning in aphasics was best when pairs of pictures were used, rather than when pictures were linked with words or words linked with words. Fitch-West recommends the use of visual imagery in aphasia since "it seems to be largely a consequence of right hemisphere processing" (p. 218); she argues that "when brain damage has severely dampened the processing strategies associated with the left hemisphere, emphasizing strategies associated with the right hemisphere is a more viable therapeutic goal than stressing linguistic recovery per se" (pp. 216–217).

The presumed latent semantic abilities of the right hemisphere have been exercised as a therapy technique by Buffery and Burton (1982). This technique, so far reported as successful with one patient, requires the right hemisphere to make semantic choices based on trimodal inputs: tactile input from the left hand that manipulates letter shapes, visual input from the left hemifield that reads a word and auditory input from the left ear that hears a word. The right hemisphere is thus invited to detect which of the three different words so presented is not semantically associated with the others. To encourage the making of this decision more by the right hemisphere than by the left, masking stimuli are given to the left hemisphere through each of the three channels. A modified application of this technique, using only dichotic listening and involving phonological decisions, has been reported by Code (1983). Burton and Kemp (1986) have investigated this technique further to stimulate the right hemisphere in aphasia. They tested explicitly the effect of semantic processing or "priming" on naming. The semantic priming took the form of hearing a word and deciding whether it matched a picture. The word was presented to the left ear, with a masking word in the unattended ear. Right hemisphere priming in this fashion was compared with left hemisphere priming and with biaural presentation. In each condition, half the attended words were the correct ones for the picture that the patient saw. For one patient changes in number of errors in naming of pictures before and after priming was the dependent variable, whereas in the other patient with a milder anomia reaction times were used. Comparison conditions were also included where the patients were asked to name, during the retest period, pictures (either primed or unprimed) they had not named before. The results of this study suggested that, far from assisting, this type of semantic priming resulted in poorer or slower naming. Words retested without the priming treatment were named more easily, showing an improvement in naming simply as a function of being allowed to have a second attempt after a delay. This is consistent with the reports in earlier studies we have discussed. Semantic priming, however, appeared to interfere with this process. From one patient there was a slight indication that there might be some facilitation from the priming, but this occurred with left hemisphere stimulation rather than right. The only information given about the language disorder in these patients is that one had Broca's aphasia and one had a moderately severe anomia. Although superficially these results can be taken as contradictory to Howard et al.'s results (1985a), it is clear that the timing and duration of semantic priming may be critical. The dichotic task in which the patients heard two words simultaneously while being asked to attend only to one may have added an extra confusion. So may the fact that for half of the pictures used in the priming task an incorrect word was presented to the attended ear. It is also possible that the disorder of naming in these two patients was not a central semantic disorder. The role of the right hemisphere in communication, and the extent to which it may be productively used in aphasia therapy, is still far from clear (see Code, 1987, for a general review).

The studies just described concern rehabilitative strategies applied to presumably unconscious modes of operation, but recently there has been increasing interest in the patient's conscious use of overt strategies to assist communication. Beauvois and Derouesné's (1982) study, already described, illustrates this with reference to one type of reading disorder. Behrman and Peelle (1967) describe how self-generated cues can be used to trigger the production of names. One patient with severe word finding difficulties could often retrieve a word if given a phonemic cue. He could also often spontaneously write the first letter. The therapists taught him, over a period of time, to acquire a strategy whereby he wrote the first letter of the word he was trying to find, then sounded out the letter, then cued himself with this sound to produce the word. This also is a "relay" strategy in Beauvois and Derouesné's terminology. Another patient described by Behrman and Peelle could produce associative words for a target word when she failed to retrieve the target word itself and could also use associates provided by the therapist as a cue to retrieval. Teaching her to regard her own utterance of associates as a productive strategy for self-cuing instead of a frustrating error facilitated her word retrieval. Some patients acquire these strategies spontaneously, as indeed nonaphasic people do in the "tip-of-the-tongue state." Some aphasic patients, however, may have to be specifically taught them and encouraged in their use. One important influence that neuropsychology has had on aphasia therapy, as a byproduct of

98 LESSER

cognitive model making, is to make therapists more aware of the need to discuss with the patient their analysis of his or her difficulties, where possible, to enhance the patient's own metalinguistic insight into suitable compensatory strategies. Green (1982) has listed some possible strategies that patients can be encouraged to develop when they fail to retrieve words.

1. use of another modality (e.g., gesturing, drawing, pointing)
2. giving the listener an associated word
3. allowing an error to be produced and then correcting it, rather than "blocking" in silence
4. giving parts of words in speech or writing and relying on context to complete the sense
5. using fillers to maintain the listener's attention (e.g., "erm," "you know") and asking the listener to wait
6. asking for help.

Specific strategies to encourage generalization of naming from an exercise in the clinic to functional communication have been advocated by Davis and Wilcox (1985). In their system for Promoting Aphasics' Communicative Effectiveness (PACE), therapist and patient have a stack of stimulus items in front of them that serve as a basis for brief conversations initiated alternatively. The stack of items, where appropriate, may include pictures of objects or actions or their written names. Any means of communicating the information is accepted from the patient, and the therapist models through his or her own behavior what is to be fostered in the patient. The PACE format provides a setting where strategies such as those listed earlier can be rehearsed.

CONCLUSION

It is clear from this summary of anomia therapies that a major limitation has been the lack of an adequate theory-based analysis of naming disorders that could be applied to individuals. Most reported studies of therapy for anomia have concentrated on the examination of a technique applied to groups of subjects, rather than on selection of a technique on a principled basis as appropriate for a specific disorder in an individual.

The component model described here provides a starting point for an analysis of an individual patient's difficulties and for planning theory-based intervention, the careful evaluation of which may in turn modify the model. Although assessment of a patient's difficulties may be initiated by the therapist's sharpened perceptions of the patient's spontaneous behavior in terms of the model, there is also a clear need for developing specific assessment materials that will assist in identifying disordered subcomponents. These materials need to control for a number of factors that, as the present paper has described, are known to influence naming, such as word frequency, length, articulatory complexity, abstractness and part of speech; such controls are more easily built into an assessment battery rather than applied post hoc to the analysis of spontaneous utterances. A battery applying psycholinguistic theories is currently being tested (Kay, Lesser and Coltheart, in preparation).

Such an assessment battery will assist in the more exact definition of an individual's disorder and in the planning of targeted therapy directed at specific components of the naming process. This is one example of the hypothesis testing approach to aphasia therapy, in which recent developments in neuropsycholinguistic theory now allow for a clear formulation of what hypotheses should be tested.

A major oversimplification of the model presented in Figure 3.1, however, is that it does not allow for the interactive processing that must be taking place when words are retrieved in their natural contexts. Nevertheless, it acts as a starting point for the devising of model-based therapy for anomia. It offers guidelines for examining anomic problems on a finer scale than is commonly proposed in clinical practice, and for attempting to match the therapeutic strategy with the hypothesized primary level or levels of deficit. The success or failure of the strategies used gives us an opportunity to refine the model, and in turn to improve the diagnosis of the underlying difficulty in the individual patient and match it with improved strategies. It is such developments, beyond ad hoc therapy and beyond therapy based on loosely defined syndromes, that herald the advent of a new era in aphasia therapy.

REFERENCES

Allport, D. A. (1983). Language and cognition. In R. Harris (Ed.) *Approaches to Language* (pp. 61–94). London: Pergamon Press.

Allport, D. A. (1985). Distributed memory modular subsystems and dysphasia. In S. Newman, & R. Epstein (Eds.), *Current perspectives in dysphasia* (pp. 32–60). Edinburgh: Churchill Livingstone.

Beauvois, M. F., & Derouesné, J. (1982). Recherche en neuropsychologie et rééducation: quels rapports? In X. Seron, & C. Laterre (Eds.), *Rééduquer le cerveau* (pp. 163–189). Brussels: Mardaga.

100 LESSER

Beauvois, M. F., & Saillant, B. (1985). Optic aphasia for colours and colour agnosia: a distinction between visual and visuo-verbal impairments in the processing of colours. *Cognitive Neuropsychology, 2,* 1–48.

Behrman, M., & Peelle, L. M. (1967). Self-generated cues: a method for aiding aphasic and apractic patients. *Journal of Speech and Hearing Disorders, 32,* 372–376.

Blumstein, S. E., Milberg, W., & Schrier, R. (1982). Semantic processing in aphasia: evidence from an auditory lexical decision task, *Brain and Language, 17,* 301–315.

Brown, J. W. (1972). *Aphasia, apraxia and agnosia.* Springfield, IL: Charles C. Thomas.

Brownell, H. H., Potter, H. H., Michelow, D., & Gardner, H. (1984). Sensitivity to lexical denotation and connotation in brain-damaged patients: a double dissociation? *Brain and Language, 22,* 253–265.

Bub, D., & Kertesz, A. (1982). Evidence for lexicographic processing in a patient with preserved written over oral single word naming. *Brain, 105,* 697–717.

Buffery, A. W. H., & Burton, A. (1982). Information processing and redevelopment: towards a science of neuropsychological rehabilitation. In A. Burton (Ed.), *The pathology and psychology of cognition* (pp. 253–292). London and New York: Methuen.

Burton, A., & Kemp, R. (1986). Hemispheric priming and picture naming in aphasics. *Paper presented at the British Aphasiology Conference,* Preston.

Butterworth, B. (1980). Some constraints on models of language production. In B. Butterworth (Ed.) *Language Production* (Vol. 1) (pp. 423–459). London: Academic Press.

Butterworth, B. (1985). Jargon aphasia: processes and strategies. In S. Newman, & R. Epstein (Eds.), *Current perspectives in dysphasia* (pp. 61–96). Edinburgh: Churchill Livingstone.

Butterworth, B., Howard, D., & McLaughlin, P. (1985). The semantic deficit in aphasia: the relationship between semantic errors in auditory comprehension and picture naming. *Neuropsychologia, 22,* 409–426.

Caramazza, A., Miceli, G., Silveri, M. C., & Laudanna, A. (1985). Reading mechanisms and the organization of the lexicon: evidence from acquired dyslexia. *Cognitive Neuropsychology, 2,* 81–114.

Cicone, M., Wapner, W., & Gardner, H. (1980). Sensitivity to emotional expressions and situations in organic patients. *Cortex, 16,* 145–158.

Code, C. (1983). Hemispheric specialisation retraining: possibilities and problems. In C. Code, & D. J. Muller (Eds.), *Aphasia therapy* (pp. 42–59). London: Edward Arnold.

Code, C. (1987). *Language, aphasia and the right hemisphere.* Chichester: Wiley.

Cohen, R., Engel, D., Kelter, S., & List, G. (1979). Kurz-und Langzeiteffekte von Benennenhilfen bei Aphatikern. In G. Peuser (Ed.), *Studien zur Sprachtherapie* (pp 350–360). Munich: Wilhelm Fink.

Colby, K. M., Christinaz, D., Parkinson, R. C., Graham, S., & Karpf, C. (1981). A word-finding computer program with a dynamic lexical-semantic memory for patients with anomia using an intelligent speech prosthesis. *Brain and Language, 14,* 272–281.

Coltheart, M. (1980). Deep dyslexia: a right hemisphere hypothesis. In M. Coltheart, K. Patterson, & J. C. Marshall (Eds.), *Deep dyslexia* (pp. 326–380). London: Routledge and Kegan Paul.

Coltheart, M. (1985). Cognitive neuropsychology and the study of reading. In M. Posner, & O. Marin (Eds.), *Attention and performance* (Vol. XI). Hillsdale, NJ: Lawrence Erlbaum Associates.

Coltheart, M., Patterson, K., & Marshall, J. C. (Eds.). (1980). *Deep dyslexia.* London: Routledge and Kegan Paul.

Davis, G. A., & Wilcox, M. J. (1985). *Adult aphasia rehabilitation: applied pragmatics.* Windsor: NFER-Nelson.

Drummond, S. S., & Rentschler, G. J. (1979). The efficacy of gestural cueing in dysphasic word-retrieval responses. *Paper presented at ASHA Conference*, Atlanta.

Ellis, A. W. (1985). The production of spoken words: a cognitive neuropsychological perspective. In A. W. Ellis (Ed.), *Progress in the psychology of language* (Vol. 2) (pp. 107–145). London: Lawrence Erlbaum Associates.

Feyereisen, P., Van der Borght, F., & Seron, X. (1988). The operativity effect in naming: A re-analysis. *Neuropsychologia, 26*, 401–415.

Fitch-West, J. (1983). Heightening visual imagery: a new approach to aphasia therapy. In E. Perecman (Ed.), *Cognitive processing in the right hemisphere* (pp. 215–228). New York: Academic Press.

Gardner, H. (1973). The contribution of operativity to naming capacity in aphasic patients. *Neuropsychologia, 11*, 213–220.

Geschwind, N. (1967). The varieties of naming errors. *Cortex, 3*, 97–112.

Green, G. (1982). Assessment and treatment of the adult with severe aphasia: aiming for functional generalisation. *Australian Journal of Human Communication Diseases, 10*, 11–23.

Grober, E., Perecman, E., Kellar, L., & Brown, J. (1980). Lexical knowledge in anterior and posterior aphasics. *Brain and Language, 10*, 318–330.

Hadar, U., Jones, C., & Mate-Kole, C. (1987). The disconnection in anomic aphasia between semantic and phonological lexicons. *Cortex, 23*, 505–517.

Hart, J., Berndt, R. S., & Caramazza, A. (1985). Category-specific naming deficit following cerebral infarction. *Nature, 316*, 439–440.

Helm-Estabrooks, N. (1983). Exploiting the right hemisphere for language rehabilitation—Melodic Intonation Therapy. In E. Perecman (Ed.), *Cognitive processing in the right hemisphere* (pp. 229–240). New York: Academic Press.

Henderson, L. (1985). Towards a psychology of morphemes. In A. W. Ellis (Ed.). *Progress in the psychology of language* (Vol. 1) (pp. 15–72). London: Lawrence Erlbaum Associates.

Honeygosky, R. (1979). Naming performance by anomic aphasics correlated to Creative Imagination Scale. *Paper presented to ASHA Convention*, Atlanta.

Howard, D., & Orchard-Lisle, V. (1984). On the origin of semantic errors in naming: evidence from the case of global aphasia. *Cognitive Neuropsychology, 1*, 163–190.

Howard, D., Patterson, K., Franklin, S., Orchard-Lisle, V., & Morton, J. (1985a). The facilitation of picture naming in aphasia. *Cognitive Neuropsychology, 2*, 49–80.

Howard, D., Patterson, K., Franklin, S., Orchard-Lisle, V., & Morton, J. (1985b). Treatment of word retrieval deficits in aphasia. *Brain, 108*, 817–829.

Humphreys, G. W., & Riddoch, M. J. (1984). Routes to object constancy: implications from neurological impairments. *Quarterly Journal of Experimental Psychology, 36A*, 385–415.

Humphreys, G. W., & Riddoch, M. J. (1986). *To see but not to see: a case study of visual agnosia.* London: Lawrence Erlbaum Associates.

John, E. R. (1982). Multipotentiality: a theory of recovery of function after brain injury. In J. Orbach (Ed.), *Neuropsychology after Lashley* (pp. 247–271). Hillsdale, NJ: Lawrence Erlbaum Associates.

Kay, J., & Ellis, A. (1987). A cognitive neuropsychological case study of anomia: implications for psychological models of word retrieval. *Brain, 110*, 613–629.

Kay, J., Lesser, R., & Coltheart, M. (in preparation). *Psycholinguistic assessments of language processing in aphasia.* London: Lawrence Erlbaum Associates.

Kay, J., & Patterson, K. (1986). Routes to meaning in surface dyslexia. In K. E. Patterson, J. C. Marshall, & M. Coltheart (Eds.), *Surface dyslexia: neuropsychological and cognitive studies of phonological reading* (pp. 79–104). London: Lawrence Erlbaum Associates.

102 LESSER

Keith, R. L. (1980). *Graduated language training: treatment manual for patients with aphasia and children with language deficiencies.* Houston: College-Hill.

Kempen, G., & Hujbers, P. (1983). The lexicalization process in sentence production and naming: indirect election of words. *Cognition, 14*, 185–209.

Kertesz, A. (1984). Neurobiological aspects of recovery from aphasia in stroke. *International Rehabilitation Medicine, 6*, 122–127.

Kohn, S. E. (1984). The nature of the phonological disorder in conduction aphasia. *Brain and Language, 23*, 97–115.

Kohn, S. E., & Goodglass, H. (1985). Picture-naming in aphasia. *Brain and Language, 24*, 266–283.

Kuhlenbeck, H. (1982). *The human brain and its universe: Vol. 2. the brain and its mind.* Basle: Karger.

Landis, T., Regard, M., & Serrat, A. (1980). Iconic reading in a case of alexia without agraphia caused by a brain tumour: a tachistoscopic study. *Brain and Language, 11*, 45–53.

Larrabee, G. J., Levin, H. S., Huff, F. J., Kay, M. C., & Guinto, F. C. (1985). Visual agnosia contrasted with visual-verbal disconnection. *Neuropsychologia, 23*, 1–12.

Lesser, R. (1973). Word association and availability of response in an aphasic subject. *Journal of Psycholinguistic Research, 2*, 355–367.

Lesser, R. (1978). *Linguistic investigations of aphasia.* London: Edward Arnold.

Lesser, R. (1985). Aphasia therapy in the early 1980s. In S. Newman, & R. Epstein (Eds.), *Current perspectives in dysphasia* (pp. 198–216). Edinburgh: Churchill Livingstone.

Maly, J., & Wikus, B. (1979). Imagery zur Therapie Aphatischer Wortfindungsstörungen. In G. Peuser (Ed.), *Studien zur Sprachtherapie* (pp. 452–461). Munich: Wilhelm Fink.

Margolin, D. I. (1984). The neuropsychology of writing and spelling: semantic, phonological, motor and perceptual processes. *Quarterly Journal of Experimental Psychology, 36A*, 459–489.

Marshall, J. C. (1988). Sensation and semantics. *Nature, 334*, 378.

Marshall, R. C., & Watts, M. T. (1976). Relaxation training: effects on the communicative ability of aphasic adults. *Archives of Physical Medicine and Rehabilitation, 57*, 464–467.

Martin, R. C., & Caramazza, A. (1986). Theory and method in neurolinguistics: the case of acquired dyslexia. In H. J. Hannay (Ed.), *Experimental techniques in human neuropsychology* (pp. 363–385). New York: Oxford University Press.

McCarthy, R., & Warrington, E. K. (1985). Category specificity in an agrammatic patient: the relative impairment of verb retrieval and comprehension. *Neuropsychologia, 23*, 709–727.

McCarthy, R. A., & Warrington, E. K. (1988). Evidence for modality-specific meaning systems in the brain. *Nature, 334*, 428–430.

Miceli, G., Silveri, M. C., Villa, G., & Caramazza, A. (1984). On the basis for the agrammatic's difficulty in producing main verbs. *Cortex, 20*, 207–220.

Milberg, G. W., & Blumstein, S. E. (1981). Lexical decision and aphasia: evidence for semantic processing. *Brain and Language, 14*, 371–385.

Miller, E. (1984). *Recovery and management of neuropsychological impairments.* London: Wiley.

Moerman, C., Saerens, J., & Guleac, J. (1985). The background of aphasia misnamings: a factor analysis of visual naming errors. *Acta Neurologica Belgica 85*, 110–122.

Monoi, H., Fukusako, Y., Itoh, M., & Sasanuma, S. (1983). Speech sound errors in patients with conduction and Broca's aphasia. *Brain and Language, 20*, 175–194.

Morton, J. (1980). Two auditory parallels to deep dyslexia. In M. Coltheart, K. Patterson, & J. C. Marshall (Eds.), *Deep dyslexia* (pp. 189–196). London: Routledge and Kegan Paul.

Morton, J. (1985). Naming. In S. Newman, & R. Epstein (Eds.), *Current perspectives in dysphasia* (pp. 217–230). Edinburgh: Churchill Livingstone.

Pease, D. M., & Goodglass, H. (1978). The effects of cuing on picture naming in aphasia. *Cortex, 14*, 178–189.

Neumann, O. (1984). Automatic processing: a review of recent findings and a plea for an old theory. In W. Prinz, & A. F. Sanders (Eds.), *Cognitive and motor processes* (pp. 255–293). Berlin: Springer.

Nicholas, M., Obler, L. K., Albert, M. L., & Helm-Estabrooks, N. (1985). Empty speech in Alzheimer's disease and fluent aphasia. *Journal of Speech and Hearing Research, 28*, 405–410.

Nolan, K. A., & Caramazza, A. (1983). An analysis of writing in a case of deep dyslexia. *Brain and Language, 20*, 305–328.

Ogrezeanu, V., & Voinescu, I. (1984). Hierarchy of stimuli and of semantic divergent techniques in rehabilitation of aphasics. *Revue Roumaine de Neurologie et de Psychiatrie, 22*, 223–235.

Parisi, D. (1985). A procedural approach to the study of aphasia. *Brain and Language, 26*, 1–15.

Patterson, K. E., Marshall, J. C., & Coltheart, M. (1985). *Surface dyslexia: neuropsychological and cognitive studies of phonological reading*. London: Lawrence Erlbaum Associates.

Patterson, K., Purell, C., & Morton, J. (1983). Facilitation of word retrieval in aphasia. In C. Code, & D. J. Muller (Eds.), *Aphasia therapy* (pp. 76–87). London: Edward Arnold.

Pena-Casanova, J., Roig-Rovira, T., Bermudez, A., & Tolosa-Sarro, E. (1985). Optic aphasia, optic apraxia and loss of dreaming. *Brain and Language, 26*, 63–71.

Podraza, B. L., & Darley, F. L. (1977). Effect of auditory prestimulation on naming in aphasia. *Journal of Speech and Hearing Research, 20*, 660–683.

Poeck, K. (1984). Neuropsychological demonstration of splenial interhemispheric disconnection in a case of "optic anomia." *Neuropsychologia, 22*, 707–713.

Ratcliffe, G., & Newcombe, F. (1982). Object recognition: some deductions from the clinical evidence. In A. W. Ellis (Ed.), *Normality and pathology in cognitive functions* (pp. 147–171). New York: Academic Press.

Reason, J. T. (1984). Absent-mindedness and cognitive control. In J. E. Harris, & P. E. Morris (Eds.), *Everyday memory, actions and absent-mindedness* (pp. 113–132). London: Academic Press.

Reason, J. T., & Lucas, D. (1984). Using cognitive diaries to investigate naturally occurring memory blocks. In J. E. Harris, & P. E. Morris (Eds.), *Everyday memory, actions and absent-mindedness* (pp. 53–70). London: Academic Press.

Regard, M., & Landis, T. (1984). Experimentally induced semantic paralexias in normals: a property of the right hemisphere. *Cortex, 20*, 263–270.

Schacter, D. L., McAndrews, M. P., & Moscovitch, M. (1988). Access to consciousness: dissociations between implicit and explicit knowledge in neuropsychological syndromes. In L. Weiskrantz (Ed.), *Thought without language* (pp. 242–278). London: Oxford University Press.

Schuell, H. M., Jenkins, J. J., & Jiménez-Pabón, E. (1964). *Aphasia in adults*. New York: Harper and Row.

Seron, X. (1982). Les choix de stratégies: rétablir, réorganiser ou aménager l'environment. In X. Seron, & C. Laterre (Eds.), *Rééduquer le cerveau* (pp. 63–76). Brussels: Mardaga.

Seron, X. (1984). Reeducation strategies in neuropsychology: cognitive and pragmatic approaches. In F. C. Rose (Ed.), *Advances in neurology: Vol. 42. Progress in Aphasiology* (pp. 317–325). New York: Raven.

Seron, X., Deloche, G., Bastard, V., Chassin, G., & Hermand, N. (1979). Word-finding difficulties and learning transfer in aphasic patients. *Cortex, 15,* 149–155.

Shallice, T. (1986). Impairments of semantic processing: multiple dissociations. In M. Coltheart, G. Sartori, & R. Job (Eds.), *The cognitive neuropsychology of language* (pp. 111–127). London: Lawrence Erlbaum Associates.

Stemberger, J. P. (1985a). Bound morpheme loss errors in normal and agrammatic speech: one mechanism or two? *Brain and Language, 25,* 246–256.

Stemberger, J. P. (1985b). An interactive activation model of language production. In A. W. Ellis (Ed.), *Progress in the psychology of language* (Vol. 1) (pp. 143–186). London: Lawrence Erlbaum Associates.

Wallace, G. L., & Canter, G. J. (1985). Effects of personally relevant language materials on the performance of severely aphasic individuals. *Journal of Speech and Hearing Disorders, 50,* 385–390.

Warrington, E. K. (1981). Neuropsychological studies of verbal semantic systems. *Philosophical Transactions of the Royal Society of London: Biological Sciences, 295,* 411–423.

Warrington, E. K., & McCarthy, R. (1984). Category specific semantic impairments. *Brain, 107,* 829–856.

Warrington, E. K., & McCarthy, R. A. (1987). Categories of knowledge: Further fractionations and an attempted integration. *Brain, 110,* 1273–1296.

Weigl, E. (1961). The phenomenon of temporary deblocking in aphasia. *Zeitschrift fur Phonetik Sprachwissenschaft und Kommunikations-forschung, 14,* 337–361.

Weigl, E. (1970). Neuropsychological studies of structure and dynamics of semantic fields with the deblocking method. In A. J. Greimas, R. Jakobson, M. R. Mayenowa, S. K. Saumjan, W. Steinitz, & S. Zolkiewski (Eds.), *Sign, language, culture* (pp. 287–290). The Hague: Mouton.

Wiegel-Crump, C., & Koenigsknecht, R. A. (1973). Tapping the lexical store of the adult aphasic; analysis of the improvement in word retrieval skills. *Cortex, 9,* 411–418.

Wepman, J. M. (1951). *Recovery from aphasia.* New York: Ronald Press.

Williams, S. E., & Canter, G. J. (1982). The influence of situational context on naming performance in aphasic syndromes. *Brain and Language, 17,* 92–106.

4 Reorganization Therapy for Memory Impairments

Martial Van der Linden
Unité de Neuropsychologie, Université de Liège
Unité de Psychologie Experimentale Cognitive, Université de Louvain

Marie-Anne Van der Kaa
Unité de Neuropsychologie, Université de Liège

Brain lesions, even when they are minor, normally affect a patient's mnemonic efficiency. Memory disorders constitute a major impairment at the individual, familial, social, and professional levels. They often produce a decrease in social interactions and a loss of autonomy, give rise to irritation on the part of relatives, and prevent the patient from reentering the work force. Moreover, these disorders prove to be expensive to society, as well as to the organizations financially involved in the care of the patients. From the frequency and high cost of memory disorders then, one would expect them to enjoy some priority in the field of rehabilitation.

Yet, most therapists who deal with such disorders can actually complain about the lack of efficient reeducational procedures. The methods used most often employ games like Kim's game and exercises requiring repetition or learning lists of words. Such tasks presuppose that memory is like a muscle that needs training and that exercises related to certain kinds of tasks will induce positive effects in other mnemonic activities including the activities of daily life. In any case, they see memory as a single and unitary function.

But cognitive psychology has shown in the past 20 years that memory is a complex function consisting of numerous subprocesses. Using these models and taking an effective part in their elaboration, neuropsychological studies have also shown that memory disorders need not constitute a homogeneous symptomatology and that impairments might be related to very different levels of the mnemonic process. As a matter of fact, the use of classical psychometrical tests in neuropsychology tended to mask the heterogeneity of the disorders. These particular methods could identify a decrease in mnemonic efficiency (by comparing some individual to a population of reference), but could not indicate more precisely the roles played by the different variables involved in the defective processes.

Now we believe that only a careful description of the memory disorder combined with the formulation of hypotheses about its nature for well-defined populations will allow therapists to select the most efficient rehabilitative strategies, or, more precisely, reorganizational strategies (Seron, 1982). The latter postulates that a single behavior may rely on several underlying processes; that a cerebral lesion will damage these processes; and that other processes usually not involved in the behavior, which remain intact, may become functional at this point. This assumes that we have at our disposal one or several models of the mnemonic processes, hypotheses about the nature of disorders, and hypotheses about the intact processes that might be used.

Thus, as far as evaluation and rehabilitation are concerned, familiarity with the experimental research in both cognitive psychology and neuropsychology proves to be absolutely necessary. Furthermore, it would be difficult to expose the logic of memory therapies without first making explicit the way in which mnemonic activities are conceived in normal subjects nowadays and the way in which the disorders appear.

THE COGNITIVE APPROACH TO MEMORY

The experimental analysis of memory actually began in 1885 with the work of Herman Ebbinghaus, whose purpose was to study the evolution of memory with respect to time. Most of his methods are still in use today, particularly in the psychometrical tests used in clinical psychology. Following Ebbinghaus (1885), numerous studies have been guided by an associationist approach, a perspective that focuses particularly on the external (spatial and temporal) contiguity between stimulus and response. As Tiberghien (1976) has pointed out, this kind of interpretation prompts the researcher to explore successively the different parts that compose the diagram and to neglect the features that cannot be observed, more particularly the subject's central activities. Research projects, therefore, have consisted of studies of the effects of the variables related to the type and characteristics of the material to be retained in memory, the temporal management of the experimental conditions (retention intervals, rate of stimulus presentation, etc.), and the mode of information outputs (recall or recognition). These studies have produced a set of interesting data at the descriptive level (forgetting curve, superiority of recognition to recall, etc.) for which the causes still await definition.

In the early 1960s, a new class of psychological models of memory made its appearance. Inspired by information processing theory, researchers tackled the structure of mnemonic systems, as well as the strategies used by subjects. The most representative theoretical model of this approach is certainly that of Atkinson and Shiffrin (1968). They propose that we distinguish among several storage units that are elicited depending on the temporal constraints of the encoding condition: the precategorical storage system (iconic memory and echoic memory), the short-term memory (STM), and the long-term memory (LTM). Iconic memory and echoic memory are both storage systems of the sensorial information and sustain the physiological representation of sensorial information during brief intervals (several hundred milliseconds). Short-term memory is defined as transitional memory that serves to maintain the information temporarily. It is characterized by a rapid decline in the trace strength, a limited capacity and the absence of organization, and a weak sensitivity to interference laws. In contrast, long-term memory is regarded as a structure for permanent storage of information and is characterized by a high level of organization. Short-term storage employs speech coding: The material is maintained in short-term memory by subvocal rehearsal, and the longer it is maintained, the more likely it is to be transferred to long-term memory, whereas, long-term storage involves semantic coding.

The distinction between STM and LTM was born in part from some observations that seemed to indicate the involvement of two distinct factors in several memory tasks. For instance, the analysis of serial position curves showed that the last words of a list were more easily recalled than other words (constituting the recency effect). These last words assumed to rest in some echo box (i.e., the STM) from which they could easily be recovered as long as there was no interference. What remained of the curve would then refer to a different mnemonic process, the information retrieval from LTM. Some operations affect one of the systems without any effect on the other. Thus, lengthening the time of words presentation improves LTM without modifying STM, but the insertion of an interfering task between the items' presentation and their recall would impair STM (the recency effect disappears) but not LTM.

To explain forgetting, the researchers of the 1960s turned to the two sources still being proposed by the associationists: the decay of the mnemonic trace and the interference phenomenon. One usually invokes the theory of interference (semantic interference) to explain forgetting in LTM and postulates an interaction between trace decay and acoustic interference when considering forgetting in STM. In sensorial memory (iconic and echoic), the theory of trace decay is generally put forward.

Brenda Milner (1959), while studying her famous patient H.M., contributed greatly to the support for this distinction between two storage units. Her patient could not store any new information permanently. At most he could memorize material that would not exceed his memory span by constantly rehearsing it. Shallice and Warrington (1970) reported in another observation the case of a patient who had sustained a left parietooccipital lesion and who was characterized by a normal LTM and an impaired STM in the auditory modality (see also Tzortzis & Albert, 1974; Basso, Spinnler, Vallar, & Zanobio, 1982).

However, the credibility of the short- and long-term memory distinction has been strongly shaken by several studies that question the basic characteristics that supported the opposition between the two systems. Agreement could never be reached on the matters of the storage capacities of the different units and the longevity of the information stored in each of the two systems. Moreover, several studies showed that the laws of interference would affect the STM, as well as the LTM, and that some semantic encoding could also be detected in STM. And finally, it is worth pointing out that Shallice's and Warrington's observation (1970) of a patient with an intact LTM and an impaired STM was inconsistent with the linear characteristic of Atkinson's and Shiffrin's model (1968).

These facts led Baddeley and Hitch (1974) to give up the idea of a single STM system and to turn to the concept of working memory. This system consists of a central processor, called the Central Executive, that coordinates a set of temporary storage systems; one slave system, which is the articulatory loop that account for the role of speech in STM; another slave system, the visuo-spatial scratch-pad, which is assummed to be concerned with the creation and the manipulation of visuo-spatial images.

Craik and Lockhart (1972) have offered another proposal, namely to eliminate those theories based on different storage systems and to focus instead on the initial operations of encoding: the theory of the depth of processing. Memory is conceived as a subproduct of the depth of an encoded item; the deeper the analysis, the stronger and more durable the corresponding mnemonic trace. They distinguish between maintenance processing (a permanent recirculation of information) and elaboration processing (the creation of deeper analyses of information). However, this approach is faced with the difficulty of precisely defining the different levels of the process.

Tulving and Thomson (1973) made the assumption of an interaction between the conditions of encoding and the conditions of retrieval, thus settling the principle of encoding specificity. According to their theory, the level of encoding depth is less important than the concordance between the cues present at the encoding stage and the cues present at the retrieval stage. This theory grants an important role to the concept of contextual association and states that at least part of the context of encoding must be present at the retrieval stage. Any modification of the context between the encoding and retrieval stages will produce a deterioration of the mnemonic performance.

The influence of the subject's activity had been neglected in the associationists approach, but for their part, the cognitive psychologists have been studying the subject's activity in the different stages of memorization, and more particularly the way in which subject organizes the material to be memorized. The activities involved in the organization of the material bring us to the problem of the nature and the format of mnemonic information, and, more broadly, to consider the organizational laws that rule the mnemonic information.

According to the dual coding theory (Paivio, 1971), information may be coded in two different formats, verbal and imaged. Several kinds of data gave a consistent empirical base to this theory. First, the intervention of imagery variables may have positive effects on the rates of acquisition and restitution for material to be memorized. Moreover, a recourse to imagery proves to be efficient in verbal learning tasks. Furthermore, one can observe that concrete words are acquired and retained more than abstract words in tests of learning. The theory assumes that the availability of the code is slightly inferior to that of the imaged code and that imaged perceptual information would be represented at same time in both a verbal and an imaged fashion, whereas verbal perceptual information would be represented almost completely in a verbal fashion. This dual coding theory is nowadays challenged by a unitary theory, which states that imaged and verbal information are both represented in a single and abstract form.

Two theoretical positions concerned with permanent memory organization have been proposed: A componential conception (Kintsch, 1974) and a conception based on the idea of a semantic network (Anderson & Bower, 1973). The componential models postulate that lexical units may be split up into a set of fundamental semantic features. These semantic features may be chunked in a propositional form based on the subject–predicate relationship. The network models envisage that semantic features are connected in a network of labeled relationships like those of superordination and subordination. The network will take a hierarchical form: The semantic features are combined to define the concept of argument and relation, the concatenation of which determines declarative (the knowing that) or procedural (the knowing how) propositions whose combinations constitute schema, scripts, or plans. The retrieval of information might follow at least two paths: the activation of superior order schemas by occurrences of the elementary features or the activation of the latter by units at a highly organized level (Tiberghien, 1983). Recent attempts to approach textual memory led to the development of theories in which high order representational structures play an important part. These studies are based on the idea that textual memory has to resort to some abstract schema (the macrostructure), which is a set of organizational principles that would be shared by every text of the same type (Kintsch, 1974; Rumelhart, 1975; Bower, 1976). Such an analysis has been developed in memory for places (Brewer & Treyens, 1981). These schemas, plans, and scripts are believed to influence the mnemonic performance in different ways and to determine particularly which objects are encoded; they might also be used as a framework for new information and might guide the retrieval process.

Might these rules of organization apply to specific and experiential rememberings? Tulving (1972) distinguishes between two classes of information: semantic memory and episodic memory. Episodic memory is conceived as a system specialized in the encoding, the storage, and the retrieval of spatially located, temporally dated, and personally experienced events and episodes. Semantic memory, on the other hand, would apply to the encoding, the storage, and the retrieval of pieces of general knowledge. In a recent publication, Tulving (1984) explains his distinction in terms of two parallel information processing systems that partially overlap. They are both systems of propositional and declarative memory and in this sense can be contrasted with the memory systems that deal with the acquisition and the use of skills and procedures, that is, the procedural memory. Although most of the authors will agree at a heuristic level with the distinction between an episodic and a semantic memory, they still will not accept the hypotheses of two distinct functional systems. The controversy is brisk and the debate far from conclusion. As noted by Tiberghien and Lecoq (1983), from a more dialectical point of view, semantic features elaborate and modify themselves through a sequence of episodes, and no episode could escape translation in a semantic network already constituted.

Shiffrin and Schneider (1977) placed this distinction between episodic and semantic memory in the framework of the distinction between automatic and controlled processes: Episodic encoding would depend on controlled process. From this perspective, Hasher and Zacks (1979) suggest that there exist variations in the attentional demands of the different encoding operations. The automatic encoding requires minimal energy from the attentional system, has a limited capacity, is effortless, and does not interfere with other ongoing cognitive activities. It is believed to be involved in the encoding of the temporal, spatial, and frequency-of-occurrence information. Under some circumstances, other automatic processes develop through practice. The effortful processes, on the other hand, require a large capacity of attention, are initiated intentionally, and interfere with other cognitive activities also requiring attentional capacity. They would especially be involved in elaborate mnemonic strategies. A progressive shift from the effortful, or controlled processes, to the automatic processes prevents the cognitive system from becoming overloaded by processing demands and, therefore, increases its capacity. It should be noted that notions, such as the level of attentional resource, the level of processing, and the capacity of the cognitive system, are used by Reason (1984) in a model whose purpose is to give an account of absent-minded errors.

Mandler (1979, 1980) has proposed a distinction between the activation and the elaboration process. According to his theory, when a word is presented to a subject, its features are automatically activated; that is, the schema that represents the word in memory is activated. Such a process temporarily increases the word's availability. A second consequence of the presentation of the word is the elaboration process: it requires cognitive effort and allows the presented word to be related to the context, as well as to other material in memory. The subject, if asked to recall the previously presented word, can find it in memory and decide whether it had been presented. The process of activation would be involved in priming, the perceptual recognition, and the word completion method.

We have broadly described the different conceptions of (a) the properties of those processes that guarantee the transcoding of information in a code suitable to the representations and that permit access to memory and the control of outputs and (b) the way in which the information is represented in the mnemonic system. Now we can examine how neuropsychology has approached the memory disorders in the light of these theoretical models.

THE NEUROPSYCHOLOGY OF MEMORY

Most of the neuropsychological studies that tackled memory disorders from a cognitive perspective involved the amnesic syndrome, a syndrome that can arise from different etiologies (Parkin, 1984). The Wernicke-Korsakoff syndrome is usually encountered as a sequelae of chronic alcoholism. The brain damage is centered on the diencephalon, with the mamillary bodies and dorsomedial thalamic nucleus being the two structures principally affected. A second cause of the amnesic syndrome is herpes simplex encephalitis. Encephalitis generates extensive lesions in the medial temporal lobe including the hippocampus, amygdala, and uncus, the diencephalic structures remaining relatively untouched. The involvement of the medial temporal lobes in memory processes has also been shown after temporal lobectomy.

Considering the neuroanatomy of memory, Markowitsch (1984) reviewed many human case reports of amnesia and concluded that a straightforward correlation between a particular brain lesion and mnemonic deficits had too often been assumed. Behavioral deficits should rather be viewed as the consequence of an altered equilibrium in an extensive network of the brain. As a matter of fact, the relevance of this remark clearly extends beyond the case of amnesic syndrome.

Amnesics generally present an undiminished level of intellectual efficiency, except in those cases associated with dementia. Short-term memory seems untouched (normal mnemonic span, typical recency effects). A retrograde amnesia exists but in varied degrees, whereas, anterograde amnesia is very severe. Residual learning capabilities can usually be observed. Parkin (1984) shows that the diencephalic and temporal amnesias differ in numerous ways (length of retrograde amnesia; disordered or preserved STM; presence or absence of the release from proactive interference, of anosognosia and of frontal lobe symptoms). Actually, one should be apprised of the fact that many studies indistinctly used the term amnesic syndrome for the different types of amnesia.

There are three major classes of hypotheses about the amnesic syndrome (Stern, 1981; Meudell & Mayes, 1982; Cermack, 1982).

Deficit in the Encoding Processes

According to Butters and Cermak (1980), problems arise from a tendency on the part of amnesics to ignore the meaningful aspects of the stimuli. As far as verbal material is concerned, they assert that the problem finds its origin in the patient's failure to encode spon-

4. THERAPY OF MEMORY   113

taneously the information at the semantic level. Several facts seem to support such a hypothesis: Amnesics do not show release from proactive interference in the Wickens' paradigm (1970). They do not benefit as much as controls from category cues that are supplied after the learning of lists of words comprising different taxonomic categories. In recognition tests, they chose more homonymous items than controls, which is interpreted as the consequence of superficial encoding, a low level analysis of the stimuli.

Baddeley and Warrington (1973) suggest that amnesics encounter difficulties when using the imagery components of semantic information, which constitutes another aspect of encoding problems. However, Baddeley (1982) gave up this hypothesis in an ulterior study.

As a matter of fact, there are two types of encoding deficit theories. The first one assigns the problem to a failure in the use of the effortful processes, involving a deep and elaborate analysis of the stimuli. The second one finds the cause of amnesia in a failure of the automatic processes that encode temporal, spatial, and frequency-of-occurrence information. For this approach, amnesics sustain a selective loss in the ability to encode background context, that is, spatiotemporal or extrinsic context. Mayes, Meudell, and Pickering (1985) show that the upholders of the contextual hypothesis give to the word "context" very different definitions and that the contextual theories not only differ in the postulated nature of the impairment (an encoding or storage impairment) but also the kinds of contextual information that are remembered deficiently.

Impairment of the Storage Processes

Either it is a failure of the consolidation process that gives the temporarily stored information a lasting status, or it is a more rapid loss or decay of information. Several arguments contradicting the hypotheses of storage have been put forward (Weiskrantz, 1978) and more specifically the fact that amnesics are still able to learn some information and that prior lists' intrusion errors in amnesics' recall protocols are commonly observed.

There is little behavioral evidence for a consolidation failure in humans. Moreover, do amnesics forget faster than normal subjects? Several studies led to conflicting results (Huppert & Piercy, 1979; Kopelman, 1985; Warrington & Weiskrantz, 1968; Williams, 1953). As a matter of fact, it seems obvious that the relevance of any comparison between the two groups of subjects suppose a similar initial level of performance.

Defective Information Retrieval

This theory has principally been defended by Warrington and Weiskrantz (1973) who state that amnesics' difficulties would be the consequence of a higher sensitivity to interference from previously learned or other irrelevant information. The irrelevant information increases the competition between responses, and so doing, originates the impairment sustained by the amnesics. As support for their theory, Warrington and Weiskrantz (1970, 1974, 1978) showed that amnesics clearly benefit from cues (initial letters of previously presented words) provided at recall, an observation that has not been made in other studies (Mayes, Meudell, & Neary, 1978; Squire, Wetzel, & Slater, 1978; Wetzel & Squire, 1982).

In a recent study, Graf, Squire, and Mandler (1984) show that amnesic patients were impaired on free recall, recognition, and cued recall tests but not on a word completion test, which differed from cued recall only in the instructions: The subjects were directed away from the memory aspects of the test and asked to complete each three-letter cue with the first word that came to mind. These results offer an explanation of the conflicting findings in cued recall tests: the instructions determine whether amnesics will perform normally. According to the authors, the fact that amnesics show normal performance on word completion would attest to the integrity of the activation process (Mandler, 1980). These data do not require a retrieval interpretation. Though amnesics could create representations sufficient to support word completion, they might still be unable to acquire other types of information, particularly the type of information that allows the recognition of a previously presented word.

It should be noted that preserved learning has been demonstrated in many other repetition priming tasks (Schacter, 1987), in which performance is facilitated as a result of a single prior exposure to the same stimulus. Several studies have also shown preserved learning abilities in motor, perceptual-motor, and cognitive tasks, though the patients cannot recognize the newly acquired skills. According to Parkin (1982), these facts might be interpreted as the relative preservation of semantic memory versus an impaired episodic memory. But Squire & Cohen (1984) think that these facts suggest instead the distinction between procedural and declarative knowledge.

Last, let's describe the hypothesis which postulates that amnesia proceeds from a lack of equivalence between the encoding and the retrieval contexts. It, therefore, would consist in a failure to use contextual information as a predominant retrieval cue. Several studies have been investigating this field (e.g., Fisher & Craik, 1977, on verbal material; Winocur & Kinsbourne, 1978, on visual material.) Prosopagnosia has also been discussed in such a framework (Damasio, 1985; Damasio, Damasio, & Van Hoesen, 1982). According to Tiberghien (1986), face recognition could be achieved in two distinct ways: either by a rapid and automatic predecision process giving rise to an overall feeling of familiarity or nonfamiliarity, or by an activity of mental reconstruction guided by context. This second mode of face recognition occurs when the predecision process has failed and consists of an attempt to retrieve the original encoding context on the basis of the recognition context.

Agreement on the nature of amnesia is far from conclusive; many theories compete and results often conflict. As Piercy (1977) pointed out, the analysis of memory disorders within the perspective of normal theories can help to throw light on the nature of the disorder and reciprocally, the memory disorders can help to clarify the nature of normal memory. Yet, the controversial aspects of these theories create problems when the concepts they involve are used to explain amnesia. The distinction between STM and LTM gives a clear example of the ambiguity that has been introduced in studies of amnesia. As seen before, this distinction between two storage systems has been discussed. Now, if we refer to studies about amnesia to confirm the hypothesis, our position becomes circular. Moreover, amnesics' performances in STM tasks cannot be accepted just as they are in order to demonstrate a dissociation between short- and long-term memory in amnesia if the distinction that the test is supposed to reveal is only justified in the performances of amnesic patients.

Another problem, described by Meudell and Mayes (1982), is that retention intervals, which allow amnesics to achieve performances above chance, induce ceiling effects in controls. In contrast, retention intervals that get controls off the ceiling decrease amnesics' performances to floor level. According to Meudell and Mayes (1982), numerous results that support the encoding, retrieval, or contextual hypothesis will not be reproduced if the general level of performance is previously equalized by varying the retention intervals across the groups. Intergroup differences, therefore, would not proceed from qualitative differences showing a selective impairment at one or another stage of the memory process but from the qualitative differences between levels of performance.

While commenting on the book *Human Memory and Amnesia* (Cermak, 1982), Morton (1985) stresses that the difference between populations of Korsakoff patients can also account for some of the inconsistencies in the results (for instance the differences between British and American patients). In a more general way, the error was to consider both the alcoholic Korsakoff syndrome (clinically defined) and amnesia (psychologically defined) as the same problem. Morton also points out several theoretical gaps, more specifically the frequent confusion made between encoding as a cognitive operation and encoding as an operation that involves putting something into memory, or else, confusion between retrieval cues and content of memory. However, though several authors claim that the three-stage model of memory (encoding, storage, and retrieval) is inappropriate and that it proves more useful to consider the interaction between encoding and retrieval, some of them are led to confuse encoding specificity with state-dependent learning. According to Morton (1985) again, models of memory are still too rough and do not allow us to explain variations in amnesia, as the models of reading in patients with acquired dyslexia do. Furthermore, most authors postulate that all amnesics sustain a central disorder and disregard the possibility of multiple functional lesions.

Finally, Morton emphasizes the current lack of comparative studies focusing on the different etiologies of amnesia. From this point of view, several recent comparative studies suggest that the memory disorders of amnesics and Huntington's disease (HD) patients have very distinctive characteristics (Butters, 1984). More especially, amnesic patients would sustain some difficulties in the recall and the recognition of data-based verbal and nonverbal information but would maintain a normal procedural memory (tested on mirror reading tasks). On the other hand, HD patients sustain difficulties in their acquisition of general skills, but cannot learn new facts when recognition tests are employed (Martone, Butters, Payne, Becker, & Sax, 1984). Moreover, the HD patients are able to use the language as a mnemonic aid for circumventing their pictorial memory problems, whereas the amnesics and patients with Alzheimer's disease cannot do so (Butters et al., 1983). Butters, Wolfe, Martone, Granholm, and Cermak (1985) provide further support for the hypothesis that the deficits of HD patients are characterized by deficiencies in retrieval mechanisms. Yet, they found that Korsakoff patients and HD patients were impaired in the acquisition of the skills necessary to solve the Tower of Hanoi puzzle, whereas Korsakoff patients had shown in the previous study a normal rate of skill learning on mirror reading tasks. These differences lead the authors to question the use of the Tower of Hanoi puzzle as a means of evaluating the role of procedural learning in memory impairment. As a matter of fact, one might rather question the definition of procedural memory.

From another perspective, the study of Nebes, Martin, and Horn (1984) reveals the presence of normal semantic priming in patients with Alzheimer's disease, which is inconsistent with recent suggestions according to which such patients sustain some deficiency in the organization of their semantic memory (Bayles, 1982). In the context of the levels of processing models memory, Martin, Brouwers, Cox, and Fedio (1985) suggest that while still able to perform different types of encoding operations (e.g., phonemic and semantic operations), patients with Alzheimer's disease cannot encode as many relevant stimulus attributes during learning as do normal subjects. Their performance would differ quantitatively though not qualitatively from normals.

The nature of memory impairments in patients with a cortical lesion has not yet been systematically investigated. Several studies have described deficits in auditory-verbal STM (Allport, 1983; Beauvois & Lhermitte, 1975; De Renzi & Nichelli, 1975; Shallice & Warrington, 1970, 1977; Vallar & Baddeley, 1984). These breakdowns in auditory-verbal STM may have at least three origins (Mayes, 1986): a disorder in the phonological processing ability, a failure in the articulatory loop system, and a reduced capacity in the central executive. Some evidence also exists for specific disorders in STM for visually presented material (Butters, Samuels, Goodglass, & Brody, 1970; Samuels, Butters & Fedio, 1972; Warrington & Rabin, 1971).

Besides disorders of STM, lesions of the neocortex can also yield two kinds of memory disorders (Mayes, 1986): (a) A deficiency in the access to previously well-established semantic memory and in the acquisition of new information (caused by posterior association cortex lesions). Some studies even described selective breakdowns of semantic memory, as for instance breakdowns in knowledge of concrete or abstract words (Warrington, 1981), animate (Warrington & Shallice, 1984), or inanimate objects (Warrington & McCarthy, 1983); these observations give rise nowadays to a brisk theoretical debate. (b) A deficiency in the ability to plan encoding and retrieval strategies (caused by frontal lesions). Hirst (1985) has also suggested that frontal patients would suffer from a "bad metamemory" in this regard; that is, they would show a poor awareness of how the memory system works and which memory strategies are efficient.

Grober (1984) has been evaluating aphasics' and subjects' performances on two memory tasks: In the first one, they were required to judge how often words in a study list were repeated and in the second one, they had to recall the spatial location in which a picture of an object had been presented. Aphasics obtained results similar to those obtained by normal subjects, no matter what their type of aphasia. Grober (1984) concludes that such data indicate that automatic processes are still properly working in aphasics and that only effortful processes are impaired.

Cermak and Moreines (1976) and Cermak, Stiassny, and Uhly

(1984) suggest that verbal memory trouble in anterior aphasics is not attributable to some inability to analyze or to recirculate particular features of words but rather to an inability to manipulate these features cognitively during a comparison or free recall portion of a task, that is, an inability to manipulate stored information. The introduction of instructions that prime appropriate feature representation might improve subjects' performances in the sense that priming might increase the representation of a specific feature of a word, and in doing so, lead to retrieval of the word. The authors are tempted to draw a parallel between these data and the naming disorders of the patients. This hypothesis guides us toward a procedural approach to memory disorders, an approach that has recently been defended in the study of aphasia (Parisi, 1985).

Several studies also addressed the question of the effects of closed head injury on memory (for a review, see Schachter & Crovitz, 1977). The most current, though controversial, interpretation states that they reflect a selective impairment of information in LTM. Richardson (1984), Richardson and Snape (1984), and Richardson and Barry (1985) showed that patients with minor closed head injuries were impaired in the free recall on concrete material but not in the free recall of abstract material. They explain this disorder as an inability of patients to encode verbal information in imaginal representation. In a recent study, Baddeley et al. (1987) compared the memory disorders of patients with moderate or severe closed head injuries with those of Korsakoff patients. Both groups presented episodic memory deficits, but they had no problems with memory span, the recency effect, and well-learned semantic information. However, unlike the Korsakoff patients, the patients with closed head injuries presented deficits in various priming tasks and retarded semantic memory access speed.

Though too succinct, this review of experimental data clearly indicates that no single model can account for the entire set of memory disorders, not to mention their complexity. However, such conclusions do not eliminate the necessity of a close coordination between clinical and experimental neuropsychology. A therapist who expects to gain some effectiveness and to play a part in the study of memory disorders should be able to refer to one or another memory processing model and hypothesis about the memory impairment before starting a memory retraining program.

As a matter of fact, however, descriptions of programs generated by definite hypothesis are not very numerous in literature. We shall now examine the most commonly used strategies.

REEDUCATIONAL STRATEGIES
FOR MEMORY DISORDERS

Most reeducational programs have resorted to classically proposed procedures for overcoming memory difficulties encountered by subjects without any cerebral lesion, that is for improving mnemonic performances in normal individuals. While analyzing the different ways of improving memory, Morris (1979) indicated that it is crucial to characterize the specific situation of memorization.

First, does one have to remember to do something (an intention) or recall some facts? Very little is known about the underlying processes for remembering intentions. Plans for future actions could be described as a hierarchy of many component actions, each component being susceptible to error or forgetting. Reason (1977) proposed four error categories:

1. Storage errors consist in forgetting some items in a plan such as forgetting to post a letter.
2. Testing difficulties within the execution of a plan can lead to errors, such as entering one's bath wearing a piece of clothing.
3. Discrimination errors may result in relevant actions at a formal level, which do not suit the conditions, for instance, tacking one's own keys while approaching a friend's home.
4. Selection problems consist in doing one irrelevant action in place of an appropriate one in the course of a plan (branching errors when actions share a common origin, forgetting, inserting, or omitting actions).

Meacham and Leiman (1982) distinguish between habitual and episodic prospective remembering: Habitual remembering concerns things that one is used to do, whereas episodic memory deals with actions that are not parts of routines. Reason (1979) relates both of these processes to two levels of attentional control, but it also seems interesting to make a distinction between single-activity and dual-activity prospective memory (Harris, 1984a). Finally, according to Baddeley and Wilkins (1984), there exist a few examples of both semantic and episodic types in several prospective memory studies. They put Reason's studies (1977) of slips of action in the semantic group, for actions that encounter errors are overlearned components of habitual behavior (for instance making coffee). Furthermore, there is a preexisting cognitive structure for the action sequence (schemata), and the precise circumstances in which this information is learned cannot be defined anymore. On the other hand, an action proposed in Wilkin's and Baddeley's study (1978), which involves a button-pressing task analogous to remembering to take one's medicine several times a day, proves to be an instance of episodic prospective memory, for it consists in a novel arbitrary action for which the circumstances of learning cannot be precise.

Furst (1986) describes a method for investigating intention memory abilities of brain-injured patients. The task chosen relies on a commercially available time-punch clock of the sort used for personal time keeping. Patients are expected to respond by punching their time card at specified moments. Pajurkowa and Wilkins (described in Harris, 1984) designed another method that could easily be incorporated into test batteries and which was administered to focal epilepsy patients. At the beginning of the session, they asked them to use a red pencil for one of the subsequent tests (drawing a bicycle) and a black pencil in the other tests. In the Rivermead Behavioural Memory Test (Wilson, Cockburn & Baddeley, 1985), some prospective memory tasks were elaborated, such as remembering to ask for a hidden belonging at the end of the session, remembering an appointment when an alarm rings, and remembering to deliver a message.

The aids usually involved to help the person to remember to do things may be either external memory aids (appointment diaries) or strategies that facilitate the storing of information (e.g., the method of loci mnemonic). In both cases, the problem of actuating the stored information at the right moment remains, and is particularly critical, in dual-activity prospective memory.

In cases where someone has to memorize a fact, does the problem consist in the encoding (how can one learn something in order to maximize the later recall?) or in the retrieval (how can one retrieve a piece of information believed to have entered the memory?)? At the encoding stage, when the material to be learned is organized and meaningful, the information shall be conditioned to manage the memory system more efficiently (active learning, self testing, etc.). In contrast, if we deal with material that is poorly structured, we shall have to impose meaning. For this purpose, one usually resorts to the classical mnemonic techniques that will make up for the lack of meaning and supply retrieval cues. At the retrieval stage, relevant cues that will elicit recall will have to be found, cues whose relevance depends on the initial encoding situation (the original learning context). In the cases where we have to remember a personally experienced event, we may try to reconstitute the situation. If what is to be recalled is a name, we may attempt to cue ourselves, for example, by

4. THERAPY OF MEMORY 121

going through the alphabet to see if the first letter may cue recall.

The memory reeducation programs in neuropsychology have generally adopted the same rationale. In effect, one may characterize a strategy with regards to its selective action on the encoding or retrieval processes. However, according to Seron (1982), one may also consider whether external aids (mental prosthesis), internal strategies (reorganizational strategies), or reestablishment strategies are involved in the reeducation. We will not dwell on reestablishment strategies. We have seen that memory is a complex function, and it seems implausible to believe that the intensive retraining, the repeated exercises on definite tasks will result in an improvement in the performance of the other memory tasks and activities of daily life. Let us rather consider which strategies are aimed at the reorganization of the processes underlying the memory function. Two principal types are generally proposed: imagery techniques and verbal strategies.

Visual Imagery Techniques

Imagery has been used in mnemonics for ages (Yates, 1966). The best known technique is the peg method, which consists of an imaged association of items to be memorized with a previously learned ordered list of peg words. It is usually asserted that such images must be as ridiculous and bizarre as possible. There are several forms of pegtype mnemonics: the phonetic system (which relies on a relationship between numbers and consonant sounds), the rhyming peg method (where the peg list is elaborated by choosing words having a rhyming relationship with a specific number, as for instance, one-bun, two-shoe, three-tree, etc.).

Many studies from experimental psychology closely investigated this procedure. The subject requires enough time to execute each of the implied activities (recalling the peg word, elaborating an image, remembering and translating it). Concrete words generally prove to be better cues for recall than abstract words. The peg method is most inconvenient in the memorization of a long list of peg words.

In the loci method (used by Veniamin, the famous mnemonist described by Luria, 1970), the peg words are replaced by locations in the real physical world (one or several streets, rooms, etc.). The first item to be memorized is associated in an image with the first distinctive characteristic of the street, etc.

Both the peg mnemonic and the loci method need to establish a connection between the items to be memorized and independent cues. In the link method, each item is related both to the preceding item and to the item which follows it, without any resort to external cues.

Another method, created to improve subjects' ability to associate a face with a name, links an imaged substitution of the name to a distinctive feature of the face. McCarty (1980) showed that the three following components of the face-name mnemonic were essential for its effectiveness: a prominent facial feature, a concrete transformation of the person's name, and an interactive image of these two elements.

Roediger (1980) indicates that the link method, the peg system, or the loci method have positive consequences for recall when compared to conditions in which normal subjects are given elaborative rehearsal or simple imagery instructions. The greatest differences appear when considering a positional criterion, for each of the three methods allow the subject to recall words in the correct order better than in any other strategy. But among the three, the peg and loci conditions seem more efficient than the link method because forgetting some item in the sequence of links shall more easily disturb the recall of other items ordered with this method. Whereas in peg and loci methods, the retention of order does not depend on previously successful recall of items. Peg and loci mnemonics seem more convenient in situations where the order of data is privileged; otherwise, the link method appears to be just as efficient.

These different memory techniques and their effects may be analyzed in the framework of Tulving's theory (1974). A good mnemonic procedure is a procedure that simultaneously supplies high quality encoding of the material and a set of efficient retrieval cues. Why use imagery during encoding? Some authors think that the main point is simply to create a condition that relates items with cues or with each other, imagery merely offering greater connection possibilities by allowing the subject to use all possible visuospatial relations between objects. Most methods require the formation of an absurd image, although several studies dispute the importance of this feature. As Morris (1979) has pointed out, it remains possible that these experimental tasks have not reproduced the same complexity and interference level as the tasks carried out by those mnemonists who praise a resort to absurd characteristics. The formation of an absurd image might also encourage the recall of numerous properties of the items, thus improving the encoding. Last, it might help to maintain motivation in subjects. Imagery techniques also include a system of retrieval cues. In the link method, each recalled item works as a cue for the other one by the creation of interactive images, whereas pegs and locations are the cues supplied in the peg and loci methods.

Numerous studies have undertaken to demonstrate the usefulness of imagery for the improvement of brain-damaged patients' performances. Most of the time, their aim is to modify the nature and depth of the patient's encoding as well as giving them relevant retrieval cues. Some of the research took its inspiration from the evidence of specific memory disorders with regards to the damaged hemisphere (and more particularly Milner's study, 1968, on left and right temporal lobectomies); it also relies on the dual-coding theory according to which the verbal code and the visual code are separately stored in memory. The basic principles of these studies rest on the aid provided by an allegedly intact visual memory to the impaired verbal memory. The methods employed mainly derive from the experimental literature (words lists, paired associates).

Patten (1972) first resorted to imagery with brain-damaged patients. Using the peg method, he clinically describes improvement in four patients with a left lesion who have maintained good visual memory capacities. Three patients did not benefit from the method: a patient with Alzheimer's disease, a patient with a third ventricular tumor, and a patient who showed a defective memory after operative clipping of an anterior communicating artery aneurysm. The three of them could hardly produce images, were anosognosic, had little motivation, and showed a deficiency of STM. After this first attempt, other patients were studied, more particularly patients showing focal left or right lesions and amnesic patients.

While using imagery as a mnemonic aid, Jones (1974) showed that it was possible to improve the impaired verbal memory of patients who sustained a left temporal lobectomy on paired-associates tasks. Not only do the subjects profit by the imagery method in the condition wherein the examiner provides the imaged link between words, but also in the condition wherein the patient creates his or her own image. The benefit specially applies to immediate recall, and to a lesser extent, to long-term recall. Unexpectedly, patients with a right lobectomy behave as normal subjects and profit by the method, despite a possible impairment of visual memory. Jones interprets this conflicting elements as the consequence of a ceiling effect due to the simplicity of the proposed verbal tasks. This assertion seems rather curious, for the presence of a ceiling effect merely means that patients with a right temporal lobectomy can actually benefit from imagery. Furthermore, no ceiling effects are observed in right temporal subjects who do not resort to imagery (as indicated by Ehrlichman & Barrett, 1983). In 1978, Jones-Gotman and Milner resumed this first study but then proposed a longer list of paired associates and compared the imagery method with a verbal strategy. Right temporal patients prove to obtain worse results than controls while using imagery but normal results while using the verbal method. Thus, the authors concluded that the right hemisphere and more particularly the right hippocampal region plays a role in the use of imagery in the verbal learning tasks of paired associates. Jones-Gotman (1979) confirmed these results in a later study where they proposed an incidental verbal learning task in order to prevent the subjects from employing strategies other than the one required by the study. In a very detailed critical review, Ehrlichman and Barrett (1983) contest the special role of the right hemisphere in mental imagery, arguing from the lack of empirical data and the different possible interpretations of the results.

Gasparrini and Satz (1979) also show that memory for paired associates can be improved by teaching left-hemisphere brain-damaged patients (CVA patients) a visual imagery technique when comparing it with another method (rote repetition with encouragement). Furthermore, Shore (1979) compares the performances of left- and right-hemisphere brain-damaged patients on imagery and verbal mnemonics. The absence of an advantage for either strategy suggests that both of them may be efficient irrespective of the laterality of the lesion.

Wishing to test the efficiency of imagery during delayed recall (after 30 minutes and after 1 week), Lewinsohn, Danaher, and Kikel (1977) submitted patients to paired-associate learning and face-name tasks. The subjects were previously trained in image formation on both types of tasks. It appeared that the use of imagery improves the patients' performances during the acquisition and after 30 minutes, with less progress being observed in the face-name tasks. Yet, the advantage of imagery training was no longer present after 1 week.

The authors wondered whether the method would not have proved to be more efficient if they had asked the patients to repeat imagery tasks at home. Furthermore, the patients were usually not satisfied with the associations with which they were supplied in the face-name task, so it would have been of a great interest to let them create images of their own. Finally, this work gave few details about the site and the extent of the lesion: unmentioned lesional variables (unilateral or bilateral character of the lesions) might give an account of the relative inefficiency of the method.

Another group of studies dealt with amnesic patients. Baddeley and Warrington (1973) compared the performances of six amnesics on free recall tasks involving one list of unrelated control words, one list of words grouped on the basis of phonemic similarity, one list of words grouped on the basis of taxonomic category membership, and finally one list of words that had to be recalled in an imagery condition (with the link method). Amnesics do not benefit from visual imagery coding but profit from the taxonomic category grouping and phonemic similarity. Every patient claimed to be able to form the images, which led Baddeley and Warrington (1973) to assume that amnesics do not sustain a simple imagery impairment, but that they fail to exploit the new interactions generated by the imagery technique. Brooks and Baddeley (described in Baddeley, 1982) have ulteriorly questioned this defective imagery hypothesis. In a first study, they did not find any significant differences between amnesics and controls in a task thought to involve the manipulation of visuospatial images (the Thurstone's Flags test). This consisted in comparing one pattern with other similar patterns and deciding whether each pattern represented a rotation of the model or whether a mirror image was involved. Kapur (1978) has also shown that Korsakoff patients obtain normal results in a modified version of an imagery test (Weber & Harnish, 1974), which consists of indicating the spatial characteristics of letters in an imaged seven letter word. Therefore, they would be able to form images. In a second experiment, Brooks and Baddeley (in Baddeley, 1982) studied the amnesics' ability to use an imagery mnemonic in paired-associate learning and contrasted this with learning based on rote repetition and on a verbal mnemonic involving linking the two words in a pair by a sentence. To ensure that they actually resorted to imagery, the patients were requested to sketch their image on a small piece of paper that was later removed. The amnesics obtained poor results overall, and no advantage for either the imagery or the sentence mnemonic could be observed. In fact, the defective imagery hypothesis would have implied that the verbal mnemonic improves the performances, whereas the imagery mnemonic does not. Baddeley (1982) suggested that the differences of results between Baddeley's and Warrington's study (1973) and the later one would proceed from some capacity of subjects to use pre-existing structure in the taxonomic category condition as opposed to the imagery mnemonic wherein retrieval depends on a newly created image.

Cermak (1975) also studied the role of imagery in Korsakoff patients. Though Baddeley and Warrington (1973) were using a recall technique involving a four-unit sequence of nouns, Cermak (1975) proposed different learning tasks on material of two units (six lists of five verbal paired associates constructed in such a way that both a verbal mediator and a visual image might be created for each pair). The learning tasks were as follows: one task of rote learning, one imagery learning task, and one verbal cued learning task (the patients were supplied with a verbal mediating link at the presentation of the pairs and the retrieval stage). When having to recall, Korsakoff patients performed significantly better on the imagery learning and verbal cued learning tasks than on the rote learning one. But in the recognition condition, imagery learning proved to work better than the two other ones that produce similar results. The fact that the imagery technique did not yield better results than the verbal cued learning method in the recall condition might be due to some loss of information occurring when the patient had to translate the images into verbal responses.

Cutting (1978) does not find any progress in Korsakoffs' performances in a task of paired associates, whether the patients produce their own interactive image or it is provided by the experimenter. Meanwhile, patients do not receive training in the use of the imagery technique, in contrast to Cermak's study (1975) where patients learn how to create an image by relating items and how to use the image at the retrieval stage. Therefore, it seems possible that Cutting's patients (1978) do not actually use the image at encoding and retrieval.

According to Howes (1983), it is difficult to interpret the contradictions between the results of the different studies for the procedures can hardly be compared. Nevertheless, he propounds some elements of a conclusion that seem consistent with the available data. The Korsakoff patients seem able to use the mental image (when verbally proposed by the experimenter) to improve their mnemonic abilities in a two-unit association task. But when they have to process more complex material (associations between four or five items), they seem to need a verbal description of the image and at the same time, an iconic stimulus representing the related items (Way, 1979, used puzzling collages of five related items). Furthermore, Howes (1983) compared the effects of imagery in Korsakoff patients' performances in two distinct situations. In the first one, the experimenter proposed the imaged relation by showing the subjects a drawing of the related items and verbally describing it. In the second one, the subject had to self-generate, draw, and verbally describe the image. Though patients profit from the two conditions, they achieve better performances when the imaged relation has been provided by the experimenter (whereas the second condition generally gives the best results in normal subjects). Improvement in the experimenter condition are maintained beyond a 24-hour delay. It should be noted that Binder and Schreiber (1980) showed that alcoholic subjects improved in a paired-associate learning task though they were only supplied with verbal instructions asking them to apply the imagery method (that is, without being given the imaged mediating link).

Hence, one may distinguish between studies wherein patients are supplied with the images and studies wherein patients generate images of their own. Another main difference among all the studies concerns the existence of a previous program of imagery learning. While discussing the difficulties encountered by some patients in imagery tasks, Crovitz, Harvey, and Horn (1979) showed that they can be overcome by a suitable learning procedure (and more particularly the difficulties encountered in the construction of absurd images). The imagery strategy belongs, along with others, to the Wisconsin Neuromemory Program (Grafman, 1984). Patients are supplied with previous imagery learning. At first, they have to imagine an animate object and describe its image in a very detailed manner. After this, they learn to generate images from audible words. Then, they must memorize a list of words in a selective reminding task without any imagery instructions. In the following trials, they have to use the individual images of each word to remember the list of words. In the next phase of training, patients are instructed to create interactive images including two or three words from the list. Finally, they are taught the loci method. The patients are given lists of words for which images are progressively harder to construct. In addition to imagery, they are trained in jointly using other strategies (verbal strategies and external aids). Of the 42 patients that followed the program, 19 showed functionally and quantitatively significant progress. Among the subjects who improved their performances, 63% were under the age of 40 and had a full-scale IQ score above 95. It is worth noticing that the 42 patients sustained memory disorders from diverse etiologies (head injury, CVA, dementia, encephalitis, epilepsy, anoxia). The nature of the memory problem was not differentiated, and each patient was reeducated on the basis of the same principles of care: the organization, association, and elaboration of information to be learned (Craik & Lockhart, 1972). This eclectic approach, therefore, neglected the diversity of impairments and gave little information about the strategy variables that led to the failure or the success of therapy. This point will be discussed later.

In our laboratory, Branle (1981) has devised a program intended to teach the sequelae aphasic patients an imagery technique. It includes three parts.

1. A training in the formation of images: The patients are taught how to process information in an imaginal way, without resorting to verbal coding.
   a. The direct visualization step that consists in the formation of an image based on some visual support (drawing of familiar objects classified in an order of increasing complexity).

128 VAN DER LINDEN AND VAN DER KAA

b. The indirect visualization step where the subject has to mentally conceive an image of an object without any visual support (the formation of an image from a word). The subject then has to describe the created image and answer questions about its details.

c. The training in the memorization of images, where subjects have to create an image from a target photograph and then pick it out from several other distractive photographs after a 10-second delay. To prevent any verbalization of material, the subjects are requested to count aloud during the observation and mental reviewing of the photographs.

2. A training in the creation of absurd imaged associations between pairs of words.

a. The subject is presented with bizarre associations while having the principles that subtend the absurd creations explained (see Crovitz et al., 1979): Objects may be pictured as fused, the size could be exaggerated, colors, and shape modified, the object situated in a unusual context, etc.

b. The subjects first have to self-generate interactive images from pairs of words that allow associations close to those of the previous stage, then from different pairs.

c. The method is applied to lists of five verbal paired-associate stimuli. The pairs are read three times with a memory trial following each reading. If the patient fails, the effectiveness of the created image is discussed again.

3. A utilization of the peg method in memorizing 15 words.

a. The patient first has to remember a peg list based on a number-object association. The morphological similarity between the object and the number constitutes a double cue. We resorted to this type of peg method because of the difficulties encountered by aphasics when memorizing the peg rhymes or phonetic systems.

b. The memorization of a 15-word list. The absurd associations refer to the peg word and the word to be memorized, the number only interposing for the ordered recall. The subjects start with lists of 5 words, then continue with 8, 10, 12, and 15 word lists.

Four right-handed patients with left-hemisphere damage (CVA patients) were presented with such a program (Table 4.1).

These patients manifested aphasic sequelae (discrete word finding difficulty, dysorthography, poor linguistic elaboration) and complained about marked impairments of verbal memory in daily life.

4. THERAPY OF MEMORY   129

TABLE 4-1
Age, Duration of Illness and Localization of Lesion

Patient	Age	Duration (Months)	Localization
1	57	6	posterior temporal
2	51	48	temporal
3	43	24	frontoparietal
4	50	9	frontoparietal

At the beginning of the program, they obtained poor results in the Rey Auditory-Verbal Learning Test (Table 4.2).

The first and second patients showed considerable evolution by the end of the program for they each remembered 11 out of 12 words after a single reading and 14 out of 15 words by resorting to the peg method. Results were the same after a 20-minute delay. They needed about 10 seconds to generate their own associations. It should be noted that the retrieval of associated words proved to be difficult when the absurd was not involved. For instance, the first patient who had only mentally leaned a ladder against a hallway wall in the ladder-hallway association did not recover the word "hallway." Both of these patients mentioned spontaneously resorting to imagery in their daily life, though not to absurd imagery. The third and fourth subjects could never create interactive images and execute the method despite the learning procedure. However, they were weakly motivated patients, showing a decrease in intellectual efficiency. Their brain damage extended to the frontal area.

We have seen that the different studies about imagery involved both methods and material issuing from experimental psychology (paired associates, lists of words, etc.) Hence, the problem of transfering the imagery technique to daily life situations and other types of material is addressed. Gasparrini and Satz (1979) did not obtain significant differences when the imagery method was applied to differ-

TABLE 4-2
Results in Rey Auditory-Verbal Learning Test

Patients	Trials					Total Score	Expected Score
	1	2	3	4	5		
1	5	6	6	5	6	28	57
2	4	7	7	10	7	35	57
3	4	7	8	7	9	35	57
4	3	6	7	6	6	28	57

ent kinds of material from that of the study. Howes (1983) also showed that Korsakoff patients did not seem spontaneously to use the method in the acquisition of new lists. Shore (1979) attributes the absence of transfer to the brevity of learning.

The causes of such failures deserve careful research, including an analysis of the principle of encoding specificity, according to which some material that has been learned in a given context would not be generalized to other contexts. Once a strategy has been mastered, we ought to ensure that it will be executed in several different environments, and so doing, consider the encoding variability versus the encoding specificity (Baddeley, 1984).

It is worth noting that according to Robertson-Tchabo, Hausman, and Arenberg (1976), elderly patients may quickly acquire an imagery technique (the loci method). Yet, they do not resort to it in a posttraining trial as long as they are not given explicit instructions to do so. Hulicka and Grossman (1967) showed that the spontaneous use of imaged mediators was generally less frequent in normal elderly subjects than in younger ones, but that if the formers were instructed to resort to the imagery method, they would show relatively more progress than the latter.

Besides, it would certainly prove useful to distinguish between learning and learning to learn (Schacter, Rich, & Stampp, 1985), that is, a distinction between the improvement generated by a mnemonic technique in the acquisition of new information and the patient's ability to acquire knowledge of when and how to use a memory aid. A distinct training that would enable patients to recognize those daily life situations wherein mnemonics might be used should be included in the whole reeducational program.

As a matter of fact, few studies approached the direct application of imagery techniques in daily life situations. Thus, one of Glasgow's patients seemed unable to use the imagery procedure (the face-name method) outside the laboratory, for the images that he created were too complex and the visualization time too long (Glasgow, Zeiss, Barrera, & Lewinsohn, 1977). A simplified method was then devised for use in daily life situations. The patient self-recorded the frequency of name forgetting, had to write the forgotten names on a sheet and at three scheduled times a day, had to read each name on the list, and, simultaneously, had to visualize the person. Such a strategy induced a significant decrease of forgettings. Wilson (1982) also presented his patients with a similar simplified procedure. In another study, Wilson (1987a) used visual imagery to teach patients the names of people they came into contact with regularly in their daily social intercourse.

As noticed by Moffat (1984), the loci method is a suitable technique, for a resort to well-known and natural locations enables the patient to avoid having to learn a long list of peg words and may also serve as an additional cue for the use of the technique. Going by these actual locations may trigger their associated images and then allow the related actions to be performed.

Another piece of information lacking in all the studies concerns the long-term maintenance of the treatment benefit. Crosson and Buenning (1984) designed a program to improve the retention of verbal material. Because their patient's profession involved interviews and supposed that he could retain their contents, the therapists decided to work from paragraphs picked up in current magazines. By using mnemonic strategies (especially visual imagery), they prompted considerable improvement in their patient's results. Nevertheless, a drop was observed in a 9-month follow-up, which was consistent with the fact that the patient mentioned no longer resorting to the mnemonic strategies.

Studies of imagery techniques face several other criticisms besides the problem related to the transfer of learning and the maintenance of acquisitions. Not the least of them is the vagueness of the hypotheses that underlie the use of imagery. As a matter of fact, most of the studies belong to an empirical approach in which the variables that might explain the occurrence of success or failure can hardly be identified.

It should be noted that two recent studies propounded a general theoretical interpretation of their results. Kovner, Mattis, and Goldmeier (1983) showed that severe amnesics were able to learn and recall lists of unrelated words when trained with a learning technique; the method used ridiculous imagery embedded in a story line, contextual and categorical cuing, and spaced repetition of learning sessions. Kovner, Mattis, and Pass (1985) observed that these patients could recall seemingly unlimited numbers of words and there were no differences between a ridiculously imaged story (RIS) and a logically imaged story (LIS) condition. The authors indicate that their subjects did not try to apply the techniques to promote recall of everyday events or control lists and only seemed able to use them if they were externally structured by the examiner. The authors, therefore, assume that some amnesics might sustain an impairment of the automatic encoding of contextual variables due to hypoactive orienting. The RIS and LIS techniques would restore the saliency of contextual cues by providing them in a structured way. While integrating their data in the framework of Grossberg's model (1982), Kovner et al. (1985) postulated that structured chunking, contextual cuing procedures, and spaced practice may slowly lead to enough conditioned reinforcer value for the contextual cues; the adaptative resonance is triggered and consequently, the items are transferred from STM to LTM.

Meanwhile, many uncertainties remain as to the real value of imagery techniques in the reeducation of memory. Stricter studies should be directed, studies that would rely on clearly defined hypotheses and whose methodology would ensure a better control of the following variables: the validation of therapy, the length of imagery training, the evaluation of associated problems, and the transfer and maintenance of acquisitions.

Verbal Strategies

As shown by several studies, amnesic patients are sensitive to manipulations that organize the information taking activities of verbal material, as for instance, gathering words in semantic or phonemic categories (Baddeley & Warrington, 1973). They also improved their performances when they were supplied with adequate semantic or phomenic cues at recall (Warrington & Weiskrantz, 1971, 1974, 1978). Moreover, Cermak (1976) showed that the presentation of a verbal mediator (i.e., linking paired associates, for instance the link "wood" for the "tree-arrow" pair) at the retrieval and the encoding stages induces better performances in amnesics on recall.

Jaffe and Katz (1975) devised a reeducational program whose logic consisted in providing cues (semantic categories) to the patient (a 52-year-old Korsakoff patient) either at the storage or the retrieval stages, or at both of them. Only the last condition (simultaneously providing cues at both storage and retrieval steps) proved to be effective. Those data were interpreted from the framework of "the encoding specificity hypothesis" of Tulving and Thomson (1973). Still, it appeared that the patient would not spontaneously use the cuing procedure and thus not acquire a learning-to-learn effect. Davies and Binks (1983) resumed Jaffe's and Katz's work (1975) with a 31-year-old Korsakoff patient. To avoid the methodological problems originally encountered by this research (the use of a single list of items with multiple testing on it), they investigated the use of cues (category names) under four conditions: recall, no cues; recognition, no cues; recall, storage and retrieval cues; and recognition, storage cues. Preliminary work showed that the storage and retrieval cues in the recognition mode led to 100% correct responses. Four replications of the four conditions were foreseen, and 16 lists of 25 words had been constructed. Results were better on recognition (60% retrieved items)

4. THERAPY OF MEMORY   133

than on recall (12%) when no cues were provided, which suggested a retrieval deficit even though the still imperfect recognition rate also signals some storage disorder. Storage and retrieval cues brought the recall results to 30% correct responses and the recognition to ceiling levels. The authors drew information from this experiment and elaborated an everyday living revalidation program in the following manner. At the acquisition stage, they prompted the patient to generate associations (in a person's name example: "Brown, you could think of John Brown's body, browned-off, a good sun tan, you could think of ways he looks brown") and to use them in retrieval of names. This procedure also involves imagery. The patient was perfectly able to carry out such tasks, but only if prompted to do so. Then the patient's spouse was asked to elicit associations at the encoding stage and to provide them at retrieval. Furthermore, relying on the superiority of recognition over recall, the spouse was requested to supply the patient with several possibilities each time he or she forgot a name or an object (which restricted his field of investigation).

Another method aimed at encouraging a deep and elaborate encoding of verbal material consists in relating the items to be memorized in a story line (Crovitz, 1979), a method that may be yoked with an imagery technique. Gianutsos and Gianutsos (1979) designed a rehabilitation program for verbal memory by modifying the task formerly developed by Peterson and Peterson (1959), which allows one to differentiate short- and long-term storage. For those conditions where long-term storage was required, they encouraged an elaborative rehearsal (Craik & Watkins, 1973) by having the patients integrate the words to be remembered in a story. Using a design involving a "multiple baseline across cases," the authors showed the positive effects of the mnemonic training by dissociating them from practice effects. Moreover, a differential analysis of each subject's results indicated among other things that efficient short-term storage is a necessary though not sufficient prior condition for long-term storage. While wondering about the functional significance of the recorded progress, they stressed the usefulness of an evaluation of the information processing required by everyday living. They finally insisted on the interest of the single case methodology in rehabilitation, more particularly to analyze the differential effectiveness of training. According to us, the combination of these three elements (the single case methodology, the study of memory in daily life, and the use of adequate evaluational methods) seems essential for an effective reeducational program. Notice should be taken of the fact that Gianutsos' and Gianutsos' program (1979), although empirical, lacked an accurate evaluation of the nature of the impairment of the four subjects, which might very well explain the heterogeneity of their results. Gianutsos (1981) adapted a similar methodology for the reeducation of a college professor who had contracted herpes simplex encephalitis. A previous evaluation had shown impairments of both short- and long-term storage and two training procedures were consequently devised, one applying to each storage system (memory span practice and use of imagery or story method). Short- and longterm recall showed some evolution (though it was rather minimal in the latter case). Except for the distinction between STM and LTM, the nature of the disorders remained imprecise, and little could be said about the way in which the training tasks brought about some improvement.

From another perspective, the first letter mnemonic may be used as an illustration of the strategy of retrieval cues. We are often able to guess the first sound or length of a name that is on the tip of the tongue. As Marshall (1979) pointed out, it is tempting to put together the normal tip of the tongue state with the aphasic anomic deficit, at least the deficit that involves the unavailability of the phonological representation. When confronted with the forgetting of a name, some people try to cue themselves by recapitulating the alphabet in hopes of aiding recall. As a matter of fact, several studies have shown that supplying the patients with the first letter might ameliorate the recall performances, especially in presenile and senile dementia patients (Miller, 1975; Morris, Wheatley, & Britton, 1983).

Jaffe and Katz (1975) successfully taught their Korsakoff patient the names of two ward staff members by means of alphabetical cuing (the first initials of the names) at encoding and recall, and fading. Actually, this patient had not been able to learn a single name for the 5 years of his hospitalization. The authors resumed this method to teach him the location of both his locker and some items in it. The main difficulty encountered by this research proceeded from the patient's inability to generate the cuing procedure by himself. Moffat (1984) described the case of a patient with a head injury who was encouraged to recapitulate the alphabet to retrieve his friends' names. To this effect, he used to wear a card with the alphabet printed on it. When a new name had to be learned, special attention was devoted to the encoding of initials.

Two strategies based upon the first letter are frequently used by normal subjects and more particularly by students. Either the first letter of words on a list that have to be remembered are chunked so as to form a meaningful word, or the first letters of the words to be remembered are used as the first letters of the other words forming a sentence that will easily be remembered. Based on studies involving normal subjects, Morris (1979) concluded that such techniques prove effective for retaining the order of well-known or easily learned items (as related words), but are not adapted for learning new items. Gruneberg, Monks, and Sykes (1977) showed that normal subjects who resorted to this alphabetical exploration strategy would spend more time on their recall attempt than controls. If available times for recall were equalized, the differences between the groups' results would also disappear. Such facts led Morris (1979) to suggest that the success of the strategy would not directly proceed from the supply of a relevant cue but rather from other variables occurring during this longer retrieval.

Few studies considered the use of these strategies in the reeducation of brain-damaged patients. Wilson (1982) applied a first letter mnemonic system to the learning of a shopping list in a patient suffering from severe memory impairment after a bilateral stroke. The first letters of the list's items were set in an order that would form for instance the words GO SHOPPING: G=Grapes, O=Oranges, S=Sugar, H=Ham, O=Olives, P=Paper, P=Pears, I=Ink, N=Nails, G=Grass seed. The procedure was greatly appreciated by the patient who could soon reach 100% success. On the other hand, the strategy failed to aid the same patient when attempting to remember short routes. Several other methods, such as following cues like a chalk line or large capital letters chalked on the corner of buildings, had not yielded any better results. Wilson (1982) indicates that the route finding problem would not result from difficulties with spatial relationships, for the patient could follow a map perfectly and perform tasks involving mazes, had a normal immediate memory for spatial tasks, and obtained a good Rey-Osterrieth copy. In any case, such details do not allow us precisely to identify the level of the patient's impairment. Byrne (1982) assumed that an impairment of topographical knowledge might affect two different types of mental representation, that is the network-map and vector-map representations, as well as updating position and maintaining position skills. Wilson's patient may have presented with a disorder of representations, whereas his updating and maintaining position skills remained preserved. Therefore, he might have been able to find his way with a map even though he had lost all cognitive representations of familiar areas. As a matter of fact, topographical disorders may constitute a heterogeneous pathology and the term spatial orientation disorders can by no means give a clear account of the phenomenon or definite indications about further reeducational strategies. Once again, it seems that an effective treatment will first have to rely on an accurate description of the problem. Recently, we conducted a study from Byrne's framework

(Van der Linden & Seron, 1987) on a patient showing a seemingly better preserved network-map representation versus impaired vector-map representation.

The first letter and the story strategies may improve learning in some cases of disordered or meaningless material. When dealing with organized and meaningful material, actively looking for relations between items at the encoding stage is generally advised (that is elaborative rehearsal). Glasglow et al. (1977) used the PQRST approach on a young woman with a head injury complaining of long-term recall difficulties of meaningful verbal or written material. The PQRST method consists of the following stages:

1. Preview: surveying the material in order to acknowledge the general content of the text
2. Question: asking the key questions about the content
3. Read: actively reading the text in order to answer the questions
4. State: repeating the information that was formerly read
5. Test: self-testing by answering the questions that have been developed, the answers constituting a summary of the text

The Q stage included four standard questions and the two first steps had been chunked to use auditorily presented material. The material provided in the laboratory situation consisted in short texts (three or four paragraphs) or in longer narrative prose (two pages). The PQRST gave better results than the rehearsal strategy, which was itself superior to the preintervention strategy. There was no effect related to the presentation modality or the length of text. Moreover, the method was successfully applied to activities of daily life: reading newspaper articles and school related material. It is worth noting that at the time, negative self-appraisals decreased. Nevertheless, the method required a greater investment of time before being actually applied and the observed improvement might still be the result of this additional time.

Grafman (1984) also used the PQRST method to organize the text material. He added a last stage (probing), wherein the examiner elicits factual, accessory information from the patient not included in the summary provided at the T stage. The material involved standardized stories. After the patient had reached a criterion of recall, he or she was presented with more complex material, afterwhich the patient was given simple stories selected from magazine articles and finally, material relevant to daily life. According to Grafman (1984), the crucial factor was the step-by-step visible organization of information to be remembered. The conclusions referred to the whole

4. THERAPY OF MEMORY   137

reeducational program (including other strategies) but without specifically discussing this strategy in particular.

Wilson (1984) described a resort to the PQRST approach to prevent a patient from constantly asking the same question: "Why have I got a memory problem?" This patient had sustained a right hemisphere subarachnoid hemorrhage following rupture of an anterior communicating artery aneurysm. After having supplied him with a summary of both his pathology and its consequences, the author turned to the PQRST procedure, the key questions being selected. Three weeks later, the patient could correctly answer all of the selected questions, but still would ask the same question several times a day. According to Wilson (1984), such behavior is similar to that described in frontal patients: The observed impairment would not be related to a specific disruption of the processes involved in the storage of information but would rather result from a loss of strategies of recall for material that has already been stored. We shall also add that such disorders could also be due to a lack of initiative, perseverative behaviors, or a difficulty in relating information spaced in time. Once again, an accurate evaluation of the disorders would have been requisite.

We have already mentioned the use made by Crosson and Buenning (1984) of an imagery method intended to improve the memory of paragraphs in a head-injured patient. In addition to imagery, they also proposed another rather successful strategy to increase the patient's interactions with the material (the paragraphs were selected from current magazines, each of them being divided into ideas similar to the paragraphs from the Wechsler Memory Scale). The patient was requested to ask relevant questions about the material that he had just read. Gianutsos (1980) also improved the performances of a patient with a left hemisphere CVA in remembering material in paragraphs: The training consisted of reading and rephrasing paragraphs. A previously begun training involving word lists had not improved the memory for paragraphs.

Despite the fact that the difficulties in reading stories or newspaper articles constitute a very frequent complaint of brain-damaged patients, the nature of such disorders has not yet been elucidated. Recent studies in cognitive psychology support the idea according to which the understanding, the production, or the retention of a text would involve an abstract schema, that is, a set of principles of organization common to all discourses of the same type. Those schema generate the macrostructure of the stories and work as rewriting rules. The requisite components of all stories are setting, theme, plot, and resolution. The setting establishes the time, location, and protagonists. The theme defines the general focus or the main goal of the story. The plot is an indefinite succession of episodes, each of which is a cluster of actions, comprising attempts to reach a subgoal and the outcomes of those attempts. The episodes may be recursively embedded in the plot structure. The resolution is the final result of the story. The theory of schemata holds that perception, comprehension, and memory are processes that involve an interaction between new information and schema-based information. In a memory task, the subject would use the macrostructure as a cue allowing him to have access to the list of propositions stored in memory. Information recall would be a function of the role of the proposition in the structure and of the level of correspondence between the story and the schema. The longer the delay between recall and encoding, the closer the story and the schema.

Several neurolinguistic studies devoted to the production and the comprehension of discourse or narrative by aphasic patients seem to indicate they were more proficient at the discourse level than at the sentence level. Differences between normal persons and aphasics were differences of degree, not of nature. Not only does the macrostructure of the story seem to be preserved but also the causal and chronological relations between events inside an episode. In the research of Ulatowska et al. (1983), the patients described as moderately aphasic showed a selective reduction of information (a smaller number of episodes); a reduction of the superstructure in stories without codas, abstracts, and evaluation; a reduction of clues; and a simplification of the plot profile. The disorders were highly selective because they only implied a reduction of elaborative material (nonessential propositions). Thus, these patients retained at their disposal some intact cognitive processes that might be able to operate for comprehending or memorizing texts. In the same way, Brookshire and Nicholas (1984) showed that aphasics and right-hemisphere-damaged subjects remembered main ideas from discourses better than details. Nevertheless, they tested both comprehension and remembering on the basis of the recognition of statements, which might not have been the most relevant procedure for the memory tests. It should be noted that models of analysis in the field of texts may not yet have reached a sophistication level equivalent to those in the field of sentences.

In our rehabilitation center, Philippe (1982) designed a program intended to improve text memory in three left-damaged patients (CVA patients), by using the concept of macrostructure. While tested on a long text of 1,030 words, analyzed in terms of 12 principal and 8 secondary items of information, all patients showed a loss of both principal and secondary information (Table 4.3). Two of them also (patients 1 and 2) sustained difficulties in linearity, such as in chronology and causal links with inventions and reinterpretations. Thus, qualitative problems were observed in both of these patients, and it could be assumed that their basic text structure had not been preserved.

In the reeducation program, the patients had to extract the different propositions from a text before reinserting them in a story schema setting (in writing). This request obliged them to closely investigate the material and to select, structure, and organize the information in the text. The patients were instructed to look for the interconnections of ideas and to logically relate them in the following written schema: setting (principal protagonists, time, location), theme, plot (actions, results), and resolution. They had to comply with a principle of economy, that is to choose key words rather than long sentences, and to connect the events to construct a chain of information that would be unrolled at retrieval. The patients were also taught how to use some rules for the reduction of information (Kintsch & Van Dijck, 1975), rules that allow a subject to elaborate the macrostructure from the microstructures (for instance, neglect inferable propositions, generalize the predicates that share the same arguments, etc.). The programs could vary in the length of the text involved (from 75 to 1,200 words), as well as in their linear and familiar characteristics. Thus, 75 to 800 word texts were typewritten and left at the disposal of the subjects who could consult them as often as they wished while filling in the story schema. Once they were finished, they were asked to tell the story from the written schema. On the other hand, when confronted with texts of 800 to 1,200 words, subjects had to read and simultaneously complete the schema. Then, they were given an opportunity to organize the information with a pencil of another color. The

TABLE 4-3
Age, Duration of Illness, Localization of Lesion,
Results in the Text Memory Evaluation

Patients	Age	Duration (Months)	Localization	Results
1	52	48	temporal	8 principal and 4 secondary items
2	26	7	frontoparietal	4 principal and 0 secondary items
3	55	24	temporal	4 principal and 3 secondary items

140   VAN DER LINDEN AND VAN DER KAA

final step was story telling. The subjects would proceed to the following step each time they had achieved the success criterion of control text. Finally, a posttest was administered involving a text of 1,000 words that was to be recalled without any written schema. Two patients (patients 1 and 2) showed good progress and could recall 17 pieces of information out of the 20 included in the text of 1,000 words. The third patient left the program during the first step (linear 200 words text) due to health complications. In general, the main difficulties dealt with nonlinear stories and the production of inferences. Interpreting the results is not a simple task, for the program is likely to have operated at two distinct levels. On one hand, it probably encouraged an active and elaborated encoding and required interrelations between the story components, which elicited from the patients the recall of more secondary information. On the other hand, the program might have constituted some sort of simulation of the normal strategy, for the written story schema and the rules for simplifying information might have supplied them with a framework for encoding and cues at retrieval.

In conclusion, it is our contention that the cognitive approach to text memory provides models and experimental data that may be used in the rehabilitation of brain-damaged patients. Nevertheless, studies on text memory give rise to numerous theoretical and methodological questions. For instance, which procedures should we resort to in memory tests: questionnaires, recognition of statements, or free recall? What are the relationships between comprehension and memory? From a neuropsychological point of view, it would also prove necessary to estimate the patients' performances on delayed recall, long texts, etc., as well as to evaluate the performances of patients with other lesional sites (more specifically frontal patients). The evaluation should be as broad as possible and apply to diversified cognitive capacities of the patient (for example, inference capacities), as well as to other types of discourse (descriptions, conversations, etc.).

Other Strategies

Several different strategies have been propounded in addition to the verbal and imaginary ones, though in a rather anecdotal way.

Relying on certain residual learning capabilities and more particularly the capacity to acquire motor skills shown by amnesics, several authors imagined that motor movements might improve memory. Moffat (1984) described the progress in learning lists of words displayed by a severely head-injured amnesic who resorted to a motor

4. THERAPY OF MEMORY   141

coding method: Each word had been associated with a sequence of actions. Turning to Moffat's example, the word "baby" would be represented by the action of moving the arms in a dangling fashion. Wilson and Moffat (1984a) also indicated that it was possible to use the same method for the learning of certain names, therein following Powell's suggestion (1981). Davies and Binks (1983) whose patient displayed a relatively intact capacity for learning skills (tested in a mirror drawing task) advised him to develop do-it-yourself type activities and prompted him to ask people to show him how to do things to copy their movements.

Several studies conducted on normal subjects seem to indicate that motor skills are retained better than verbal skills (Annett, 1979), but major methodological problems hinder the interpretation of the results, especially the difficulty of establishing task equivalencies for all variables (except for the verbal-motor distinction), as well as the absence of a unified scoring system. Moreover, the verbal or motor nature of the coding occurring in certain tasks could not be firmly defined. The question of the generalization from laboratory tasks to practical situations was also addressed, which, in Annett's terms (1979), is a question related to the lack of a generally agreed taxonomy of tasks. Actually, the evaluation of the usefulness of the motor method in neuropsychology still has to be accomplished and will encounter the same difficulties as the studies conducted on normal subjects.

A common strategy used by people in daily life to retrieve personally experienced information is the reconstruction-of-context method, which would prove to be effective insofar as recall would involve a cue related to the initial encoding situation. According to Lindsay and Norman (1980), information recovery in normal subjects proceeds from active and reconstructive research among the accessible rememberings. The subject does not attempt directly to recall the information but rather divides the task into a sequence of problems and partial questions followed, as long as the subject can provide answers, by more and more precise questions. As noticed by Tiberghien and Lecoq (1983), the recovery of past information does not merely consist in a mnemonic action, but also proceeds from a double decision, first when the subject must decide whether he will start an activity of mnemonic research and second, when he has to choose a firm response at the end of the conditional investigation. Finally, let us remark that a recovery failure often proceeds from a mistake in the initial orientation of the memory investigation toward a context irrelevant to the questions involved. In this vein, Baddeley (1982) distinguishes between relatively automatic retrieval processes and the active problem-solving aspects of recall that he terms "recollection." He suggests that amnesics could not recollect although they might still be able to run off procedures involving learned associations. Thus, their impairments might refer to some difficulty either in using incidental details to confirm that what was retrieved was correct, either in rejecting incorrect associations produced by the automatic procedures, or else, in carrying out the different operations that consist of checking items evoked by semantic memory or reasoning on the basis of their episodic characteristics. Patients with an intellectual impairment might also sustain some disability in their capacity to reason about retrieved items. As noted by Morton (1985), this conception is more dynamic and confronts us with real memory phenomena. Yet, its use in neuropsychology supposes that we knew more about the recollection process in normal subjects.

The reconstruction-of-context method has not been frequently used in the reeducation of brain-damaged patients. As pointed out by Moffat (1984), if this method is praised when an object has been lost, it would prove even more effective if an imaginal association had previously been made between the object involved and its location (for instance, we might create the image of a huge pair of scissors cutting off the diningroom table to ulteriorly retrieve the fact that we have put the pair of scissors on the diningroom table).

In another direction, Gardner (1977) reported the case of a patient with a gross memory disorder who was still able to learn a body of facts embedded as lyrics in a song. This patient, an accomplished pianist, could sing the melody of songs that he had previously learned on the piano and even recite the words without the melody. Yet, he could not remember both the lyrics and the music simultaneously, and the patient sometimes needed prompting. Three months after the training process, the patient was able to perform both the music and the lyrics without too many difficulties. Gardner (1977) related these data to the fact that severely demented patients might still be able to sing compositions and even learn simple melodies. These observations should give rise to further studies examining the role of melody in learning. It would surely be tempting to combine these data with the use of melody within aphasics as it occurs in the Melodic Intonation Therapy (Van Eckhout, Pillon, Signoret, Deloche, & Seron, 1982). It is worth noticing Moffat's suggestion (1984) that Gardner's patient took advantage of the rhyming format of the lyrics. Rhymes are better retained than prose because the knowledge of the rhyming relations restrains the range of possible responses (Bower & Bolton, 1969).

According to Schacter et al. (1985), all of these strategies, which attempt to modify the patient's encoding (visual imagery mnemonics, verbal strategies), are characterized by a major problem: They all require such extensive cognitive resources that the patient can hardly use them in everyday life. While wondering about the possibility of less exacting methods, they suggested resorting to a spaced retrieval technique (Landauer & Bjork, 1978). The strategy is based on a property of memory systems: The act of retrieval exerts an effect on the subsequent memorability of a retrieved item. Therefore, it consists in maximizing the benefit of recalling a previously studied item. In a study conducted on normal college students, Landauer and Bjork (1978) showed how it might be advantageous to try to retrieve the information at various intervals after presentation. Schacter et al. (1985) evaluated the usefulness of this technique with four patients that had to learn characteristics associated with faces (name, hometown, occupation, and hobby). The experiment comprised four stages: (a) a baseline, (b) a cued-training phase wherein the subject was verbally cued by the experimenter to use spaced retrieval during the presentation-recall delay (that is recalling the face characteristics at various intervals), (c) a self-cued training wherein the experimenter progressively faded the verbal cues intended to prompt spaced retrieval, and (d) an evaluation stage. Spaced retrieval improved the four patients performances but the analysis of results led the authors to assume that the technique would only prove useful when applied to a relatively small amount of information or when the information was tested after a short delay. Indeed, the real use of this less demanding method on long-term retention remains to be established, and the causes of the phenomenon should be further investigated. From a more general perspective, however, it seems important that the distribution of practice be taken into account in reeducation programs, whatever strategy is involved. As Baddeley (1983) remarked, the principle of "few and often" is a good learning rule, and it is probably just as true when one has to learn material over a long period of time. Likewise, Baddeley and Longman (1978) demonstrated that a training rate of 1 hour per day was more profitable (both for the learning rate and for the subsequent retention) than two sessions of 2 hours per day, one session of 2 hours per day, or two sessions of 1 hour per day. This principle would also find an application at a microlevel and, therefore, constitutes a microdistribution practice. Thus, when a patient is presented with a single item twice, recall will be better if both presentations are spaced than if they are given in a rapid succession. On the other hand, memory will reinforce more when information is self-remembered than when it is provided by the experimenter. A successful recall has positive effects on motivation and works as a second

144 VAN DER LINDEN AND VAN DER KAA

training trial. Now, the sooner the item is tested, the more likely it is to be recalled, which pulls in the opposite direction from the distribution of practice principle. According to Baddeley (1984), a solution might be found by adopting a flexible strategy. The subject is presented with an item and tested after a short delay; then, as the item becomes better and better learned, recall delays are progressively increased until they reach the longest interval at which the patient is still able to recall the item.

Schacter et al. (1985) also showed that while using an adapted program, two patients demonstrated learning to learn effects, that is, a spontaneous use of spaced retrieval. As seen earlier, the distinction between learning and learning to learn gives rise to much more general issues and points to the necessity of a training program in daily life intended to identify the situations in which the mnemonic strategies may be employed.

As another alternative to the approach of learning mnemonic strategies, Schacter and Glisky (1987) suggested that it may be more productive or more useful to teach memory-disordered patients domain-specific knowledge, that is, knowledge that enables the patients to perform a task important for everyday functioning. Glisky, Schacter and Tulving (1986) develop a study designed to teach four memory-impaired patients a small vocabulary of computer-related terms. While relying on different works that showed that severely amnesic patients' retention of individual words was improved by letter-fragment cues (Diamond & Rozin, 1984; Graf et al., 1984; Warrington & Weiskrantz, 1970, 1974, 1978), they attempted to teach the patients a new lexicon by giving the initial letter of target words as cues. To accomplish this, they used an errorless learning procedure (Seron, Lambert, & Van der Linden, 1977; Skinner, 1958), which they called the method of "vanishing cues." This method requires the subject be actively involved in the learning process and minimizes the probability of erroneous responses or omissions by supplying him or her with prompts that produced the desired response initially. The stimulus control of behavior is progressively decreased by fading out the provided stimulus information. For example, the patient is led to recall the word "software," defined as "programs that the computer carries out." The first letter S is given to the subject, and if it fails to produce the correct word, the next letters of the word are successively added until the subject is able to furnish the correct response. When compared with a standard anticipation procedure, the method of vanishing cues provides higher levels of learning and retention. Moreover, it is better appreciated by patients and proves to be more successful on transfer tasks. From a theoretical point of view, the authors

4. THERAPY OF MEMORY   145

assume that this sort of learning shares some characteristics with the kinds of learning involved in the experiments concerning priming effects (Schacter, 1987): Once they have studied a list of words, the memory-disordered patients show an enhanced tendency to complete letter fragments with recently presented words, even if they do not explicitly remember having learned the words. Priming effect and explicit remembering would derive from an independent process, which would, therefore, mean that the vanishing cues method would employ processes involved in priming effect. As indicated by the authors, the vanishing cues method might be used to teach the information necessary to carry out some activities of everyday life, and more precisely, would allow the patients to acquire the data needed to use microcomputers in the revalidation process. In another study, Glisky and Schacter (1987) have shown that patients with memory disorders can learn to perform basic operations on the microcomputer. Glisky and Schacter (1988) have also shown that a severely amnesic patient can acquire the knowledge and skills needed to perform a complex computer job in true working environment.

From a functional perspective, Davies and Binks (1983) rested their rehabilitative program on a principle propounded by Miller (1978), which recommended modifying the environment to reduce the demands placed on memory. They trained their patients to use a prompt card intended to be shown to the persons they met with to (a) legitimize the memory disorder and (b) encourage the acquaintances to prompt the patient in a relevant manner. The patient was also taught how to use a notebook and to casually ask someone to put down information in his book (role playing training). Furthermore, the patient's spouse was given some instructions and advised to structure her husband's environment to afford him encoding in propitious conditions (for instance, by making sure that only one person talked to him at a time). Follow-up after 1 year showed that this memory support system had continued.

In the same way, Milton (1985) devised an according-type cardboard file system with alphabet sections and content cue cards on the front of the file. The card consists of an alphabetic letter followed by selected file headings for that letter. Following are some examples found on the content cue card, which is intended to aid the patient to organize and retrieve personal papers:

B: Birthday list; Bank
C: Coupons; Cassette players; Cleaners; Church
I: Insurance; Index cards; Invitations

146 VAN DER LINDEN AND VAN DER KAA

The patient can use the card to decide under which heading a new entry will be filed, as well as to retrieve a paper by reviewing the card to spot the place where a paper may be filed.

A second strategy was elaborated by Milton (1985). A modified bus schedule card was designed to overcome problems in planning a route and carrying it out, as well as difficulties in remembering information such as bus number, bus stop location, and time of departure. The use of external memory aids and cuing devices has to be accurately studied; Harris (1984b) detailed its conditions of utilization.

Another approach propounded by Wilson and Moffat (1984b) involved the organization of memory groups. Group work not only proves interesting for the acquaintances that a patient can make among persons sustaining the same type of impairments but especially for the fact that it provides a setting in which one may recreate conditions similar to everyday living. It would, therefore, constitute a valuable tool for learning transfer.

CONCLUSION

For now, the cognitive approach has only made its first steps in the field of the reeducation of memory disorders. Its basic principle consists in palliating the impairment of memory by supplying the patient with alternative strategies that involve preserved or normally nonfunctional subprocesses. It is essential that the therapeutic program be devised by relying on hypotheses that define the nature of the disorder and by considering the possible forms of memory impairment, as well as the residual capabilities of the patients. A single-subject paradigm will be especially encouraged in this regard (Wilson, 1987b). Yet, the experimental data are still sparse or inconsistent. Furthermore, the generality or vagueness of certain concepts decrease their operational value in the field of revalidation. Despite the fact that therapeutic progress is a function of the development of experimental studies, one ought never wait for experimental data to be clarified before clinically testing the strategies they generate. On the contrary, such an approach affords therapists the opportunity to play a clarifying role in selecting from among the theoretical hypotheses that compete today. Research work and rehabilitation are involved in a kind of dialectical relationship wherein each enriches the other. This, needless to say, assumes the application of rigorous methodological principles dealing with both the pretherapy evaluation and the validation of treatment.

Thus, strategies are too often chosen without any prior accurate evaluation of the disorder. If most of the memory tests applied in current clinical practice can detect a decrement of mnemic efficiency in a patient (that is, detect a score inferior to the expected one in a population of normal subjects), very few could give information about the nature of the disorder. As a matter of fact, very similar quantitative rates may occur in patients sustaining problems with very different characteristics. As Butters (1984) pointed out, the research data must be integrated to forge adequate evaluational tools. These investigative tools will further have to be adapted or completed with regards to the progress of research and the new problems encountered by the patients. As indicated by Buschke (1984a, 1984b), insofar as remembering and learning depend on attention, use of an effective strategy and cognitive abilities to carry out that strategy, the control of cognitive processing during learning and recall is absolutely necessary. This author proposes to use the method of cued recall in the evaluation of clinical memory impairments because it affords a control of the processing during learning by a search procedure in which the patient uses specific cues to identify target items, and a control of processing during recall by the presentation of appropriate cues. Furthermore, cued recall also gives an opportunity to assess storage and retention. On the basis of this method, we have devised several tests involving different ways of encoding and different cues, and presented them to varied memory-impaired patients (Van der Linden, 1988).

Although evaluation in a standardized situation may inform us about the nature of the trouble and its specific characteristics, it will supply us with very few details about the concrete difficulties encountered by the patient in his everyday life because the conditions in which mnemic efficiency is usually tested are very different from the actual conditions of daily life. In the latter situations, noise, weariness, interruptions during tasks, and the subject's simultaneous involvement in several other activities are factors that may influence the memory disorder. As indicated by Sunderland, Harris, and Baddeley (1984), the demands placed on memory by the environment and the life style of a patient will partly determine the frequency of problems. Finally, some phenomena are not easily elicited by standardized situations, as for instance remembering to do things, emotional and motivational variables. All of these problems led researchers to exit from the laboratory (Baddeley & Wilkins, 1984) and clinical practitioners to design other evaluational tools, such as questionnaires and memory diaries (Van der Linden, 1988). These methods raise several problems regarding validity, but as Sunderland et al. (1984) noted, they may provide mainly qualitative information about the forms of memory failure, information that can be used by the therapist to simulate the activities of daily life that provoke such difficulties. The Rivermead Behavioral Memory Test (Wilson, Cockburn & Baddeley, 1985) is an example of a behavioral evaluation procedure wherein several everyday living tasks are simulated and the patient is requested to remember information similar to that of daily life.

After having described the patient's behavior and proposed a rehabilitative strategy, one must be able to measure its effects and firmly establish that the observed progress actually proceeds from the therapy and not from external causes. Such a goal may be efficiently reached by resorting to a multiple-baseline paradigm, the subject constituting his or her own control (Hersen & Barlow, 1976).

If it is essential to identify the causes that make a method successful, it also appears indispensable that the therapeutic benefits be transferable to other situations and be maintained for the long term. It sometimes proves more effective to place rehabilitation directly in the real environment of the patient, thus avoiding the problems of learning transfer. Otherwise, one will have to turn to a progressive program of transfer by securing a step-by-step removal from relatively artificial reeducation conditions to the everyday situations actually met by the patient. In the same connection, the patient will also be taught when spontaneously to apply the previously learned strategies (the distinction between learning and learning to learn).

Most of the time, studies involved in the reeducation of memory have been confined to the analysis of retention over rather short delays. Nevertheless, it seems obvious that the maintenance of the benefits of treatment ought to be tested after long delays, in order to estimate real effectiveness of the strategy.

Such principles as the detailed pretherapeutic analyses, the measurement of the effects of treatment and the validation of the therapy, the transfer of learning, and the maintenance of the acquisitions are classically found in behavior modification (Bruyer et al., 1982; Seron et al., 1977). They constitute the standards to which the reeducation field may evolve, for they give access to the causes of the success or failure of a therapy, and they allow everyone to use and test the method because the different variables are identified.

We saw that the reeducational programs took several orientations. The first and major one is the use of mnemonics whose effectiveness when used by normal subjects has been known for ages. The second and more restricted one is the elaboration of methods relying on variables that experimental studies assumed to be able to improve the patient's performance. Their logic was either to modify the nature of the encoding, to provide retrieval cues or to resort as much as possible to residual capabilities. In most of the cases, however, there were numerous methodological and/or theoretical gaps.

The approach that combines a detailed pretherapeutic evaluation, firm hypotheses, and some methodological rigor requires large amounts of time and cannot be applied easily in rehabilitation centers. Yet, there is considerable demand for treatment, and it is tempting to adopt those methods that previously proved successful in one case or another. The danger in doing so is that it encourages large-scale development of ready-made programs. The disproportionate ratio between well-established experimental data and the complex, numerous, and urgent problems that long to be solved may lead the practitioner to adopt some pragmatic approach. Although such a position may afford a short-term solution to some concrete difficulties, by no means does it constitute an efficient long-term strategy. From this point of view, the cognitive approach to reeducation is anything but secure, for there exists no structured theory giving a clear account of the pathological data and more particularly of the memory disorders. This insecurity will be increased even more if we consider the fact that learning and remembering strategies vary with the tasks, situations, individuals, etc.

The cognitive orientation in reeducation is characterized by a will to understand the structure of the disorder, to identify those processing components that are disrupted. It appears to us that a functional analysis should be conducted in a parallel direction with such structural analysis, which could focus particularly on the contingencies of reinforcement that control and maintain the memory disorders. Its purpose would mainly involve the investigation of the reactions to the patient's impairment and complaints and the possible secondary benefits that the patient might obtain from the situation. For instance, overprotective reactions from the relatives often prevent the patient from properly using the acquired strategies or residual capacities. Finally, the part played by motivational factors in both appearance of the mnemonic disorders and course of the reeducation also must be delineated.

We shall end by mentioning several variables that have been studied in the framework of the reeducation of aphasics (Seron, 1979) and that are still poorly taken in account in the case of memory disorders: anosognosia, duration of illness, age, and socioeconomic level of the patient. The study of interindividual differences in the mnemonic strategies and the self-knowledge of the functioning of the mnemonic system (metamemory) should also see further development in the coming years.

150   VAN DER LINDEN AND VAN DER KAA

We believe that it is now possible to devise reeducation strategies for memory disorders, which meet methodological rigor, and rely on those hypothesis propounded by the theories of memory. However, well-established facts are still sparse and the variables to be studied quite multiple, and only a future increase in strict and controlled reeducation interventions will lead to a solution.

ACKNOWLEDGMENTS

We are very grateful to J. M. Grailet who offered helpful comments on a previous draft of this chapter. We are also indebted to J. M. Grailet, M. Overvold, and A. Overvold for assistance in chapter translation and to E. Grailet for patiently typing the various drafts of the manuscript.

REFERENCES

Allport, D. A. (1983). Auditory-verbal short-term memory and conduction aphasia. In H. Bouma, & D. Bouwhuis (Eds.), *Attention and performance*, Vol. 10. Hillsdale, NJ: Lawrence Erlbaum Associates.

Anderson, J. R., & Bower, G. H. (1973). Human associative memory. Washington: Winston.

Annett, J. (1979). Memory for skill. In M. M. Gruneberg, & P. E. Morris (Eds.), Applied problems in memory (pp. 215–248). London: Academic Press.

Atkinson, R. C., & Shiffrin, R. M. (1968). Human memory: a proposed system and its control processes. In K. W. Spence, & J. J. Spence (Eds.), *The psychology of learning and motivation*, Vol. 2. pp. 89–195. New York: Academic Press.

Baddeley, A. D. (1982). Amnesia: a minimal model and an interpretation. In L. S. Cermak (Ed.), *Human memory and amnesia*. Hillsdale, NJ: Lawrence Erlbaum Associates.

Baddeley, A. D. (1984). Memory theory and memory therapy. In B. A. Wilson, & N. Moffat (Eds.), *Clinical management of memory problems.* (pp. 5–27). Rockville: An Aspen Publication.

Baddeley, A. D., & Hitch, G. J. (1974). Working memory. In G. A. Bower (Ed.), *The psychology of learning and motivation*, Vol. 8. (pp. 47–91). New York: Academic Press.

Baddeley, A. D., & Longman, D. J. A. (1978). The influence of length and frequency of training sessions on rate of learning to type. *Ergonomics, 21*, 627–635.

Baddeley, A. D., & Warrington, E. K. (1973). Memory coding and amnesia. *Neuropsychologia, 11*, 159–165.

Baddeley, A. D., & Wilkins, A. (1984). Taking memory out the laboratory. In J. E. Harris, & P. E. Morris (Eds.), *Everyday memory, actions and absent-mindedness* (pp. 1–17). London: Academic Press.

Baddeley, A. D., Harris, T., Sunderland, A., Watter, K. P., & Wilson, B. (1987). Closed head injury and memory. In H. Levin & H. Eisenberg (Eds.) *Neurobehavioral recovery from head injury* (pp. 235–317). New York: Oxford University Press.

4. THERAPY OF MEMORY 151

Basso, A., Spinnler, H., Vallar, G., & Zanobio, M. E. (1982). Left hemisphere damage and selective impairment of auditory verbal short-term memory. A case study. *Neuropsychologia, 20,* 263–274.

Bayles, K. A., (1982). Language function in senile dementia. *Brain and Language, 16,* 265–280.

Beauvois, M. F., & Lhermitte, F. (1975). Deficits mnésiques électifs et lésions corticales restreintes. *Revue Neurologique, 131,* 3–22.

Binder, L. M., & Schreiber, V. (1980). Visual imagery and verbal mediation as memory aids in recovering alcoholics. *Journal of Clinical Neuropsychology, 2,* 71–74.

Bower, G. H. (1976). Experiments on story understanding and recall. *Quarterly Journal of Experimental Psychology, 28,* 511–534.

Bower, G. H., & Bolton, L. S. (1969). Why are rhymes easy to learn? *Journal of Experimental Psychology, 82,* 453–461.

Branle, P. (1981). *Elaboration d'un programme rééducatif de la mémoire auditivoverbale pour des sujets aphasiques.* Unpublished, Neuropsychology Unit, University of Liège.

Brewer, W. F., & Treyens, J. C. (1981). Role of schemata in memory for places. *Cognitive Psychology, 13,* 207–230.

Brookshire, R. H., & Nicholas, L. E. (1984). Comprehension of directly and indirectly stated main ideas and details in discourse by brain-damaged and non brain-damaged listeners. *Brain and Language, 21,* 9–31.

Bruyer, R., Rectem, D., Lepoivre, H., & Seron, X. (1982). Le point de vue méthodologique. In X. Seron & C. Laterre (Eds.), *Rééduquer le cerveau: logopédie, psychologie, neurologie.* (pp. 77–89). Bruxelles: Pierre Mardaga.

Buschke, H. (1984a). Cued recall in amnesia. *Journal of Clinical Neuropsychology, 6,* 433–440.

Buschke, H. (1984b). Control of cognitive processing. In L. R. Squire, & N. Butters (Eds.), *Neuropsychology of memory* (pp. 33–40). New York: The Guilford Press.

Butters, N. (1984). The clinical aspects of memory disorders: contributions from experimental studies in amnesia and dementia. *Journal of Clinical Neuropsychologia, 6,* 17–36.

Butters, N., Albert, M. S., Sax, D. S., Miliotis, P., Nagode, J., & Sterste, A. (1983). The effect of verbal elaborators on the pictorial memory of brain-damaged patients, *21,* 307–323.

Butters, N., & Cermak, L. S. (1980). *Alchoholic Korsakoff's syndrome: an information-processing approach to amnesia.* New York: Academic Press.

Butters, N., Samuels, I., Goodglass, H., & Brody, B. (1970). Short-term visual and auditory memory disorders after parietal and frontal lobe damage. *Cortex, 6,* 440–459.

Butters, N., Wolfe, J., Martone, M., Granholm, E., & Cermak, L. S. (1985). Memory disorders associated with Huntington's disease: verbal recall, verbal recognition and procedural memory. *Neuropsychologia, 23,* 729–743.

Byrne, R. W. (1982). Geographical knowledge and orientation. In A. W. Ellis (Ed.), *Normality and pathology in cognitive functions.* New York: Academic Press.

Cermak, L. S. (1975). Imagery as an aid to retrieval for Korsakoff patients. *Cortex, 11,* 163–169.

Cermak, L. S. (1976). The encoding capacity of a patient with amnesia due to encephalitis. *Neuropsychologia, 14,* 311–326.

Cermak, L. S. (1982). *Human memory and amnesia.* Hillsdale, NJ: Lawrence Erlbaum Associates.

Cermak, L. S., & Moreines, J. (1976). Verbal retention deficits in aphasic and amnesic patients. *Brain and Language, 3,* 16–27.

152 VAN DER LINDEN AND VAN DER KAA

Cermak, L. S., Stiassny, D., & Uhly, B. (1984). Reconstructive retrieval deficits in Broca's aphasia. *Brain and Language, 21,* 95–105.

Cohen, N. J., & Squire, L. R. (1980). Preserved learning and retention of pattern-analyzing skill in amnesia: dissociation of knowing how and knowing that. *Science, 210,* 207–210.

Craik, F. I. M., & Lockhart, R. S. (1972). Levels of processing: a framework for memory research. *Journal of Verbal Learning and Verbal Behavior, 11,* 671–684.

Craik, F. I. M., & Watkins, M. J. (1973). The role of rehearsal in short-term memory. *Journal of Verbal Learning and Verbal Behavior, 12,* 599–607.

Crosson, B., & Buenning, W. (1984). An individual memory retraining program after closed-head injury: a single-case study. *Journal of Clinical Neuropsychology, 6,* 287–301.

Crovitz, H. F. (1979). Memory retraining in brain-damaged patients: the airplane list. *Cortex, 15,* 131–134.

Crovitz, H. F., Harvey, M. T., & Horn, R. W. (1979). Problems in the acquisition of imagery mnemonics: three brain-damaged cases. *Cortex, 15,* 225–234.

Cutting, J. (1978). A cognitive approach to Korsakoff's syndrome. *Cortex, 11,* 163–169.

Damasio, A. R. (1985). Prosopagnosia. *T.I.N.S.,* March, 132–135.

Damasio, A. R., Damasio, H., & Van Hoesen, G. W. (1982). Prosopagnosia: anatomic basis and behavioral mechanism. *Neurology, 32,* 331–340.

Davies, A. D., & Binks, M. G. (1983). Supporting the residual memory of a Korsakoff patient. *Behavioral Psychotherapy, 11,* 62–74.

De Renzi, E., & Nichelli, P. (1975). Verbal and non-verbal short-term memory impairment following hemispheric damage. *Cortex, 11,* 341–354.

Diamond, R., & Rozin, P. (1984). Activation of existing memories in the amnesic syndrome. *Journal of Abnormal Psychology, 93,* 98–105.

Ebbinghaus, H. (1885). *Uber das Gedächtniss: untersuchungen zur experimentellen psychologie.* Leipzig: Dunker et Humblot.

Ehrlichman, H., & Barrett, J. (1983). Right hemispheric specialization for mental imagery: a review of the evidence. *Brain and Cognition, 2,* 55–76.

Fisher, R. P., & Craik, F. I. M. (1977). The interaction between encoding and retrieval operations in cued recall. *Journal of Experimental Psychology: Human Learning and Memory, 3,* 701–711.

Furst, C. (1986). The memory derby: evaluating and remediating intention memory. *Cognitive Rehabilitation, 4,* 24–26.

Gardner, H. (1977). *The shattered mind: the person after brain damage.* London: Routledge and Kegan Paul.

Gasparrini, B., & Satz, P. (1979). A treatment for memory problems in left hemisphere CVA patients. *Journal of Clinical Neuropsychology, 1,* 137–150.

Gianutsos, R. (1980). What is cognitive rehabilitation? *Journal of Rehabilitation, 46,* 36–40.

Gianutsos, R. (1981). Training the short- and long-term verbal recall of a postencephalitic amnesic. *Journal of Clinical Neuropsychology, 3,* 143–153.

Gianutsos, R., & Gianutsos, J. (1979). Rehabilitating the verbal recall of brain-injured patients by mnemonic training: an experimental demonstration using single-case methodology. *Journal of Clinical Neuropsychology, 1,* 117–135.

Glasgow, R. E., Zeiss, R. A., Barrera, M., Jr., & Lewinsohn, P. M. (1977). Case studies on remediating memory deficits in brain-injured individuals. *Journal of Clinical Psychology, 33,* 1049–1054.

Glisky, E., Schacter, D. L., & Tulving, E. (1986). Learning and retention of computer-related vocabulary in memory-impaired patients: method of vanishing cues. *Journal of Clinical and Experimental Neuropsychology, 8,* 292–312.

4. THERAPY OF MEMORY 153

Glisky, E., Schacter, D. L., & Tulving, E. (1987). Computer learning by memory-impaired patients: acquisition and retention of complex knowledge. *Neuropsychologia, 24*, 313–328.

Glisky, E., & Schacter, D. L. (1987). Acquisition of domain-specific knowledge in organic amnesia: training for computer-related work. *Neuropsychologia, 25*, 893–906.

Graf, P., Squire, L. R., & Mandler, G. (1984). The information that amnesic patients do not forget. *Journal of Experimental Psychology: Learning, Memory and Cognition, 10*, 164–178.

Grafman, J. (1984). Memory assessment and remediation in brain-injured patients: from theory of practice. (pp. 151–189). In B. A. Edelstein, & E. T. Couture (Eds.), *Behavioral assessment and rehabilitation of the traumatically brain-damaged.* New York: Plenum Press.

Grober, E. (1984). Nonlinguistic memory in aphasia. *Cortex, 20*, 67–73.

Grossberg, S. (1982). *Studies of mind and brain: neural principle of learning, perception, development, cognition and motor control.* Boston, MA: D. Reidel Publishing Co.

Gruneberg, M. M., Monks, J., & Sykes, R. N. (1977). The first letter mnemonic aid. *I R C S Medical Science: Psychology and Psychiatry, 5*, 304.

Harris, J. E. (1984a). Remembering to do things: a forgotten topic. In J. E. Harris, & P. E. Morris (Eds.), *Everyday memory, actions and absent-mindedness* (pp. 71–92). London: Academic Press.

Harris, J. E. (1984b). Methods of improving memory. In B. A. Wilson, & N. Moffat (Eds.), *Clinical management of memory problems* (pp. 46–62). Rockville: An Aspen Publication.

Hasher, L., & Zacks, R. T. (1979). Automatic and effortful processes in memory. *Journal of Experimental Psychology: General, 108*, 356–388.

Hersen, M., & Barlow, D. H. (1976). *Single case experimental designs: strategy for studying behaviour change.* New York: Pergamon.

Hirst, W. (1985). Use of mnemonic in patients with frontal lobe damage. *Journal of Clinical and Experimental Neuropsychology, 7*, 175.

Howes, J. L. (1983). Effects of experimenter- and self-generated imagery on the Korsakoff patients memory performance. *Neuropsychologia, 21*, 341–349.

Huppert, F. A., & Piercy, M. (1979). Normal and abnormal forgetting in organic amnesia: effect of locus of lesion. *Cortex, 15*, 385–390.

Hulicka, I. M., & Grossman, J. L. (1967). Age-group comparisons for the use of mediators in paired-associate learning. *Journal of Gerontology, 22*, 46–51.

Jaffe, P. G., & Katz, A. N. (1975). Attenuating anterograde amnesia. *Journal of Abnormal Psychology, 84*, 559–562.

Jones, M. K. (1974). Imagery as a mnemonic aid after left temporal lobectomy: contrast between material-specific and generalized memory disorders. *Neuropsychologia, 12*, 21–30.

Jones-Gotman, M. (1979). Incidental learning of image-mediated or pronounced words after right temporal lobectomy. *Cortex, 15*, 187–197.

Jones-Gotman, M., & Milner, B. (1978). Right temporal-lobe contribution to·image-mediated verbal learning. *Neuropsychologia, 16*, 61–71.

Kapur, N. (1978). Visual imagery capacity of alcoholic Korsakoff patients. *Neuropsychologia, 16*, 517–519.

Kintsch, W. (1974). *The representation of meaning.* Hillsdale, NJ: Lawrence Erlbaum Associates.

Kintsch, W., & Van Dijck, T. A. (1975). Comment on se rappelle et on résume des histoires. *Langages, 40*, 98–116.

154 VAN DER LINDEN AND VAN DER KAA

Kopelman, M. D. (1985). Rates of forgetting in Alzheimer-type dementia and Korsakoff's syndrome. *Neuropsychologia, 23*, 623–638.

Kovner, R., Mattis, S., & Goldmeier, E. (1983). A technique for promoting robust free recall in chronic organic amnesia. *Journal of Clinical Neuropsychology, 5*, 65–71.

Kovner, R., Mattis, S., & Pass, R. (1985). Some amnesic patients can freely recall large amounts of information in new contexts. *Journal of Clinical and Experimental Neuropsychology, 7*, 395–412.

Landauer, T. K., & Bjork, R. A. (1978). Optimum rehearsal patterns and name learning. In K. M. Gruneberg, P. E. Morris, & R. N. Sykes (Eds.), *Practical aspects of memory* (pp. 625–632). London: Academic Press.

Lewinsohn, P. M., Danaher, G. G., & Kikel, S. (1977). Visual imagery as a mnemonic aid for brain-injured persons. *Journal of Consulting and Clinical Psychology, 45*, 717–723.

Lindsay, P. H., & Norman, D. A. (1980). *Traitement de l'information et comportement humain: une introduction à la psychologie.* Saint-Laurent: Etudes Vivantes.

Luria, A. R. (1970). *Une prodigieuse mémoire.* Neuchâtel: Delachaux et Niestlé.

Mandler, G. (1979). Organization and repetition: organizational principles with special reference to rote learning. In L. G. Nilsson (Ed.), *Perspectives in memory research* (pp. 293–327). Hillsdale, NJ: Lawrence Erlbaum Associates.

Mandler, G. (1980). Recognizing: the judgment of previous occurence. *Psychological Review, 87*, 252–271.

Markowitsch, H. J. (1984). Can amnesia be caused by damage of a single brain structure? *Cortex, 20*, 27–47.

Marshall, J. C. (1979). Disorders of language and memory. In M. M. Gruneberg, & P. E. Morris (Eds.), *Applied problems in memory* (pp. 249–260). London: Academic Press.

Martin, A., Brouwers, P., Cox, C., & Fedio, P. (1985). On the nature of the verbal memory deficit in Alzheimer's disease. *Brain and Language, 25*, 323–342.

Martone, M., Butters, N., Payne, M., Becker, J., & Sax, D. (1984). Dissociation between skill learning and verbal recognition in amnesia and dementia. *Archives of Neurology, 41*, 965–970.

Mayes, A. R. (1986). Learning and memory disorders and their assessment. *Neuropsychologia, 24*, 25–39.

Mayes, A. R., Meudell, P. R., & Neary, D. (1978). Must amnesia be caused by either encoding or retrieval disorders? In M. M. Gruneberg, P. E. Morris, & R. N. Sykes (Eds.), *Practical aspects of memory* (pp. 712–720). London: Academic Press.

Mayes, A. R., Meudell, P. R., & Pickering, A. (1985). Is organic amnesia caused by selective deficit in remembering contextual information? *Cortex, 21*, 167–203.

McCarty, D. L. (1980). Investigation of a visual imagery mnemonic device for acquiring face-name associations. *Journal of Experimental Psychology: Human Learning and Memory, 6*, 145–155.

Meacham, J. A., & Leiman, B. (1982). Remembering to perform future actions. In U. Neisser (Ed.), *Memory observed: remembering in natural contexts* (pp. 327–337). San Francisco: W. H. Freeman and Company.

Meudell, P. R., & Mayes, A. R. (1982). Normal and abnormal forgetting: some comments on the human amnesic syndrome. In A. W. Ellis (Ed.), *Normality and pathology in cognitive functions* (pp. 203–239). London: Academic Press.

Milner, B. (1959). The memory deficit in bilateral hippocampal lesions. *Psychiatric Research Reports, 11*, 43–52.

Milner, B. (1968). Disorders of memory after brain lesion in man. Preface: materialspecific and generalized memory loss. *Neuropsychologia, 6*, 175–179.

Miller, E. (1975). Impaired recall and the memory disturbance in pre-senile dementia. *British Journal of Social and Clinical Psychology, 14*, 73–79.

4. THERAPY OF MEMORY   155

Miller, E. (1978). Is amnesia remediable? In M. M. Gruneberg, P. E. Morris, & R. N. Sykes (Eds.), *Practical aspects of memory*. London: Academic Press.

Milton, S. B. (1985). Compensatory memory strategy training: a practical approach for managing persisting memory problems. *Cognitive Rehabilitation, 3*, 8–16.

Moffat, N. (1984). Strategies of memory therapy. In B. A. Wilson, & N. Moffat (Eds.), *Clinical management of memory problems*. (pp. 63–83). Rockville: An Aspen Publication.

Morris, P. E. (1979). Strategies for learning and recall. In M. M. Gruneberg, & P. E. Morris (Eds.), *Applied problem in memory*. London: Academic Press.

Morris, R., Wheatley, J., & Britton, P. (1983). Retrieval from long-term memory in senile dementia: cued recall revisited. *British Journal of Clinical Psychology, 22*, 141–142.

Morton, J. (1985). The problem with amnesia: the problem with human memory. *Cognitive Neuropsychology, 2*, 281–290.

Moscovitch, M. (1982). Multiple dissociations of function in amnesia. In L. S. Cermak (Ed.), *Human memory and amnesia* (pp. 337–370). Hillsdale, NJ: Lawrence Erlbaum Associates.

Nebes, R. D., Martin, D. C., & Horn, L. C. (1984). Sparing of semantic memory in Alzheimer's disease. *Journal of Abnormal Psychology, 3*, 321–330.

Paivio, A. (1971). *Imagery and verbal processes*. New York: Rinehart and Winston.

Pajurkova, E. M., & Wilkins, A. J. (1983). Prospective remembering in patients with unilateral temporal or frontal lobectomies. *Paper presented at the Sixth European Conference of the International Neuropsychological Society*, Lisbon.

Parkin, A. J. (1982). Residual learning capability in organic amnesia. *Cortex, 18*, 417–440.

Parkin, A. J. (1984). Amnesic syndrome: a lesion-specific disorder? *Cortex, 20*, 479–509.

Parisi, D. (1985). A procedural approach to the study of aphasia. *Brain and Language, 26*, 1–16.

Patten, B. M. (1972). The ancient art of memory: usefulness in treatment. *Archives of Neurology, 26*, 25–31.

Peterson, L. R., & Peterson, M. J. (1959). Short-term retention of individual verbal items. *Journal of Experimental Psychology, 58*, 193–198.

Philippe, C. (1982). *Elaboration d'un programme de rééducation de la mémoire de textes*. Unpublished manuscript, Neuropsychology Unit, University of Liège.

Piercy, M. F. (1977). Experimental studies of the organic amnesic syndrome. In C. W. M. Whitty, & O. L. Zangwill (Eds.), *Amnesia* (2nd ed.). London: Butterworths.

Powell, G. E. (1981). *Brain function therapy*. Aldershot: Gower Press.

Reason, J. T. (1977). Skill and error in everyday life. In M. Howe (Ed.), *Adult learning: psychological research and applications*. London: Wiley.

Reason, J. T. (1984). Absent-mindedness and cognitive control. In J. E. Harris & P. E. Morris (Eds.), *Everyday memory, actions and absent-mindedness* (pp. 113–132). London: Academic Press.

Richardson, J. T. E. (1984). The effects of closed head injury upon intrusions and confusions in free recall. *Cortex, 40*, 413–420.

Richardson, J. T. E., & Barry, C. (1985). The effects of minor closed head injury upon human memory: further evidence on the role mental imagery. *Cognitive Neuropsychology, 2*, 149–168.

Richardson, J. T. E., & Snape, W. (1984). The effects of closed head injury upon human memory: an experimental analysis. *Cognitive Neuropsychology, 1*, 217–231.

Robertson-Tchabo, E. A., Hausman, C. P., & Arenberg, D. (1976). A classical mnemonic

156   VAN DER LINDEN AND VAN DER KAA

for olders learners: a trip that works. *Educational Gerontology: An International Quarterly, 1,* 215–226.

Roediger III, H. L. (1980). The effectiveness of four mnemonics in ordering recall. *Journal of Experimental Psychology: Human Learning and Memory, 6,* 558–567.

Rumelhart, D. E. (1975). Notes on a scheme for stories. In D. Bobrow, & A. Collins (Eds.), *Representation and understanding* (pp. 211–236). New York: Academic Press.

Samuels, I., Butters, N., & Fedio, P. (1972). Short-term memory disorders following temporal lobe removals in humans. *Cortex, 8,* 283–298.

Schacter, D. L. (1987). Implicit memory: history and current status. *Journal of Experimental Psychology: Learning, Memory and Cognition, 13,* 501–518.

Schacter, D. L., & Crovitz, H. F. (1977). Memory function after closed head injury: a review of the quantitative research. *Cortex, 13,* 150–176.

Schacter, D. L., Glisky, E. L. (1986). Memory remediation: Restoration, alleviation and the acquisition of domain-specific knowledge. In B. Uzzel & Y. Gross (Eds.), *Clinical neuropsychology of intervention* (pp. 257–282). Boston: Martinus Nijhoff.

Schacter, D. L., Rich, S. A., & Stampp, M. S. (1985). Remediation of memory disorders: experimental evaluation of the spaced-retrieval technique. *Journal of Clinical and Experimental Neuropsychology, 7,* 79–97.

Seron, X. (1979). *Aphasie et Neuropsychologie.* Bruxelles: Mardaga.

Seron, X. (1982). Les choix de stratégies: rétablir, réorganiser ou aménager l'environement? In X. Seron, & C. Laterre (Eds.), *Rééduquer le cerveau: logopédie, psychologie, neurologie* (pp. 63–76). Bruxelles: Mardaga.

Seron, X., Lambert, J. L., & Van der Linden, M. (1977). *La modification du comportement: théorie, pratique, éthique.* Bruxelles: Mardaga.

Shallice, T., & Warrington, E. K. (1970). Independent functioning of verbal memory stores: a neuropsychological study. *Quarterly Journal of Experimental Psychology, 22,* 261–273.

Shallice, T., & Warrington, E. K. (1977). Auditory-verbal short-term memory impairment and conduction aphasia. *Brain and Language, 4,* 479–491.

Shiffrin, R. M., & Schneider, W. (1977). Controlled and automatic human information processing. II. Perceptual learning, automatic attenting and a general theory. *Psychological Review, 84,* 127–190.

Shore, D. L. (1979). Memory deficit remediation in patients with unilateral brain damage. *Archives of Physical Medecine and Rehabilitation, 60,* 542 (Abstract).

Skinner, B. F. (1958). Teaching machines. *Science, 128,* 969–977.

Squire, L. R., Wetzel, C. D., & Slater, P. C. (1978). Anterograde amnesia following E C T: an analysis of the beneficial effect of partial information. *Neuropsychologia, 16,* 339–347.

Stern, L. D. (1981). A review of theories of human amnesia. *Memory & Cognition, 9,* 247–262.

Sunderland, A., Harris, J. E., & Baddeley, A. D. (1984). Assessing everyday memory after severe head injury. In J. E. Harris, & P. E. Morris (Eds.), *Everyday memory, actions and absent-mindedness* (pp. 191–206). London: Academic Press.

Tiberghien, G. (1976). Mémoire. In R. Droz, & M. Richelle (Eds.), *Manuel de psychologie.* (pp. 393–430). Bruxelles: Mardaga.

Tiberghien, G. (1983). Une, deux ou plusieurs mémoires: réalités et théories. *Bulletin de la Société de Neuropsychologie de Langue Française, 1,* 21–29.

Tiberghien, G. (1986). Context effects in recognition memory of faces: Some theoretical problems. In M. D. Ellis, M. Jeeves, F. Newcombe, & A. W. Young (Eds.), *Aspects of face processing (pp.88–104). Dordrecht: Martinus Nijhoff Publishers BV.*

Tiberghien, G., & Lecoq, P. (1983). *Rappel et reconnaissance.* Lille: Presses Universitaires de Lille.

4. THERAPY OF MEMORY 157

Tulving, E. (1972). Episodic and semantic memory. In E. Tulving, & W. Donaldson (Eds.), *Organization of memory* (pp. 382–404). New York: Academic Press.

Tulving, E. (1974). Cue-dependent forgetting. *American Scientist, 62,* 74–82.

Tulving, E. (1984). Precis of elements of episodic memory. *The Behavioral and Brain Sciences, 7,* 223–268.

Tulving, E., & Thomson, D. M. (1973). Encoding specificity and retrieval processes in episodic memory. *Psychological Review, 80,* 352–373.

Tzortzis, C., & Albert, M. L. (1974). Impairment of memory for sequences in conduction aphasia. *Neuropsychologia, 12,* 355–366.

Ulatowska, H. K., Freedman-Stern, R., Weiss Doyel, A., Macaluso-Haynes, S., & North, A. J. (1983). Production of narrative discourse in aphasia. *Brain and Language, 19,* 317–335.

Vallar, G., Baddeley, A. D. (1984). Fractionation of working memory: Neuropsychological evidence for a phonological short-term store. *Journal of Verbal Learning and Verbal Behavior, 23,* 151–161.

Van der Linden, M. (1988). L'évaluation des troubles de la mémoire en neuropsychologie: différenciation des niveaux d'analyse. Unpublished doctoral dissertation, The University of Liège.

Van der Linden, M., & Seron, X. (1984). A case of dissociation in topographical disorders: the selective breakdown of vector-map representation. In P. Ellen, & C. Thinus-Blanc (Eds.), *Cognitive processes and spatial orientation in animal and man* (pp. 173–181). Dordrecht: Matinus Nijhoff Publishers BV.

Van Eeckout, Ph., Pillon, B., Signoret, J-L., Deloche, G., & Seron, X. (1982). Rééducation des réductions sévères de l'expression orale: la thérapie mélodique et rythmée. In X. Seron & C. Laterre (Eds.), *Rééduquerle cerveau: logopédie, psychologie, neurologie* (pp. 109–121). Bruxelles: Mardaga.

Warrington, E. K. (1981). Concrete word dyslexia. *British Journal of Psychology, 72,* 175–196.

Warrington, E. K., & McCarthy, R. (1983). Category specific access dysphasia. *Brain, 106,* 859–878.

Warrington, E. K., & Rabin, P. (1971). Visual span of apprehension in patients with unilateral cerebral lesions. *Quarterly Journal of Experimental Psychology, 23,* 423–431.

Warrington, E. K., & Shallice, T. (1984). Category specific semantic impairments. *Brain, 107,* 829–854.

Warrington, E. K., & Weiskrantz, L. (1968). A study of learning and retention in amnesic patients. *Neuropsychologia, 6,* 283–291.

Warrington, E. K., & Weiskrantz, L. (1970). Amnesic syndrome: consolidation or retrieval? *Nature, 228,* 628–630.

Warrington, E. K., & Weiskrantz, L. (1971). Organizational aspects of memory in amnesic patients. *Neurpsychologia, 9,* 67–73.

Warrington, E. K., & Weiskrantz, L. (1973). An analysis of short-term and long-term memory deficits in man. In J. Deutsch (Ed.), *The physiological basis of memory* (pp. 365–395). London: Academic Press.

Warrington, E. K., & Weiskrantz, L. (1974). The effect of prior learning on subsequent retention in amnesic patients. *Neuropsychologia, 12,* 419–428.

Warrington, E. K., & Weiskrantz, L. (1978). Further analysis of the prior learning effect in amnesic patients. *Neuropsychologia, 16,* 169–177.

Way, G. (1979). *The development and application of a multidimensional memory battery.* Unpublished doctoral dissertation, The University of Western Ontario.

Weber, R. J., & Harnish, R. (1974). Visual imagery for words. *Journal of Experimental Psychology, 102,* 409–414.

158   VAN DER LINDEN AND VAN DER KAA

Weiskrantz, L. (1978). A comparison of hippocampal pathology in man and other animals. In *Functions of the Septohippocampal System C I B A Foundation Symposium 58* (new series) (pp. 373–387). Oxford: Elsevier.

Wetzel, C. D., & Squire, L. R. (1982). Cued recall in anterograde amnesia. *Brain and Language, 15,* 70–81.

Wickens, D. D. (1970). Encoding categories of words: an empirical approach to meaning. *Psychological Review, 77,* 1–15.

Wilkins, A. J., & Baddeley, A. D. (1978). Remembering to recall in everyday life: an approach to absent-mindedness. In M. M. Gruneberg, P. E. Morris, & R. N. Sykes (Eds.), *Practical aspects of memory* (pp. 27–34). London: Academic Press.

Williams, M. (1953). Investigation of amnesic defects by progressive prompting. Journal of Neurology, *Neurosurgery and Psychiatry, 16,* 14–18.

Wilson, B. A. (1982). Success and failure in memory training following a cerebral vascular accident. *Cortex, 18,* 581–594.

Wilson, B. A. (1984). Memory therapy in practice. In B. A. Wilson, & N. Moffat (Eds.), *Clinical management of memory problems.* Rockville: An Aspen Publication.

Wilson, B. A. (1987a). Rehabilitation of memory. New York: Guilford Press.

Wilson, B. A. (1987b). Single-case experimental designs in neuropsychological rehabilitation. *Journal of Clinical and Experimental Neuropsychology, 9,* 527–544.

Wilson, B. A., Cockburn, J., & Baddeley, A. (1985). The Rivermead Behavioural Memory Test. Thames Valley Test Company.

Wilson, B. A., & Moffat, N. (1984a). Rehabilitation of memory for everyday life. In J. E. Harris & P. E. Morris (Eds.), *Everyday memory, actions and absent-mindedness.* (pp. 204–233). London: Academic Press.

Wilson, B. A., & Moffat, N. (1984b). Running a memory group. In B. A. Wilson & N. Moffat (Eds.), *Clinical management of memory problems* (pp. 171–198). Rockville: An Aspen Publication.

Winocur, G., & Kinsbourne, M. (1978). Contextual cueing as an aid to Korsakoff amnesics. *Neuropsychologia, 16,* 671–682.

Yates, F. A. (1966). *The art of memory.* London: Routledge and Kegan Paul.

5 A Treatment for Surface Dyslexia[1]

Max Coltheart
Psychology Department, Macquarie University

Sally Byng
Department of Psychology, Birkbeck College

Acquired dyslexia, impaired ability to read caused by brain damage in a previously literate person, takes a variety of forms. This fact is now frequently interpreted by arguing that the information processing system we use when we read is complex, with various subcomponents. The consequences of damage to this system will depend on which of its subcomponents remain intact and which no longer operate normally. Different constellations of preservations and impairments of the components of the reading system will correspond to different patterns of symptoms, that is, to different forms of acquired dyslexia.

Many current models of the reading system (see, for example, Patterson and Shewell, 1987) belong to the class of *dual-route* models. Such models all incorporate the idea that two different processing procedures can be applied to the task of reading aloud. Various terms have been used to describe the two procedures. Sometimes they are referred to as the assembling of phonology and the addressing of phonology (Patterson, 1982; Patterson & V. Coltheart, 1987). An alternative terminology, the one we will use here, distinguishes between a lexical procedure and a nonlexical procedure for reading aloud (e.g., Coltheart, 1985). Whichever terms are used, the distinction appears to be an important one for the analysis of cases of acquired dyslexia because in many such cases it is plausible to interpret the patient's

---

[1]This work was supported by Grant No. G 8218596 from the Medical Research Council of Great Britain. A brief summary may be found in Byng and Coltheart (1986).

160   COLTHEART AND BYNG

reading by supposing that one of the two procedures is impaired whereas the other is relatively intact.

Reading aloud by the *nonlexical* procedure depends on the use of general rules specifying correspondences between orthographic segments and their phonological equivalents (very roughly, "lettersound rules"). This procedure is nonlexical precisely in the sense that it can yield correct responses even to letter strings that do not exist as individual entries in the mental lexicon, that is, printed nonwords. A set of rules specifying correspondences between orthography and phonology can correctly translate *slint* into "/slʊnt/", or *shoaph* into "/ʃoɷf/", despite the absence from the lexicon of these orthographic and phonological forms.

Reading aloud by the *lexical* procedure works by retrieving from the lexicon learned phonological forms, by accessing the lexical entry corresponding to the printed stimulus and using such access to retrieve the pronunciation of that stimulus. This procedure is lexical precisely in the sense that it can only yield correct responses to letter strings that exist as individual entries in the mental lexicon, that is, words. If the input is a nonword, the lexical procedure cannot function, because no lexical entry will be accessed. Just as the lexical procedure fails for one type of stimulus (the nonword), so the nonlexical procedure errs for one type of stimulus, the irregular word or exception word. English possesses words whose pronunciations violate standard correspondences between orthography and phonology: words such as "pint" or "yacht."

If these two separate processing procedures exist, and if it is possible for brain damage to harm one while sparing the other, then one ought to observe two particular forms of acquired dyslexia. When the nonlexical procedure is affected, the reading of words will be possible, but the reading of nonwords will not be. This form of acquired dyslexia has been observed and is known as phonological dyslexia (see e.g., Beauvois and Derouesne, 1979; Funnell, 1983; Patterson, 1982).

If, on the other hand, the lexical procedure has been affected by brain damage, the patient will have to rely on the nonlexical procedure for reading. This will be sufficient if the stimulus is a nonword, or a regular word (one which obeys standard letter-sound correspondences). However, if the stimulus is an irregular word, it will be misread: When the rules are applied to *pint*, the response will be "/pʊnt/", and when they are applied to *yacht* the response will be "/jætʃt/". Such errors are known as regularization errors. This form of acquired dyslexia has been observed and is known as surface dyslexia (see e.g., Coltheart, Masterson, Byng, Prior, & Riddoch, 1983;

5. SURFACE DYSLEXIA TREATMENT   161

Marshall and Newcombe, 1973; Patterson, Marshall, & Coltheart, 1985).

REHABILITATION

The kinds of theoretical interpretations we have been discussing have obvious implications for the treatment of acquired dyslexia. There would seem little point in treating surface dyslexia by training the patient in phonics, that is, in the use of letter-sound rules, when this aspect of reading remains well preserved or even intact and when the use of a rule-based reading procedure is in fact what is causing the patient's paralexias. Conversely, a whole-word approach, that is, training the patient to recognize words as familiar orthographic sequences, would not seem appropriate in phonological dyslexia because the patient may not have lost any capacity for this form of processing.

This point is a perfectly general one, of course. Any theoretical interpretation of any disorder of cognitive processing, whether it be an aphasia, an agnosia, an amnesia, or anything else, aims at identifying which aspects of cognitive processing are impaired and which remain intact. If such identification is successful, then a focus for treatment is provided. Without the prior theoretical analysis, treatment can only be unfocused.

We illustrate this approach with reference to the treatment of a case of acquired dyslexia, specifically, surface dyslexia, interpreted as a selective impairment of the lexical procedure for reading.

CASE REPORT

E.E., a 40-year-old left-handed postal worker, was admitted to hospital on October 1, 1980. He had fallen off a ladder on the previous day and had been knocked unconscious. Skull x-rays showed a linear fracture to the left frontal region extending to the base of the skull. A scan showed extensive hemorrhagic contusion of the right temporal lobe with mass lesion effect displacing the lateral ventricles to the left. There was also a large subdural hematoma extending over the left temporal lobe onto the left parietal lobe. Surgery was performed on October 1, 1980: A right temporoparietal craniotomy and evacuation of acute subdural hematoma and hemorrhagic contusions of the right temporal lobe. Three days later the craniotomy was reopened and the hematoma reevacuated. E.E. slowly regained consciousness and start-

162   COLTHEART AND BYNG

ed talking, though there was a gross element of dysphasia. A repeated scan showed resolution of the midline shift but persistence of the left-sided subdural hematoma, so surgery was performed on October 15, 1980. A left parietal burr hole was performed for drainage of the hematoma; at operation this was found to be an extradural hematoma, which necessitated craniectomy for evacuation. The patient was discharged for convalescence, physiotherapy (for left-sided weakness), and speech therapy (for residual dysphasia) on October 21, 1980.

We first tested E.E.'s reading on March 2, 1981. He was given 25 high-frequency monomorphemic concrete nouns and 25 nonwords derived from these nouns by a single-letter change (e.g., *charch, nater, floon*), one at a time, in random order, and asked to classify each as a word or nonword. He made three errors, classifying as words the three nonwords we have just listed.

With words not so high in frequency, however, E.E.'s acquired dyslexia was apparent; and appropriate testing revealed that this took the form of surface dyslexia. He was given a test of reading aloud single words using 39 irregular words and 39 words that were regular in their spelling-sound correspondence. The two sets of words (see Coltheart, Besner, Jonasson, & Davelaar, 1979) were matched pairwise on word frequency, number of letters, number of syllables, part of speech and, at least roughly, on concreteness. He read correctly 12 of 39 irregular words and 23 of 39 regular words ($p < .02$, McNemar's Test). His less-than-perfect performance with the regular words indicates that the nonlexical procedure for reading was by no means intact, unlike other patients with surface dyslexia, such as H.T.R. (Shallice, McCarthy, & Warrington, 1983) or M.P. (Bub, Cancelliere, & Kertesz, 1985). Nevertheless, the fact that he was much worse at reading irregular words than regular words indicated the presence of surface dyslexia, particularly since numerous regularization errors were observed: *pint*-"/pʌnt/", *flood*-"/flud/", and *castle*-"/kæstəl/", for example.

Second, he was given a homophone matching task. Pairs of printed words were presented, and he was asked to judge whether they were identical in pronunciation or not. The pairs were either regular words (e.g., lacks/lax), contained irregular words (e.g., know/no), or were nonwords (e.g., hyle/hile). Orthographic similarity was matched across the three conditions, and in each condition there were 25 same trials and 25 different trials. E.E. scored 74% correct with regular words, 70% correct with nonwords, but only 52% correct with irregular words, a significant disadvantage ($\chi^2_{(2)} = 6.064, p = .048$).

Because E.E. had suffered a major disruption of the lexical procedure for reading, it was decided to focus treatment on this aspect of his language impairment to attempt to improve his ability to read lexically.

We have already argued that if treatment is to be sufficiently focused it needs to be preceded by some form of theroetical analysis of the patient's disorder, and we have shown how this was accomplished with E.E., a specific impairment of the lexical procedure for reading having been demonstrated. We next wish to indicate why this is insufficient for providing guidelines for rational treatment and why something further needed to be done before the selection of a treatment program.

Symptoms and Syndromes

Surface dyslexia is one of the syndromes of acquired dyslexia, and the regularization error is one of its symptoms. However, like other syndromes, surface dyslexia is not uniform across patients: It can arise in different ways in different patients. What is crucial here is that this is true also for the regularization error. Coltheart and Funnell (1987), discussing surface dyslexia in relation to the model of reading offered by Patterson and Shewell (1987), showed that this single and highly specific symptom can arise in seven different ways. That is, seven distinct patterns of damage to the model would all result in the production of regularization errors. We will briefly describe the three most important of these, as follows:

1. If processing of words by a visual word-recognition system fails, printed words will not gain access to the lexicon, so reading aloud will have to be nonlexical.
2. If access to the visual word-recognition system is normal, but communication from this system to a phonological output lexicon (via a semantic system, for example) fails, reading aloud again will have to be nonlexical.
3. If retrieval of phonological word forms from a phonological output lexicon fails, once again reading aloud will have to be nonlexical.

Although these three patterns of impairment yield the same symptom, the impairments are obviously very different: One is an orthographic deficit, one involves semantic impairment, and one is an anomia. These differences are surely such that different treatments would be indicated in the different cases. It follows that, although a specific syndrome (surface dyslexia) has been diagnosed, and a highly

164　COLTHEART AND BYNG

specific symptom (regularization error) has been demonstrated, theoretical interpretation is still not specific enough to guide one's choice of treatment.

This issue is a general one, not at all confined just to a single form of acquired dyslexia. Consider agrammatic Broca's aphasia: How might it be treated? Since we now know that agrammatic sentence comprehension and agrammatic sentence production can dissociate, one cannot simply think of agrammatism as an entity to be treated. Expressive agrammatism itself comes in different forms (see, e.g., Berndt, 1987; Parisi, 1987). Sometimes what is seen is structural simplification; in other patients morphology proves especially problematic. Although in both types of case there is agrammatism of production, it takes different forms and perhaps different treatments. Even at a highly specific level of analysis, the level of morphology, there are indications of dissociations between inflectional and derivational morphology (Miceli & Caramazza, 1987; Parisi, 1987). Thus, it is generally true that if the point of theoretical interpretation is to provide a means of deciding what treatment is appropriate, such interpretation may need to be extremely detailed.

Specifying the Source of E.E.'s Surface Dyslexia

In the case of E.E., we have indicated three of the ways in which his regularization errors might arise and have taken the view that one must decide which of these is relevant to E.E. before devising any treatment method. There are various ways of making such decisions. For example, if E.E.'s paralexias were anomic in origin (i.e., Pattern 3 was the source of his difficulties), it would be expected that he would also exhibit anomia in other tasks, such as picture naming and spontaneous speech. As it happens, E.E. was rather anomic in general, and certainly some of his paralexias were of an anomic character, such as

> *shampoo* - "washing the hair . . . I know that but I can't say it . . . /ʃæpɒn/".
> *yacht* - "/jɒ/, /jɔ:/ . . . that's a boat, /jɔ:tʃ/ . . . don't know".

However, these were the only two occasions when he knew the meaning of the word even when he could not read it aloud. Most often, when he misread a word, he also failed to understand it. Hence the major determinant of his surface dyslexia was not an anomia.

Nor could his surface dyslexia be a consequence of an impairment at the semantic level (i.e., Pattern 2 described earlier). On the English Picture Vocabulary Test, which measures comprehension of single

5. SURFACE DYSLEXIA TREATMENT   165

words, he achieved a raw score of 95 with spoken input. If his dyslexia were due to a semantic impairment, this would affect reading comprehension and auditory comprehension equally. The fact that reading comprehension was far worse than auditory comprehension indicates that there is an impairment of the reading system at some stage earlier than the semantic level.

These results suggest that the major source of E.E.'s surface dyslexia was an impairment at the level of visual word recognition (i.e., the first of the three impairment patterns we listed earlier). We documented this by using a test of written homophone comprehension.

Suppose you present the written homophone *I* and ask a patient, not to read it aloud, but to say what it means. A patient who is simply anomic will provide an appropriate (though perhaps circumlocutory) definition. A patient with an impairment to the semantic system might respond "I don't know" or produce a semantic error, or an abnormally vague definition. Neither kind of patient, however, would produce a response like *I*—"got two" (accompanied by pointing to the eyes). This type of error, the homophone confusion, arises because there is a failure at the level of the visual word recognition system or its communication to the semantic system. When such a failure occurs, an alternative stratagem can be used: The stimulus can be translated to phonology by the nonlexical procedure, and the resulting phonological representation comprehended (i.e., transmitted to the semantic system via an auditory word-recognition system). If the stimulus, however, is a homophone, this stratagem will yield ambiguity: There will be no way of deciding between the stimulus and its homophone. Hence homophone confusions in reading comprehension will arise.

Therefore, we presented E.E. with single printed words that were homophones and asked him what they meant. Abundant homophone confusions were the result; for example,

stake - "dinner"
daze - "six in a week" (sic)
witch - "which way you turn"
billed - "build a house"
blew - "colour"
rays - "going to work raising money"

There were many others, including the remarkable *knows*—"one down the Old Kent Road." Why is this a homophone confusion? Because E.E. reads *knows* as "/kənaɒz/" (a regularization); in his di-

166   COLTHEART AND BYNG

alect, the word "canal" is pronounced "/kenaɷ/"; and there was indeed a canal near the Old Kent Road.

The frequent occurrence of homophone confusions in reading comprehension licenses the conclusion that a major source of E.E.'s surface dyslexia was at the level of visual word recognition. Having arrived at this conclusion, we were then in a position to develop a focused program of treatment because we now had a target at which to aim: the improvement of visual word recognition.

We wanted not only to carry out a treatment program that might improve E.E.'s reading, but also to know whether any improvements that occurred were actually due to the specific program instituted (rather than being due to "spontaneous recovery", to practice effects, or to nonspecific treatment effects such as might result from a therapist's attention or encouragement). There are, of course, ways of designing treatment programs that allow one to make decisions between these alternative explanations for improvements (see, e.g., Coltheart, 1983), and we adopted such methods.

Therapy Study 1

This study specifically concerned E.E.'s ability to read words containing a sequence of two vowels followed by the letters GH: for example, *though*, *through*, and *cough*. These words were chosen because they are among the most irregular of English words because there are no predominant pronunciations for any of the vowel digraphs, and the GH is, unpredictably, either silent or pronounced /f/. We used 24 such words. Not surprisingly, E.E. read these words poorly, scoring only 5 of 24 correct in a pretreatment test of reading aloud and producing such errors as *plough* → "/plʌf/", *ought* → "/oɷʌft/", *dough* → "/du:/" and *nought* → "/no ɷgʌt/".

The method of therapy aimed at restoring his ability to read these very irregular words was a kind of whole-word training. For each of the words, a mnemonic aid was provided: a card containing the printed word plus a picture representing the meaning of the word. The word *borough*, for example, was accompanied by a small map of part of London, and the word *bough* by a drawing of a tree. The use of these cards was explained to the patient, and it was arranged that he would spend 15 minutes per day at home, every day, reading aloud the treated words from their cards with the help of the mnemonic pictures, recording his daily progress on a chart provided for this purpose.

As mentioned earlier, we wanted to design this study in such a way as to be able to decide at the end of the study whether the therapy method really had improved E.E.'s reading. We did this by dividing the 24 words into two matched groups: Group 1 and Group 2. After a pretherapy pretest of all 24 words, the mnemonic therapy was used for Group 1 words, and no treatment was applied to Group 2 words. If, after a period of therapy, E.E. read the Group 1 words better than the Group 2 words, this would be evidence for the specific efficacy of the therapy because nonspecific treatment effects, or spontaneous recovery, should affect both groups of words equally. To confirm a specific therapy effect, if one appeared, we also included a period after treatment of the Group 1 words in which they were no longer treated, whereas the Group 2 words *were* treated.

This therapy study lasted 5 weeks. Once a week for 5 weeks we gave E.E. all 24 words to read aloud (without the mnemonic aids). The first of these sessions was a pretherapy pretest. For the next 2 weeks E.E. worked at home on the Group 1 words. For the final 2 weeks he worked at home on the Group 2 words. The results are shown in Table 5.1.

During weeks 2 and 3, when the Group 1 words were being treated, they were read more accurately than the Group 2 words (Mann-Whitney Test, $Z = 2.52$, $p = .012$). Therefore, there was a specific effect of the therapy.

What was unexpected, however, was that the *untreated* words also improved over this 3-week period (Cochran's Q, chi-squared = 8.0, $p = .02$).

The superiority of the treated over the untreated words indicates that there was a specific treatment effect: the mnemonic effect did specifically improve the reading of the words with which this technique was used. There was also an additional effect operating, which affected the untreated words (and, presumably, the treated words to the same degree). This could have been either spontaneous recovery or else a generalization effect of some kind. This was studied further

TABLE 5-1
Number of Words Correctly Read Each Week in Therapy Study I

	Pretest	Group 1 words treated		Group 2 words treated	
	Week 1	Week 2	Week 3	Week 4	Week 5
Group 1 words	$4/11$*	$7/11$*	$12/12$	$11/12$	$12/12$
Group 2 words	$1/12$	$3/12$	$7/12$	$9/12$	$12/12$

*By oversight, only 11 Group 1 words were tested on these occasions.

168   COLTHEART AND BYNG

in the second and third treatment programs carried out with E.E.; we discuss these shortly.

In the last 2 weeks of the first treatment program, the treatment was applied to the Group 2 words (which had previously received no treatment), and the treatment of the Group 1 words was discontinued. At the end of this period, performance was perfect with both sets of words. A year later this perfect performance had been maintained.

Therapy Study II

The aim of this study was to extend the first study using different materials, a slightly different mnemonic technique, and a modification to the design which would allow one to decide whether, if once again it were found that the untreated words improve during a period of therapy, this is a spontaneous-recovery effect.

E.E. was first given 485 words to read aloud, the 485 most frequent words in the norms of Kucera and Francis (1967). He misread 54 of these words. These 54 words were then given to E.E. to read aloud on two occasions (two pretherapy baselines) separated by 1 week. On these two occasions he scored 13 of 54 and 19 of 54 correctly; this difference did not approach significance, providing some evidence that spontaneous recovery was not occurring to any important degree.

The 54 words were then divided at random into two groups of 27 words. A mnemonic therapy, carried out by E.E. at home as in the first study, was applied to one of these groups. Instead of the word being paired with a picture, some kind of mnemonic symbol was drawn on the word, using a different color to dissociate it from the word. E.E. helped to choose these symbols. For example, for the word "work" an envelope shape was drawn against the final letter because E.E. was a postman and thought that this would remind him of the word's meaning. Similarly, for the word "society" faces were drawn inside the circular letters and curves of the S.

E.E. went through this regimen at home for a week. Then all 54 words were retested, and, after a period of 4 weeks during which no therapeutic work occurred, there was a second posttest of all the 54 words. The results are shown in Table 5.2.

Pretest performance was no different for T versus U words ($Z = .388, p = .7$). At posttest, the T words were superior ($Z = 6.10, p < .001$). However, for both sets of words, posttest performance was better than pretest performance ($Z = 4.315, p < .001$ for U words; $Z = 4.73, p < .001$ for T words). Just as with the first treatment program, then, there were two effects: a specific treatment effect (T words better

5. SURFACE DYSLEXIA TREATMENT 169

TABLE 5-2
Proportion of Words Correctly Read in Therapy Study II

	Pretreatment		Posttreatment	
	Pretest 1	*Pretest 2*	*Posttest 1*	*Posttest 2*
Treated words	.19	.44	1.00	.96
Untreated words	.47	.44	.85	.74

than U words) and a nonspecific effect (U words improve, although not as much as T words). However, the design of the second study allowed us to investigate the nonspecific effect in more detail because we used two pretests rather than only one. If the nonspecific effect is due to spontaneous recovery, or if it is simply a practice effect, then one would expect performance to be better in the second pretest than in the first. However, this did not occur. Hence the nonspecific effect appears to be produced *by the treatment*—the mnemonic technique benefits treated words more than untreated words, but it also improves the reading of untreated words to some degree.

Therapy Study III

Similar results were obtained in the third and final treatment program, which took place in the period after the completion of the second program. The third program used the next 388 words in the Kucera-Francis norms. E.E. misread 101 of these. The misread words were divided at random into two groups or 51 treated (T) words and 50 untreated (U) words. After two pretest sessions reading the 101 words, the mnemonic therapy was used with the T words. Then there were two posttest sessions reading all 101 words. The results are given in Table 5.3.

Pretest performance was not different for the two groups of words ($Z = .57, p = .56$). Performance on the T words was superior to performance on the U words at posttest ($Z = 8.46, p < .001$). However,

TABLE 5-3
Proportion of Words Correctly Read in Therapy Study III

	Pretreatment		Posttreatment	
	Pretest 1	*Pretest 2*	*Posttest 1*	*Posttest 2*
Treated words	.45	.63	1.00	.96
Untreated words	.48	.52	.78	.70

170 COLTHEART AND BYNG

performance on both groups of words improved between pretest and post-test (for U words, $Z = 3.5$, $P < .001$; for T words, $Z = 5.6$, $P < .001$). The difference between the two pretests was not significant for the U words ($Z = .447$, $P = .65$) but was just significant for the T words ($Z = 2.07$, $P = .04$).

Conclusions

These three studies of rehabilitation in acquired dyslexia provide evidence that it is possible to use a whole-word technique to restore at least partially the ability to use the lexical procedure for reading aloud after the use of this procedure has been impaired by neurological damage. The effects observed cannot be ascribed to spontaneous recovery or practice; the treatment has a highly specific effect (assisting only the particular words treated) and in addition a second, more general, effect (giving some assistance to untreated words and treated words alike).

More generally, we hope that the work reported in this chapter illustrates how fruitful the interplay between theory and therapy can be. The therapy we reported, which was successful, was guided by theory in ways we have explained. In turn, the results of the therapy may have implications for theory; we conclude by examining this possibility.

POSTSCRIPT: VISUAL WORD RECOGNITION AND DISTRIBUTED PROCESSING

Current models of reading generally distinguish among a letter level of processing, a word level, and a semantic level. However, there are two fundamentally different theoretical approaches as far as characterizing the nature of these levels is concerned. The two approaches might be described as the *item-specific* versus the *distributed-representation*.

Item-specific models view each processing component as a collection of individual elements corresponding in a one-to-one fashion to the set of stimuli that the component can identify. So, the letter level consists of a set of letter detectors, the word level consists of a set of word detectors, and the semantic level consists of a set of semantic representations of particular words. The function of each level is for the element corresponding to the stimulus to be activated with all the other elements at that level not activated. Examples of such models may be found in Morton and Patterson (1980), Coltheart (1981), and Johnston and McClelland (1980).

5. SURFACE DYSLEXIA TREATMENT 171

Distributed-representation models also view each level as consisting of a set of elements, but these elements do not correspond to particular stimuli. Instead, any stimulus will excite to some degree many or all of the elements at a particular level. The particular pattern of activation across the set of elements is responsible for stimulus identification: Each stimulus will evoke a different and unique pattern of activation of the set of elements. Models of this sort have been applied in numerous domains (see, e.g., Hinton and Anderson, 1981; Hinton, McClelland and Rumelhart, 1986). A model specifically concerned with reading has recently been proposed by Hinton, McClelland, and Rumelhart (1986) Figure 5.1, from their paper, outlines this model. The model involves three levels. At the letter level, distributed processing has not been invoked. Each unit represents a particular letter in a particular position; for example, d/3 is the unit for detecting d in the third position of a word. The next level, the word-set level, however, does use distributed processing. The elements at this level are word sets, and each word set will be activated by many different words. In the simplified example of Figure 5.1, there is a word set for all words beginning "ca" and a word set for all words ending "at." Because any word will activate many word sets and any word set will be activated by many different words, word identification cannot depend on which particular word set is activated; it must depend on the pattern of activation across all the word sets.

The third level, the semantic level, consists of individual semantic features. Each word set excites every semantic feature of every word in its set.

The efficiency of the model is increased by two specific properties. First, the strength of activation exerted by any particular interlevel connection is assumed to be incremental or decremental by learning. Second, there are horizontal interactions among units at the semantic level, so that familiar patterns of activation at this level are boosted and unfamiliar patterns of activation are suppressed.

Hinton et al. (1986) report the results of a simulation of this model using 30 letter units, 20 word-set units, and 30 semantic units. This network was taught to associate each of 20 different letter strings with a different pattern of activation at the semantic level. Accuracy reached 99.9% after a prolonged period of learning.

An acquired dyslexia was then induced; the network was damaged by adding noise to every connection that involved a word-set unit. Performance declined to 64.3%. A further program of rehabilitation was then carried out; that is, a further period of learning.

Two interesting findings emerged. The first was that relearning

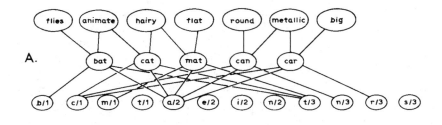

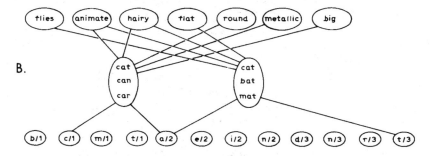

FIGURE 5.1. *A:* A three-layer network. The bottom layer contains units that represent particular graphemes in particular positions within the word. The middle layer contains units that recognize complete words, and the top layer contains units that represent semantic features of the meaning of the word. This network uses local representations of words in the middle layer. *B:* The top and bottom layers are the same as in (*A*), but the middle layer uses a more distributed representation. Each unit in this layer can be activated by the graphemic representation of any one of a whole set of words. The unit then provides input to every semantic feature that occurs in the meaning of *any* of the words that activate it. Only those word sets containing the word *cat* are shown in this example. Notice that the only semantic features which receive input from *all* these word sets are the semantic features of cat. Reprinted from Hinton, McClelland, and Rumelhart (1986).

was much faster than initial learning. This was predicted by an argument demonstrating that connection strengths perturbed by noise have certain special properties. Still more interesting was the second finding. To quote Hinton et al. (1986) in full

> An even more surprising effect occurs if a few of the words are omitted from the retraining. The error rate for these words is substantially reduced as the retraining proceeds. . . . The 'spontaneous' recovery of words that the network is not shown again is a result of the use of distributed representations. *All* the weights are involved in encoding

5. SURFACE DYSLEXIA TREATMENT   173

the subset of the words that are shown during retraining, and so the added noise tends to be removed from *every* weight. A scheme that used a separate unit for each word would not behave in this way, so one can view spontaneous recovery of unrehearsed items as a qualitative signature of distributed representations.

It will be seen that the treatment applied by Hinton and the treatment we applied had exactly the same effect. Words used during this treatment were relearned better than words not treated, but the untreated words also improved. If one agrees with Hinton's proposal that this pattern of response to treatment is indicative of a system based on distributed representations, then our treatment study of E.E. could be taken as evidence for the view that the visual word recognition system is based on distributed representations.

REFERENCES

Beauvois, M. F., & Derouesne, J. (1979). Phonological alexia: three dissociations. *Journal of Neurology, Neurosurgery and Psychiatry, 42*, 1115–1124.

Berndt, R. S. (1987). Symptom co-occurrence and dissociation in the interpretation of agrammatism. In Coltheart, M., Job, R. and Sartori, G. (Eds.), *The Cognitive neuropsychology of language* (pp. 221–232). London: Lawrence Erlbaum Associates.

Bub, D., Cancelliere, A., & Kertesz, A. (1985). Whole-word and analytic translation of spelling to sound in a non-semantic reader. In Patterson, K. E., Marshall, J. C., & Coltheart, M. (Eds.), *Surface dyslexia: cognitive and neuropsychological studies of phonological reading* (pp. 15–34). London: Lawrence Erlbaum Associates.

Byng, S., & Coltheart, M. (1986). Aphasia therapy research: methodological requirements and illustrative results. In Hjelmquist, E., & Nilsson, L-G. (Eds.), *Communication and handicap* (pp. 191–213). Elsevier Science Publishers B.V., North-Holland.

Coltheart, M. (1981). Disorders of reading and their implications for models of normal reading. *Visible Language*, Vol XV, No. 3, 245–286.

Coltheart, M. (1983). Aphasia therapy research: a single-case study approach. In Code, C. and Muller, D. J. (Eds.), *Aphasia therapy* (pp. 194–202). London: Edward Arnold.

Coltheart, M. (1985). Cognitive neuropsychology and the study of reading. In Posner, M. I., & Marin, O. S. M. (Eds.), *Attention and performance XI* (pp. 3–37). Hillsdale, NJ: Lawrence Erlbaum Associates.

Coltheart, M., Besner, D., Jonasson, J. T., & Davelaar, E. (1979). Phonological recoding in the lexical decision task. *Quarterly Journal of Experimental Psychology, 31*, 489–508.

Coltheart, M., & Funnell, E. (1987). Reading and writing: one lexicon or two? In Allport, A., Mackay, D., Prinz, W., & Sheerer, E. (Eds.), *Language perception and production* (pp. 313–339). London: Academic Press.

Coltheart, M., Masterson, J., Byng, S., Prior, M., & Riddoch, J. (1983). Surface dyslexia. *Quarterly Journal of Experimental Psychology, 35A*, 469–495.

Funnell, E. (1983). Phonological processes in reading: new evidence from acquired dyslexia. *British Journal of Psychology, 74*, 159–180.

Hinton, G. E., & Anderson, J. A. (Eds.). (1981). *Parallel models of associative memory.* Hillsdale NJ: Lawrence Erlbaum Associates.

Hinton, G. E., McClelland, J. L., & Rumelhart, D. E. (1986). Distributed representations. In D. R. Rumelhart, & J. L. McClelland (Eds.), *Parallel distributed processing* (Vol. 1, pp. 71–109). London: Bradford Books.

Johnston, J. C., & McClelland, J. L. (1980). Experimental tests of a hierarchical model of word identification. *Journal of Verbal Learning and Verbal Behaviour, 19*, 503–524.

Kucera, H., & Francis, W. N. (1967). *Computational analysis of present-day American English.* Providence: Brown U.P.

Marshall, J. C., & Newcombe, F. (1973). Patterns of paralexia: a psycholinguistic approach. *Journal of Psycholinguistic Research, 2*, 175–199.

Miceli, G., & Caramazza, A. (1987). Dissociations of inflectional and derivational morphology. In *Reports of the Cognitive Neuropsychology Laboratory* (pp. 1–26). Baltimore, Johns Hopkins University.

Morton, J., & Patterson, K. E. (1980). A new attempt at an interpretation, or, an attempt at a new interpretation. In Coltheart, M., Patterson, K. E., & Marshall, J. C. (Eds.), *Deep dyslexia* (pp. 91–118). London: Routledge and Kegan Paul.

Parisi, D. (1987). Grammatical disturbances of speech production. In Coltheart, M., Job, R., & Sartori, G. (Eds.) *The Cognitive Neuropsychology of Language* (pp. 201–219). London: Lawrence Erlbaum Associates.

Patterson, K. E. (1982). The relation between reading and phonological coding: further neuropsychological observations. In Ellis, A. W. (Ed.), *Normality and pathology in cognitive function* (pp. 77–111). London: Academic Press.

Patterson, K. E., & Coltheart, V. (1987). Phonological processes in reading: a tutorial review: In Coltheart, M. (Ed.), *Attention and performance XII* (pp. 421–448). London: Lawrence Erlbaum Associates.

Patterson, K. E., Marshall, J. C. and Coltheart, M. (Eds.). (1985). *Surface dyslexia: cognitive and neuropsychological studies of phonological reading.* London: Lawrence Erlbaum Associates.

Patterson, K., & Shewell, C. (1987). Speak and spell: dissociations and word-class effects. In Coltheart, M., Job, R., & Sartori, G. (Eds.), *The cognitive neuropsychology of Language* (pp. 273–292). London: Lawrence Erlbaum Associates.

Shallice, T., McCarthy, R., & Warrington, E. (1983). Reading without semantics. *Quarterly Journal of Experimental Psychology* (Vol. 35A, pp. 111–138).

6 Writing Rehabilitation in Brain Damaged Adult Patients: A Cognitive Approach[1]

Sergio Carlomagno
Vincenzo Parlato
Instituto di Scienze Neurologiche,
Facoltà di Medicina e Chirurgia,
Università di Napoli, Italy

The study of writing impairment in brain-damaged adult patients has usually been considered a secondary aspect of their communication disorders. This view arose from clinical and theoretical reasons. First, in clinical experience, dissociated disorders of writing and speaking abilities are quite rare. For instance, in their study concerning 500 left brain damaged patients Basso, Taborelli, and Vignolo (1978) found that 14 subjects showed this kind of dissociation, only two of them being considered cases of "pure agraphia." On the other hand, writing, at least in the alphabetic writing systems, has usually been considered a purely mechanical transformation of phonemes into their graphemic counterparts. For instance, in Luria's (1969) view ". . . the fundamental condition of writing is the acoustic analysis of words . . . The second component of the process of writing is the operation of correlation of each isolated sound with the corresponding letter. . . ." (p. 417).

Writing rehabilitation has suffered from the same kind of limitations, its practice being considered only a tool contributing to the recovery of speech or the patient's occupation in everyday life. Before the seminal paper of Hatfield and Weddel (1976), in fact, experimental works on this topic were notable exceptions in the neuropsychological rehabilitation literature.

---

[1]Preliminary results of this study have been presented at "Acute Brain Ischemia" 1985, Siena, Italy and at "Joint Conference of Experimental Psychology Society and Divisione Ricerca di Base (SIPs)", Padova, 1986.

176   CARLOMAGNO AND PARLATO

However, the recent neuropsychological studies carried out by Sasanuma (1975) in the framework of the nonalphabetic writing systems Kana and Kanj and by Beauvois and Dérouesné (1981), Shallice (1981), and Bub and Kertesz (1982) in the context of the alphabetic ones pointed out that writing cannot be considered as a mere graphemic translation of spoken language. These studies have suggested a more fruitful approach to the study of writing disorders in the framework of an information processing analysis. This approach aims to identify which cognitive processes are disturbed in writing disorders rather than classify the disorder on a clinical basis, that is, in relation to other language impairments. Therefore, the study of writing disorders in brain-damaged patients was itself becoming of interest for neuropsychology, (see Ellis, 1982; Margolin, 1984; and Hatfield and Patterson, 1984 for reviews). On the other hand, the information processing approach has proven to be fruitful for the rehabilitation of writing disorders (Hatfield, 1982, 1984).

We will briefly survey the literature on writing rehabilitation. Then we will offer an example of reorganization of writing function based on the information processing models. Finally, the major implications of the information processing analysis for the writing rehabilitation in brain-damaged patients will be discussed.

WRITING REHABILITATION: A SURVEY
OF THE LITERATURE

In 1967 Pizzamiglio and Roberts presented data concerning the ability of aphasic patients to learn written verbal material (written naming and sentence completion) through a machine-aided technique. This machine, controlled by a punch tape, provided a typed sentence with the final word missing. The patient had to write the word by means of an external keyboard. When he punched an incorrect key, the correct one was illuminated, guiding the patient to complete the word without frustration. Patients were found to learn these written tasks and to retain what they had learned at least 1 week after the terminal experimental session. Furthermore, a daily treatment was shown to be more fruitful than treatment on alternate days. A number of experimental restrictions render the data of this pioneer study not very useful to our discourse. For instance, no baseline or learning transfer evaluations or detailed clinical variables were reported. However, from the rehabilitation point of view, patients were supposed to have lost the ability to produce written language and the hypothesis of the study was to replace the lost information through this teaching technique.

A quite different approach was described in 1969 by Luria, Naydin, Tsveskova and Virnarskaya in their review on the restoration of higher cortical functions. As previously outlined, in his view writing function is considered as a multicomponent system that involves translation of the individual sounds of words into their graphemic counterparts. Consequently, the proposed rehabilitation strategy aims first to identify, in the various clinical forms of writing disorder, the damaged component of this system (acoustic analysis, phonemic sequencing, correlation of each isolated sound with the corresponding letter, and recoding of the visual image of letters in its graphic outline). Therefore, the rehabilitation exercises move toward offering the patient a self-monitoring system by means of visual, acoustic, and kinesthetic feedbacks for each damaged component. For instance, in the case of efferent motor aphasia, the writing disorder is conceived of as a deficit of successive organization of the elements leading to transposition of letters, omission of vowels and consonants, and so on. The patient is trained to identify the composition of a spoken word and to retain the correct order of sounds by picking out the sounds and counting them with the help of external aids (sticks) and then filling an optic scheme composed of ordered squares by the appropriate letters. In this case, the patient's ability to serially order sounds, and consequently the corresponding letters, is reorganized by means of acoustic and optic aids that would be progressively faded out and finally removed. Unfortunately no experimental data or clinical descriptions were reported.

Note that there are two consistent differences between this approach and the previous study by Pizzamiglio and Roberts (1967). First, the latter proposes a direct training of the function, and the patient is supposed to relearn to write by storing the written form of words as in the prelesional situation. On the contrary, in Luria et al.'s (1969) suggestion, the patient is supposed to recover writing functions by recourse to alternative spared neuropsychological components that can support the function. On the other hand, the teaching technique of Pizzamiglio and Roberts (1967) proposes a retraining of some selected written items, whereas Luria's approach suggests that general rules of writing can be restored (i.e., translation from the acoustic to the graphemic form of a word).

The two strategies were experimentally tested and discussed by Hatfield and Weddel in their valuable work of 1976. They presented data concerning writing retraining in severe aphasic patients by using three different methods. Only two of them are relevant to our discourse, the third being the global stimulation type, defined by the authors as an "umbrella approach . . . which weakens consolidation of any theory" (p. 77). The first one, visual-kinesthetic method consisted of a step-by-step passage from copy and copy from memory to write without model. Two patients suffering from severe expressive aphasia were treated. They showed a significant improvement of their spelling ability of treated words. However, 1 month after treatment completion, no retention was found for the first patient and no significant improvement at posttraining test for the second patient. Comparing her results with Pizzamiglio and Robert's data (1967), Hatfield and Weddel suggested that failure of retention could have been attributed to lack of more frequent sessions or revision of target items. As a matter of fact, some learning (initial letter, approximate word length, and consonant-vowel structure) was found to be retained. In the second method, recalling Luria's et al. suggestion (1969), they treated two patients by practicing auditory phonemic analysis of words and some phoneme-grapheme correspondences. The first patient progressed in the phonemic analysis and splitting of words but did not show any mastering of correspondences. Furthermore, the nature of her spelling errors was suggested to be attributed to the persistence of fragmentary visual images of words. The second patient appeared to be more sensitive to this kind of retraining. Unfortunately, she was Austrian and improvement could not be demonstrated because of the intrusions by German phoneme-grapheme correspondences, which accounted for half of her spelling errors at posttraining testing. Discussing their results, Hatfield and Weddel (1976) stressed that it was impossible to generalize the effectiveness of their method, as the two subjects were incomparable from the clinical point of view. A further major suggestion was that the peculiarities of the German and English writing systems, that is, regularity of spelling in one but not the other, could have influenced the two different responses to this kind of training.

A further notable investigation on the treatment of writing disorder in aphasic patients was carried out by Seron, Deloche, Moulard, and Rousselle (1980). They presented data concerning the treatment of aphasic patients by means of a computer-aided technique. The technique was aimed at retraining patients by typewriting from dictation, with particular emphasis on the choice and serial ordering of letters within a controlled situation of reinforcement. Progression was assured by the fading out of cues and by increasing the orthographic complexity of the stimuli being treated. Furthermore, in the testing sessions a separate list of stimuli was used and patients were requested to use handwriting to test for learning transfer. A first posttest, after completion of the training program, showed a significant improvement in all subjects for percentage of words correctly written, for total number of errors, and for similarity between responses and target items. At the second posttest, 6 weeks later, no retention of the improvement was found except in the case of one patient whose improvement, according to the authors, may have been due to spontaneous recovery. What is relevant to our discussion is the error analysis reported by the authors. A marked tendency to write using audiographic relationships (phoneme-grapheme correspondences) was demonstrated by the percentage of plausible phonemic errors. Furthermore, the orthographic complexity of target items was found to be a major source of errors because performance on words with as many letters as phonemes was significantly better than with other words. Therefore, the technique may have implemented writing by audiographic correspondences. However, this one-way interpretation was not entirely supported. Additional compensatory strategies, such as prepositioning of some letters of target items (writing in nonlinear order) or other visuokinesthetic behaviors, were reported by the authors as being used successfully by the patients. Consequently, one might suppose that patients should have used, at least in some cases, a quite different strategy instead of audiographic relationships (perhaps the persistence of fragmentary visual images of words; see Hatfield, 1985, for a detailed description of these strategies in a patient). This raises the issue that these strategies could be developed in future programs.

A considerable theoretical improvement in dysgraphic rehabilitation was supplied by a further work by Hatfield (1982, 1984) using information processing models. A detailed discussion of these models is beyond the scope of this chapter. A simplified version for writing and reading functions, which shares major similarities with the models put forward by Morton (1980), Ellis (1982), Margolin (1984), and Hatfield and Patterson (1984), is presented in Figure 6.1. Briefly it can be summarized as follows. Writing, like reading, involves two primary routes. The first entails the direct retrieval of a word's spelling, which is stored in the orthographic output lexicon (direct or semantic route). The second route entails segmental translation from phonology to orthography (phoneme-grapheme conversion route). According to Hatfield and Patterson (1984), this phoneme-grapheme processing involves several stages: (a) the analytical parsing of a spoken word into phonological segments, (b) assigning to each of the obtained segments its orthographic counterpart on the basis of rules peculiar to the patient's writing system, and (c) assembling these orthographic segments to obtain the written form of the word. Note that this procedure shares surprising similarities with Luria et al.'s schema (1969) of the entire writing function. However, it should be recalled that in Luria et al.'s formulation, audiographic transcoding

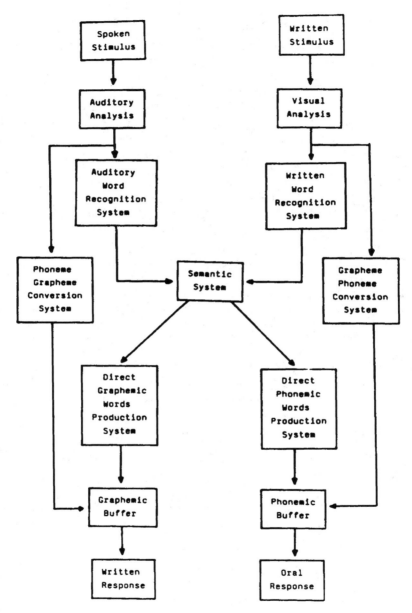

FIGURE 6.1. A simplified version of the "dual route" model for reading and writing.

is the fundamental mechanism of writing. On the contrary, in the psycholinguistic models, phoneme-grapheme conversion is only one of the writing routines and is quite insufficient to produce a correct spelling in a lot of words.

The first step of Hatfield's work (1982, 1984) was to classify dysgraphic impairments into surface or lexical (Beauvois & Dérouesné, 1981), phonological (Shallice, 1981), and deep dysgraphic (Bub & Kertesz, 1982) by means of analogy with the terminology proposed for the acquired dyslexias by Coltheart, Patterson, and Marshall (1980). Hatfield presents a detailed investigation of four patients, attempting to classify them according to the proposed model. Three patients were shown to exhibit the writing pattern of deep dysgraphia; the fourth exhibited the pattern of surface dysgraphia. Then she proposed to reorganize the writing function of the patients, using the better preserved of the two routes rather than attempting to restore the entire writing function through direct training. For instance, in the case of the deep dysgraphic patients who were unable to write function words, which are of practical importance for daily life situations, she sought to exploit their better performance on content words arising from the spared semantic route. The training method involved instructing the patient to write, by means of the spared direct route, a content word that was homophonic or quasihomophonic with the target function word and then to correct the spelling. For example, to write the word "on" the patient was instructed to write the Christian name "Ron" and then to delete the "r." In this case the word "Ron" accomplished the task of bypassing the impaired access to the spelling of word "on." The results of the study were interesting. Patient B.B.'s score on function words, for instance, improved from 34% to 63.5%. It should be noted that Hatfield's results were, of necessity, restricted to this particular aspect of the deep dysgraphic patient's disorder. Therefore, the experimental paradigm she applied could not verify all the theoretical implications of her therapeutic program. However, it was suggested that writing function could be reorganized by recourse to a spared component of the writing system.

Moreover, it must be noted that Hatfield's suggestions have been recently exploited by De Partz (1986) in her work on rehabilitation of a French deep dyslexic patient. She has presented data concerning treatment of grapheme-to-phomeme reading of such a patient by recourse to the partially preserved direct route of reading. In her approach, the patient who was unable to obtain the appropriate phoneme for a grapheme could produce this conversion by recourse to a code name, which is well processed by the direct route and contains this unit in the first position, i.e., "p" → "papa" → /papa/ → /p/. This

182   CARLOMAGNO AND PARLATO

analytical strategy allowed the patient to obtain a left-to-right sequential grapheme-to-phoneme translation of the word until the target phonological output was obtained. A detailed discussion of the method is beyond the scope of this chapter; however, Hatfield's approach (1984) to the rehabilitation of writing and reading functions has been confirmed by the successful results of such a therapeutic project.

We will present here a similar rehabilitation program of writing functions based on a reorganizational rationale. The procedure takes place in a more structured experimental situation and is intended to verify the reorganizational approach to writing disorders in the framework of psycholinguistic models.

THE REORGANIZATIONAL RATIONALE: A SINGLE CASE STUDY

Our patient is a 60-year-old right-handed man. He received a high school education and worked until June 1982 as a railway clerk. One year before being referred to our Neuropsychological Unit he had a cerebrovascular accident. Computed tomography (CT) showed infarction involving left frontotemporoparietal areas. At the time of our examination his speech was fluent and well articulated, and he complained only of reading and writing disturbances and of mild sensory impairment to the right hand. Aphasia testing showed no spoken language impairment except for a few self-corrected phonemic paraphasias in repetition and naming. The patient scored 30 of 36 on the shortened version of the Token Test (De Renzi & Faglioni, 1978), 38 of 40 on semantic comprehension tasks devised by Gainotti, Caltagirone, Miceli, & Masullo (1981), and 48 of 50 in a syntactic comprehension task of semantically reversible sentences. His phonemic discrimination was within normal levels according to Miceli, Gainotti, Caltagirone, & Masullo (1980). Oral expression was fluent, grammatically correct, and well articulated. He scored 42 of 50 in object naming, the remaining 8 items being successful "conduites d'approche," and correctly repeated 19 of 20 letters, 72 of 80 words, and 22 of 30 pronounceable nonwords.

Mental and written calculation were poor. Digit span was 4 forward and 3 backward. Rey's memory test for words was at a lower normal level but Corsi's block tapping test was normal. He scored 27 of 36 on Raven's Coloured Progressive Matrices. A mild buccofacial dyspraxia was present.

Reading Assessment

The patient's reading abilities were extensively studied during a period of 15 months, two sessions a week. The main results of the study, reported by Carlomagno et al. (1988), allowed us to classify his reading impairment as surface dyslexia syndrome (Table 6.1). He exhibited both the peculiar errors predicted by Job, Sartori, Masterson, & Coltheart (1984) and Coltheart (1984) for an Italian surface dyslexic patient. Namely, the stress assignment error on irregularly stressed words suggested that this patient was using the nonlexical grapheme-to-phoneme conversion system for reading. Furthermore, the inability to use the visual configuration of the letter strings (accent or apostrophe) indicated that he relied on the phonological form of the stimulus for his reading comprehension. For instance, his word reading was about 80% correct, but he scored only 50% correct on irregularly stressed words ($x^2 = 12.86$, $p < .001$), and he was completely unable to discriminate between "parlo" (I talk) and "parlò" (he talked), whose phonological form is the same except for the stress placement, or "lago" (lake) and "l'ago" (the needle), which sound alike.

Our patient was competent in handling the main orthographic rules (involving context and parsing) peculiar to written Italian. For instance (Table 6.1), he always respected softening of C and G before E and I (context) and correctly applied parsing procedures that assign one phoneme to two- or three-letter sequences as in the case of "ch" → /k/ or "sci" → /ʃ/. This peculiarity led us to conclude that his reading disturbance was quite different from the previously reported cases of such a reading disorder (i.e., patients J.C. and S.T. reported by Marshall and Newcombe, 1973; patient R.O.G. reported by Shallice and Warrington, 1980; patient A.D. reported by Deloche, Andreewsky, and Desi, 1982; and patient P.T. reported by Kay and Lesser, 1985), where this kind of error, that is, misapplication of parsing procedure and of context rules, represented a striking reading feature. On the other hand, in the same way as the previously mentioned cases of surface dyslexia, our patient showed, in reading aloud, a marked tendency to give a word as the erroneous response (lexical tendency). This tendency had usually been considered as a major indication that the reading of surface dyslexic patients results from the "... matching of successively larger candidate segments ... obtained by means of left-to-right segmentation ... to existing lexical addresses ..." (Marcel, 1980a, p. 256) stored in the phonological output lexicon. For instance, according to Marcel's interpretation, an error such as "unite" → "unit" results from a context insensitive left-to-right seg-

TABLE 6-1

Reading Features

General	
Word reading	80% correct
Nonword reading	30% correct*
Stimulus length	no consistent effect
Grammatical class	no consistent effect
Concrete vs. abstract	no consistent effect
Frequency	no consistent effect
Evidence of Surface Dyslexic Reading	
Stress regularization on irregularly stressed words	50% correct*
example: ésile (thin)–esìle (nonword)	
Ignoring marked stress (reading comprehension)	chance level
example: parlò (he talked) vs. parlo (I talk)	
Nonhomographic/homophones confusion (reading comprehension)	chance level
example: lago (lake) vs. l'ago (the needle)	
Knowledge of Italian Orthographic Rules (see text)	
Parsing, i.e.: "chi"– ki/	92% correct
Context, i.e.: "ci"– tʃi/	92% correct
Double consonant, i.e.: "itto"– itto/	94% correct
Consonant clusters relative frequency	significant effect†
example: fe(rt)ile vs. su(bd)olo	
Evidence of Lexical Strategy in Reading	
Reading of nonword homophonic with an idiomatic expression	80% correct‡
example: "per conto" (for account) → "perconto"	
Matching of dictated CV nonsense syllables with their written form	36% correct
example: /ka/ → "ca"	
Matching of dictated CV nonsense syllables with their written form embedded in a town name	96% correct§
example: /ka/– "(Ca)tania"	

The reading performances are expressed as overall percentages of correct responses obtained on three reading lists. List 1 (108 words and 108 pronounceable nonwords) and 2 (200 words and 30 pronounceable nonwords) wer controlled for stimulus length, grammatical class, concrete vs. abstract and frequency. List 2 was controlled for orthographic complexity, half of the stimuli requiring application of Italian orthographic rules (context and parsing). List 3 (84 words and 84 nonwords) was devised to assess the effect of the relative frequency of consonant clusters: 48 words containing infrequent consonant clusters, the remaining being words matched for frequency, grammatical class, concrete vs. abstract, length and CV structure but containing the most common Italian consonant clusters. Conversely 36 nonwords were generated to contain the infrequent consonant clusters, and the remaining were generated to have control nonwords matched for length and CV structure containing common Italian consonant clusters.

The test for assessing nonhomographic/homophone confusion was devised by Job

(continued)

6. WRITING REHABILITATION 185

TABLE 6-1
(Continued)

et al. (1984). The test for assessing sensitivity to marked stress was constructed in a similar way. The two matching tasks, each consisting of 80 items, are described in the text.

*$P < .001$ when compared to overal word reading
†$P < .02$ when compared to reading of matched words
‡$P < .02$ when compared to reading of non-words matched for CV structure
§$P < .001$ when compared to the analogous matching task

---

mentation until the obtained segment "unit" leads the patient to retrieve from the phonological output lexicon a possible pronounciation. Therefore, context and parsing errors are produced owing to a segmentation strategy where . . . "letter segmentations early in the string are not overridden by letters later in the string . . . " (Marcel, 1980a, p. 251). Further instances of such a reading strategy have been supplied in the case of A.D. by Deloche et al. (1982) and in the case of P.T. by Kay and Lesser (1985). However, in the case of our patient, who never produced errors of context rules and parsing procedure misapplication, the lexical tendency was shown to be independent of the segmentation procedure. Furthermore, we were able to demonstrate that the relative frequency of consonant clusters played a role in his reading in the sense that words containing very infrequent consonant clusters such as "pz," "tn," and so on were very difficult to read and led him, in the same way as stress regularization and the lexical tendency, to produce substitution, transposition, deletion, or addition errors. The last feature was not consistent with the interpretation that the grapheme-to-phoneme conversion of surface dyslexic patients operates at a level of single graphemes (Coltheart, 1984). Both our results (i.e., the consonant cluster effect and the spontaneous handling of context and parsing rules) suggested that our patient carried out grapheme-to-phoneme conversion by segmenting the letter string at the syllabic level and then mapping these multigraphemic sequences onto their phonological counterparts. Evidence for such a possibility has also been put forward in a different context by Shallice, Warrington, and McCarthy (1983).

In addition to the deficit of the direct route for reading, our patient also had some damage to the grapheme-phoneme conversion route. This impairment was suggested by his poor nonword reading (i.e., less than 30% correct, which was significantly worse than his word reading [$P < .001$]). This additional deficit gave rise to a lot of substitution, addition, deletion, and transposition errors, although in the absence of misapplication of the previously mentioned orthographic rules. In this sense, the deficit was comparable to the impairment of

186 CARLOMAGNO AND PARLATO

"phonemic processing" described by Dérouesné and Beauvois (1979) in two of their four cases of phonological dyslexia. These two patients were quite well able to handle the orthographic rules peculiar to written French; that is, they respected the rules that assign one phoneme to a multigraphemic sequence (parsing rules) as in "zou" → [z] + [ou] → /z/ + /u/. These patients, on the other hand, were shown to be using a spontaneous lexical strategy to attain the proper phonetic output for the stimulus, their performance being significantly better on nonwords homophonic with a word than on other nonwords. In the same way, our patient, who did not show errors resulting from parsing and context rule misapplication, had a significantly better performance on nonwords homophonic with a word than on other nonwords ($P < .02$). This difference, in our opinion, could account for his performance in word reading (by the grapheme-phoneme route), which was better than nonword reading. In this case, as in the case of homophonic nonwords, a spontaneous lexical aid must arise in attaining phonetic output. Other evidence of use of the lexical strategy in reading was furnished by his dissociated performance in a task of nonsense CV syllable recognition. In this case, (October 1984), where he had to match eight CV nonsense syllables, uttered one at time by the examiner, with concurrent presentation of their written form, he achieved a 30% accuracy rate. We gave him the same task using, for the written form, nouns of Italian towns that contained the same syllables in the first position such as Ca-tania, Pa-lermo, and so on. He succeeded at a 96% level of accuracy, which was significantly different from his performance on the previous test ($P < .001$).

Writing Assessment

Our patient was severely agraphic. Script and copying were performed correctly, but spontaneous writing and writing to dictation were performed almost totally incorrectly. He correctly wrote 18 of 19 single letters (May, 1983) and about 30% of 30 consonant-vowel nonsense syllables (October, 1984). Writing of words and nonwords to dictation was assessed on several occasions before starting the rehabilitation program: May 1983, July 1983, October 1983, January 1984, and October 1984 (Table 6.2). On all these occasions, we used stimuli from a list of 200 words and 30 pronounceable nonwords. This list was controlled for grammatical class, frequency, abstractness/concreteness, and length, the latter varying from four to eight letters. The list was also balanced for orthographic complexity, half of the stimuli requiring application of at least one orthographic rule of the Italian writing system.

6. WRITING REHABILITATION 187

TABLE 6.2
Writing Assessment

	Number	% Correct
Written Naming (May 1983)	37	10.4
Writing from Dictation		
May 1983		
4–8 Letter words	38	31.5
4–8 Letter nonwords	6	0
July 1983		
3- to 7-letter words	23	27
October 1983		
Total	143	37.7
3-letter words	53	56.6
4-letter words	47	36.1
6-letter words	43	16.2
January 1984		
4- to 7-letter words	42	29
4- to 6-letter nonwords	18	16
October 1984		
4- to 6-letter words	51	33
CV syllables	30	30

We should recall that Italian written language is very transparent as far as grapheme-to-phoneme conversion rules are concerned. For instance, in most cases one-to-one grapheme-to-phoneme correspondences apply. Indeed, there are a few occasions where one phoneme is translated into two or three graphemes, i.e.: /ŋ/ → "gn", /ʃ/ → "sci"; or one phoneme can be converted into two different alternatives, i.e.: /k/ → "c" or "ch" depending on the following context. It must be noted however, that, in any case, the context required for selecting the correct alternative is never wider than a syllabic unit, (see Coltheart, 1984, for a discussion).

In all the testing sessions, we used stimuli from the previously mentioned list, which were chosen, on each occasion, to control part of speech, frequency, length, grammatical class, orthographic complexity, and concreteness/abstractness, resulting in a sublist of at least 40 stimuli. However, because of his high error rate, our patient got easily discouraged and, on occasion, after some attempts refused to write. Therefore, in each testing session, he was not given a complete sublist (Table 6.2). In July 1983, for example, he accepted to write only 21 stimuli of a sublist plus two three-letter words. In May 1983, he was given a written naming task using the same stimuli of oral naming, and he scored 4 of 37 correct, the remaining stimuli being refused. In

188 CARLOMAGNO AND PARLATO

the same period, he was requested to give a short example of spontaneous writing by asking him "what do you do in the morning?" or "tell me about the painting session of last Sunday." The examples are reported in Appendix 6.2. In October 1983, he was given a supplementary three-letter word list to control the length effect. This list was controlled as much as possible for concreteness/abstractness and grammatical class (15 nouns, 11 verbs, 4 adjectives, 20 function words, and 3 polysemous words). On this occasion, the better overall performance on this sublist had a positive psychological effect and a more extensive testing was possible.

Pretherapy Results

In the initial testing sessions (May and July 1983) our patient preferred cursive handwriting; however, because it was sometimes nearly illegible (see Appendix 6.2), we forced him to write in capital letters. This gave rise to many self-corrections, even if this did not lead to significant improvement, probably because, when writing in capitals, he more often read his own written response and got dissatisfied. The major finding, concerning our rehabilitation experimental design, was that, from a quantitative point of view, no significant improvement was observed during testing period (Table 6.2). The slightly better performance recorded in October 1983 is due to the significant effect of stimulus length. On this occasion, in fact, his performance was 56% correct on three-letter words, 36% on four-letter words, and only 16% on six-letter words.

The second notable result is that the patient's writing impairment can be demonstrated in all writing tasks. As a matter of fact, in the sample of spontaneous writing, 25 words were correctly written, but 14 of them were one- to three-letter words. With the 12 four- to five-letter words in this sample, there were eight errors (33% correct). This result was no different from results in writing to dictation. On the other hand, in written naming he correctly wrote only 3 of 21 four- to five-letter words. The latter performance was slightly worse than the others and was probably biased by a minor tendency to self-correct (only five times in this sample). From a qualitative point of view, in the sample obtained in May 1983 (writing from dictation, see Appendix 6.1) no word-class effects were found. For instance, he scored 7 of 19 on high frequency words versus 5 of 19 on low frequency words, 10 of 30 on content words versus 2 of 8 on function words, and 3 of 7 on concrete words versus 1 of 8 on abstract words. A slight length effect was observed: 8 correct responses were recorded on 18 four- to five-letter words and only 4 on 20 six- to seven-letter words.

We have mentioned that a more careful investigation of this topic (October 1983) showed that this effect was significant, ($x^2 = 19.69$, df $= 2$, $P < .001$). On the other hand, we should note that nonword writing was usually worse than word writing. However, in this case our patient did not show any tendency to self-correct, perhaps quite consciously regarding to his poor nonword reading, and a few times a wrong repetition of the stimulus accounted for an error.

His errors resulted from a number of insertions, deletions, and substitutions, usually producing pronounceable nonwords. For instance only one error: "tra" (between) → "rtra" violated the legal structure of the Italian writing system and only two verbal, but not semantically related, paragraphias were produced: "rango" (rank) → "rancio" (ration) and "ciocca" (tuft) → "cacca" (dirt). Furthermore, he usually respected the syllable number of the stimulus, with few exceptions (i.e., 6 of 33 errors in written naming and 3 of 33 errors in writing to dictation).

To sum up, the severity of the writing impairment and the lack of a particular pattern easily suggested that both routes to writing, the direct route and the phoneme-to-grapheme route (Hatfield & Patterson, 1984), were seriously damaged.

Rationale of the Therapy Project

Our main purpose was to improve the patient's writing by phoneme-grapheme segmental translation. According to the strong regularity of the Italian writing system discussed earlier, the patient should be able to obtain general rules for writing that could allow him to write almost all Italian words. In this sense, a final outcome of "surface dysgraphia" would have been sufficient for an Italian-speaking patient in everyday life. We must recall, at this point, that he had been treated for 1 month at least, by the visuokinesthetic method described by Hatfield and Weddel (1976). However in all postsession testings no improvement was found. On other occasions, he was invited to write nouns, which were widely diffused on boards, by evoking the relative visual images, but this approach also failed to produce any significant improvement. A further possibility was that our patient could use in writing the same abilities he showed in reading. Within this framework, his orthographic competence and his ability to use a lexical relay strategy in reading words (by grapheme-phoneme conversion) were considered prerequisites for our rehabilitation program. Orthographic competence allowed our patient to segment the letter string at the syllabic level without making context or parsing errors. The spontaneous lexical aid could then arise,

190 CARLOMAGNO AND PARLATO

owing to the phonological form of the stimulus (see Dérouesné and Beauvois, 1979, for a discussion of this possibility). Therefore, our general objective was to instruct the patient to apply an analogous strategy of lexical relay between the phonological form of a syllabic group and the graphemic form using code names as lexical relay for accessing his orthographic competence. According to Beauvois and Dérouesné (1981) and Roeltgen and Heilman (1984), orthographic competence in reading and writing are supported by different systems. Therefore, our interpretation of the therapy is not theoretically supported. However, there were some practical reasons for our choice to retrain his phoneme-to-grapheme translation by using syllabic units instead of single letters. The first was that writing in syllabic units would be less laborious and time-consuming than writing by one-to-one sound-to-letter correspondences. The second reason was that in the Italian writing system, almost all the orthographic rules operate at the syllabic level. Finally, our main purpose was to offer our patient a self-monitoring system. On this view reading could easily be used by him to control what he was writing, and his reading had been shown to operate at the syllabic level.

However, in October 1984, the patient was asked to write 30 names of Italian towns or Christian names. These names contained in the first position the 30 consonant-vowel syllables he had written scoring 9 of 30 correct (see earlier discussion). Even though his general performance was again very poor (less than 30% correct), the first syllable was always correct. Therefore, this dissociated performance in writing paralleled somehow his reading ability with nonsense syllables, suggesting that some analogous orthographic (syllabic ?) competence was present in writing as well as in reading. In this regard, it was interesting that he usually respected in his writing responses the number the syllables of the stimulus, and his errors never violated the proper consonant-vowel structure of the Italian language.

Procedure

The method we used and the therapy stages are summarized in Table 6.3. The therapy lasted about 5 months, with 2 sessions per week.

Stage One. The first step of treatment consisted of searching for code names, usually names of Italian towns or Christian names, which contain in the first position about 30 consonant-vowel syllables to be treated. Our patient easily succeeded in searching for the appropriate code name for almost all the syllables. He had been a railway clerk and could promptly evoke a name of an Italian town

6. WRITING REHABILITATION   191

TABLE 6.3
Rehabilitation Program

Rationale of the method: Phoneme-grapheme segmental (syllabic) conversion + lexical relay strategy

Procedure:

Stage 1 (1 month)

Therapy on : 30 CV syllables
Training : word writing from dictation
Method : a) syllabic seg-   b) searching for   c) writing of the
mentation   code-nomes   syllabic units

/parola/			"pa + ro + la"
/pa/	→	[Pa] lermo	↑ ↑ ↑
/ro/	→	[Ro] ma	
/la/	→	[La] ura	

Stage 2 (2 months)

Therapy on : other 40 CV syllables + ~20 syllables requring orthographic competence (example /ki/– "chi")
Training : nonword writing from dictation
Method : as in the first stage

Stage 3 (2 months)

Therapy on : consonant clusters and diphthongs
Training : nonword writing from dictation
Method : as in stage one and two + further segmentation of diphthongs and consonant cluster

/kanka/				"ca + n + ca"
	/ka/	[Ca]	rlo	↑ ↑ ↑
/kan/				
	/n/	[Na]	poli→n	
/ka/		→ [Ca]	rlo	

that contained the target syllable in the first position. However, in a few cases the therapist offered him the appropriate syllable by using town or Christian names. In each session, 8 of 10 of these names, handwritten in capital letters by the therapist, were vertically arranged on a paper sheet. The patient was trained to match spoken syllables uttered by the therapist with its code name then code names with words, always uttered by the therapist, containing the relative syllable in first position. Finally he was requested to write the syllable without a model. After a few sessions, he achieved the established criterion of 95% correct in writing the 30 treated syllables and the next step was begun. We devised lists of words composed of two or three of these syllables. The patient was trained to make a syllabic segmentation of these stimuli in acoustic form and to recall for each segment the corresponding code name. For example, when the therapist dictated the word "mito" (myth) he had to segment orally the word into [MI] + [TO] and to say [MI] = MILANO, [TO] = TORINO. At this time he was invited to write the syllables to obtain the target stimulus. On a few occasions, the therapist proposed written words to be segmented. However, this practice was limited to the first two or three sessions to give the patient positive feedback by means of the final goal of the therapy. When the established criterion of 95% correct both in stimulus segmentation and in code name recall was achieved after 1 month of treatment, he was given a control writing list of two- to four-syllable words (consonant-vowel; 40 items). Half of these were words containing only treated syllables and half contained at least one untreated syllable. He scored 80% correct on words containing only treated syllables and 50% correct on the other words. It is interesting to note that he always attempted to write using the learned strategy and, in the case of the words with untreated syllables, he spontaneously searched for a new code name. For example, in the case of "dove" (where) the syllable "ve", which had not been treated, led him to spontaneously say: "ve as in Venezia." Then he promptly wrote the correct segment. At this time, most of his errors on treated syllables reflected marginal aspects of defective application of the strategy. For instance, in some cases with infrequent words, a wrong repetition of a syllabic unit led him to search for an inappropriate code name. This difficulty was more marked with untreated syllables.

Stage Two. In the Italian writing system there are 5 vowels and 14 pronounceable consonants that comprise 70 consonant-vowel syllables. During the second stage of treatment we attempted to introduce the remaining approximately 40 consonant-vowel syllables of written Italian. To automate the procedure, to expand his segmentation ability to four- to five-syllable stimuli (memory load), and to improve his phonemic discrimination, the patient was given a treatment program using only nonwords. Learning was very fast: After 2 months our patient mastered all 70 Italian consonant-vowel syllables at 90% accuracy.

During the same period, he was occasionally given some syllables where one phoneme is correctly translated into two or three letters. In these cases, the strictly syllabic structure of the Italian language made it possible for our patient to apply the same strategy as for the consonant-vowel syllables. For example, in the case of /Ki/ → "chi" or /ɲo/ → "gno," these units were spontaneously subsumed by our patient under specific code names: "chi" under the town name [Chi]eti and "gno" under family name of the first author "Carloma[gno]," the latter being the only case where he used the last syllable of a code name. In the same way, for the G softening, /dʒo/ → "gio," he used the possibility of a relay with the code name [Gio]vanni (John) and so on. Therefore, no specific treatment was needed for Italian orthographic rules according to our prediction, and we treated these syllabic units during the same period, as well as the CV syllables, without additional effort.

Stage Three. The fifth month of treatment was spent in training the patient on consonant cluster and diphthong decomposition. For the nonword "ancai," he spontaneously segmented the stimulus as [an] + [ca] + [i] and promptly offered as code-names [An]cona + [Ca]tania + [I]mola, even though "an" and "i" were untreated units. Note that this segmentation is consistent with the syllabic composition of the stimulus. Obviously, if you consider all the VC, CCV, CVC, CCVC syllables and the diphthongs, this kind of strategy would have been affected by the statistical impossibility of finding a proper code name. Likewise, the total number of code names would have increased to an unmanageable level. This problem led us to consider the possibility of adopting, for these cases, a different strategy for decomposition, namely at the single letter level. To facilitate his efforts, he was instructed to decompose CVCCV nonwords or diphthongs embedded in nonwords. He was forced to slowly repeat the syllabic unit containing the consonant cluster or a diphthong then to separate each phoneme of the cluster. For example a CVCCV nonword was segmented at [CV] + [C] + [CV] level and CVVCV nonword at [CV] + [V] + [CV] level. Then he had to search a corresponding code name for the isolated consonant or vowel and to write only the initial consonant or final vowel of the code. However, note that in Italian a CVCCV letter string can be segmented (at the syllabic level) as [CVC] + [CV] or at [CV] + [CCV], according to the consonant content, i.e.: "canca" → "can" + "ca" but "caspa" → "ca" + "spa." Despite our aim of retraining him for both possibilities with this more analytical segmentation strategy, he did not agree. Instead, he always attempted first to segment the stimulus at the syllabic level and, subsequently, to find a new code name by using all kinds of geographic knowledge: "spa" = "Spagna" (Spain) and so on. For instance, in almost all cases of VC and CCV syllables he preferred to use the syllabic instead of the single letter strategy. The latter was confined to the diphthongs, to more complex CCCV syllables such as "stra," and, sometimes, to the CVC syllables for which he could not spontaneously find any code name.

The last problem we had the opportunity to treat was represented

194 CARLOMAGNO AND PARLATO

by the double consonant rule. The Italian writing system requires that the correct writing of words as /kassa/ (box) is "cassa" since "casa" is the correct spelling of the word /kasa/ (house) and many Italian words differ only in the presence of a single/double consonant. This last rule, to write a double consonant where the double phonetic value is pronounced, was treated similarly to the consonant clusters for just two sessions. Finally, during all the sessions of the last month, the patient was also instructed to mark the stress on the last syllable if necessary as in the Italian word "parlo'" (he talked). However no particular strategy was offered to our patient for these two topics, and treatment was confined to the acoustic discrimination of related pairs, such as "parlo" versus "parlo'" or "casa" versus "cassa".

We have described the intermediate evaluation of the effect of therapy on treated syllables and words containing these syllables. Another intermediate assessment concerned the mastery of all 70 consonant-vowel Italian syllables plus syllables requiring the application of orthographic rules (about 20). This test yielded the result of about 90% correct in both cases. For the third stage (consonant cluster and diphthong decomposition), no intermediate test result was available because our patient suffered an epileptic seizure and missed two therapy sessions.

In the next session he was discouraged and told us that he did not feel up to continuing. It has to be recalled that he was living in Sorrento and it usually took him at least an hour to come to our unit. On this occasion no appropriate test list was available. Therefore, we decided to measure his overall improvement by using the same task of spontaneous writing that we had used in the pretherapy assessment. A second test was possible 2 months later (July 1985) when the patient underwent a medical consultation in the neurological unit of Prof. R. Cotrufo. On this occasion he underwent a testing session lasting 1 hour. He was requested to write a number of words to dictation and he wrote 36 items from the list of May 1983, 6 idiomatic expressions requiring apostrophe (three to four words for each expression), and another 23 words from a list we had devised for a qualitative evaluation (see later). No more data are available because the patient refused to return for other sessions.

Posttherapy Quantitative Evaluation

Immediate Assessment. The first test, April 1985, consisted of spontaneous writing of two short paragraphs. The sample, which is 71 words long, can be compared with the analogous pretherapy sample, which was 45 words in length (May 1983) and which concerns the same topic. The pretherapy sample contained 20 writing errors, 17 neologisms and 3 real words that were grammatically or semantically implausible. The posttherapy sample contained many successful self-corrections but only three errors of phoneme-to-grapheme conversion: "pennello" → "pennelo," "prendo" → "brendo" and "campagna" → "campania", $\chi^2 = 39.63$, $P < .001$. A fourth one, "e'" → "e" could be predicted on the basis of this writing procedure (see later for a qualitative discussion). Therefore, a considerable improvement was observed at the time therapy stopped. Note that the whole sample required about 15 minutes.

Delayed Assessment. In the list we administered 2 months later to test writing to dictation there were 36 items (30 words and 6 nonwords) of the 44 stimuli that had been used in the pretherapy evaluation of May 1983. Again, a significant improvement was observed. While in the pretherapy evaluation, the patient made 31 errors with these 36 stimuli; in the second he made only 5 errors plus 3 successful selfcorrections ($\chi^2 = 29.59$, $P < .001$). Thus, the improvement by our rehabilitation procedure had been maintained 2 months after training completion. Note that this improvement was stronger than one could evaluate with this limited sample. In fact, performance was error free with regard to phoneme-grapheme conversion in writing the idiomatic expressions (20 words). Furthermore most of the errors of grapheme-phoneme conversion reported in this sample are linked to the peculiarities of our experimental design (see qualitative evaluation).

These two results argue in favor of the effectiveness of our rehabilitation program. In Figure 6.2, the evolution of our patient's reading and writing abilities during the entire study period is reported. Thus, according to the single case paradigm described by LaPointe (1976), the improvement cannot be ascribed to spontaneous recovery, but is strongly linked to the effectiveness of our rehabilitation program. On the other hand, we have stressed that our patient was initially (from May to July 1983) trained by other methods. However, his writing did not improve with this type of treatment (Figure 6.2).

Posttherapy Qualitative Evaluation

The major theoretical interest concerning our reorganizational hypothesis is that our patient demonstrates that writing improvement is due to the learned strategy. This hypothesis is strongly supported by the temporal correlation between the improvement itself and the

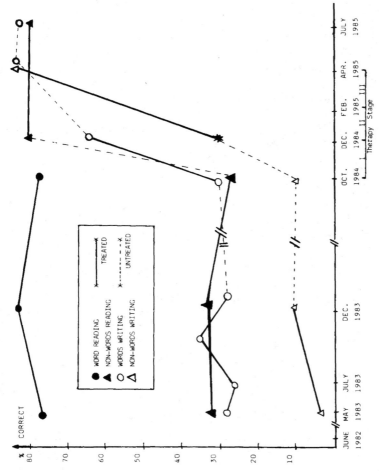

FIGURE 6.2. Performance of our patient in reading and writing during the entire study period. Dashed lines (training) are used for word and nonword reading from May 1983 to October because of the continuous testing sessions for his reading disorder and for nonword reading from December 1984 to April 1985 because of peculiarities of the therapy (see text). Dashed lines are also used for word and nonword writing from May 1983 to January 1985 because of training by means of visuokinesthetic method, repeated testing sessions, or other attempts.

therapy (LaPointe, 1976). However, we want to discuss here some other findings corroborating that our patient actually writes by the learned strategy. The first evidence would arise from the possibility that our patient could use it in other untreated tasks. For instance we have stressed that the difference between our patient's word and nonword reading (and writing) is linked to the lack of spontaneous lexical aid in nonword reading (and in writing) as shown by the better performance on pseudohomophonic nonwords. The learned strategy offers our patient the general possibility of obtaining a lexical relay to access his orthographic competence. Thus, the prediction is that nonword reading would improve by learning transfer at the same rate as writing. The second line of evidence would be provided by the nature of his actual writing errors, in the sense that they must be predicted on the basis of his actual writing procedure, which consists in the experimental design of phoneme-to-grapheme conversion mostly at the syllabic level.

Learning Transfer. As shown by Figure 6.2 the final results agree with the prediction of learning transfer. At the end of the first stage of therapy (December 1984) we had him read a 30 nonword list he read 2 months before at 50% accuracy. He now scored 80% correct, which is significantly different from the previous result ($x^2 = 5.93, P < .02$). The patient demonstrated a clear use of the learned strategy when he attempted to read this kind of written material. For instance, when requested to read the nonword "tarola" he suddenly segmented the stimulus by covering alternatively one or two syllables with his forefinger and said: "This is Taranto, ta . . . , this is Roma, ta-ro, this is Laura . . . O.K. ta-ro-la." At this time we had never used nonwords for the therapy, and some nonwords contained consonant-vowel-consonant and consonant-consonant-vowel syllables, which had not been treated. Therefore, improvement of non-word reading at the same rate as word writing must be considered a good example of learning transfer. A further assessment was made in July 1985, using a 30 nonword list the patient was given in December 1983. Whereas on the first occasion he scored 10 of 30 correct, in the second he scored 22 of 30 correct ($x^2 = 11.38, P < .01$). We have to remember that in the second and third stages of therapy we used nonwords, and some training of nonword reading must be considered a possibility. However, 2 months after therapy stopped, the strategy was widely applied, and results were consistent with the improvement he had previously shown.

Nature of Errors in Writing. The second clue is offered by the nature of his writing errors. Indeed, some of them may reflect marginal aspects of defective application of the learned strategy. For instance, consider the three substitutions, 'rango' (rank) → 'rongo' (n-w), 'invano' (vainly) → 'imvano' (n-w) and "prendo" (I take) → "brendo" (n-w), or the deletion, 'giornale' (newspaper) → 'gionale' (n-w). These errors can be explained as due to lack of appropriate relay or faulty phonological processing of the dictated stimulus. For instance, in the case of "rango" the patient correctly repeated and segmented the word: "ra-n-go" but wrote "ro" instead of "ra;" in the case of "imvano" he correctly repeated the word but in segmenting the stimulus said: "im . . . as in [Im]peria" and wrote "im;" in the case of "brendo" he made the same error, "bre as in [Bre]scia;" and in the case of "gionale" he segmented according to the syllabic composition: "gior-na-le" then forgot "r." All these errors could have been assessed using an appropriate list specifically devised for testing his ability to carry out a correct phonemic segmentation of dictated stimuli. For instance, infrequent consonant clusters represented a major problem: "riflettere" (reflect) → "rifettere" or "etnico" (ethnic) → "entico" or "opzione" (option) → "opizione," but it could be due either to the fact that he was unable to monitor what he had written owing to his reading features (see earlier) or to the fact that he was unable to obtain a correct phonological representation of these words, particularly when the components of the clusters were members of two syllables (see Marcel, 1980b). Unfortunately, this assessment was not possible because of the patient's unexpected medical problems.

However none of these errors are inconsistent with the application of the learned strategy. On the other hand, on two occasions he missed Italian orthographic rules/ "ciliegia" (cherry) → "ciliega" (n-w) and "campagna" → "campania". Because /ʎ/, /ʃ/, /tʃ/ and /dʒ/ orthographic translation was missed on no other occasion, a lack of appropriate relay could easily account for this error. In the second case we must remember that /ɲ/ is almost never in the first position in an Italian word and the patient probably had difficulty in finding an appropriate relay; that is, for /ɲo/ he used the last syllable of family name of the first authors.

In any case, according to our prediction that by using a syllabic code the patient would easily obtain a correct mastering of the Italian orthographic rules, his ability (16 of 18 correct) must be considered clear evidence that he was using the strategy. On the contrary some errors are of interest because of the predicted final outcome of "surface dysgraphia." This final outcome would parallel the peculiar features of the patient's reading by using phoneme-to-grapheme conversion, for instance difficulty in handling stress or apostrophe. Some errors at posttherapy assessment reported in the Appendix 6.1: "quassu'" (up here) → "quassu", "parlo'" (he talked) → "parlo" (I talk), "apri'" (he opened) → "apri" (open) and "e'" (is) → "e" (and), reflect a difficulty of stress assignment, as well as in reading. The same difficulty was shown when he had to use the apostrophe in the idiomatic expressions, i.e.: "l'inizio d'anno" (the beginning of year) → "linizio danno." In all these occasions he missed (7 of 7). Thus, his writing procedure was accomplished by phoneme-to-grapheme translation.

With regard to some "irregular" Italian words where the phoneme /k/ corresponds to the grapheme "q" instead of "c," (see Appendix 6.1), one must say that his performance was not consistent with our prediction of a final "surface dysgraphia." The sample is too limited to draw any conclusions, and it was not clear which code names he applied in these cases. Nevertheless, he used "cu → [Cu]neo" for the words ("cuore" (heart) and "cuoco" (cook). However, we should note that in written Italian the syllabic units /kwa/ and /kwε/, which are always written "qua" and "que," are widely diffused and no /kua/ or /kuε/ exist. Conversely, the syllabic unit /kwo/ → "quo" exists only in the case of the word "quota" (quota) and its derivatives, but /kuo/ → "cuo" exists in some Italian words. It is possible that in the case of the error "cuota," faulty phonemic analysis (/kwo/ → /kuo/) led him to use the code name Cu-neo, and conversely for "qua" and "que" he used the most frequent orthographic representation of these segments. Therefore, this result could be considered consistent with our prediction of final "surface dysgraphia" whose phoneme-to-grapheme system operates at the syllabic level.

All the results reported here agree with our reorganizational hypothesis. First, the use of the temporal single case paradigm, where the absence of spontaneous recovery can easily be demonstrated, proves the effectiveness of such a rehabilitation approach. The peculiar features of the patient's writing errors confirm that our patient writes by phoneme-to-grapheme conversion and agree with the prediction that the conversion itself operates, according to the learned strategy, mostly at the syllabic level. Finally, the strategy itself is easily applied by learning transfer to another untreated task (nonword reading).

It is true that the transparent structure of the Italian writing system has greatly facilitated our program. However, the effectiveness of a reorganizational hypothesis in the framework of current psycholinguistic models of writing and reading processes is clearly shown by our results.

GENERAL DISCUSSION

The major theoretical approach to brain function restoration by means of reorganization of fundational systems was first suggested by A. Luria. We have briefly described how such a strategy applies to writing disturbances in brain damaged people according to the Luria et al.'s (1969) formulation of the writing function. However, we have recalled that recent neuropsychological studies carried out by Sasanuma (1975), Beauvois and Dérouesné (1981), Shallice (1981), and Bub and Kertesz (1982) have clearly demonstrated that audiographic transcoding, as in the formulation of Luria et al. (1969), is insufficient to account for all writing mechanisms in normal adults. Furthermore, these studies have supplied a detailed representation of cognitive processes involved in writing and have provided considerable diagnostic tools aimed at identifying, in the context of pathology, defective and intact processes. This theoretical and clinical improvement allowed Hatfield (1982, 1984) and present authors to test the effectiveness of a reorganizational hypothesis in the treatment of writing disorders in a well-defined experimental situation. Following Seron (1984), in fact, to effect a reorganization of the processes underlying behavioral deficiencies it is necessary (a) to have a sufficiently clear picture of the processes and the manner in which they interact to produce normal function, (b) to be able to advance some plausible hypotheses aimed at identifying both defective and intact processes, and (c) that processes to which one proposes to have recourse are sufficiently efficient to permit the reappearance of the function.

Hatfield's results and those reported here were developed in the context of a detailed and widely accepted model of writing and reading functions (prerequisite a). Furthermore, in both studies analytical testings clearly assessed damaged and intact processes (prerequisite b). For instance, in the case of B.B., P.W., and D.E. (Hatfield 1982, 1984), their writing patterns displayed a marked inability to use phoneme-grapheme conversion rules and partial preservation of the direct semantic route for writing. The latter allowed them to write a number of content words. These patients on occasion wrote, instead of a function word, a content word homophonic with it. This phenomenon was considered a spontaneous strategy used to access the target function word. In this case it was considered that the homophonic content word should accomplish the role of bypassing the impaired access (prerequisite c). Therefore, a number of function words were treated following this strategy and the resulting improvement did agree with the prediction.

In our case we have supposed, according to the results of the reading and writing assessment (Carlomagno et al., 1988), that this patient has some nonlexical orthographic knowledge (i.e., grapheme-phoneme and, perhaps, phoneme-grapheme correspondences at the syllabic level). However he was unable to access this knowledge without a relay via the phonological output lexicon. A program was developed to get the patient to apply a phoneme-grapheme segmental translation by means of code names for each syllabic or subsyllabic unit of the stimulus to be written. Again, as in the case of Hatfield's work, our results do agree with the prediction: The clear single case temporal paradigm, as suggested by LaPointe (1976), proves the effectiveness of our reorganizational hypothesis. It should be recalled that, in the case of the Hatfield's work, some limitations of the experimental procedure raise the issue of the real processes underpinning the observed improvement. However, in our case, a significant learning transfer to nonword reading was observed. If one supposes that, by means of the learned strategy, the patient gains access to his still stocked orthographic knowledge, the prediction would be that the strategy could be used for nonword reading as far as it spontaneously arose in word reading. Furthermore, also relevant to the reorganizational hypothesis, if one supposes that the improvement is linked to the learned strategy, then the patient's writing errors, after training, must be consistent with the strategy itself. Quantitative results and error analysis do agree with these predictions. On the whole, these and Hatfield's data comply with the theoretical prerequisites involved in the reorganizational hypothesis (Seron, 1984) and confirm the effectiveness of such an approach to the restoration of writing disturbances.

Returning to the "state of the art" of writing rehabilitation some practical and theoretical limitations of Hatfield's experience and our own should be considered. At present we do not know the number of such selective semiologic cases to whom these analytical strategies might be applied (Seron, 1984). Although Roeltgen and Heilmann (1984) have provided evidence that lexical and phonological spelling systems can be independently disrupted by focal lesions in distinct brain regions, extensive brain damage might produce less clear semiology and add to the clinical profile disturbing symptoms. For instance, it should be recalled that our patient was nonaphasic and his phonemic discrimination and repetition abilities were quite preserved, thus constituting a major practical prerequisite for the therapy. Agrammatism, for instance, constituted a real problem in the case of Hatfield's patients and could have limited her therapeutic project.

Another serious limitation from the clinical point of view is that Hatfield's experience, as is also the case for the majority of works we have discussed, concerns writing from dictation. If writing rehabilitation is regarded as a tool for supplementing and replacing spoken language (i.e., severe Broca's aphasia), the real effectiveness of the therapy should be demonstrated in patient's spontaneous writing. On the other hand, an improvement of spontaneous writing occurred in our patient, but it was supported by a self-dictation strategy. Therefore, in the case of a severe nonfluent aphasia, the phoneme-grapheme segmental translation obtained by means of such a strategy must lack any practical interest.

Indeed, from the theoretical point of view, one can raise the issue of the number of code names (link-words in Hatfield's terminology) that a patient must store and, perhaps, to keep available to realize his writing procedure. This quantitative aspect was not experienced or discussed in Hatfield's work (1982, 1984). We directly treated about 100 code names: 70 consonant-vowel syllables plus Italian orthographic units where one phoneme is translated into two or three graphemes. In the case of diphthongs, VC, CCV, CVC, and CCCV syllables, in order not to give the patient too large a memory load, we proposed a more analytic single letter strategy. However, we have stressed that our patient consistently preferred to find a new code name by himself for most of VC, CVC, and CCV syllables. This means that the real memory load was probably smaller than we had supposed, in the sense that he did not store code names but applied an active search strategy on occasions. It was significant that he was a railway clerk, and at least nine times out of ten he preferred names of towns instead of Christian names that we had initially proposed. Furthermore, the spoken language of our patient was fluent and well articulated. This probably allowed him to spontaneously or quite easily find the appropriate code name, but one could doubt the possibility of use of such a strategy for a nonfluent aphasic patient who did not have a sufficient capacity to repeat or with word retrieval difficulties.

On the other hand, the number of code names could have been drastically reduced to the 21 letters of the Italian writing system if a strategy of code names for single letters had been used. A similar approach has been successfully applied by De Partz (1986) for the treatment of grapheme-phoneme reading in a French deep dyslexic patient. However, as described by the author, a single letter strategy requires the relearning of some orthographic rules peculiar to the patient's writing system by means of classic paedagogic methodology. Our patient was observed to master, at least for reading, orthographic competence at the syllabic level (Carlomagno et al., 1988). Therefore, we chose the syllabic unit for remediation. From the practical point of view, even if a larger number of code names was necessary, writing would perhaps have been less laborious and time consuming, and it would not have needed specific treatment for Italian orthographic rules.

It should be noted that the therapy took about 5 months, with 2 sessions a week. Furthermore, our patient's major motivation was mainly psychological because he had left his job after the cerebrovascular accident, and this motivation suddenly failed when he suffered an epileptic seizure. Thus, one might wonder whether such a strategy could easily apply to writing disturbances of an aphasic patient whose less clear semeiology and motivation might require a more intensive and prolonged treatment.

The final serious limitation for reproducing our therapeutic project arises from the peculiarities of the writing system. Italian is considered to have a very transparent writing system where one-to-one grapheme-to-phoneme correspondences are usually quite sufficient and few orthographic rules are needed. Furthermore, almost all of these rules can be predicted in the context of a single syllable. This transparent structure greatly facilitated our experimental design. This raises the issue of the possibility of applying an analogous strategy in the case of writing systems where the same regularity of spelling does not apply. For instance, the phoneme /o/ in written French has multiple graphemic correspondences such as 'o', 'eau' or 'au' whose choice cannot be predicted in a syllabic nonlexical context. Therefore, a patient should choose the correct one without any appropriate criterion. In this case, phoneme-grapheme translation, although supported by a well-defined strategy, as of lexical relay, again must lack practical interest. For instance, the treatment of T.P., the surface dysgraphic patient described by Hatfield (1984), was confined to a few correspondences. In the same way, as pointed out by Seron et al. (1980), audiographic transcoding was a strategy of limited value for their French patients.

These theoretical implications and practical limitations might claim, at least, a reevaluation of more traditional teaching methodology, such as the visuokinesthetic method described by Hatfield and Weddel (1976). However, as pointed out earlier, results that concern experimental testing of such a strategy are conflicting, and it is very difficult to reach a conclusion as to what extent the damaged brain can relearn written items. In our opinion, further experimental testing using a similar approach, perhaps with reference to the previously discussed psycholinguistic models, should be considered.

ACKNOWLEDMENTS

We are grateful to Professor R. Cotrufo for allowing us to investigate this patient. Major suggestions on the therapeutic program were

204 CARLOMAGNO AND PARLATO

kindly provided in Bressanone (January, 1984) by F. M. Hatfield. We are also indebted to C. Burani, X. Seron, G. Deloche, and J. Masterson for their helpful criticism. O.G.'s constructive and friendly cooperation is also acknowledged.

REFERENCES

Basso, A., Taborelli, A., & Vignolo, L. A. (1978). Dissociated disorders of speaking and writing in aphasia. *Journal Neurology, Neurosurgery and Psychiatry, 41,* 556–563.

Beauvois, M. F., & Dérouesné, J. (1981). Lexical or orthographic agraphia. *Brain, 104,* 21–49.

Bub, D., & Kertesz, A. (1982). Deep Agraphia. *Brain and Language, 17,* 146–165.

Carlomagno, S., Colombo, A., Iavarone, A., Buongiorno, G. C., & Parlato, V. (1988). Differenti patterns di lettura in pazienti italiani con "surface dyslexia". *Archivio Italiano di Psicologia, Neurologia e Psichiatria,* in press.

Coltheart, M., Patterson, K. E., & Marshall, J. C., Eds. (1980). *Deep dyslexia.* London: Routledge and Kegan Paul.

Coltheart, M. (1984). Writing systems and reading disorders. In Henderson, L. (Ed.), *Orthographies and reading.* Hillsdale, NJ: Lawrence Erlbaum Associates.

Deloche, G., Andreewsky, E., & Desi, M. (1982). Surface dyslexia: a case report and some theoretical implications to reading models. *Brain and Language, 15,* 11–32.

De Partz, M. P. (1986). Reeducation of a deep dyslexic patient: rationale of the method and results. *Cognitive Neuropsychology, 3,* 149–177.

De Renzi, E., & Faglioni, P. (1978). Normative data and screening power of a shortened version of the token test. *Cortex, 14,* 41–49.

Dérouesné, J., & Beauvois, M. F. (1979). Phonological processing in reading: Data from alexia. *Journal of Neurology, Neurosurgery and Psychiatry, 42,* 1125–1132.

Ellis, A. W. (1982). Spelling and writing (and reading and speaking). In Ellis, A. W. (Ed.), Normality and pathology of cognitive functions. London: Academic Press.

Gainotti, G., Caltagirone, C., Miceli, G., & Masullo, C. (1981). Selective semanticlexical impairment of language comprehension in right-brain-damaged patients. *Brain and Language, 13,* 201–211.

Hatfield, M. F., & Weddel, R. (1976). Re-training in writing in severe aphasia. In Lebrun, Y., & Hoops, R. (Eds.), Recovery in aphasics. Amsterdam: Swets and Zeitlinger.

Hatfield, M. F. (1982). Diverses formes de desintegration du language écrit et implication pour la réeducation. In Seron, X., & Laterre, C. (Eds.), Réeduquer le cerveau. Brussels: Mardaga.

Hatfield, M. F., & Patterson, K. E. (1984). Interpretation of spelling disorders in aphasia: impact of recent developments in cognitive psychology. In Rose, F. C. (Ed.), *Advances in neurology: Vol. 42. Progress in Aphasiology.* New York: Raven Press.

Hatfield, M. F. (1984). Aspect of acquired dysgraphia and implication for re-education. In Code, C., & Muller, D. J. (Eds.), *Aphasia therapy.* London: Edward Arnold Publisher.

Hatfield, M. F. (1985). Visual and phonological factors in acquired dysgraphia. *Neuropsychologia, 23,* 13–29.

Job, R., Sartori, G., Masterson, J., & Coltheart, M. (1984). Developmental surface dyslexia in Italian. In Malatesha, R. N., & Whitaker, H. (Eds.), *Dyslexia: a global issue.* The Hauge: Martinus Nijhoff Publisher.

6. WRITING REHABILITATION   205

Kay, J., & Lesser, R. (1985). The nature of phonological processing in oral reading: evidence from surface dyslexia. *Quarterly Journal of Experimental Psychology, 37A*, 39–81.

LaPointe, L. (1976). Base-10 programmed stimulation: task specification, scoring, and plotting performance in aphasia therapy. *Journal of Speech and Hearing Disorders, 42*, 90–105.

Luria, A. R., Naydin, V. L., Tsveskova, L. S., & Virnarskaya, E. N. (1969). Restoration of higher cortical function following local brain damage. In Vinken, P., & Bruyn, G. N. (Eds.), *Handbook of Clinical Neurology*, Vol. 3. Amsterdam, North Holland.

Marcel, A. J. (1980a). Surface dyslexia and the beginning reading: a revised hypothesis of the pronunciation of print and its impairments. In Coltheart, M., Patterson, K. E., & Marshall, J. C. (Eds.), *Deep Dyslexia*. London: Routledge and Kegan Paul.

Marcel, A. J. (1980b). Phonological awareness and phonological representation: investigation of a specific spelling problem. In Frith, U. (Ed.), *Cognitive processes in spelling*. London: Academic Press.

Margolin, D. I. (1984). The neuropsychology of writing and spelling: semantic, phonological, motor, and perceptual processes. *The Quarterly Journal of Experimental Psychology, 36*, 459–489.

Marshall, J. C., & Newcombe, F. (1973). Patterns of paralexia: a psycholinguistic approach. *Journal of Psycholinguistic Research, 2*, 175–199.

Miceli, B., Gainotti, G., Caltagirone, C., & Masullo, C. (1980). Some aspects of phonological impairment in aphasia. *Brain and Language, 11*, 159–169.

Morton, J. (1980). The logogen model and the orthographic structure. In Frith, U. (Ed.), *Cognitive processes in spelling*. London: Academic Press.

Pizzamiglio, L., & Roberts, M. (1967). Writing in Aphasia: a learning study. *Cortex, 3*, 250–257.

Roeltgen, D. P., & Heilman, K. M. (1984). Lexical agraphia, further support for the two system hypothesis of linguistic agraphia. *Brain, 107*, 811–827.

Sasanuma, S. (1975). Kana and Kanji processing in Japanese aphasics. *Brain and Language, 3*, 369–383.

Seron, X., Deloche, G., Moulard, G., & Rousselle, M. (1980). A computer based therapy for the treatment of aphasic subjects with writing disorders. *Journal of Speech and Hearing Disorders, 45*, 45–58.

Seron, X. (1984). Reeducation strategies in neuropsychology: cognitive and pragmatic approaches. In Rose, F. C. (Ed.), *Advances in neurology: Vol. 42. Progress in aphasiology*. New York: Raven Press.

Shallice, T., Warrington, E. K. (1980). Single and multiple component central dyslexic syndromes. In Coltheart, M., Patterson, K. E., & Marshall, J. C. (Eds.), *Deep dyslexia*. London: Routledge and Kegan Paul.

Shallice, T. (1981). Phonological agraphia and the lexical route in writing. *Brain, 104*, 413–429.

Shallice, T., Warrington, E. K., & McCarthy, R. (1983). Reading without semantics. *Quarterly Journal of Experimental Psycholygy, 35A*, 111–138.

206 CARLOMAGNO AND PARLATO

Appendix 6.1 Written Responses (Writing from Dictation)

Section A reports written responses of pretherapy (May 1983) and posttherapy assessment (July 1985) to the dictated stimuli from the controlled writing list.

Section B reports written responses to the dictated stimuli from a list for qualitative assessment (July 1985). These stimuli were mixed with the other stimuli of the posttherapy assessment. Because of the peculiarities of the Italian writing system, widely discussed in the text, no phonological transcriptions are reported.

APPENDIX 6.1
Written Responses (Writing from Dictation)

Section A Stimulus	Responses of May 1983	Responses of July 1985
sole (sun)	+	+
persona (person)	pana	+
momento (moment)	pamento	+
buono (good)	bono	+
ultimo (last)	+	
fare (to do)	rafe	+
sapevo (I know)	+	
come (how)	+	
durante (during)	catende	+
amico (friend)	+	+
giorno (day)	giongo	+
ragione (reason)	ganone	
caro (dear)	+	+
giovane (young)	vebente	+
dice (he says)	cice	+
capire (to	capere	+
understand)		+
poco (few)	coppo	+
nessuno (nobody)	tessuno	+
valvola (valve)	valvana	+
ozio (leisure)	ozino	
pudore (decency)	rutore	
vano (vain)	+	+
rotondo (round)	gostinte	+
spara (he shoots)	+	
sputare (to spit)	supare	
salve (hello)	+	imvano
invano (vanly)	anvano	+
ciocca (tuft)	cacca (dirt)	ciliega
ciliegia (cherry)	cigia	rongo
rango (rank)	rancio (ration)	
canone (canon)	+	+
goffo (clumsy)	foffo	+

(continued)

APPENDIX 6.1
(Continued)

Section A Stimulus	Responses of May 1983	Responses of July 1985
cinico (cynical)	ginico	+
corro (I run)	+	+
leggevo (I read)	legivo	quassu
quassù (up here)	ussù	
sebbene (although)	abente	+
durto (non-word)	rutio	+
mafo (non-word)	zafo	+
suno (non-word)	sunso	umo
fareco (non-word)	rarevo	+
aldiamo (non-word)	altano	+
ludare (non-word)	sutanle	+

Section B Stimulus	Responses
aprii (I opened)	apri (you open)
parlò (he talked)	parlo (I talk)
aprì (he opened)	amii
quota (quota)	cuota
quadrato (square)	+
cuore (heart)	+
cuoco (cook)	+
quadro (picture)	+
questi (these)	+
quaderno (copy-book)	+
etnico (ethnic)	entico
atlante (Atlas)	+
atleta (athlete)	+
opzione (option)	opizione
riflettere (to reflect)	rifetteré
bacchette (stick)	+
giornale (newspaper)	gionale
scialle (shawl)	+
gioco (play)	+
occhio (eye)	+

208 CARLOMAGNO AND PARLATO

Appendix 6.2 Spontaneous Writing

Section A is a photograph of an original sample of the pretherapy assessment: "What do you do in the morning?" No useful transcription was possible for this sample (May 20, 1983).

Section B reports the cursive transcription of the other sample from the pretherapy assessment (May 29, 1983): "Tell me about the painting session of last Sunday." Target items, uttered by the patient himself, were recorded during his performance by the examiner and are reported in capital letters.

Section C is a photograph of the analogous posttherapy sample obtained by asking the patient: "Do you remember that two years ago you wrote about what you were doing in the morning and about a painting session? Try to write now about the same things." Target items were again recorded by the examiner. The arrows indicate his writing errors in this sample (April 2, 1985).

Appendix 6.2   Section A

APPENDIX 6.2
Section B

| Alle | ade | 6 | scanari | e | con | la | tela | | andi | sella |
| | ORE | | ? | | | | | | ANDAI | ALLA |

| scuola | a | rintrarla | | oto | | bartii | | con | i | colore | e |
| | | RITIRARLA | ALLE | OTTO | PARTII | | | | COLORI | |

| nantai | in | famfangio | a | fare | il | papigo | | orti |
| ANDAI | | CAMPAGNA | | | | PAESAGGIO | PARTII |

| aresto | | le | 6 | e | lo | consegnio | alle | 10 | antai | a |
| PRESTO | ALLE | | | | | CONSEGNAI | | | ANDAI |

| casa | e | utti | riteri | rubiti | alla | senta | anteno |
| | | TUTTI | ? | SUBITO | | SERA | ANDAMMO |

| a | vedere |

6. WRITING REHABILITATION 209

Appendix 6.2 Section C

MI ALZO ALLE SETTE, VADO IN BAGNO,
PRENDO IL PENNELO, IL SAPONE. E MI
FACCIO LA BARBA.
MA SENZA IL CONTROPELO PERCHE
MI FACCIO MALE

MI ALZO ALLE SEI PRENDO LA TELA
E LA "CASCETTA" (COME SI DICE A NAPOLI)
DEI COLORI E VADO A FARE UN
PAESAGGIO DI CAMPANIA.
IL GIORNO DOPO SI FA LA PREMIAZIONE
E SE IL PRIMO (RA) CLASSIFFCATO PIGLIA
IL PRIMO PREMIO IL QUALE E RISULTATO
IL SOTTOSCRITTO

7 Coordination of Two Reorganization Therapies in a Deep Dyslexic Patient with Oral Naming Disorder

Noëlle Bachy-Langedock
Unité de Neuropsychologie Expérimentale de l'Adulte (NEXA),
Bruxelles, Belgium

Marie-Pierre de Partz
Centre de Revalidation Neuropsychologique; Cliniques Universitaires
Saint-Luc, Bruxelles, Belgium

In this chapter, we describe the reeducational strategies applied with a patient presenting a deep dyslexia (de Partz, 1986) and an oral naming disorder. The therapy of naming had the peculiarity of being dependent in its execution on the improvement obtained in reading therapy. For this reason, we will present the analyses, hypotheses, and therapeutic programs carried out by two different therapists for both disorders.

A considerable amount of clinical description and theoretical discussion on acquired reading disorders has followed the publication of the works of Marshall and Newcombe (1966, 1973, 1980). After this fundamental study, different reading disorders were described in terms of specific alterations in the architecture of a multicomponent processing system underlying normal reading behavior rather than in physiopathological (Benson, Brown, & Tomlinson, 1971; Hécaen, 1967) or linguistic (Dubois, 1971) terms. Most of these models admit the coexistence of at least two distinct and generally noninteractive routes in converting a written word into a sound form. The *lexical* procedure would be responsible for the treatment of familiar words. After visual analysis, familiar words are categorized in the visual logogen system and then addressed to the cognitive system where they receive semantic characterization. This process is followed by activation of the corresponding phonological code previous to the verbal output. The *nonlexical procedure* would be used for the treatment of unfamiliar words (nonwords and uncommon words). As in the lexical procedure, the letter string first receives a visual analysis.

211

Because it does not belong to the reader's internal lexicon, systematic conversion rules are used for the pronunciation of letters and groups of letters.

Among these models, the logogen model of Morton (1980) and its subsequent versions (1982, 1984) (Figure 7.1) have become classic. In its present form, it postulates the existence of three different routes to account for normal reading activity: Two direct routes insure transformation of the written form into a sound form without phonic mediation and with or without semantic mediation depending on the route; the indirect route allows access to a sound form by means of the application of a number of conversion rules for letters or groups of letters.

To describe and to interpret the anomic disorder of our patient and to justify the logic of the therapy, we also used Morton's naming model (1984). Using a theoretical background common to reading and naming activities had the major advantage of requiring coherence between the theoretical interpretation of both disorders. Indeed, the oral production model presented by Morton has the peculiarity of requiring different processing components in function of the entering stimuli (reading, oral naming, repetition, and spontaneous speech), and it also postulates common mental processing systems and common mental representations. For instance, Morton assumes the uniqueness of the phonological output lexicon, which puts constraints on the dissociations theoretically possible. The use of a common model for both tasks required that we interpret any disturbance occurring on the level of a process involved in both tasks by taking into account the errors observed in both tasks; conversely, when encountering errors specific to a task, we tried to identify as an underlying cause a process specific to that task or at least one that does not intervene in the other task.

In Morton's model (1984), the naming processes begin with the visual analysis of the picture or object. The results of this analysis provide data to the pictogene system, which is responsible for categorizing the pictures, collecting data on it, and recognizing it. From there, the information is sent to the cognitive system for semantic interpretation and classification. The appropriate phonological form is recovered in the next stage, the logogen output system, which itself contains the stock of phonological codes. The information is finally transmitted to the response regulator, which creates the appropriate articulatory code that allows the word to be verbalized.

In the case of our patient, S.P., a dissociation appeared between oral naming, which was defective, and a written naming, which was partially preserved. A few examples are cited in the literature of this

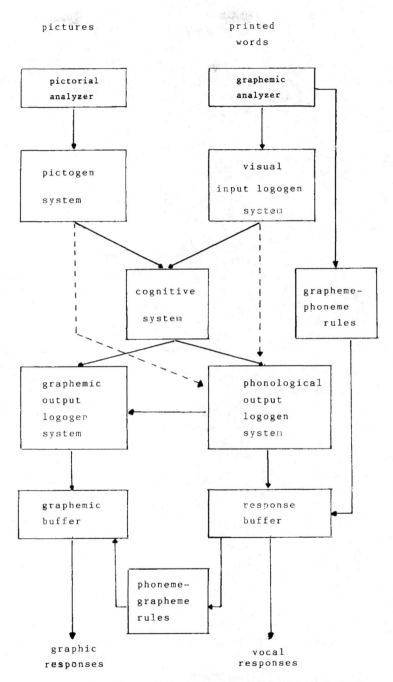

FIGURE 7.1. Schema derived from Morton's model (1980–1984).

type of dissociation (Hier & Mohr, 1977; Bub & Kertesz, 1982). These authors account for this dissociation by positing the existence of a route that permits direct conversion of the lexical information into a graphemic code. This route could be used when the connection between the lexical system and the phonological code is disturbed. This lexicographic route has been described by Ellis (1982, 1984), and we used it as a relay for oral naming.

CLINICAL CASE

Medical History

The patient, S.P., was a left-handed 31-year-old man, who was an executive in a small firm. He was admitted to our hospital after a sudden left cerebral hemorrhage. At the time of his admission, neurological examination of his sensory-motor status revealed a right hemiparesis with pyramidal signs, a right hemihypoesthesia, and a right lateral homonymous hemianopsia. Computerized tomography scans showed a major left parietotemporal intracerebral hematoma.

Neuropsychological Evolution

The first neuropsychological examination was administered two weeks after surgical evacuation of the hematoma. At this time, the patient's speech output was fluent but contained numerous phonemic paraphasias, occasional neologisms, and semantic paraphasias and evidenced severe anomia and paragrammatism. Repetitive speech was severely disturbed, the errors being mainly phonemic paraphasias or neologisms. Only isolated phonemes could be repeated correctly. Object and picture naming was impossible, but oral comprehension, though not perfect, was considerably superior to expression. In written language, the deficits were clearly more severe: The patient was completely unable to write spontaneously or from dictation, but he could copy correctly, albeit slowly. His reading was also severely impaired: The oral reading of letters and words was impossible, the majority of the responses being "no response."

The initial diagnosis was Wernicke's aphasia with total agraphia and alexia. Given the difficulties in oral expression and the initial anosognosia, the therapy concentrated initially on oral language. The subject received therapy sessions twice a day for 3 months. The objectives were to establish specific control of the phonemic deviance present in the verbal output and to improve communication efficiency (PACE therapy, Davis & Wilcox, 1981). Significant improvement in his oral language was achieved in 3 months: His fluent verbal speech output had become more informative, but paragrammatic components, word finding difficulties, and incomplete sentences were observed. Phonemic paraphasias were still present, but they were generally followed by spontaneous attempts at self-correction. Occasional semantic paraphasias occurred. At this stage he was capable of repetitive speech, but some phonemic difficulties persisted in word repetition. His oral comprehension was still superior to his expressive abilities, but clinical observation and detailed testing allowed us to identify specific disturbances. No semantic errors were observed in a short standard examination, but some difficulties were still revealed in tests examining particular semantic fields (colors, body parts, locative prepositions, days of the week, and other semantic fields involving serial relations). In these semantic fields, he performed better when the presentation was written.

Reading disorders seemed to be more structured than previously and suggested a dissociation of processes similar to that described in deep dyslexia, sparing the direct access to meaning and disturbing the transcoding process (Coltheart, Patterson, & Marshall, 1980).

Spontaneous writing was still impossible, and writing from dictation gave rise to "no response" or to jargonagraphia.

Nevertheless, it is important to note that S.P. was able to commence the written word he was not able to name orally. According to these selective impairments in reading and naming, detailed analyses were made to design a specific therapeutic program.[1]

Disorder Analysis

Reading Disorder Analysis

To verify the clinical intuition of deep dyslexia, an extensive reading examination was conducted. This complex syndrome is distinguished by the co-occurrence of symptoms, such as an incapacity to derive phonology from written nonsense words by utterance of semantic, derivational, and visual paralexias, and by difficulty in reading function words and less imageable words. All these symptoms were considered to be due to a disturbance of the visuophonological transcoding process, sparing the visual input system and the verbal output system and leaving direct access to meaning relatively undamaged.

---

[1]More information about reading analysis and reeducation can be found in *Cognitive Neuropsychology*, 1986, 3(2), pp. 149–177.

Visuophonological Transcoding Nature of the Deficit. To verify that the dyslexia was related neither to a specific (visual) mode of presentation of the stimulus nor to an oral response modality, seven single-letter processing tests were constructed with three modalities of stimulus presentation (auditory, visual, and tactilokinesthetic) and two response modalities (oral and visual). In five tests, the production of letter names was required by reading aloud letters visually presented, by reading aloud letters by means of passive kinesthetic recognition, and by repetition. In the two reading aloud tests, two written modes of printing were compared (hand-written small letters in script form and capital letters in print form). In the two other tests, a non-verbal response was required: In an auditory-visual test, the patient was asked to point to the letter named by the examiner on a board containing the entire alphabet. In a visuo-verbal test, the patient was asked to match physically dissimilar letters (lower-case handwritten letters and upper-case printed letters). The results showed that letters could not be read correctly whatever the modality of stimulus presentation or of response (Figure 7.2).

When S.P. made errors in the reading aloud tasks and in the visual pointing tasks, the letters uttered or pointed to had no visual similarity to the letter stimuli. In the letter matching test, the correct

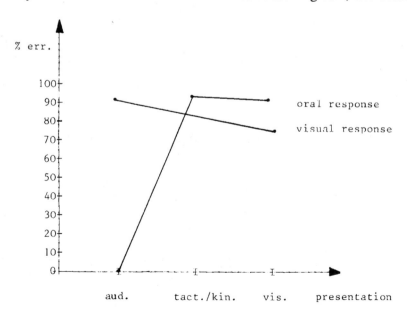

FIGURE 7.2. Percentages of errors according to the three modalities of stimulus presentation.

responses in six cases concerned letters having some visual similarities in the two typographies (e.g., o-O, c-C, k-K, t-T, u-U, x-X). Such poor performance in these tasks is unusual among deep dyslexics, for they can normally do this matching easily (Saffran & Marin, 1977). However, there is one report of a patient who could read words but could not match across letter case and type (AR- Warrington & Shallice, 1979). In spite of this matching difficulty, S.P. showed no dissociation between visual and kinesthetic afferences as do agnosic alexics. Thus, his reading disorder did not involve the modality of letter presentation. Nor was the response modality the cause since at this time S.P. could repeat all the letters perfectly.

Lexical Route in Reading. In lexical decision tasks, deep dyslexic patients are expected to have preserved their ability to categorize linguistic stimuli as words and nonwords, even if nonwords differ by only one letter from words (Patterson, 1979) and even if nonwords are homophones of real words (Patterson & Marcel, 1977).

The lexical task administered to the patient contained 80 items, 40 words and 40 nonwords. The nonwords were of four types (10 nonwords of each type): Nonwords having an illegal phonotactic and graphotactic structure in French (e.g., DIRTZ, /dirts/), nonwords having an acceptable structure (e.g., PUKO, /pykɔ/), nonwords visually similar to words (e.g., BUNE, /byn/- DUNE (dune)), and nonwords that were homophones of real words (e.g., KOK, homophone with COQ, cock). In all the cases, the items were handwritten.

On the whole, the error percentage in the lexical decision task was slightly higher (18%) than what is usually reported. Errors were found in nonwords visually similar to words and could have been due to frequent metathesis of adjacent pairs of letters (e.g., LIRVE, /lirv/) leading to confusion with existing words (LIVRE, book). Within the framework of the dual reading models, authors assume that isolated use of the lexical route in reading would prevent the patient from reading linguistically meaningless material, for reading it would require the derivation of phonology from print. Thus, the patient would present important difficulties in reading isolated letters and nonwords.

In the reading aloud tasks, the results showed that letters could not be read correctly whatever the modality of stimulus presentation (visual or tactile) or response (oral or visual). An important dissociation came to light between words and nonwords, 45% and 93% errors, respectively, when the patient had to read words and nonwords, a test previously presented in the lexical decision task (Figure 7.3).

Other relevant stimulus dimensions were introduced to clarify the

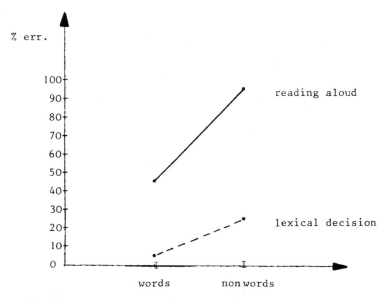

FIGURE 7.3. Percentages of errors in the lexical decision task and in reading aloud words and nonwords.

lexical involvement in reading aloud: The effects of the part of speech, the imageability dimension, and frequency of use. The length and regularity of spelling were expected to have no effect on the deep dyslexic performance (Patterson, 1981, 1982). These lexical variables were investigated by means of four tests. The first test (Figure 7.4) contrasted content words to function words (pronouns, prepositions, and conjunctions) matched for length and frequency of use as far as possible. For the 26 function words, a distinction was made between function words that were not homographs or homophones of content words (e.g., CHACUN, each; CHEVEU, hair), function words that were not homographs but were homophones of content words (e.g., IL, he; ILE, island), and function words that were homophones and homographs of content words (e.g., CAR, because or bus according to the context).

The second test (Figure 7.5) consisted of 70 words and compared different grammatical categories: nouns, adjectives, adverbs, prepositions, pronouns, and verbs (infinitives and finite forms). The results indicated a clear effect of part of speech on S.P.'s performances: In the first test, the error percentage for function words (89%) was greatly superior to that for content words (49%); in the second test, he scored better with nouns than with any of the other grammatical classes.

7. COORDINATION OF TWO THERAPIES   219

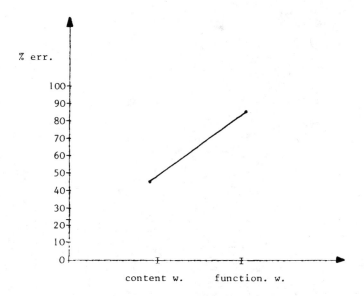

FIGURE 7.4. Percentages of errors in reading aloud content and functional words.

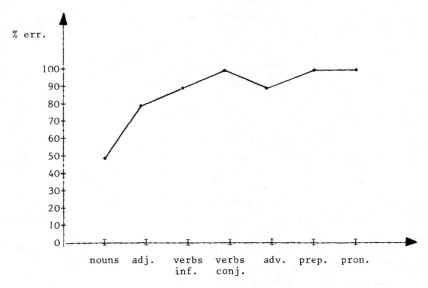

FIGURE 7.5. Percentages of errors in reading aloud single words according to part of speech.

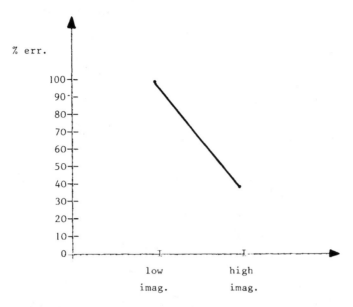

FIGURE 7.6. Percentages of errors in testing imageability dimension in reading aloud.

In the third test (Figure 7.6), high imagery words were compared to low imagery words. Imagery and concreteness dimensions often have a positive effect on the performance of deep dyslexics. Twenty words matched for length and frequency of use were chosen from the two extreme categories of a French list (Hogenraad & Orianne, 1981) (e.g., low imagery word: CAS (case) and high imagery word: EAU [water]). A clear effect of imagery was observed: The patient was unable (0%) to read the low imagery words but he could read correctly 60% of the high imagery words.

The fourth test compared regular words with irregular words (Beauvois & Derouesné, 1981). The irregular word list contained phoneme-grapheme mappings, which are exceptional in French (for example, the French word AUTOMNE (autumn), in which the letter M is irregularly pronounced as /n/). This test consisted of 15 items of each category and were matched for length and frequency of use. No significant difference between regular words (67%) and irregular words (74%) was observed.

The error rates for lexical words from this test seemed to be slightly higher than those for lexical words from the test opposing functional lexical words. This disparity could be explained by the lower frequency of some regular and irregular words and indicated an effect of the frequency of use on the patient's reading.

7. COORDINATION OF TWO THERAPIES   221

In the reading aloud tests, a qualitative analysis of types of errors according to Coltheart's (1980) criteria was made. The majority of errors were "no responses" (42%); the others were semantic (12%), visual (8%), derivational (7%) or function word substitutions (3%) (Table 7.1).

S.P.'s written comprehension was tested by means of two different tasks: a picture-written word matching task and an odd-word-out test. The picture matching task contained two subtests: In the first, a semantic matching test (nine items), the patient pointed to the picture corresponding to a printed word stimulus on a board containing several pictures, the distractors being semantically related to the target (e.g., printed word HIVER (winter) was used with a response set of pictures representing summer, winter, autumn, and spring). In the second subtest, the derivational matching test, the distractors were of a derivational nature (e.g., for the printed word PLUMAGE (plumage), the response set was (pictures) plume (feather), plumier (pen-tray), plumage (plumage), and plumeau (feather-broom).

TABLE 7.1
Examples of Types of Errors in Reading Aloud

a) No responses (59%)

b) Semantic Errors (17.5%)
   CERCLE (circle)—"rond" (round)
   SECOND (second)—"C'est le deux" (it's two)
   JEUNESSE (youth)—"scout" (boy scout)
   RIVIERE (river)—"barque . . . rame" (boat . . . string)
   DEMAIN (tomorrow)—"mercredi" (Wednesday)
                        (the following day was in fact Wednesday)
   CEDRE (cedar)—"olivier" (olive tree)
   TUILE (tile)—"brique" (brick)
   VISAGE (face)—"figure" (figure)

c) Visual Errors (10.5%)
   PAGNE (loincloth)—"page" (page)
   COUDE (elbow)—"coudre" (to sew)
   GRAVE (serious)—"gravier" (gravel)
   CHEZ (among)—"chef" (chief)

d) Derivational Errors (9.5%)
   JOURNEE (day)—"journal" (newspaper)
   OUVERTE (opened)—"ouvrir" (to open)
   JAMBE (leg)—"jambon" (ham)
   FIN (end)—"fini" (ended)

e) Function Words Substitutions (3.5%)
   TOI (you)—"nous" (we)
   NOTRE (our)—"nous . . . il" (we . . . he)

According to Patterson (1979), deep dyslexic patients demonstrate relatively impaired comprehension of written nouns, for she observed few errors in a picture matching test (Peabody) and more errors in a synonym test. Affixed words would induce more derivational paralexias in reading aloud and would disturb comprehension.

In the second test, the patient was asked to locate the semantically irrelevant word on a list of six words (Albert, Yamadori, Gardner, & Howes, 1973). Two types of lists were constructed: In the first type (10 lists), the irrelevant word was unrelated to the five other words; in the second type (also 10 lists), there were visual resemblances between one of the five words and the irrelevant word (e.g., AIGUILLE (needle), the irrelevant word in a list of fish names, could be visually confused with ANGUILLE (eel)).

In matching semantically similar words, a considerable number of mistakes were observed (45%). Paralleling the results of the reading aloud task, S.P. had difficulties in matching derivational words (89%). In an odd-out test, he was unable to point to the unrelated word, when this was visually similar to a word semantically expected in the test. Thus, there was obvious written comprehension impairment.

In conclusion, it was clear that S.P. presented a severe reading impairment if we took into account the 72% error rate on the reading aloud battery as a whole. As concerns the influence of linguistic and cognitive parameters on his reading efficiency, the patient was particularly sensitive to the meaningfulness of the stimuli, to the degree of imagery, and to the frequency of use. However, the length of the words and regularity of spelling did not influence his performance. Reading errors consisted in "no response", semantic, visual, and derivational paralexias, and functional substitutions. Written word comprehension was disturbed by morphological and semantic confusions.

This symptomatology corresponds well to the classic picture of deep dyslexia and was due to significant impairment of visuophonological transcoding and partial alteration of direct access to meaning.

Naming Disorder Analysis

Oral Naming Assessment. To make this assessment, we used an oral naming battery that tested the incidence of various parameters described in the literature as acting either positively or negatively in the naming task (Kremin & Koskas, 1984; Williams, 1983).

The oral naming general battery consisted of 108 black and white drawn items matching the variables of frequency and length of the words. The frequency levels taken into account (Vikis-Freibergs's table, 1974) were: frequent words (occurrence of 20 or more in 125,000 words), moderately frequent words (occurrence between ten and two times in 125,000 words), and unusual words (no occurrence in the 125,000 words). Three word lengths were selected: one, two, and three syllables.

On this general naming battery, S.P. scored 52% correct responses. The errors were distributed among 40% no responses, 29% phonemic approaches, 19% graphemic approaches, and 12% semantic paraphasias (Figure 7.7). When there were several false productions for the same item, only the first one was taken into account in the analysis. As can be seen in Figure 7.8, most of the difficulties occurred on items of low frequency and on items of more than one syllable. The error rates show significant statistical differences between the extreme frequencies and lengths (low/high frequency: $\chi^2 = 14.2, P < .001$; one syllable/three syllable length: $\chi^2 = 6.7, P < .01$). As indicated in Figure 7.7, the

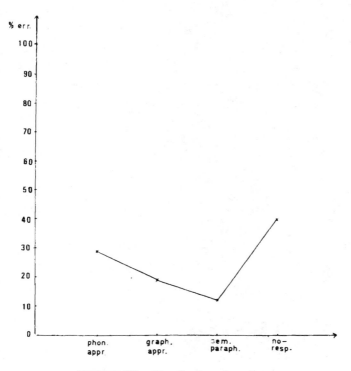

FIGURE 7.7. Distribution of error types.

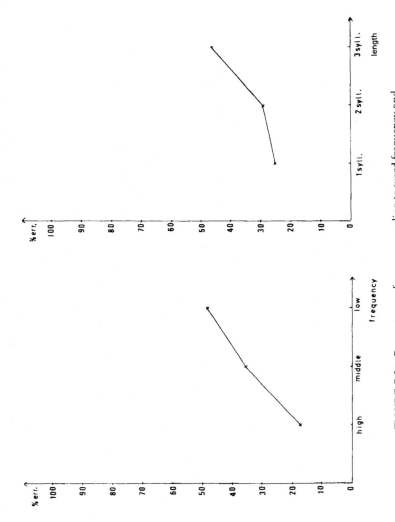

FIGURE 7.8. Percentages of errors according to word frequency and word length.

7. COORDINATION OF TWO THERAPIES   225

rate of the no responses predominates over the other errors, especially for long words.

A graphemic approach was counted as often as the patient tried to write down the name of the object. This occurred for 18% of the items. A third of these productions were correct, but they could not always be used by the patient because of his reading difficulties.

The phonemic approaches found in naming were also present in other oral tasks such as spontaneous speech and repetition. It has been reported for some conduction aphasics that the rate of appearance of phonemic approaches is lower in reading (Lecours & Lhermitte, 1979). The semantic paraphasias were infrequent and were near the target in the semantic field.

Table 7.2 shows these different types of errors. For example, confronted by the picture of a tram (tram) the patient adequately wrote the name but failed to read it and said "metro" (underground). This semantic error was probably the result of the lexicosemantic reading procedure even if a phonemic and morphologic similarity was also present in this case.

With regard to the reading skills, we see that the error rate noted in naming task is similar to the reading error rate. In both tasks, the no responses are more frequent, and the semantic errors, though present, are less frequent. The error rate noted in picture naming is

TABLE 7.2

Examples of Picture Naming Productions (Oral Naming or, in the Case of a Nonoral Response, Graphemic Naming)

Verbal Semantic Paraphasias

Target items		*Responses*	
arrosoir	(watering can)	"pomme"	(rose)
évier	(sink)	"bassin"	(basin)
jambon	(ham)	"cochon"	(pig)

Phonemic Paraphasias

Target items		*Responses*
cosmonaute	(astronaut)	[kastramot]
cadenas	(padlock)	[kalma]
hélicoptère	(helicopter)	[elisɔtɛr]

Literal or Morphological Paraphasias (I;2)
Written naming misread (3)

Target items		*graphemic approaches*	*reading attempts*	
éléphant	(elephant)	ELEPH	[elefãsɔ]	(1)
caravane	(caravan)	CARANTE	?	(2)
tram	(tram)	TRAM	[metrɔ]	(3)

also comparable with the reading aloud error rate for the items with a high mental imagery level.

It should also be noted, as is frequently reported with regard to conduction aphasia, that the phonemic approximation error rate is greater in naming than in reading. Unlike in reading, where it has no influence, the length (i.e., the number of syllables) has a negative effect on the oral naming skills.

With regard to writing, we have noted that the patient sometimes produced written responses (incompletely or totally) upon seeing a picture he could not name orally. This production is striking in view of the virtually complete inability of the patient to write spontaneously or from dictation. Other authors (Hier & Mohr, 1977) have also reported patients with oral naming and written naming dissociation.

The battery testing the effect of different "cues" or "prompts" contained six series assessing the efficiency of six different cues proposed in cases of misnaming. These cues were as follows:

1. A phonemic and semantic cue (e.g., "fouetter" (to whip) for the item fouet (whip))
2. A phonemic final cue (e.g., /lɛt/ for the item squelette (skeleton))
3. A graphemic initial cue (e.g., P for the item pyramide (pyramid) or PY for this same item)
4. A phonemic initial cue (e.g., /s/ for the item cimetière (cemetery) or /si/ for this same item)
5. An oral contextual cue (e.g., "un noeud de . . ." (to knot one's . . .) for the item cravate (neck-tie))
6. A cue by definition (e.g., a small, white flower, offered May 1 for the item muguet (lily of the valley))

The results obtained by the patient on this battery confirm the predominant efficacy of a graphemic initial cue in the form of the first syllable. When the patient failed to name, giving him the first written syllable of the word induced the word in 83% of cases. It must be noted that the cue was never the real prefix of the target word. The highest efficacy was observed for the contextual and semantic cues, but they cannot be taken into account because they appeared in too few items. Table 7.3 summarizes the results.

The efficacy of cuing with the first written syllable may seem paradoxical in view of the patient's difficulties in reading isolated letters and nonsignificant syllables in the reading set. The condition re-

TABLE 7.3
Efficiency of Cues

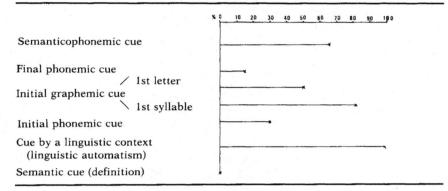

ported here, however, differs from the classic reading condition as information is given simultaneously by the target picture. The decoding asked for by the cuing letter or the cuing syllable could be assisted by the picture presentation.

Beyond this general naming set, we tested the patient with two different phonological sets. These sets consisted of monosyllabic items and was based partly on the work of Zaidel and Peeters (1981) and on the work of Bub and Kertesz (1982). These sets of items attempt to assess the residual internal phonological representation, without oral production by the patient.

The first part tested the phonological representation underlying pictures, written words, or written nonwords. These different types of stimuli were presented in five tests. Each test had 20 series, 10 series for the processing of homophones and 10 for the processing of rhymes and alliterations. Distractor phonemic and semantic items were also included, for example

1. Find the homophones among four drawings cor (horn), corps (body), flûte (flute), and nord (north) (Figure 7.9).
2. Find the homophone of the word sel (salt) among three drawings selle (stool), poivre (pepper), cercle (circle).
3. Find the homophones among four written words BAR (bar), BARRE (rod), VERRE (glass), BARBE (beard).
4. Find the homophones among four nonwords THAIR /tɛr/, TERE /Tɛr/, THAR /tar/, TIERE /tjɛr/.
5. Find the homophone of the nonword NEUX /nø/ among the drawings noeud (Knot), nez (nose), yeux (eyes).

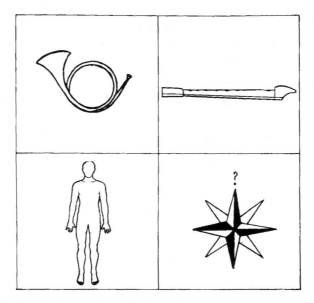

FIGURE 7.9. Examples of the phonological representations underlying four pictures.

The second part of the phonological battery tested phonological representation of oral stimuli. Four tests, each of them consisting of either 20 or 30 items, involved processing homophones, rhymes, and alliterations. Distractor semantic and/or phonemic items were also included in the tasks. The stimuli were either drawings, words, or nonwords, each being either written or oral, such as:

1. Find among three drawings, carte (playing card), cage (cage), and livre (book), the word that rhymes with /paʒ/ (Figure 7.10).
2. Decide about the homophony of two pronounced items /pɛ̃/ /bɛ̃/.
3. Find the homophone of the word /fɑ̃/ among three written words FAON (fawn) VENT, (wind), FOIN (hay).
4. Find the homophone of the nonword /viʃ/ among three written nonwords VICHE /viʃ/ VIJE /viʒ/ JICHE /ʒiʃ/.

The results indicated that S.P. treated successfully the phonological representation underlying the monosyllabic words. The following assumption can then be made: Without being able to pronounce the name of some pictures, S.P. probably preserved some information

FIGURE 7.10. Examples of the phonological representations underlying an oral word and three pictures (find on basis of the rhyme).

related to the spoken form of the word. This assumption was valid at least for the monosyllabic[2] words and had to be related to their superiority on polysyllabic words in the oral naming task.

Synthesis and Therapeutic Assumptions. These data on naming have to be situated within the schema derived from Morton's model (1984) and compared with the reading deficits.

With regard to picture processing, the patient's visual analysis seemed to be very adequate, and the pictures seemed to have been identified. The content of the periphrases and the comments made by the patient revealed good recognition of the depicted object. Furthermore, in other investigations of object matching with different visual and/or functional variables, the results indicated the absence of visual agnosia (investigations with agnosia tests in use in our unit). In addition, we noted no visuosemantic errors (Bishop & Byng, 1984). Thus, S.P. could probably apprehend the relevant features in the pictures and could identify the stimuli.

Semantic paraphasias were rare and were in the target semantic field (e.g., with the picture of a tire-bouchon (corkscrew), the patient

---

[2]At the time of the observations, we did not have a set checking polysyllabic phonological representations.

said "vin" (wine) "bouteille" (bottle)). Frequently, the incorrect semantic productions were recognized to be wrong by the patient, and he would then try another production, for example, with the picture of a arrosoir (watering can), the patient said "pomme" (rose) and then said "no, it is not;" with the picture of a faon (fawn) he said "paon" (peacock) and then said "no it is not" and wrote FA, the first two letters of the target.

Accordingly, for pictured and concrete stimuli, the semantic categorization could be assumed to be almost undamaged. This integrity was also indicated by the dissociation observed in some productions. The example of the picture of a verre (glass), simultaneously orally named /vɛ̃/ (wine) and written verre (glass), showed that the patient comprehended the semantic information.

With regard to the phonological representations, some data are stressed here because they were be used for the interpretation of the disorder. The phonological results attested to the patient's ability to access the phonological representations of most words, at least the monosyllables. However, the examination of the phonemic approximation sequences in the way proposed by Valdois, Joanette, & Nespoulous (1986, see appendix) indicated a high incomplete representation rate. This rate is higher (77%) for the three- or four-syllable words than the bisyllabic words rate (43%). A specific analysis of the utterances showed that the first syllable was nearly as often correct in both word types (for the three- and four-syllable words, 55% correct first syllables; for the bisyllabic words, 63% adequate first syllable).

Particular for the long words was their provocation of many "no response." For these words, the initial syllabic graphemic prompt was often the only one effective. The analysis also indicated good segmental content preservation (emitted target phoneme maintenance) from one approximate sequence to the other. For the long words (three syllables and more) as well as for the bisyllabic words, the patient maintained in most cases the target phonemes up to the last attempt (78% and 86% of the cases, respectively).

S.P. had no any arthric difficulties; his errors were phonemic but not phonetic (in the sense defined by Lecours and Lhermitte 1979). The phonemes were separately well realized with regard to their articulation features, but their seriation was inadequate. The phonemical distortions were not constant; they appeared in the oral naming task but not in other oral tasks like reading aloud.

After this description of the main processing components of naming let us recall that the patient had at this task an error rate of 48%. For 19% of the cases, he could use written naming. This was complete and correct for 30% of the cases, incomplete but correct for 60% of the

7. COORDINATION OF TWO THERAPIES   231

cases, the last 10% being paragraphias. Note, too, for anomia, that graphemic initial cues were the best facilitation in the form of the first written word syllable. This cue was effective for 83% of the cases.

These data indicate that a differentially located deficit could be assumed. For some long words, the deficit could be situated on the level of access to the phonological representation or on the level of this phonological representation itself. However, when the phonological representation was intact, the difficulty could be situated in the phonemic assembly stage, as suggested by the less frequent phonemic approaches in reading aloud than in spontaneous speech and oral repetition. In reading one may suppose that the assembly process found elements for sequentialization in the written support. The written naming residual capacities led us to assume that access to graphemic representation was relatively better preserved than access to phonemic representation. These representations nonetheless remained insufficient and incomplete. The skill improvement in using graphemic cues in cases of oral misnaming argued for an oral naming therapeutic program with a written relay. The therapy was planned to make use of the superiority of the graphemic representations access and to induce a cue for sequentialization.

The patient was asked to visualize the word's written form and to use this mental representation as a support for the production of the oral equivalent.

Stimulation and preliminary training on paper for the written production was a necessary requisite, first to automate the relay and then to verify the adequacy of the written form, which could be partial or complete. As the written form produced had to be decoded and then uttered aloud, the oral naming therapy was subordinate to the reading therapy; it was started only when a minimal grapheme decoding made it possible to decode the mental image of the written word.

Reeducation

Reading Reeducation

The reading therapy aimed at reorganizing the grapheme-phoneme transcoding process. The strategy was to use the patient's residual knowledge and, more specifically, his spared lexical knowledge as a relay between simple and complex graphemes and their pronunciation.

The program was thus divided into three main stages: reconstructing simple grapheme reading, reconstructing complex grapheme reading, and learning graphemic contextual rules.

Stage 1: Reconstructing Simple Grapheme reading. The first step of stage one was association letters /lexical code/ phonological code. During the three months preceding the therapy, some interesting incidental observations were made. For example, although the patient was totally incapable of reading letters aloud, he did seem able to associate some letters with some familiar words (i.e., the letter C was associated with his wife's name "Carole"). Such spontaneous responses have been reported by Hatfield (1982) in a deep dysgraphic patient and by Funnel (1983) in a case of phonological dyslexia. The first step in the therapy consisted of expanding these spontaneous responses. For each letter, a lexical relay code was established that associated the sight of a letter with the verbalization of a word.

The training sessions were then devoted to teaching these visuolexical associations by presenting written letters as stimuli, the patient's responses being the word codes (A: "Allo", B: "Bébé", C: "Carole", etc.). The process was laborious, and only after 52 sessions (five half-hour sessions a week) were the associations firmly established.

The second step was association of letters with the first phonemes of the word codes. Once the word code associations had become completely automatic, the second step was then to associate the sight of the letter with the first phoneme of the word code. To do this, the patient was asked to stress the word code's first phoneme by emphasizing and lengthening his emission. Thus, when confronted with the letter A, the patient said "Aaallo" and was then asked to say only the first phoneme /a/. This procedure of accentuating the first phoneme and then its splitting was mastered relatively rapidly by the patient, but he had more difficulty with stop consonants (P-T-K-B-D-G), which are not continuous. More exercises were necessary to automate the isolation of such phonemes, and a tendency to associate the written letter with the first syllable was often observed (e.g., D was said /de/ instead of /d/). After 3 months of such exercises, the sight of a letter automatically generated the word code followed by the production of the first phoneme. The patient was then asked to fade the vocal production of the word code and to speak only the required phoneme (e.g., F: "France" (silent) -/f/ aloud). He was then able to produce isolated correct phonemes in response to stop consonant letters. At this step of the therapy, if the patient vocalized an incorrect phoneme, he was asked to return to the vocal production of the word code, but this was rarely necessary. Note that several letters have more than one pronunciation in French depending on the context. For instance, the letter C is pronounced /k/ when it is followed by the vowels A, O, and U, and /s/ when followed by E and I. At this step of the program, the most frequent pronunciation was selected, so the letter C was associated with the word code "Carole" and, thus the phoneme /k/.

The third step was letter reading in nonwords and regular words. The paradox of the therapy took place at this stage: After having used a lexical code based on the patient's lexical knowledge for the reorganization of isolated letter reading, we inhibited his attempts to read by direct access to the signification by having him first read nonwords. We hoped to prevent any use or interference of direct semantic access processing reading and to reinforce the obligation of recourse to analytical processing. The exercises were performed with nonwords. The patient was asked to pronounce separately each of the phonemes corresponding to the different letters of the nonwords and then to try to combine these phonemes in a simple oral production (e.g., Allo -/a/ . . /k/ . . /ɔ/ then /akɔ/).

After these exercises, short words were introduced that were selected so that their pronunciation could easily result from the concatenation of single-letter reading. At this step, it was stressed that it was necessary to maintain analytical reading. Nevertheless, for some content words, the patient continued to produce semantic paralexias. To prevent such interference and to reinforce the obligation of recourse to analytical processing, the patient was asked to say the word code of the first letter of the content word before reading aloud the intended word (e.g., for ami (friend), he first said "allo," the word code for the letter A and then /ami/).

Stage 2: Reconstructing Complex Grapheme Reading. Before this step, the patient was still unable to read the different pronunciations of the letters, and he could not apply graphemic rules. For example, he was able to read correctly the isolated letters *O* and *U* but was unable to say the correct phoneme /u/ in response to the digraph OU.

To reorganize the reading of these groups of letters, we used the "relay strategy" proposed by Hatfield (1982, 1983) for the reeducation of writing a finite group of function words in cases of deep dysgraphia. It consisted of using the patient's residual ability to write content words homophonous with functional words. In a similar vein, we used the ability of the patient to read some content words that were homophones (or almost homophones) of some frequent complex graphemes, including several letters (e.g., OU /u/ with "houx" (holly); AU /o/ with "eau" (water)). The other letter groups, having no word homophones, were associated with frequent words containing these groups to remind the patient of their pronunciation (e.g., /ɛ̃/) was associated with "lapin" (rabbit). This association recalls the lexical analogy theories (Marcel, 1980; Henderson, 1982,

1984), according to which pronunciation of a meaningless group of letters can be obtained because of activation of words containing this group. Together with the relay words, we presented corresponding pictures to avoid semantic paralexias. Nine sessions later, S.P. could read aloud the different groups of letters without pictures and without relay words. The training was checked by reading aloud nonwords and words differentiated only by the groups of letters previously learned (examples of nonwords KOURA-KOIRA-KONRA-KINRA; examples of words SON [his, its], SOU [money], SOI [himself, itself]). When he hesitated or gave an erroneous response, the patient was asked to return to the first association picture or picture name.

After 9 months of intensive therapy, the complete reading battery was readministered to the patient. He performed all the letter processing tests correctly. Thus, no difficulties remained in reading aloud letters whatever the input modality (visual or gestural), in matching physically different letters without saying their word code, or in printing letters presented orally. At this stage of the therapy, therefore, the patient could transcode each letter into its corresponding phoneme and vice versa.

Progress was evident for the rest of the battery and could be quantified by comparing the 72% error score at the pretherapeutic baseline with the present 14% error score at this point in the therapy. More interesting was the insensitivity of some variables that had characterized the initial reading disorder (Figure 7.11). The word-nonword opposition was no longer significant. The variability of performance by grammatical class tended to disappear except for conjugated verbs. A discrete effect of imagery still persisted. Furthermore, an effect of the regularity of spelling, not observed previously but characteristic of the surface dyslexia syndrome (Marshall & Newcombe, 1973), now appeared. This partial disappearance of errors classically encountered in cases of deep dyslexia was accompanied by the appearance of classes of errors unusual in this condition (Figure 7.12). Errors resulting from an erroneous application of grapheme/phoneme transcoding rules predominated. These visuophonological transcoding errors arose from:

1. insufficient automatism in transcoding some letter strings previously learned in the therapy (e.g., AI /ɛ/ in the adjective LAID [ugly] and in the verb AIDAIT [helped] could not be read)
2. the impossibility of transcoding complex graphemes not yet learned (e.g., EUIL /œj/)
3. the erroneous application of grapheme/phoneme transcoding

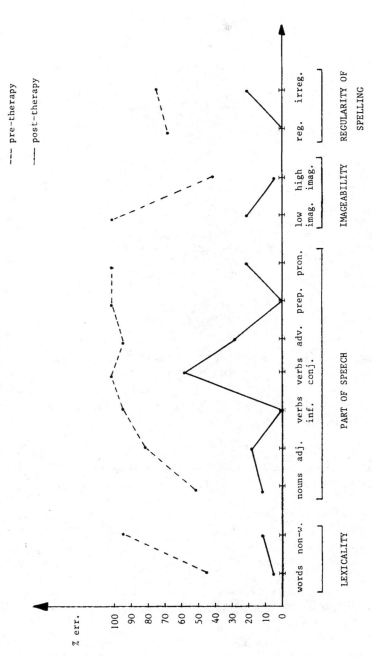

FIGURE 7.11. Intermediate therapy results according to some linguistic and cognitive variables characteristic of initial reading disorder.

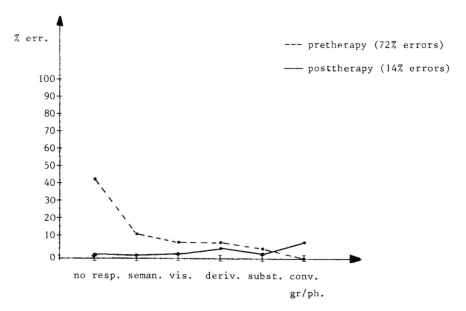

FIGURE 7.12. Distribution of error types after 6 months of reading therapy.

rules when the letter pronunciation was dependent on the context (e.g., CELLE /sɛl/ [the one] was read /kɛl/)
4. difficulties in reading words whose irregularity depended on a silent final consonant (e.g., CAS /ka/ [case] read /kas/; SECOND /səgɔ̃/ [second] read /səgɔ̃d/)

In numerous respects, these errors corresponded to what is classically described in surface dyslexia (Marshall & Newcombe, 1973; Marcel, 1980; Kremin, 1982; Deloche, Andreewsky, & Desi, 1982) and seemed to have been induced largely by the therapy, which, in reorganizing the visuophonological transcoding, was far from having exhausted the set of transcoding rules. Contrary to what may be expected in surface dyslexia, we observed that S.P. was disturbed by "homophony" variable in the lexical decision task. For the 80 items proposed, four errors were produced in response to one nonword homophone: One real word, two nonwords visually similar to French words, and one nonword having an acceptable structure in French.

In addition, his reading performance with irregular words was clearly superior to what is observed in surface dyslexia. It may be surprising that a patient trained to use a strategy of transcoding

7. COORDINATION OF TWO THERAPIES   237

grapheme-phoneme rules succeeded in reading so many irregular words. Even if the therapy had temporarily aimed at inhibiting lexical reading strategy, it was not as yet abolished. In this respect, the approximations made by S.P. are of particular interest. First, we observed that the lexical strategy would be used first when reading an irregular concrete word and permit spelling irregularities to be distorted (e.g., FEMME [woman] was read "Madame . . . non . . . c'est /f/ . . . /fam/" "Madam . . . no . . . it is /f/ . . . /fam/ [woman]"). Second, we noted that the patient also produced a few normalizations of pronunciation of irregular words by giving nonwords as a surface dyslexic would do. Third, we also observed that he would attempt to approach an irregular word analytically until he obtained a French word (an example of a correct response: PATIENT [patient] . . . /pat/ . . . /pati/ . . . /patiā/ . . . /patjās/ . . . /patjā/ . . . . /pasjā/; an example of an erroneous response SECOND [second] /sǝkɔ̃d/ . . . . non /sǝgɔ̃d/).

To eliminate the possibility that the disorder was situated on a strictly phonological level (the patient still presented phonemic paraphasias), we regularly verified his phonological processing by means of a battery derived from the work of Zaidel and Peters (1981) and described previously. The results were obvious: S.P. performed perfectly when he had to select two homonyms from pictorial material (e.g., cerf /sɛr/ [stag]; biche /biʃ/ [hind]; sel /sɛl/ [salt]; serre /sɛr/ [greenhouse]) or select two rhymes (e.g., coq /kɔk/ [cock]; oie /wa/ [goose]; phoque /fɔk/ [seal]; col /kɔl/ [neck]), but when confronted with written words and nonwords, his performance dropped to the 35% and 65%, respectively.

In these two testing situations, the patient's responses were influenced only by graphic similarities rather than by a real transcoding of rhymes and alliterations.

His written word comprehension had improved over his previous performances. The semantic matching task was correctly performed, and only one error remained in the derivational matching task: Vitrier (glazier) was confused with vitre (window pane) in the picture set vitrail (leaded glass window), vitrine (shop window), vitrier (glazier), vitre (window pane). In odd-word-out tests, S.P. still made errors in the visual resemblance condition. Error regularities led us to adjust the third stage of the therapy.

Stage 3: Relearning Contextual Graphemic Conversion Rules. The purpose here was to reinforce previous learning and to consider learning of three graphemic conversion rules accountable for the majority of the patient's errors in the previous phonological tests.

1. The conversion rules for letters C and G, their most frequent phonemic value being respectively /k/ and /g/ but changing to /s/ and /ʒ/ when appearing with vowels E or I.
2. The conversion rule of the letter S, which is pronounced most frequently /s/ but which changes to /z/ in an intervocalic position.
3. The conversion rule of the letter E, usually read /œ/ but changing to /ɛ/ in a double consonant context.

This relearning took 65 sessions and used nonwords and abstract words. After this particular training, the error rate of the reading aloud tests was 2%, the letter processing and reading comprehension tasks yielding no errors. The effects of variables, such as imagery value and regularity of spelling, that had appeared before this stage of the therapy had now disappeared. The residual errors were atypical.

At this point, the patient was able to read correctly but slowly. His reading procedures were mixed. While reading phrases, the patient had recourse simultaneously to analytical reading with grapheme-phoneme codes and to reading procedures controlled by direct access to meaning. The former was used more frequently for verbs, functional words, abstract words, and words with affixes, and the latter aided by the former, when he read concrete words and very common function words. This was indicated by differences in his reading. When S.P. read syllabically and used phonemic approaches, he was probably apprehending the word analytically, but concrete words were most often produced in one single oral emission, which, if incorrect, he would correct syllable by syllable. Thus, one may presume that the analytical procedure was used conjointly with the global process as a means of checking it.

Oral naming Reeducation

Let us now recall the basic strategy of the therapy: To create a relay using the mental visualization of the written word and to have the patient make use of this visualized written form to suggest oral production. The purpose of using an internal representation of a written word over a cue written on paper was to have the patient become more autonomous in his naming activities. Written relay transposition to daily life is indeed easier using this form. The oral naming therapy started after the first step of the reading reeducation, that is, after the reorganization of single grapheme reading. It was necessary for the patient to be able to transcode and read aloud the mental image of the written word.

In response to a stimulus to name, the patient was asked the following:

1. To construct the mental image of the word in its written form
2. To decode the written word using the code learned in the reading therapy
3. To utter the word subvocally
4. To pronounce the word aloud

The subvocalization of the word was intented to give a sequentialization cue previous to the vocal production. As noted earlier, stimulation and preliminary training for written transcription on paper had been given during the examination time, for it was necessary to make sure that the patient, upon seeing the picture, could write the corresponding word correctly, either completely or partially.

During the therapy, when the patient failed to find the mental visual written word form, real paper writing procedure was reverted to. The therapist would give him a cue in the form of the first written letter or the first written syllable of the word, which generally induced the emergence of the complete written word on paper and its letter-by-letter decoding. In some cases, this cue of the beginning of the written word was sufficient to induce the relay step; the word would then be mentally pictured and decoded. The reeducation tempo was, at this time, three sessions a week. This first therapy step took 12 weeks. At this reeducation stage, difficulties persisted for words with irregular or ambiguous writing that had not been worked on in reading therapy. The decoding step, therefore, was difficult to achieve.

Oral Naming Intermediary Results. A check of the oral naming therapy, 6 months after the first evaluation, confirmed the efficiency of the relay step.

For the general naming set, the rate of misnamed or unevoked words decreased from 49% to 16%, and the error distribution changed; the residual errors were more clearly concentrated on long words and on uncommon words (Figure 7.13). It is important to note here that the words of the battery checking set were never used during the therapy. Therefore, these results cannot be attributed to the words having been explicitly taught. Rather, the graphemic strategy for access to the phonological form was responsible for these improved results.

Some examples of naming productions at this time are presented

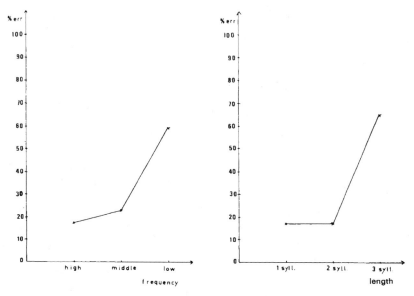

FIGURE 7.13. Distribution of errors after 3 months of naming therapy with relay use by the written word.

TABLE 7.4
Examples of Picture Naming Production After 3 Months
of Relay Therapy to the Written Words

---

a) Phonemic approaches (and, in some cases, graphemic cues)
    Target items   Responses
    bracelet (bracelet)   "[brasjɛl], [brasɛl]".
    sécateur (pruning shears)   "[ɛskatœr], (cue: S) [sekatœr]".
    araignée (spider)   " ? (cue: AR) [arɛɲe]".

b) Semantic, phonemic or literal approaches (and the "relay" by the mental image of the written word)
    Target items   Responses
    bol (bowl)   "for coffee, . . . B . . . O . . . I see the photo of the word, [bɔl]".
    kangourou (kangaroo)   "[kɔla] [kɔl rala] [kɔala]" I see the word [kãguru]".

c) Approaches by the written form and decoding
    Target items   Responses
    cerf-volant (stag beetle)   "[sɛrpãtẽ] . . . no . . . C as the first letter to write Carole . . . C . . . E . . . R".
    chronomètre (chronometer)   "the first letters to write cheval . . . CH . . . R . . . [ʃrɔ]".

7. COORDINATION OF TWO THERAPIES   241

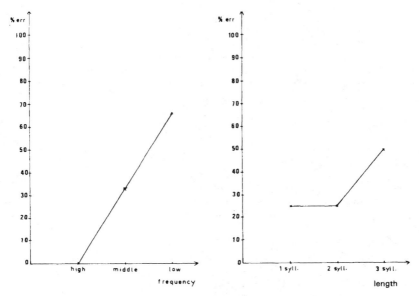

FIGURE 7.14. Distribution of errors after 6 months of naming therapy.

in Table 7.4. The examples give (a) the residual errors; (b) the cue of the first character or the first syllable given in some cases by the therapist; (c) the relay use, clearly attested by the patient ("I see the word's photo"); and (d) the use of the code introduced in reading reeducation to decode the visualized words.

Our patient was well disposed to continue this kind of therapy and frequently used the relay in his daily life conversation. Reeducation was thus continued with the same aim of intensifying the relay use and automate it in cases of oral evocation difficulties.

After 12 more weeks of therapy at the rate of three sessions a week, the assessment again showed modest improvement. The error rate on our general set had decreased to 11%. Again there were phonemic transformations as residual errors, a higher error rate on uncommon and long words (Figure 7.14), and difficulties in decoding irregular writing words (Table 7.5).

Final Assessment of the Naming Therapy. One year after the first assessment, naming was nearly normal (6% errors), and word evocation in normal conversation was good. The obvious persistent difficulties were limited to very uncommon words. To conclude the presentation of the therapy for S.P., a program synthesis is illustrated in the Figure 7.15.

242 BACHY-LANGEDOCK AND de PARTZ

TABLE 7.5
Examples of Naming Production at the Third Evaluation
after 6 Months of Relay Therapy with Written Words

Target Items		Responses
éclair	(lightning)	[ekrɛr] . . . [éclair]
xylophone	(xylophone)	[siglɔfɔn] . . .
coquelicot	(red poppy)	[kɔr] . . . [krɔl] . . . [kɔlriɔ] . . . [coquelicot]
sécateur	(pruning-shears)	[ɛskatœr] . . . [rɛskatœr] . . .
agenda	(diary)	[aʒɛrn] . . . [agnəda] . . agenda
bouquet	(bunch (of flowers)	[bɔ] . . . [bu] . . [buʃ] . . . [bouquet]

Phonemic approximations occurred on uncommon words, on graphically irregular words and on compound words

Complementary Reeducation to Improve Phonological and Graphemic Representation

Though we had assumed correct phonological representation for monosyllabic words, this assumption was dubious for long words. Therefore, complementary therapy was developed parallel with the naming therapy. We attempted to improve phonological representation by estimation tasks for rhymes or alliteration similarity with oral stimuli. Other comparison tasks of vocalized forms underlying words and pictures were also included in the programme.

In addition, spelling and spelled word reconstruction drills were administered to ensure correct graphemic representation and adequate written programming. The difficulty of these exercises was gradually increased in function of the progress in reading therapy. After the first 6 months of naming therapy and in relation to the progress obtained both in naming and in reading aloud, we continued these exercises on the word form. Though checking their specific impact was impossible, these exercises were intended to provide a secure base for the naming relay therapy.

After reading recovery for the complex or irregular writing words, we introduced other exercises: Finding words phonologically near a written proposed form, with a similarity with either the beginning or the end of the source word (e.g., find a word with a end that sounds like the end of the word FILLE); and finding words graphemically near a spoken form (e.g., to find a word the end of which is written like the written end of /vil/ or of /fij/ as pronounced). The spelling exercises and the spelled word reconstruction exercises were also made more complex by using words and nonwords with irregular or ambiguous spelling.

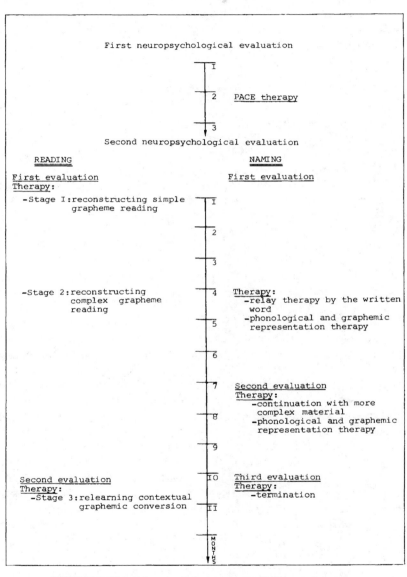

FIGURE 7.15. Schema of the progress of the two therapies.

244 BACHY-LANGEDOCK AND de PARTZ

In summary, three therapies were synchronized: Reading therapy with relay code establishment, naming therapy with the use of a graphemic relay, and a set of exercises focused on the improvement of phonological representations.

CONCLUSIONS

This analysis presents two particular patterns of disorders in the same patient: first, a deep dyslexia with an impairment in visuophonological transcoding and relative preservation of the direct access route to meaning, and second, a major difficulty in oral naming with residual capabilities in written naming. These residual abilities were exploited to design two distinct courses of therapy. To reeducate deep dyslexia, we tried to reorganize the impaired grapheme-to-phoneme process by using spared lexical knowledge as a relay between graphemes and their pronunciation. To remedy oral naming difficulties, we trained the patient to maximize his written naming abilities. An interaction between the two therapies proved necessary insofar as the use of the written relay in naming therapy required a degree of visuophonological transcoding.

This interaction was possible on the basis of a common theoretical model. In the reading and naming tasks, the patient's performances were subjected to specific analyses and comparisons to obtain logical and consistent interpretations. For instance, we observed more phonemic approach sequences in naming and spontaneous speech than in reading aloud. This difference was explained by attributing assistance in sequentialization to the written support. This observation was one of the reasons for using the written relay system in the naming therapy. The interaction among the therapies and the recourse to a single theoretical model to explain the patient's problems were possible because of the extent and the dissociation of his pathological forms of behavior. They were also the occasion for persistent interrogation. For instance, the level of disturbed processes responsible of oral naming disorders was not easy to establish and seemed to be limited to lexical variables. Our double description shows that the two therapies were complementary and were enhanced by the theoretical coherence and close collaboration among therapists.

The question remaining at the end of the therapy was whether the patient had really well automated the different relays trained.

We observed that the use of the lexical code in reading was spontaneously transferred to other linguistic activities. In some cases of incomprehension of proper names, the use of the lexical code permitted the patient to grasp the meaning of the name via the intermediary

7. COORDINATION OF TWO THERAPIES   245

stage of its graphemic representation. For example, "Pekin" (Peking) was not understood when presented orally, so the patient proceeded as follows: "Papa" - "Eté" - "Kilo" - "O.K." "It's the capital of China". In addition, we established that when the patient was unable to use the relay trained—when the presentation of words on computer screen was too rapid—he would again utter semantic paralexias, which did not happen when there were no temporal constraints.

With regard to naming, we noted, a transfer of relays from naming to spontaneous speech; when S.P. encountered naming difficulties in spontaneous speech, he would stop, using the relay and utter the correct word.

We also observed at the end of therapy residual difficulties for naming less frequent and long words. If the patient was then invited to spell these words aloud, he would make spelling errors. Because of his inability to utter a correct graphemic representation, the patient would make naming errors.

ACKNOWLEDGMENT

We would like to thank Xavier Seron and Gérard Deloche for their critical comments.

REFERENCES

Albert, M. L., Yamadori, A., Gardner, H., & Howes, D. (1973). Comprehension in alexia. *Brain, 96*, 317–328.

Beauvois, M. F., & Derouesné, J. (1981). Lexical or orthographic agraphia. *Brain, 104*, 21–49.

Benson, D. F., Brown, J., & Tomlinson, E. B. (1971). Varieties of alexia: word and letter blindness. *Neurology, 21*, 951–957.

Bishop, O., & Byng, S. (1984). Assessing semantic comprehension: methodological considerations and a new clinical test. *Cognitive Neuropsychology, 1*, 233–243.

Bub, D., & Kertesz, A. (1982). Evidence for lexicographic processing in a patient with preserved written over oral single word naming. *Brain, 105*, 697–717.

Coltheart, M. (1980). Reading, phonological recoding, and deep dyslexia. In Coltheart, M., Patterson, K. E., & Marshall, J. C. (Eds.), *Deep dyslexia*. London: Routledge and Kegan Paul.

Coltheart, M., Patterson, K. E., & Marshall, J. C. (1980). *Deep dyslexia*. London: Routledge and Kegan Paul.

Davis, L. A., & Wilcox, J. (1981). Incorporating parameters of natural conversation in aphasie treatment. In Chapey, R. (Ed.), *Language intervention strategies in adult aphasia* (pp. 163–193). Baltimore: Williams & Wilkins.

Deloche, G., Andreewsky, E., & Desi, M. (1982). Surface dyslexia: a case report and some theoretical implications to reading models. *Brain and Language, 15*, 12–31.

Dubois-Charlier, P. (1971). Approche neurolinguistique du problème de l'alexie pure. *Journal de Psychologie normale et pathologique, 1*, 39–68.

Ellis, A. (1982). Spelling and writing (and reading and speaking). In Ellis, A. (Ed.), *Normality and pathology in cognitive functions* (pp. 113–145). London: Academic Press.

246 BACHY-LANGEDOCK AND de PARTZ

Ellis, A. W. (1984). *Reading, writing and dyslexia: a cognitive analysis.* London: Lawrence Erlbaum Associates.

Funnel, V. (1983). Phonological processes in reading. *British Journal of Psychology, 33A,* 465–495.

Hatfield, F. M. (1982). Diverses formes de désintégration du langage écrit et implications pour la rééducation. In Seron, X. & Laterre, C. (Eds.), *Rééduquer le cerveau* (pp. 133–156). Bruxelles: Mardaga.

Hatfield, F. M. (1983). Aspects of acquired dysorthographia and implications for reeducation. In Code, C. & Müller, D. (Eds.), *Aphasia therapy* (pp. 157–169). London: Edward Arnold.

Hécaen, H. (1967). Aspects des troubles de la lecture (alexies) au cours des lésions cérébrales en foyers. *Word, 23,* 265–287.

Henderson, L. (1982). *Orthography and word recognition in reading.* London: Academic Press.

Henderson, L. (1984). *Orthographies and reading: perspective from cognitive psychology, neuropsychology, and linguistics.* London: Lawrence Erlbaum Associates.

Hier, D. B., & Mohr, J. P. (1977). Incongruous oral and written naming. Evidence for a subdivision of the syndrome of Wernicke's aphasia. *Brain and Language, 4,* 115–126.

Hogenraad, R., & Orianne, E. (1981). Valences d'imagerie de 1.130 noms de la langue française parlée. *Psychologica Belgica, 21, 1,* 21–30.

Kremin, H. (1982). Theory and research. In Malatesha, R. N. & Aaron, P. G. (Eds.), *Neuropsychology of developmental dyslexia and acquired dyslexia: Varieties and treatments* (341–363). New York: Academic Press.

Kremin, H., & Koskas, E. (1984). Données de la pathologie sur la dénomination. *Langages, 76,* 31–76.

Lecours, A. R., & Lhermitte, F. (1979). *L'aphasie.* Paris: Flammarion.

Marcel, T. (1980). Surface dyslexia and beginning reading: a revised hypothesis of the pronounciation of print and its impairments. In Coltheart, M., Patterson, K. E., & Marshall, J. C. (Eds.), *Deep dyslexia* (227–258). London: Routledge and Kegan Paul.

Marshall, J. C., & Newcombe, F. (1966). Syntactic and semantic errors in paralexia. *Neuropsychologia 4,* 169–176.

Marshall, J. C., & Newcombe, F. (1973). Patterns of paralexia: a psycholinguistic approach. *Journal of Psycholinguistic Research, 2,* 175–199.

Marshall, J. C., & Newcombe, F. (1980). The conceptual status of deep dyslexia: an historical perspective. In Coltheart, M., Patterson, K. E., & Marshall, J. C. (Eds.), *Deep dyslexia* (pp. 1–21). London: Routledge and Kegan Paul.

Morton, J. (1980). Two auditory parallels to deep dyslexia. In M. Coltheart & J. C. Marshall (Eds.), *Deep dyslexia.* London: Routledge and Kegan Paul.

Morton, J. (1984). La dénomination. *Langages, 76,* 19–30.

Morton, J., & Patterson, K. E. (1980a). A new attempt at an interpretation or, an attempt at a new interpretation. In Coltheart, M., Patterson, K. E., & Marshall, J. C. (Eds.), *Deep dyslexia.* (91–118). London: Routledge & Keagan Paul.

Morton, J., & Patterson, K. E. (1980b). Little words-"no!". In M. Coltheart, Patterson, K. E. & Marshall, J. C. (Eds.), *Deep dyslexia.* (pp. 270–285). London: Routledge and Keagan Paul.

Morton, J. (1982). Desintegrating the lexicon: information processing approach. In: Mehler, J., Walker, E. & Garrett, N. (Eds.), *Perspectives on mental representation* (pp. 89–109). Hillsdale, NJ: Lawrence Erlbaum Associates.

Partz, M. P. (de) (1986). Re-education of a deep dyslexic patient: rationale of the method and results. *Cognitive Neuropsychology, 3,* 149–177.

Patterson, K. E. (1979). What is right with "deep" dyslexic patients? *Brain and Language, 8,* 111–129.

7. COORDINATION OF TWO THERAPIES   247

Patterson, K. E. (1981). Neuropsychological approaches to the study of reading. *British Journal of Psychology, 72*, 151–174.

Patterson, K. E. (1982). The relation between reading and phonological coding: further neuropsychological observations. In Ellis, A. W. (Ed.), *Normality and pathology in cognitive functions* (pp. 77–111). London: Academic Press.

Patterson, K. E., & Marcel, T. (1977). Aphasia, dyslexia, and the phonological encoding of written words. *Quarterly Journal of Experimental Psychology, 29*, 307–318.

Saffran, E. M., & Marin, O. S. M. (1977). Reading without phonology: evidence from aphasia. *The Quarterly Journal of Experimental Psychology, 29*, 515–525.

Valdois, S., Joanette, Y., & Nespoulous, J. L. (1986). Intrinsic Organization of sequences of phonemic approximations in conduction and Wernicke's Aphasia. *Meeting of Babble* (Niagara Falls).

Vikis-Freiberg, V. (1974). *Fréquence d'usage des mots au Québec.* Presses de l'Université de Montréal.

Warrington, E. K. & Shallice, J. (1979). Semantic access dyslexia. *Brain, 102*, 43–63.

Williams, S. E. (1983). Factors influencing naming performance in Aphasia: a review of the literature. *Journal of Communication Disorders, 16*, 357–372.

Zaidel, E., & Peters, A. (1981). Phonological encoding of ideographic reading by the disconnected right hemisphere: two case studies. *Brain and Language, 14*, 205–234.

APPENDIX

In a communication made to the French Society of Neuropsychology (Toulouse, May, 1986), Valdois suggested that sequences of phonemic approximations could be analyzed.

To determine if the patient has access to the whole phonological representation of target word in the course of sequences of phonemic approximations, Valdois compares the number of phonemes in the target word with the number of target phonemes appearing for the first time in each attempt. For instance, if the target word /kart/ (four phonemes) produces the three successive attempts /a/ . . . /akt/ . . . /kart/, the sequence equals the four phonemes expected. In this case, Valdois considers that the patient has preserved an adequate phonological representation of the target word. However, if the sequence produced is /a/ . . . . /ar/ . . . . /art/, which equals three phonemes, it is considered to correspond to an incomplete phonological representation.

To determine the internal consistency among the different attempts or, in other words, the efficiency of phonemic attempts, Valdois compares the sum of all target phonemes appearing for the first time in every attempt with the number of target phonemes produced in the last attempt. If all the target phonemes produced at a given time in successive attempts are retrieved in the last approximation, Valdois concludes that the segmental content has been preserved and the attempt is efficient. This is the case in the two examples cited earlier.

8 Reeducation of Number Transcoding Mechanisms: A Procedural Approach

Gérard Deloche
INSERM, Hôpital de la Salpêtrière, Paris, France

Xavier Seron
Unité NEXA, Cliniques Universitaires, St. Luc, Bruxelles, Belgium

Isabelle Ferrand
INSERM, Hôpital de la Salpêtrière, Paris, France

Developmental studies (Fuson, Richards, & Briards, 1982; Gelman & Gallistel, 1978), data from brain-damaged patients (Deloche & Seron, 1982, 1987a; Grewel, 1969; Henschen, 1922; McCloskey & Caramazza, 1987; Warrington, 1982), and formal analyses (Hurford, 1975; Power & Longuet-Higgins, 1978) have led to the two widespread notational systems for numbers (Arabic digits and alphabetically written numeral forms) being considered as specific semiotic codes presenting some degrees of autonomy with reference to language. These two coding systems may be viewed as microlinguistic systems with three common features that clearly distinguish them from languages: a very limited number of lexical primitives (the 10 digits from 0 to 9 and 25 words for French numerals from 0 to 999,999), easily formalizable syntaxes, and unambiguous semantics. These reasons make the universes of numbers and numerals a very favorable locus for in-depth componential analyses of transcoding mechanisms, that is, of the processes implied in the production of the notational form expressed in a target code (like Arabic digits) that unambiguously correspond to the form given in a different source code (like alphabetic numeral writing). Transcoding numbers into numerals and the reverse are applications to the particular domain of numerical activities of the general class of transcribing processes dealing with natural language, such as reading aloud, writing to dictation, or translation.

The neuropsychological models of transcoding mechanisms in repetition, reading, and writing can be classified into two formal categories based on different theoretical frameworks (Coltheart, Patterson,

250 DELOCHE, SERON, FERRAND

& Marshall, 1980; Deloche & Andreewsky, 1982). First are semantic models where target forms are deduced from source code forms through the intermediate mediation of semantic representations. Second are asemantic models where the target code forms are the direct results of the application to source code forms of a set of rewriting rules. The relevance of the two kinds of models is now well established in the field of normal and impaired language processing, and numbers and numerals have similarly recently led to well described semantic (McCloskey & Caramazza, 1987; Power & Longuet-Higgings, 1978) and asemantic (Deloche & Seron, 1982; Seron & Deloche, 1984, 1987) numerical transcoding models.

This chapter presents two single-case studies that illustrate rehabilitation programs designed for patients with impaired numerical transcoding abilities. The two treatment programs (from Arabic numbers to alphabetic numerals and the reverse) were framed according to the asemantic model: The patients were simply taught small sets of rewriting rules. The very restricted size of lexical primitives sets and the simplicity and understandability of the few procedures to be mastered favor such a direct rules training approach, which could hardly be used with language at large.

The two models of number-numeral transcoding operations resort to a multicomponent information processing analysis (Deloche & Seron, 1987b). The data-driven models are tailored to the formal structural features that we assume to be relevant for the processing of number and numeral lexical primitives (Table 8.1). In such a precise theoretical framework, the transcoding mechanisms may be viewed as consisting of psycholinguistic procedures operating essentially in stacklike environments. Digit-number lexicon primitives are unambiguously specified by their position information (e.g., the seventh position in the digit file refers to 7). Most alphabetic numeral lexicon primitives are specified by two independent pieces of categorizing information, the file they belong to (stack information), and their position within the file (position information). Three sequential files or stacks are considered: unit names, that is words from UN (1) to NEUF (9); teen names in French, (from ONZE [11] to SEIZE [16]), and decade names. The last three decade names are actually combinations of two or three one-word numerals. However, for the sake of training program consistency, these three composed decades were listed in the numeral lexicon vocabulary.

The multicomponent structure of the transcoding models distinguishes four main components, the impairment of which should induce identifiable errors. The architecture as a whole is controlled by a task supervisor, which can apply repair procedures in cases

8. NUMBER TRANSCODING REEDUCATION   251

TABLE 8.1
Lexical Structures of French and Arabic Digit Numerical Coding Systems

Digit Number Lexicon	Positions	Alphabetic Numeral Lexicon		
		Numeral	Lexical	Categories
		Units	Teens	Decades
9	9th	Neuf (9)		Quatre vingt dix (90)
8	8th	Huit (8)		Quatre vingts (80)
7	7th	Sept (7)		Soixante dix (70)
6	6th	Six (6)	Seize (16)	Soixante (60)
5	5th	Cinq (5)	Quinze (15)	Cinquante (50)
4	4th	Quatre (4)	Quatorze (14)	Quarante (40)
3	3nd	Trois (3)	Treize (13)	Trente (30)
2	2nd	Deux (2)	Douze (12)	Vingt (20)
1	1st	Un (1)	Onze (11)	Dix (10)

Miscellaneous
0   ZERO
• (,)   ET (and)
            CENT (hundred)
            MILLE (thousand)

where errors are detected. The training exercises were structured and arranged in such a way that the occurrence of the different types of errors would be prevented by the modularity of the programs, the experimental working constraints, and the facilitation information. Both programs were thus hierarchized into separate levels devoted to particular transcoding patterns. Each level was then subdivided into different steps focusing on a specific rule and its associated exception cases (subrules). Finally, each step could be worked under several experimental conditions (vanishing cues). Throughout the therapy, a criterion of 90% correct responses determined the patient's progression in the exercises. The items to be transcoded were selected so that their processing never implied other rules than those that had already been learned and the rule under consideration at that step.

The asemantic transcoding algorithms have been detailed elsewhere (Deloche & Seron, 1987). We simply recall here the main features of the four components of the production models and the related types of disturbances observed in the cases of errors. The *parsing process* has to isolate the lexical primitives in the source code form. Errors may be left-to-right direction violations (CINQ CENT [500] → 105 [CENT CINQ]), segmentation errors (QUATRE VINGT TROIS [83] → 4 [QUATRE] 23 [VINGT TROIS] or 204 → VINGT [20] QUATRE [4]), and overlapping/skipping errors (CENT QUATRE VINGT TROIS [183] → 123 [CENT

VINGT TROIS]). The *lexical categorization/identification component* had to extract the lexical information attached to the source code primitives (just isolated by the parsing process) and required by the transcoding algorithm per se. Categorization concerns position information in the case of digits and numerals plus stack information for numerals. Identifications are required for some primitives like CENT (hundred) and the separators ("," or MILLION and THOUSAND), which indicate the boundaries where the source code form may be truncated in substrings on which the production process operates repeatedly.[1] There may be position errors in both coding systems (QUATORZE [14] → 13; 7 → HUIT [8]) and stack errors with numerals (TRENTE [30] → 13). The *transcoding process* per se is a set of rewriting rules triggered by the lexical information received from the preceding component. The result consists in loading an output buffer with the information specifying the target code lexical primitives to be produced. Errors may be full or partial lexicalizations (QUARANTE CINQ [45] → 405, *CENT* CINQUANTE TROIS [153] → 10053). Another frequent error type is erroneous term-by-term correspondence, which assigns an object coding system primitive to each primitive of the source-code form (usually with 0 or 1 for thousand and hundred), as in TROIS MILLE HUIT CENT VINGT TROIS (3,823) → 308123. Thousand and hundred, depending on whether they are purely lexical additive constants (non-multiplicand as in MILLE CENT VINGT QUATRE [1,124]), or multiplicand preceded by a multiplier (as in the previous example) may induce particular errors (123 → UN CENT VINGT TROIS instead of CENT VINGT TROIS; 469 → CENT QUATRE SOIXANTE NEUF or QUATRE CENT SOIXANTE NEUF [469] → 4169). Finally, the *output encoding process* writes down the target code elements selected by the lexical specifications delivered by the transcoding process. Paragraphias may occur at that component level (14 [QUATORZE] → QUATROZE or 40 [QUARANTE] → QUATRANTE]).

We will now present two transcoding treatment programs administered to two different patients, in the first case from Arabic digit strings to alphabetic numeral forms; in the second, from numerals to

---

[1]Writing alphabetic integers from Arabic digit strings involves the repeated application of transcoding three-digit substrings (previously grouped in sets of three digits from right to left) with the proper insertion of the separator "million," "mille" (thousand) between each run of the algorithm: 345,345 is: "trois cent quarante cinq mille trois cent quarante cinq". In the reverse direction, the same remark applies, the alpabetic lexical primitives substrings to the left and to the right of "mille" (thousand) are well-formed numerals on their own ("trois cent quarante cinq") that can be independently transcoded by the same processes, thus producing the two digital substrings separated by a comma (345,345).

numbers. The rationale, structure, and precise administration modalities will be detailed. The two patients entered the experimental training long enough from onset so that modifications in performances profiles could not be attributed to spontaneous recovery. The treatment effects will be assessed by comparing prerehabilitation evaluations to posttest scores administered at the completion of the therapy program (short-term training effects) and then several months thereafter (long-term training effects). Pretesting and posttesting concerned not only the transcoding operations that were trained (specific effects), but also other tasks dealing with numerical concepts (training transfers).

TESTING BATTERIES FOR THE INVESTIGATION OF THE PATIENTS' NUMERICAL SKILLS

A standard examination battery was devised for documenting the patients' number and numeral transcoding abilities and their general abilities in dealing with the semantic and the syntax of the numerical coding systems. Depending on the performance profiles, some special studies were also considered.

Transcoding Tasks

The two transcoding tasks involving Arabic digits and alphabetic numerals served for selecting the type of treatment program. The third system for coding integers simply represented quantities on tokens of different values depicted by printed dot clusters of 1, 10, 100, and 1000 points, respectively. Although the transcoding tasks from/to tokens to/from the two notational systems were introduced to gain information about the patients' comprehension of the meaning of number and numeral forms (the quantities referred to), it is clear that this type of magnitude representation is bound to the base 10 digit system. Moreover, manipulating the tokens does not necessarily reflect semantic encoding-decoding processes into/from number or numeral forms because asemantic transcoding algorithms can also be implemented between each of the two numerical coding systems and the token system. The six transcoding tasks (Figure 8.1) comprised three practice trials and 62 test items (the same 62 values to be produced from and into the three coding systems).

The 62 items could be categorized in different ways, depending on the formal descriptions of the source code and the object code and on the parameters that seem relevant in the framework of the transcod-

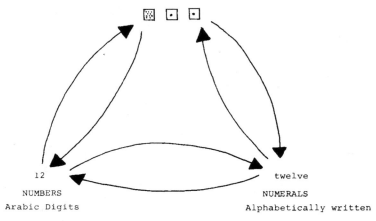

FIGURE 8.1. The six transcoding tasks between three quantity coding systems.

ing model. Suffice it to say here that these 62 items, ranging from 1 to 7,001 presented the following patterns:

1. 23 alphabetical lexical primitives (nine units, six teens, six simple decades, hundred, and thousand) and the three composed decades (70, 80, 90)
2. 15 cases with a 0 in the unit position (60, 420, 4,030 . . .)
3. 47 cases with a nonzero digit to be transcribed by unit name (32 items) in the unit position (7, 84, 1,309, . . .) or by a teen name (15 items) as in 15, 1,016, 1,791, . . .)
4. 10 cases with a 0 in the decade position (108, 1,700, 7,001 . . .)
5. 43 cases with a nonzero digit in the decade position, to be transcribed either by a simple decade name (20 items: 28, 60, 1,134, . . .) or by a composed decade (13 items: 193, 583, 5,475, . . .) or by a teen name (10 items: 15, 616, 6,012)
6. Six cases with a 0 in the hundred position (1,000, 4,030, 6,012, . . .)
7. 21 cases with a nonzero digit in the hundred position, to be transcribed either by cent (hundred) without a multiplier (six items: 108, 139, 1,134 . . .) or by a unit name as a multiplier and hundred as a multiplicand (15 items: 616, 842, 5,475, . . .);
8. 15 four-digit figures: nine items with 1 in the thousand position to be transcribed into MILLE without a multiplier (1,001, 1,245,

8. NUMBER TRANSCODING REEDUCATION 255

1,791 . . .) and six items to be transcribed by a unit name as a multiplier and thousand as a multiplicand (3,823, 6,012, 7,001, . . .).

Other Numerical Tasks

The patient's comprehension of numerical forms was further assessed in three different tasks involving the manipulation of numerical values. Each task was performed first with alphabetic forms and then with Arabic digits.

Number Line Positioning. An horizontal number line with the origin marked 0 and the end marked 100 (to the right) was presented to the patient. A place was indicated on the line with a cross and the patient had to select from a five- element multiple-choice array the numerical form whose value corresponded to that place. The distractors were items whose value was relatively close to the target or whose alphabetic numeral forms shared some lexical properties with the correct response (same position value but different stacks: QUINZE (15) for CINQUANTE (50); same primitives but sequenced differently: QUATRE VINGT (80) for VINGT QUATRE (24). There were six items in this test.

Magnitude Comparison. Following two practice trials, the patients were shown 38 cards in succession, each card presenting two numerical forms. For each pair, the instructions were simply to indicate which of the two forms had the largest value. In the Arabic digit condition, the length varied from one (e.g., 4) to six (e.g., 200,000), and the two digit forms differed in length in 18 pairs. In the alphabetic condition, the number of words varied from one (e.g., six [6]) to four (e.g., QUATRE CENT CINQUANTE NEUF [459]) and the two numerals to be compared differed according to the number of words in only five out of the 38 test pairs.

Numerical Serial Ordering. Given six different numerical forms printed on separate cards, the patient had to place the cards in the correct order from smaller to larger. There were ten items in this test, and the numbers ranged from 4 to 8,003. The number of words in alphabetic forms varied from one (lexical primitives) to five.

Numeral Grammaticality Judgment. This test consisted in asking the patients to find out which sequences of two to four alphabetic lexical primitives were not well-formed numerals. Following three practice trials, 132 items were administered among which were 66

256   DELOCHE, SERON, FERRAND

illegal sequences that violated rejection rules operating on adjacent (TROIS VINGT [three twenty]) or nonadjacent (TRENTE CINQ CENT NEUF [thirty-five hundred nine]) numeral primitives categorized into lexicosyntactical classes (Deloche & Seron, 1986).

FIRST THERAPY PROGRAM: FROM NUMBERS TO NUMERALS

The patient, a 42-year-old man, was a carpenter who worked for the district police. In November 1979, he was hospitalized for general epileptic injuries, followed by right upper and lower limb hemiplegia, a Broca's aphasia, and obnubilation. Computed tomography (CT) showed an encephalomalacia in the left sylvian area due to a sylvian embolic obstruction. There was no hemianopsia or sensitive disorders, and the lower limb hemiplegia cleared rapidly. A neuropsychological examination in January 1980 showed no intellectual deterioration (IQ of 108 on the Progressive Matrix 38) but some elements of an ideomotor apraxia, significant dyscalculia, and still a severe Broca's aphasia.

After 3 years and 7 months of classic speech therapy, the patient still complained about troubles with number tasks. A language examination was then administered with the French version of the Goodglass and Kaplan aphasia test (Mazaux & Orgogozzo, 1982). The performance profile indicated classic Broca's aphasia, with reduction of oral and written language, discrete articulation difficulties, significant agrammatism, and some residual difficulties in text comprehension. Oral comprehension was considered fairly good.

Specific Pretherapeutic Testing on Numerical Tasks (3 years 7 Months Postonset)

Transcoding tasks showed major difficulties in the production of alphabetically written numeral forms, both from numbers and tokens (error rates: 45% and 37%, respectively), without comparable impairment in the other transcoding directions (from 2% to 6% errors; see Figure 8.2).

Writing numerals from numbers or quantities showed a structurally similar pattern of errors. About 25% of the error total were either literal or verbal paragraphias. The improper production of ZERO accounted for 25% and 30% of the errors from numbers and quantities respectively. In both tasks such errors occurred on 9 out of the 14 items with 0 in the decade or hundred position as in 907 →

8. NUMBER TRANSCODING REEDUCATION   257

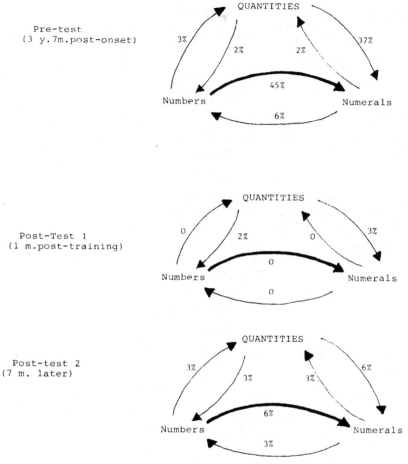

FIGURE 8.2. Case 1: Performance profile (error percentages) for the six transcoding tasks before training (pretest) and after the number → numeral transcoding treatment program (posttests 1 and 2).

NEUF ZERO SEPT; 7 T (seven tokens of thousand) 1 U (one unit token) (7,001) → SEPT MILLE ZERO UN. The 15 cases with 0 in the unit position only gave one such error (from number to numeral). Errors occurred frequently in the production of teen names (45% and 30% of the opportunities from numbers and quantities respectively) that were not integrated into one single word (114 → UN CENT DIX QUATRE, 9D (nine decades tokens) 6U (96) → QUATRE VINGT DIX SIX) or transcribed by a verbal or literal paragraphia. Other errors occurred on items requiring the production of CENT (hundred) either inserted in a multiplier multiplicand structure (four errors out of 15 items in both tasks: 420 → QUATRE DEUX or 1T 7H (seven hundred tokens) (1,700) → MILLE SOIXANTE DIX CENT) or not (two and one errors out of six cases from numbers and quantities, respectively: 108 → MILLE HUIT, 1H 1D 4U (114) → UN CENT QUATIEME). The 15 four-digit figures produced only two errors on the thousand structure in transcoding numbers into numerals.

The types of errors produced in writing numerals thus seem to reflect common impaired processing in the two transcoding tasks whose source codes are tied to the same base 10 system (Arabic digits and decimal tokens) and whose common target code is the alphabetic written numeral system. The literal paragraphias result from lexical impairment concerning mainly the triad of lexical primitives whose morphological similarities are very high QUATRE (4), QUARANTE (40), QUATORZE (14). The other errors seem to result from the syntax of the transcoding rules to be applied in the production of numerals (Deloche & Seron, 1987b).

The few errors observed in the four other transcoding experiments concerned parsing (four errors) or two cases of erroneous processing of CENT (hundred), two cases where the values of hundred tokens were confounded with decades, and perseverations (two cases).

The Positioning on a Number Line of Arabic digit forms or alphabetic written numerals was performed without error. There were no error in the Numerical Serial Ordering of numbers in both digit and alphabetic coding systems. The Magnitude Comparison Test was perfect on digit forms and showed only three unsystematic errors out of the 38 item pairs in the alphabetic presentation condition.

The Numeral Grammaticality Judgment Test indicated significant error percentages in both nonrecognitions of well-formed numerals (20%) and false recognitions of illegal numeral strings (30%). Teens and composed decades were a special source of difficulty and often caused the rejection of legal items. False recognitions often corresponded to some violation of rejection rules that have acceptation exceptions. For instance, QUATRE (4) was accepted to the left of any decade name, whereas it can legally be followed only by VINGT (20) either in QUATRE VINGT (80) or in QUATRE VINGT DIX (90).

Given the specific difficulties the patient had in writing alphabetic numerals from digit forms, the training program specifically addressed this transcoding ability.

The Treatment Program: From Numbers to Numerals

The program is divided into five specific levels plus a review level (see Table 8.2 for the detailed structure).

Table 8.2
Structure of Treatment Program 1

Level	Conditions	Items	VP*	SF†	RF‡	Items	RRP§	SF†	RF‡	Items	RRP§	SF†	RF‡
				Step 1				*Step 2*				*Step 3*	
1 Most decade	1	60	colored	colored	colored	22	present	colored	2 lines	40	present	blank	1 line
unit figures	2	60	colored	colored	blank	22	present	blank	2 lines	40	removed	blank	1 line
	3	60	colored	blank	blank	22	removed	blank	1 line				
	4	60	removed	blank	blank								
2 Most 3-digit	1	24	colored	colored	2 lines	20	RRP	blank	blank				
figures				+ Cent	+ arrow	20	removed	blank	blank				
	2	24	colored	blank	+ arrow								
	3	24	removed	blank	2 lines								
	4	24	removed	blank	blank								
3 "O" in decade/	1	25	RRP	blank	blank								
unit positions	2	25	removed	blank	blank								
4 4- to 6- digit	1	Positioning the comma				34		colored + mille	3 lines + arrow	24	present	blank	blank
figures	2	Mille with multiplier				34		blank	3 lines	24	removed	blank	blank
	3	Mille without multiplier				34		blank	1 line				
						34		blank	blank				
5 the case of ET	1	30	RRP	blank	blank								
(and)	2	30	removed	blank	blank								
6 General Re-	1	30	without cues										
caputilative													

*VP = vocabulary panel
†SF = stimulus frame
‡RF = response frame
§RRP = rewriting rules panel

260 DELOCHE, SERON, FERRAND

Level 1: Transcoding of Most Decade Unit Figures

The exercises concern the transcoding of most two-digit numbers. The principles will then directly apply to the two rightmost digits in the more general case of three-digit numbers, and also to the leftmost fifth and fourth digits of six-digit numbers, etc.

Step 1: Simple Decades and Composed Decades Without Teens. The general transcoding rule to be applied here can be stated as follows: "Write the decade name corresponding to the digit to the left followed by the unit name of the digit to the right." For example, 27 had to be written VINGT SEPT by 2 giving the decade name VINGT followed by unit name SEPT for 7.

Step one contained four conditions with 60 items each. During condition one, the alphabetic lexicon (vocabulary panel = VP) arranged in two colored columns was placed in front of the patient (Figure 8.3). The red part on the left side of the VP contained the nine decade names from the bottom DIX (ten) to top QUATRE VINGT DIX

Vocabulary Panel

9	QUATRE VINGT DIX (ninety)	9	NEUF (nine)
8	QUATRE VINGT (eighty)	8	HUIT (eight)
7	SOIXANTE DIX (seventy)	7	SEPT (seven)
6	SOIXANTE (sixty)	6	SIX (six)
5	CINQUANTE (fifty)	5	CINQ (five)
4	QUARANTE (forty)	4	QUATRE (four)
3	TRENTE (thirty)	3	TROIS (three)
2	VINGT (twenty)	2	DEUX (two)
1	DIX (ten)	1	UN (one)

Number Stimulus Frame

2	7

Numeral Response Frame

VINGT	SEPT

FIGURE 8.3. From the digital to the alphabetic coding systems: vocabulary panel, number stimulus frame and numeral response frame. The left hemipart is red, the right blue.

8. NUMBER TRANSCODING REEDUCATION 261

(ninety), each name being indexed by the associated position digit (from 1 to 9). Similarly, the blue part on the right contained the unit names and their digit counterparts (from bottom 1 UN [one] to top 9 NEUF [nine]). The number to be transcoded was presented in two rectangle frames (stimulus frames). The left rectangle was red for decades; the right one was blue for units. The response frame also consisted of two rectangles colored in the same way. Thus, the same color cues in the same position underlined the decades and the units, in the vocabulary pannel, in the number stimulus frame, and in the numeral response frame.

Thus, in order to transcode the digit string 27, the patient only needed to proceed from left to right in the following manner:

1. Consider the left red digit 2 in the stimulus frame.
2. Find its alphabetic decade name in the left, red column of the vocabulary panel, at the position pointed to by 2.
3. Write down this decade name in the left, red empty rectangle of the numeral response frame.
4. Apply exactly the same procedure with the right, blue digit 7, pointing to SEPT in the right, blue column of the vocabulary panel of alphabetic digit names.

In Condition 2 the color cues were deleted from the numeral response frame, which was reduced to a single horizontal line broken in its middle. Color cues were deleted from the stimulus frame in Condition 3 and the vocabulary panel was removed in Condition 4.

Step 2: Composed Decades with Teens. The preceding digit unit transcoding rule directly applied to a digit substring like 73 (SOIX-ANTE TREIZE) would give the illegal numeral form SOIXANTE DIX TROIS by 7 → SOIXANTE DIX and 3 → TROIS. The purpose of Step 2 was to teach the patient how to avoid such erroneous productions. This step contained three conditions each with 22 items.

In Condition 1, a panel illustrating the six rewriting rules (like DIX TROIS → TREIZE) of decades units into teens was presented in one column from ONZE at the bottom to SEIZE at the top. The stimulus frame was a bicolored double rectangle. The response frame was composed of two horizontal lines. The first or top line was divided into two parts: The left part is reserved for decade names, the right one for unit names. The second or bottom line is unbroken (Figure 8.4).

With this arrangement, the patient had to proceed as follows:

1. Write down, in the left part, on the first (top) line the decade name (e.g., digit 7 in 73 must be transcribed SOIXANTE DIX).

262   DELOCHE, SERON, FERRAND

SOIXANTE DIX   TROIS

FIGURE 8.4. Numeral response frame for transcribing Arabic numbers (e.g., 73) into alphabetic numerals with teens imbedded in composed decades.

SOIXANTE TREIZE

2. Write down the unit name on the right part of the same line; the 3 must be written TROIS.
3. Transform the illegal numeral (SOIXANTE DIX TROIS) into the correct one by applying to the incorrect alphabetical substring DIX TROIS the corresponding rewriting rule presented on the panel.

In Condition 2, the color cues are deleted from the stimulus frame. In Condition 3, a direct transcription of teens was required, so the panel of rewriting rules was removed and the response frame contained only one continuous line.

Step 3: Isolated Teens and Items from Steps 1 and 2. This step contained some items already presented together with new items aimed at teaching the transcoding of isolated teen names. The main reasons for mixing Step 1 and Step 2 items with this new step were the following: First, there had to be no overgeneralization of the rewriting subrules of Step 2 to the cases of Step 1 to which they did not apply. Such an overgeneralization could produce illegal numerals like QUARANTE TREIZE instead of QUARANTE TROIS. Second, the writing of isolated teens obeyed the same rewriting rule learned in the preceding Step 2 and thus did not seem to require a specific training. The battery contained 40 items: three times the six isolated teens, 11 composed decades with teens (from Step 2) and 11 simple digit-unit figures (from Step 1).

In Condition 1, the stimulus frame was a double blank rectangle, the response frame was a continuous line, and the panel with the rewriting rule from Step 2 was present. The patient was invited to check carefully whether he had to use a rewriting rule before producing the alphabetic form. The panel was removed in Condition 2.

Level 2: Transcoding of Most Three-digit Numbers

Exercises show the two different uses of CENT (hundred) in French numerals.

Step 1: Transcoding into Cent with Multiplier. The general transcoding rule for digits in the hundred position was to write down their unit name followed by CENT (hundred). The remaining decade-unit pattern could then be processed according to the transcoding procedures for two-digit figures already learned. Thus 456 was transcribed QUATRE CENT CINQUANTE SIX by 4 → QUATRE CENT and 56 → CINQUANTE SIX. There were four conditions with 24 different items each.

In Condition 1, the stimulus frame, was situated just above the response frame and divided into three rectangular boxes. The leftmost box corresponding to the hundred position was blue with the word CENT printed on top at the right. A vertical arrow originated from CENT and pointed downwards to a slot in the numeral response frame (Figure 8.5).

The blue unit name vocabulary panel was presented to the patient. With this arrangement, transcoding had to proceed from left to right through these successive operations:

1. Look at the first, blue digit in the stimulus frame.
2. Pick out in the vocabulary panel the alphabetic unit name indexed by this digit.
3. Write the name on the first part of the horizontal line of the response frame.
4. Copy on the second part of the line the word CENT as indicated by the vertical arrow.
5. Transcode the remaining decade unit substring.

In Condition 2, the word CENT (hundred) and the color blue were removed from the stimulus frame. The vocabulary panel and the arrow were removed in Condition 3. Finally, in Condition 4 the broken lines were removed from the response frame. This was done up to Level 4.

Step 2: Transcoding into Cent Without a Multiplier. Overgeneralization of the transcoding rule stated in Step 1 would cause the patient to transcode *1* in hundred position by UN CENT as in 143 → UN CENT QUARANTE TROIS instead of the correct CENT QUARANTE TROIS.

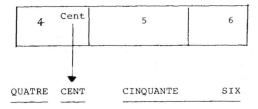

FIGURE 8.5. Number stimulus frame and numeral response frame for transcribing the hundred digit into CENT with multiplier.

264   DELOCHE, SERON, FERRAND

This step thus concerns an exception. It contained two conditions. There was one list of 20 items among which "1s" in the hundred position occurred 12 times, the others items being from Step 1. In Condition 1, the stimulus frame was made of three uncolored boxes (as in Step 1, Condition 4) and the panel with the rewriting subrule UN CENT → CENT was present. This panel was removed in Condition 2.

Level 3: Transcoding of "0" When in Decade and/or Unit Position

In a digit string "0" does not represent a quantity but is merely a position indicator; thus the digit name ZERO must not appear in alphabetical forms. This special case causes errors such as 403 being transcoded into QUATRE CENT ZERO TROIS. Notice that "0" never appeared in the vocabulary panels presented to the patient.

There was a single step with two conditions, each with a new battery of 25 three-digit items and each item containing one or two occurrences of "0." In Condition 1, a panel illustrating the erasing rule 0 (ZERO) → RIEN (nil) is present. The stimulus and response frames were the same as shown earlier (three colorless boxes and one horizontal line). The panel was removed in Condition 2.

Level 4: Transcoding of Four- to Six-digit Numbers

This level concerned the writing of MILLE (thousand) in numerals.

Step 1: Positioning the Comma. Because Arabic digit strings were presented without comma, this separator first had to be inserted by the patient. Four- to six-digit numbers were written on a sheet of paper. The patient indicated the comma by placing a large green mark between the third and fourth digits (counted from right to left).

Step 2: Transcoding into Mille with Multiplier. The exercises focused on the transcoding of most typical four-, five-, and six-digit numbers. The general rule is to run the transcoding algorithm for three-digits numbers once on the digit substring to the left of the comma, then to write the separator MILLE (thousand), and finally to run the transcoding algorithm on the remaining three-digit substring. There were four conditions, each with a new battery of 34 items.

In Condition 1, the stimulus frame consisted of two groups of three boxes separated by a green mark symbolizing the comma. MILLE (thousand) was written above the green mark (Figure 8.6). From this word, a vertical arrow pointed down toward a slot in the response frame.

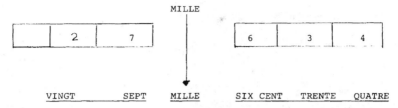

FIGURE 8.6. Number stimulus frame and numeral response frame for transcoding four- to six-digit figures.

With such an arrangement the patient had to proceed from left to right in the following manner:

1. Transcode the first digit substring (three, two, or one digits).
2. Copy down mille.
3. Transcode the group of three digits to the right.

In Condition 2, the green mark and the word MILLE were removed. In Condition 3, the response frame occupied a single line, and the stimulus frame was now a single group of six boxes without a mark for the comma. The patient had first to place the comma and then to proceed as in the preceding conditions. In Condition 4, the response frame was removed, as was the case for the subsequent exercises.

Step 3: Transcoding into Mille Without a Multiplier. This step concerned the exception to the above general rule for the cases where the digit was a "1." In French, the "1" is not transcribed into its unit name when it starts a number (1,000 is MILLE [thousand] and not UN MILLE [one thousand]), but "1" is marked by UN in other cases like DEUX CENT UN MILLE (201,000). This step had two conditions. The battery had 24 items, some of which were taken from Step 2 to check for overgeneralization of the exception subrule to the general case. A panel presenting the two cases was shown to the patient in Condition 1, and then removed in Condition 2 (Figure 8.7).

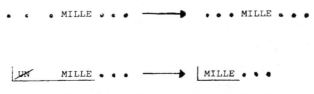

FIGURE 8.7. The two cases for transcribing "1s" in thousand position.

Level 5: The Arithmetical Operator Et (And).

Et (and) must be inserted in the alphabetic numeral forms corresponding to some digital forms with "1s" in the first or the fourth positions (from right to left). A battery of 30 six-digit items, all illustrating at least once the ET problem in one of the two-digit substrings around the comma, was used. The six cases where ET was needed were shown in column on a panel (Condition 1), from the bottom VINGT UN → VINGT ET UN to the top SOIXANTE ONZE → SOIXANTE ET ONZE. The panel was removed in Condition 2.

Level 6: General

Because all the transcoding rules had now been trained but one facilitation procedure still remained, this level contained only one step and one condition: the uncued situation. The 30 numbers to be transcoded were representative of the different transcoding pictures, the lengths varied from three to six digits, the digit strings were presented without being justified to the right (there was no longer a stimulus frame), and the alphabetic transcription had to be directly written to the right of the digit string.

Results

Treatment Sessions

The training program consisted of 25 sessions (three sessions a week for 2 months). The sessions lasted from 30 minutes to 1 hour. The progression in the program was regular because the criterion of 90% correct responses was always met. However, three complementary exercises were decided on during the course of the program. One concerned literal paragraphias mixing QUATRE and QUARANTE; the others were devoted to the transcoding of MILLE without a multiplier (Level 4, Step 3) and to the case of ET (and) (Level 5).

Treatment Effects

Performance profiles to the training battery for numerical abilities were measured 1 month after completion of the treatment program and the 7 months thereafter (Figure 8.2).

Posttest 1. The patient's performances on Posttest 1 showed a general improvement. Transcoding into numerals was perfect from numbers and showed only 2 errors from the tokens quantities. Three literal paragraphias occurred on QUARANTE and QUATORZE, but they were self-corrected spontaneously. Positioning a numerical value on a number line, numerical serial ordering, and magnitude comparisons were performed without errors in both the Arabic digit and the alphabetic numeral systems. The Numeral Grammaticality Judgment Test showed four false recognitions and one nonrecognition out of the 66 items in each category. The false recognitions all occurred on the same decade unit hundred structure where the patient scored at chance level (four acceptations out of eight items like QUARANTE TROIS CENT (forty-three hundred)).

Posttest 2. The long-term stability of the effects of the treatment program was reassessed 7 months after Posttest 1. The results indicated either unchanged performances or small increases in error rates relative to Posttest 1, but in each case the patient still performed better than on the pretest.

The general improvement observed after completion of the rehabilitation program extended to other situations involving numbers and numerals than those already described. For instance, the patient now introduced in his (poor) spontaneous speech topics dealing with quantities (the money earned by his daughter-in-law at her new job) and wrote his checks by himself. Reading aloud, which had been impossible for numerals and rarely correct for numbers on the pretest, was now deblocked, but oral productions involved some errors (100 → /UN CENT/; VINGT CINQ [25] → /VINGT SEPT/ [27]) and numerous self-corrections, with silent or filled pauses often being inserted between lexical primitives.

SECOND THERAPY PROGRAM: FROM NUMERAL TO NUMBER

Born in 1958, the patient was right-handed and worked as an unskilled laborer in a printing plant. In January 1983, he presented with purulent sinusitis with right hemiplegia and mutism. The CT scan revealed a left-hemispheric subdural empyema. Two operations were performed, one in February 1983 to resect the empyema, another in November 1984 to insert a boneplasty of a skull defect. A CT scan administered between the two operations indicated a left frontoparietal hypodensity.

The language disorders were initially important: quasitotal mutism and marked impairment of oral and written comprehension, but some language abilities recovered rapidly. Language therapy using the classic French reeducation method (Ducarne, 1986) was com-

268 DELOCHE, SERON, FERRAND

menced immediately after the first operation and was still being continued 2 years later at the rate of three sessions a week.

A complete neuropsychological examination was performed just before the patient entered the treatment program, 1 year after onset (January 1984). The French version of the Boston Clinical Examination of Aphasia indicated an obvious reduction of the verbal output: The mean length of utterance was four words and the verbal output was disrupted by frequent pauses. There were no paraphasic substitutions in spontaneous speech; but phonemic paraphasias were present in oral repetition, in naming, and in reading aloud. Oral and written comprehension was good. There were no apraxia or memory deficits. The patient scored 35 on the PM 47, which gave an IQ of 110 by extrapolation.

Specific Pretherapeutic Testing on Numerical Tasks (1 Year Postonset).

Writing alphabetic numerals from digit numbers or from tokens collections was impossible, and difficulties occurred in the two transcoding tasks with numerals as the source forms. However, the error rates were very low for the transcriptions between the two nonalphabetic base 10 notational systems, digit, and tokens (one error and two errors from numbers to quantities and from quantities to numbers, respectively out of 62 items; see Figure 8.8).

Transcoding from numerals was always disturbed in the items with composed decades. The nine items with QUATRE VINGT . . . (8x or 9x) all showed the nonintegration of the alphabetical primitives into one single decade because QUATRE was transcribed either into its lexical context-free value, the digit 4 (QUATRE VINGT [80] → 42); or into the decade value with the same fourth position, 4D (QUATRE VINGT [80] → 4D 2 D, the two collections of decades tokens being clearly individualized). In the same way, the two items with SOIXANTE DIX . . . (7x) were erroneously transcoded without integration in the composed decade SOIXANTE DIX (70) → 610 or 6D 1D; SOIXANTE DIX HUIT (78) → 618 or 6D 1D 8U. Teen names were a source of trouble and were processed as the corresponding unit names, especially when they appeared embedded in a composed decade like CINQ MILLE QUATRE CENT SOIXANTE QUINZE (5,475) → 5465 or 5T 4H 6D 5U (five and four errors out of five items in producing numbers and quantities, respectively). Transcoding numerals that require intercalary "0s" showed five and three errors in numbers and tokens, respectively (MILLE SEPT CENT [1,700] → 1070 or → 1T 7D [1,070]). In the numeral → quantity direction, there were three cases of overlapping errors in the left-to-

8. NUMBER TRANSCODING REEDUCATION   269

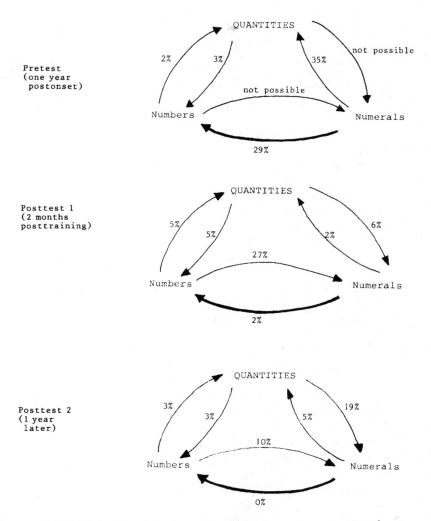

FIGURE 8.8. Case 2: Performance profiles (error percentages) to the six transcoding tasks before training (pretest) and after the numeral → number transcoding treatment program (Posttests 1 and 2).

right parsing of the (unit name, hundred) structure. Taken together, the results to the two transcoding tasks performed with alphabetic numerals as the source code seemed to indicate that the same cases (mainly composed decades, figures requiring intercalary "0s") gave problems to the patient, whatever the precise form of the two non-alphabetical base 10 object codes.

As already indicated, the two tasks that required the production of

270 DELOCHE, SERON, FERRAND

alphabetic numerals could not be administered because the patient was unable to write numeral forms spontaneously. However, since copying was preserved, a reduced version (12 items) of the testing battery was presented. The patient transcoded Arabic numbers into alphabetic numerals by first building the sequence of numeral primitives with individual cards that had been placed at random on the table, each card displaying a lexical primitive, and then, copied the form produced. Difficulties occurred in the production of composed decades and numbers with intercalary "0s." Oral number naming was generally preserved for both Arabic digits and alphabetic written forms. Incidental errors were one phonemic paraphasia (16 /sɛz/ → /trɛz/ [13]), three stack errors (ex: SIX CENT SIX [606] → SIX CENT SEIZE [616]), and one error on a composed decade name. Although all these erroneous readings had induced the production of the object code form corresponding to reading and not to the source item, there were also instances where correct readings accompanied written transcoding errors.

Positioning a Numerical Form on a Number Line was perfect with Arabic digits, but two errors were made with alphabetic numerals: (DIX [10] was chosen instead of VINGT QUATRE [24] and QUARANTE DEUX [42] for QUATRE VINGT [80]). Transcoding errors similar to the latter were made with the composed decades (QUATRE [4] in QUATRE VINGT . . . → 4D [40] or QUATRE read aloud /QUARANTE/ [40]). Numerical Serial Ordering was preserved with Arabic numbers, but at least one out of the six forms was not correctly ordered in five series with alphabetic numerals. The errors involved the misplacement (twice) of a form with a composed decade. Magnitude Comparison was perfect in the Arabic digit system, but two errors occurred on the 38 items presented in alphabetic forms: TRENTE SIX (36) and SOIXANTE SEPT (67) were both considered greater than QUATRE VINGT (80).

The 18 errors observed in the Numeral Grammaticality Judgment Test were 10 false recognitions of illegal sequences of alphabetic primitives and 8 nonrecognitions of well-formed numerals (error percentages: 15% and 12%, respectively). Seven out of the eight numerals erroneously rejected involved composed decades (QUATRE VINGT [80], CENT QUATRE VINGT QUINZE [195]). Three out of the ten false recognitions occurred on items like TRENTE HUIT CENT (thirty-eight hundred) or SOIXANTE QUATRE VINGT (sixty for twenty) where the two two-word substrings deduced from the three-word sequences were, in isolation, legal (both SOIXANTE QUATRE [64] and QUATRE VINGT [80] refer to well-formed numerals) but their concatenation was illegal.

Because the patient was unable to produce alphabetic forms but could write Arabic digits numbers, albeit with significant error rates,

8. NUMBER TRANSCODING REEDUCATION 271

his treatment program was designed to improve his residual performances.

The Treatment Program: From Numerals to Numbers

The program was divided into three specific levels and one final recapitulative level (Table 8.3).

Level 1: Decades Units Figures

These exercises concerned the cases where the digital form to be produced was a two-digit number.

Step 1: Identifying Composed Decades Names. Composed decades (SOIXANTE DIX [70], QUATRE VINGT [80], and QUATRE VINGT DIX [90]) are cases where the parsing component must simultaneously consider several (from two to three) adjacent words in the alphabetic string to integrate them into a single unit for further processing.

Step 1 contained two conditions, with 50 items in each case. In Condition 1, the composed decade panel in red was placed on the table in front of the patient. The patient was instructed to color red as a whole the composed decade name embedded in the numeral strings. The items all contained one or two composed decades, but the lexical primitives DIX, VINGT, and SOIXANTE never appeared as simple decades or QUATRE as a unit or multiplier of thousand or hundred. In Condition 2, the list did contain items with composed decades, and the four lexical primitives of DIX, VINGT, SOIXANTE, and QUATRE did appear elsewhere than in composed decades.

Step 2: Simple Decades and Composed Decades Without Teens. The general transcoding rule stated in Program 1 still applied, the source and object coding systems being exchanged "write the digit corresponding to the decade name, immediately followed by the digit whose unit name was to the right of the decade name." Three conditions were used in this step, with two lists of 40 and 34 items, respectively.

In Condition 1, the alphabetic numeral stimulus form to be transcribed was printed (in colors) in the top left portion of a page. A number response frame was printed to the right of the numeral. It consisted of an array of six rows and three colums. The first row contained three "0s", which represented the initial state of the transcoding process devices (Figure 8.9).

TABLE 8.3
Structure of Treatment Program 2

Level	Step	Conditions	Items	VP*	SF†	RF‡	Miscellaneous
1 Decade unit figures	1 Identifying composed	1	50				CDP§
	decades	2	50				CDP
	2 Simple and	1	40	colored	colored	colored	
	composed decades	2	34	colored	none	blank	
	without teens	3	40	removed	none	blank	
	3 Isolated teens	1	18	colored	none	colored	
		2	18	colored	none	blank	
		3	18	removed	none	blank	
	4 Teens in composed	1	24	colored	none	colored	
	decades	2	24	colored	none	blank	
		3	24	removed	none	blank	
	5 Summary	1	30		no cues		
2 Figures with "cent" (hundred)	1 Identifying the "hundred group"	1	30				HGP‖
	2 Writing 3-digit	1	30		none	colored	HGP
	numbers	2	30		none	blank	HGP

		3	30		none	blank	removed
		4	30		none	2 rows	removed
3 Figures with "mille" (thousand)	1 Identifying "mille"	1	32				
	2 "Mille" when multiplicand	1	30	none	none	2 arrays + Mille and arrow	
		2	30	none	none	arrow removed	
		3	30	none	none	"mille" removed	
	3 "Mille" when nonmultiplicand	1	30	none	none	2 arrays	RRP¶
		2	30	none	none	2 arrays	none
4 General	1 Summary	1	25	none	none	1 array	
		2	25	none	none	1 row	
		3	25		no cues		

*VP = vocabulary panel
†SF = stimulus frame
‡RF = response frame
§CDP = composed decade panel
‖HGP = hundred group panel
¶RRP = rewriting rules panel

274 DELOCHE, SERON, FERRAND

Vocabulary Panel

QUATRE VINGT DIX (ninety)	9	NEUF (nine)	9
QUATRE VINGT (eighty)	8	HUIT (eight)	8
SOIXANTE DIX (seventy)	7	SEPT (seven)	7
SOIXANTE (sixty)	6	SIX (six)	6
CINQUANTE (fifty)	5	CINQ (five)	5
QUARANTE (forty)	4	QUATRE (four)	4
TRENTE (thirty)	3	TROIS (three)	3
VINGT (twenty)	2	DEUX (two)	2
DIX (ten)	1	UN (one)	1

Numeral Stimulus   Number Response Frame

QUATRE VINGT SEPT (eighty-seven)

O	O	O
O	8	O
O	8	7
++	8	7

FIGURE 8.9. From alphabetic to digital coding system: vocabulary panel, numeral stimulus and number response frame. The left half of the vocabulary panel and the middle column of the number response frame are red; the right half of the vocabulary panel and the right column of the number response frame are blue.

The vocabulary panel was shown to the patient. The correspondence between the vocabulary panel and the number response frame was still indicated by color cues: Decade names, their corresponding digits, and the middle column of number response frame were in red, whereas Unit names, their associated digits, and the rightmost column of number response frame were in blue. The patient was instructed to transcode the numeral stimulus through the following successive operations:

1. Consider the entire alphabetic string before starting the transcoding mechanisms, operate from left to right in both the numeral stimulus and the number response frame.
2. Cross the decade name in the numeral stimulus string (either simple or composed decade), then look at the vocabulary panel and write the corresponding digit in the middle column of

number response frame; copy from Row 1 the number of heading "0"s (one in this case), and the remaining "0" to the right.

3. Cross the next lexical primitive in the numeral stimulus; copy, in the third row, the two leftmost characters of the second row; then write in the unit position the digit found in front of the unit name in the vocabulary panel.

4. Because no lexical primitive remains to be processed in the numeral stimulus, transcoding requires only erasing the heading "0", which is obtained in the next row by replacing it by a special character (#) to indicate the beginning of the digit string; the digits to the right being copied from Row 3, without modification. In Condition 2, the number response frame was now empty. The vocabulary panel was removed in Condition 3.

Step 3: Isolated Teen Names. Although several lexical primitives (two or three) are given one single digit counterpart in the case of composed decades, isolated teen names present the reverse figure: two digits are required to transcode one single word: a 1 as the decade value and the digit corresponding to the position of the teen name in its lexical file as the unit value.

This step had three conditions, using 18 items in each case (three times the six teen names). In Condition 1, a vocabulary panel was presented to the patient. The left-hand part displayed the six teen names from bottom ONZE (eleven) to top SEIZE (sixteen). The right-hand part consisted of two colored columns; the first (red) indicated that something (unspecified) was related to the red decades column of number response frame, and the second (blue) contained the digits associated with the teen name positions (Figure 8.10).

The patient was instructed to transcode the numeral stimulus following these successive operations:

1. Consider the one-word item to be transcribed.

2. Cross the word in the numeral stimulus, look up to its position in the vocabulary panel, and write the digit found in the blue rightmost column of the number response frame. A small "1," like a carry, was then written to the left, in the right top of the red cell; and the two leftmost "0s" were copied from Row 1 to Row 2.

3. Copy, from left to right, Row 2 into Row 3 while adding the two digits in the red column $(0 + 1 \rightarrow 1)$.

4. Produce the final result in Row 4 where the heading "0" was replaced by the special character "#."

276 DELOCHE, SERON, FERRAND

Vocabulary Panel

SEIZE (sixteen)	6
QUINZE (fifteen)	5
QUATORZE (fourteen)	4
TREIZE (thirteen)	3
DOUZE (twelve)	2
ONZE (eleven)	1

red blue

Numeral Stimulus   Number Response Frame

QUINZE (fifteen)

0	0	0
0	0^1	0
0	1	5
#	1	5

red blue

FIGURE 8.10. Transcoding teen names from the alphabetic to the digital coding systems.

The reasons for the unusual right-to-left writing of the digit string in Row 2 will be given in the section on the transcoding of teens imbedded in composed decades (Step 4).

In Condition 2, the colors were removed from the number response frame. The vocabulary panel was removed in Condition 3.

Step 4: Teens in Composed Decades. The decade value embodied in teen names reacts to the digital transcription of the decade names that may precede them, as in *SOIXANTE* TREIZE → *6* TREIZE → *6* (13) → 7 3. There is thus a carry from the teen to the decade slot. This step contained three conditions with 24 items each, all composed decades with imbedded teen names.

In Condition 1, the material (vocabulary panel for teens and the number response frame both colored) was identical to that of Step 3, Condition 1 cited earlier.

For instance, for the numeral stimulus SOIXANTE TREIZE, the patient had to

8. NUMBER TRANSCODING REEDUCATION 277

1. Consider the entire alphabetical string.
2. Cross the decade name SOIXANTE in the numeral stimulus and write from left to right "060" in Row 2 of the number response frame.
3. Cross the teen name TREIZE in the numeral stimulus, copy in Row 3 the first two digits from Row 2, then write in the right-most column the digit "3" associated to the teen and, in the top-right part of the decade cell the carry "1." Row 3 was thus "0 6¹3".
4. Copy Row 3 to Row 4, performing the addition of decade and carry: 0 7 3.
5. Finally, erase the heading "0" in Row 5: # 7 3.

The right-to-left digital writing of teens required in Step 3 acquires its meaning here where the same technique highlights with the carrying process the backward modification exerted by teens on decades. In Condition 2, the color cues were removed from number response frame, and the vocabulary panel was removed in Condition 3 where the number of operations in the digital writing was reduced by instructing the patient to perform the carry directly. The successive stages in transcribing SOIXANTE TREIZE thus become "000," "060," "073" (from left to right), and "#73."

Step 5: Summary—Items from Steps 2, 3, 4. Because Steps 2, 3, and 4 were specifically designed to handle transcoding procedures into two-digit numbers, a mixed list of 30 items from these steps was then used to check for overgeneralization of a particular process. There was one single uncued condition (no colors, no panels).

Level 2: Figures with Cent (Hundred)

The exercises concerned the case of numerals to be transcoded into three-digit numbers.

Step 1: Identifying the "Hundred Group". Either one word (CENT in CENT VINGT TROIS [123]) or two adjacent words (SEPT and CENT in SEPT CENT VINGT TROIS [723]) gave one single digit in the hundred slot of the number response frame. Identification of this group of one or two alphabetic lexical primitives thus constituted a precondition for the transcoding process. A list of 30 numerals was presented to the patient, who was instructed to color (in blue) each hundred group, as a whole. Ten items contained no such group; one half of the 20 remaining contained CENT preceded by a digit name; the other half contained CENT alone as the first word of the numeral.

278   DELOCHE, SERON, FERRAND

This step had only one condition. A vocabulary panel for hundreds names was shown to the patient. The nine hundred groups were arranged in a column from bottom CENT to top NEUF CENT and printed in blue.

Step 2: Writing Three-digit Numbers.   The transcoding rule for the hundred group was to write the digit corresponding to the digit name preceding CENT, or to write 1 when CENT was not preceded by a digit name, and then to process the alphabetic substring to the right of CENT as indicated in Level 1 for decade unit figures.

There were four conditions in this step with three lists of 30 items. In Condition 1, a vocabulary panel for the hundred group was presented with the nine alphabetic forms (from CENT to NEUF CENT). The corresponding digits, from bottom 1 to top 9, were also indicated. These two columns of the vocabulary panel were printed in blue, as was the leftmost column of the number response frame. The transcoding instructions obeyed the same principles as stated earlier for two-digit numbers: proceed from left to right; cross successively the hundred, decade, unit, or teen group in the numeral stimulus before actually writing the corresponding digits in the hundred, decade, and unit positions of the number response frame on different rows. For instance, SEPT CENT TRENTE SIX → 000 (Row 1); 700 (Row 2); 730 (Row 3); 736 (Row 4). In Condition 2, the color cue in the leftmost column of number response frame was no longer present. In Condition 3, the vocabulary panel was removed, and the patient now had to transcribe directly the decade units or decade teens figures by mentally performing the intermediate operations—thus, QUATRE CENT SOIXANTE DOUZE → 000; 400 (Row 2); 472 (Row 3). In Condition 4, the number response frame was reduced to two rows, the first, 000 still indicating the initial state of the transcription that had to be written directly from left to right onto the second row after crossing the entire numeral string. Together with three-digit numbers, this list contained four one-digit and eight two-digit numbers that the patient had to justify to the right of the number response frame when producing the Arabic number forms.

Level 3: Figures with Mille (Thousand)

This level concerned the writing of numbers from four to six digits.

Step 1: Identifying the Separator Mille.   Because the general rule was to apply separately and successively to the two substrings to the left and to the right of MILLE the transcoding technique for the case of three-digit numbers, the first step was to identify the separator. The patient was instructed to color in green each occurrence of MILLE found in a list of 32 numerals.

Step 2: Mille (Thousand) When Multiplicand. In this case, MILLE actually separates two substrings that have to be processed independently. There were three conditions, with different lists of 30 items. The items were four, five, or six digits long, with 20 of them requiring at least one intercalary "0" in their digital writing.

In Condition 1, the number response frame was made by juxtaposing the two arrays of two rows and three columns. The word MILLE was written just above the junction between the two arrays, and a vertical arrow pointed downward to this place, where a comma was to be inserted in the digital form. The transcoding proceeded from left to right according to the general principles already stated. The entire substring to the left of MILLE was crossed and then transcribed into the left hemipart of the number response frame. MILLE was then crossed and a comma written. The remainders of the numeral stimulus was then crossed and transcribed to the right of the comma. The digital transcription thus occupied only one row (the second) in the number response frame; the six "0"s in the first row facilitated the writing of intercalary "0"s when necessary.

In Condition 2, the word MILLE was no longer printed above the number response frame, but the arrow still indicated the proper positioning of the digit string to the right. The arrow was suppressed in Condition 3, so the patient had to position the digits without a spatial cue.

Step 3: Mille (Thousand) in the Initial Position. In numerals beginning with MILLE, this word is not really a separator because the numeral substring to its left is reduced to null. The unqualified application of the transcoding rules stated earlier would induce errors like *MILLE* DEUX CENT TRENTE → , 2 3 0, instead of 1,230. A rewriting rule panel of the form MILLE . . . → 1, . . . was presented to the patient. A vertical bar just before MILLE stressed that this rule was valid only in the first position of numerals. This step contained two conditions, with one new list of 30 items in each case. The numbers to be produced ranged from four to six digits. One half of the items required the rewriting rule, the other half did not, so overgeneralization could be controlled.

In Condition 1, the number response frame was an array of two rows and six columns, with "0"s in the first row. The rewriting rule panel was shown to the patient. The panel was removed in Condition 2.

280 DELOCHE, SERON, FERRAND

Level 4: General

This final state of the rehabilitation program contained just one summarizing step.

Items of the different kinds were mixed together. The same list of 25 items of two-digit to six-digit numbers was used in three conditions.

In Condition 1, the number response frame contained the array of two rows and six columns. The numbers had to be correctly justified to the right by the patient. In Condition 2, the number response frame array was reduced to one single row of six columns. Intercalary "0"s had to be produced by the patient when necessary, and positioning to the right was still required. The number response frame was removed in Condition 3. All facilitation devices were thus progressively removed.

Results

Treatment Sessions

The therapy took 8 weeks, comprising a total of 17 sessions of 30 minutes to 1 hour each. The patient always achieved the 90% criterion of response accuracy, so no supplementary sessions were needed.

Treatment Effects

The effects of the training program were first measured 2 months after the therapy was completed and also 1 year thereafter. (Figure 8.8).

Posttest 1. Improvement was noted not only in the *transcoding task* that was specifically taught (from a 29% error rate on the pretest to 2%), but also in the transcription of numeral forms into the base 10 token system for quantities (from a 35% error rate to 2%). In addition to this training transfer in the decoding of alphabetic numerals, a deblocking effect seems to have occurred because the patient was able to write numerals without having to copy the primitives printed on cards.

The errors produced in writing numerals from Arabic digit forms were 11 literal paragraphias, which mainly concerned the unit name QUATRE (4) and its corresponding teen name QUATORZE (14), three composed decade numbers, and one item (13) that could not be transcribed at all. There were also some errors that the patient spontaneously corrected himself, sometimes by checking his responses by reading them aloud. Transcoding quantities into numerals was performed some days later, whereupon only four errors were made, three literal paragraphias and one substitution of the unit name for its decade name. Self-corrected errors were frequent and concerned mainly literal paragraphias but also some incidental transcoding errors like 6D (60) → SIX (6), then SOIXANTE (60). The deblocking effect observed in the writing of alphabetic numeral forms may thus have been due to the presentation of well-formed numerals during both training and testing. Reading aloud was used by the patient for checking his productions. This was slightly easier with numerals than with numbers (three and five errors respectively out of the 62 items). The errors were phonemic paraphasias (/sɛz/ (16) for /tRɛz/ (13) in 193 → /CENT QUATRE VINGT SEIZE/ (196)), stack errors (4 → /QUARANTE/ [40]) and confusions between thousand and hundred (583 → /CINQ MILLE QUATRE VINGT TROIS/ (5,083); 4,030 → /QUATRE CENT TRENTE/ [430]).

The few errors produced in transcribing the forms of one base 10 coding system into the other involved erroneous countings.

Positioning on a Number Line, was correct in both coding systems on only four out of the six trials. The errors were 14 for 4, 10 for 24, QUARANTE TROIS (43) for VINGT CINQ (25), and QUARANTE DEUX (42) for VINGT QUATRE (24).

Numerical Serial Ordering was perfect with Arabic numbers but there were four incorrect sequences out of the 10 items with numerals. The errors mainly concerned numerals with composed decades (SOIXANTE SEPT [67] coming after QUATRE VINGT [80]).

Magnitude Comparisons were performed without error in both the Arabic and the alphabetic coding systems. This result, which could seem at variance with the error rates observed in the sequencing of numerals according to their value, could be tentatively reconciled with the data by considering that handling six numerals at the same time may be more resource consuming than dealing with only two. This hypothesis was supported by the finding that the patient was able to detect his errors when he was presented the 10 sequences he had produced and instructed to successively check the adjacent numerals by groups of two. The Numeral Grammaticality Judgment Test was performed with some hesitation, but only one nonrecognition occurred and all illegal forms were correctly rejected.

Posttest 2. The long-term effects of training were similar to those obtained at Posttest 1, thus indicating that the improvements over the pretraining performance level were significant and stable. In fact, the only source of discrepancies between the two posttests occurred in the two transcodings with alphabetic numerals as the object code and were due to occasional and nonstable literal paragraphias that were sometimes self-corrected by the subject, who read aloud as a means of checking his transcriptions. There were no errors in the transcoding task, that had been trained (from Arabic numbers to alphabetic numerals). The other transcoding tests showed non-systematic errors. Positioning a Numerical Form on a Number Line, Numerical Serial Ordering, and Magnitude Comparisons were performed without any error, in both the Arabic digit and alphabetic-numeral systems. The Numeral Grammaticality Judgment Test showed no errors.

The main results of this single case therapy thus concern the transfer of training in the decoding of alphabetically written numeral forms, the deblocking effects on the written production of numerals, the long-term efficiency of training, and the progressive improvement in dealing with the values of numeral forms. Reading numbers, numerals, and tokens collections aloud was often spontaneously used to check the responses. Improvements also extended to the metalinguistic skills involved in the Numeral Grammaticality Judgment Test. It thus seems that the training of a set of local transcoding rules, without reference to comprehension and the syntactical components of number-numeral processing, had progressively reorganized these numerical abilities. The residual literal paragraphias might be reduced because they were localized in the writing of the unit- teen-decade triad whose lexical elements share the highest morphological similarities (QUATRE, [4], QUATORZE [14], and QUARANTE [40]).

CONCLUSION

The therapies presented here both derive from the "reconstitution of function" approach proposed by Luria (1966), which employs the patient's intact capabilities to inculcate operating procedures corresponding to formalized analyses of the tasks under consideration. Such approaches have already been successfully applied to a variety of domains like memory and language using the single-case paradigm (see for instance Beauvois and Derouesné [1982] for a general discussion and case reports). Here, the structural characteristics of the notational systems for numerical codings strongly contribute to the feasibility and efficiency of the treatment program: The number of the rules required for transcribing the whole set of numbers or numerals is very limited, and the rules do not manipulate abstract representations or use obscure notations but are stated in very simple terms. In short, the bridge between Arabic digital numbers and alphabetic numeral forms resides in the core of the same lexical "position" information concept that is common to the file structures of the two systems. It turns out that what "position" means for digits and unit names coincides with the usual meaning of one-digit numbers used to represent positions (i.e., the values from 1 to 9), which is readily understandable. The therapies may, of course, seem odd in the sense that children are not taught such rules when learning to handle numbers and because the procedures do not imply numerical comprehension operations involving semantic representations. However, because the asemantic algorithms also achieve the functional results of transcodings, their efficiency for rehabilitation purposes had to be considered. The structure of both therapies obeyed the general principles of programed learning. The exercises were highly specific for exemplifying the use of one rule/subrule or another and were hierarchized in such a way that any level in the program did not require more knowledge than that already acquired. The progression thus followed logically organized steps. For example, parsing numeral alphabetic forms into lexical primitives preceded the assignment of digit specifications, and the exceptions were presented after stating the general rule, not only because this seemed more natural, but also because it was the occasion to make the patient aware of why he had made overgeneralization errors like the 1 in the hundred position transcribed by UN CENT instead of CENT. The case of teens is even more instructing because the erroneous forms (16 [SEIZE] → DIX SIX) had to be actually written as an intermediate production before reaching the right numeral forms. The constant criterion of correct response percentage to be passed ensured that learning the rule of the particular step was sufficiently established so that it could be instantiated later on when necessary. However, it appeared that some errors did not occur at random on the items that exemplify the same transcoding pattern, but sometimes exclusively concerned lexical primitives with a high degree of morphological similarities (the triad QUATRE [4], QUATORZE [14], QUARANTE [40]). Such a limited and purely lexical disorder does not invalidate the logical structure of the treatment program for learning syntactic rules for operation on lexical categories (units, teens, decades) but simply requires a pause in the general therapy and exercises specifically designed for the lexical primitives that give problems. (Another possibility would be to begin rehabilitation with a program for the alphabetic numeral lexicon before entering syntactic rule exercises.)

The two experimental treatment programs reported here were administered to patients who had passed beyond the point of spontaneous recovery. The performance profiles were measured before therapy, at the end of the program, and again several months later. The modifications observed were obvious and stable, so they can reasonably be attributed to the effect of training.

The first case was a success in the transcoding direction trained, and this effect was not limited to the items used during therapy (the error rate dropped from 45% to 6% on the assessment battery). The results of the other transcodings between the three notational systems for quantities (Arabic digits, alphabetic numerals, collections of dots tokens) indicated a similar progression in writing numerals from tokens (from 37% to 6% errors) and no change in the tasks where performances were initially good (probable ceiling effect). It may thus be that producing alphabetic numerals from digits or tokens makes use of one common component, or that performances similarities simply reflect the structural similarities of the transcoding processes operating from the two base 10 representation systems to the alphabetic code, or finally that one task mediates the other. Although the route from tokens to numerals via the number code would be expected to produce a combined error rate of 47%, whereas the observed error rate from tokens to numerals was only 37%, several arguments favor such a hypothesis. First, the patient always arranged the tokens in groups of decimal values serially and horizontally from left to right, like digit strings (the 1,000s, 100s, 10s, and 1s). Second, he declared at the end of the task that he used Arabic digit forms as temporary representations and consequently had some trouble with items with embedded "0"s as in 7H 2U (702) → SOIXANTE DIX (70) DEUX (2) presumably transcribing 702 erroneously parsed into 70 and 2, or 1H 8U (108) → CENT ZERO HUIT where the word ZERO stands for nothing present in the collection of tokens, or 9H 7U (907), which was spontaneously written in the digit system before being transcoded. Third, the difficulties in writing alphabetical numerical forms (as opposed to digit forms) also appeared in writing from dictation (14 and 0 errors, respectively out of the 62 items of the battery). Finally we note that such impairments in producing written numerals were manifested in the context of controlled transcoding operations clearly dealing with the universe of numbers, but neither when numerals had to be produced in open-ended idioms "se mettre sur son trente et un" (to dress up; literally to put on one's 31s); "faire le tour du monde en quatre-vingts jours" (around the world in 80 days); "faire les quatre cents coups" (to commit all sorts of excesses; literally do the 400 strokes) nor in the context of historical events or in writing the counting sequence (Seron & Deloche, 1987).

Because the three tasks that tentatively tapped the patient's numerical comprehension skills (positioning, sequencing, and magnitude comparisons) were not disturbed, one may conclude that the tasks are not sensitive enough to numerical semantic representation processing or that numerical transcodings do not necessarily rely on such semantic procedures (see McCloskey & Caramazza [1987] for semantic models), or finally that semantic operations were performed but that the patient's disorder was located elsewhere in the transcoding mechanisms. The improvements observed in judging the grammaticality of sequences of alphabetic lexical primitives may be explained by the effects of the structure of the transcoding treatment program on the particular error types. Before therapy, most transcoding errors (86%) were dyssyntactic, and false recognitions in the grammaticality judgments occurred on forms whose structure corresponded to erroneous transcriptions actually produced. The decrease of false recognitions (from 30% to 6%) seemed to be because only correct numeral forms were written during therapy, the use of explicit rewriting rules panels pointing to illegal forms (ZERO → nil or DIX SIX → SEIZE, . . .) and also because the lexicalization of composed decades that removes the ambiguity from the complex decade-unit-decade item TRENTE QUATRE VINGT (thirty four twenty) where both TRENTE QUATRE (thirty-four) and QUATRE VINGT (eighty) are well formed into the clearly illegal decade-decade (thirty eighty) pattern. The modification of nonrecognition scores from 20% to 2% may be attributed to the patient having been trained to produce legal numeral forms covering the whole range of acceptable structures. Syntactical abilities in handling the grammar of numerals thus seemed in this case to be linked to transcoding abilities (or to depend on a commonly used component) and not necessarily to be involved in tasks that presumably manipulate numerical semantic representations. The long-term improvements of the performance profiles of the patient (Case 2) engaged in the treatment program for writing numbers from numeral forms did not seem to be obscured by his surgery (insertion of a boneplasty of a skull defect) that took place between the two posttests because no clinical or behavioral modifications were observed. The error percentage decreased from 29% to 2% in the treated transcoding direction, and was not item specific. Improvement was also marked in the task that concerned the same source coding system but used the other base 10 notations (dots-tokens) as the object code. As in the first case, the global therapy effect hypothesis may be dismissed on the grounds that errors on the pretest resulted from the same erroneous parsing of the numeral string (non-integration of the elements of composed decades and of the multiplier-multiplicand unit name, hundred figures), such structures being extensively worked on during the therapy. The improvement observed in

286 DELOCHE, SERON, FERRAND

writing alphabetic numerals (almost impossible initially) receives no evident interpretation in the framework of componential models of number processing. If such a deblocking did occur, it may be related to the exposure of the patient to numerals throughout the program and to his ability to copy them in pretherapeutic evaluation. The clearing of errors in numeral grammaticality judgments can be similarly explained in the case of nonrecognitions by the presentation of well-formed sequences and in the case of false recognitions by their locus that concerned trained structures (integration of composed decades). Finally, residual errors were observed in the semantic representation tasks. The finding of impaired numerical transcoding abilities that may co-occur and independently evolve (this patient) or not (first patient) in reference to semantic processes does not seem to support the basic hypothesis underlying semantic transcoding models according to which semantic representations of numerical forms are necessarily required in transcoding operations. On the contrary, the assumption that transcoding may be performed without mandatory comprehension of the numerical values represented by surface forms seems to be strengthened. However, the fascinating question of the mechanisms involved in the comprehension of complex numerical forms, those not restricted to one-digit numbers, still remains open.

REFERENCES

Beauvois, M. F., & Derouesné, J. (1982). Psychologie cognitive et rééducation neuro-psychologique: quels rapports? In Seron, X., & Laterre, C. (Eds.), *Rééduquer le cerveau*. Bruxelles: Mardaga.

Coltheart, M., Patterson, K., & Marshall, J. C. (1980). *Deep dyslexia*. London: Routledge & Kegan Paul.

Deloche, G., & Andreewsky, E. (1982). From neuropsychological data to reading mechanisms. *International Journal of Psychology, 17*, 259–279.

Deloche, G., & Seron, X. (1982). From one to 1: an analysis of a transcoding process by means of neuropsychological data. *Cognition, 12*, 119–149.

Deloche, G., & Seron, X. (1986). Grammaticality judgments by aphasics of alphabetically written numeral forms. *Psychologica Belgica, 26*, 17–42.

Deloche, G., & Seron, X. (Eds.). (1987a). *Mathematical disabilities: a cognitive neuropsychological perspective*. Hillsdale, NJ: Lawrence Erlbaum Associates.

Deloche, G., & Seron, X. (1987b). Numerical transcoding mechanisms: a general production model. In Deloche, G., & Seron, X. (Eds.), *Mathematical disabilities: a cognitive neuropsychological perspective*. Hillsdale, NJ: Lawrence Erlbaum Associates.

Ducarne, B. (1986). *Rééducation sémiologique de l'aphasie*. Paris: Masson.

Fuson, K. C., Richards, J., & Briards, D. J. (1982). The acquisition and elaboration of the number word sequence. In Brainerd, C. J. (Ed.), *Children's Logical and Mathematical Cognition*. New York: Springer Verlag.

Gelman, R., & Gallistel, C. R. (1978). *The child's understanding of number*. Cambridge, MA: Harvard University Press.

8. NUMBER TRANSCODING REEDUCATION 287

Grewel, G. (1969). The acalculias. In Vinken, P. J., & Bruyn, G. (Eds.), *Handbook of clinical neurology* (Vol. 3). Amsterdam: North Holland.

Henschen, S. E. (1922). *Klinische und anatomische beitrag zür pathologie des gehirns.* Stockholm: Nordiske Bofhandelen.

Hurford, J. R. (1975). *The linguistic theory of numerals.* Cambridge: University Press.

Luria, A. R. (1966). *Higher cortical functions in man.* London: Tavistock.

Mazaux, J. M., & Orgogozzo, J. (1982). *Examen de l'aphasie.* Issy les Moulineaux: Editions Scientifiques et Psychologiques.

McCloskey, M., & Caramazza, A. (1987). Cognitive mechanisms in normal and impaired number processing. In Deloche, G., & Seron, X. (Eds.), *Mathematical disabilities: a cognitive neuropsychological perspective.* Hillsdale, NJ: Lawrence Erlbaum Associates.

Power, R. J. D., & Longuet-Higgings, H. C. (1978). Learning to count: a computational model of language acquisition. *Proceedings of the Royal Society, London, 200,* 391–417.

Seron, X., & Deloche, G. (1984). From 2 to two: an analysis of a transcoding process by means of neuropsychological evidence. *Journal of Psycholinguistic Research, 13,* 215–235.

Seron, X., & Deloche, G. (1987). The production of counting sequences by aphasics and children: a matter of lexical processing? In Deloche, G. & Seron, X. (Eds.), *Mathematical disabilities: a cognitive neuropsychological perspective.* Hillsdale, NJ: Lawrence Erlbaum Associates.

Warrington, E. K. (1982). The fractionation of arithmetical skills: a single case study. *Quarterly Journal of Experimental Psychology, 34A,* 31–51.

9 A Retrospective Analysis of a Single Case Neglect Therapy: A Point of Theory

Xavier Seron
Ucl. Unité Nexa. Brussel

Gérard Deloche
Service du Prof. Deseilligny. Hopital de la Salpétrière Paris

Françoise Coyette
Centre de Revalidation Neuropsychologique Cliniques Universitaires,
St. Luc., Brussel

Several authors have noted that, taken as a group, left hemiplegics recover to a lesser degree and adjust socially less adequately than do right hemiplegics (Hurwitz & Adams, 1972; Marquardsen, 1969; Weinberg et al., 1977; Weisbroth, Esibil, & Zuger, 1971). Investigating the role of concomitant neuropsychological factors on the outcome of recovery in right and left hemiplegics, Denes, Semenza, Stoppa, & Lis (1982) noted that the presence of a unilateral spatial neglect seems to be a crucial factor, whereas confusional states, intellectual deterioration, or emotional factors do not significantly affect the outcome of recovery. Even if these authors did not interpret the negative incidence of neglect symptoms on recovery (which may be either a causal factor or a symptom coincident with other, unnoticed factors) its status as a predictor of poor recovery and its negative effect on driving (Lorenze & Cranco, 1962), reading (Weinberg & Diller, 1968), and daily-life activities (Diller & Weinberg, 1970, 1977) render the development of accurate therapeutic methods that focus on neglect disorders of crucial importance.

NEGLECT RECOVERY

Little is known about spontaneous evolution of hemineglect disorders. Gainotti (1968) has claimed that neglect is principally evident in the early stages, and may in some cases completely disappear after

3 years postonset, whereas Zarit and Kahn (1974) have found evidence of persisting inattention up to 12 years postonset. In a more systematic investigation, Campbell and Oxbury (1976) examined two small groups of patients with right hemisphere lesions 3 to 4 weeks and 6 months after stroke. One group (six patients) had neglect symptoms; the other (eight patients) did not. At 6 months, the neglect group still performed significantly worse than the other group on several visuospatial tasks (Block design, cube counting, Goldin Incomplete Pictures, etc.) even though four patients out of the six could then make complete drawings. Campbell and Oxbury (1976) suggested that improved drawing performance may be the result of a local compensatory strategy rather than the expression of the spontaneous recovery of a more general, underlying disturbed mechanism that is responsible for the neglect symptoms. They did not analyze the influence of physiological or neuropsychological variables on symptom evolution.

Analysis of the effect of such physiological variables was done by Hier, Mondlock, and Caplan (1983a) for a larger group of patients. These authors analyzed recovery of function after right hemisphere damage by compiling several measures of neglect, prosopagnosia, denial of illness, constructional apraxia, hemianopia, dressing apraxia, leg weakness, arm weakness, etc., as well as the role of different variables such as sex, age, and size, type, and localization of lesions. The results indicated no effect of sex and a rapid rate of recovery for left neglect and unilateral spatial neglect (USN) in drawing (median duration to recovery being 8 weeks for USN on drawing and 9 weeks for neglect of left space, no range values were presented). Nevertheless, the rating of neglect was only clinical and not clearly described from a methodological point of view (Hier, Mondlock, & Caplan, 1983b), and the recovery was clearly less rapid on more complex visuospatial tasks such as block designs and the Rey-Osterrieth figure (16 weeks median duration each). One may thus suggest that the task these authors used to rate neglect symptoms were not sufficiently sensitive to provide evidence for persistent underlying spatial attentional deficits. Whatever these limitations, these authors observed that recovery of neglect is influenced by stroke type (patients with a hemorrhage recovered faster than those with an infarct), lesion size (faster recovery for small lesions), age (patients younger than 60 years recovered more quickly from prosopagnosia and unilateral spatial neglect on drawing), and the absence of a frontal lesion (which has a positive effect on neglect recuperation).

Taken together, these studies do not provide a clear picture of spontaneous recovery of neglect. The existing studies are clearly too few in number for an analysis of the differential influences of variables, such as age, sex, and size, type, and localization of lesion.

The problem is also methodological. There is a manifest need for adequate and more widely accepted criteria to assess unilateral visuospatial neglect deficits, but the establishment of such criteria is obviously dependent on a theory of the underlying neglect behavior deficits. If it seems necessary to use more than one index of neglect in recovery studies, it remains, as Campbell and Oxbury have stressed, that these different indicators have to be correlated with each other to clarify the underlying factors. Such an enterprise requires an integrated theoretical framework, which we still do not have.

NEGLECT REEDUCATION

Compared with aphasia rehabilitation, reeducation of neglect is presently not common in neuropsychological rehabilitation. In the literature, we have only single-case reports by Lawson (1962) and Seron and Tissot (1973), the more extensive work by Diller and his coworkers (Diller et al., 1974), the subsequent works these studies have stimulated (Gouvier, Cottam, Webster, Beissel, & Wofford, 1984; Sivak, Olson, Kewman, Won, & Henson, 1981), and recent reeducational programs using microcomputers (Deloche et al., 1983; Hart, Carbonari, & Sheer, 1984; Larsen, Ahrensberg, Carlsen, & Mejding, 1984). Lawson's reeducational approach involved two patients. It was not systematic and was limited to reading treatment. The first patient, a 45-year-old woman, was cooperative, fully orientated in space and time, and had no memory defect and no dysphasia. When therapy was commenced 9 weeks postonset, she presented a left lower quadrantal and homonymous defect in the visual field and severe left hemiphegia. The performance of the patient on different spatial tasks indicated symptoms of neglect of variable severity. Reading was difficult: omission of the left side of the material, difficulty and hesitation in finding the beginning of a line, and no awareness of the disorder when the incorrectly read text was incoherent. Nevertheless, visual constructive disorders were not observed during manikin assembly or arrangement of simple geometric shapes, and drawings were not grossly altered although there was a displacement of the subject matter to the right side of the page and a neglect of some detail on the left side of drawings. No details of the rehabilitation procedure were given. It simply seems to have consisted in advising the patient to "look to the left" when she was unable to make sense of a passage. This instruction was repeated as often as necessary when the patient was reading. Two retests were administered to evaluate the effect of therapy, one "some weeks later", the other "three months later." Progress was observed in reading behavior on two reading tasks: one of meaningful arrangement of words, the other of a random list of words. Aside from reading performance, no clear transfer of progress was observed in drawing or picture exploration. This may have been due to a ceiling effect because these tasks indicated less alteration than did reading before reeducation, and reading itself was not completely reorganized. Lawson's second case, again a woman, was more handicapped. The patient showed, in addition to a full, homonymous left hemianopsia, a massive neglect for the left side. The identification of words, pictures, and objects was restricted to a narrow right-hand strip. The simple correcting instruction "look to the left" was ineffective, so the author had recourse to additional cues like "spotlighting the print with a flashlight or by pointing with a pencil." After the patient was observed to react better to her own finger pointing than to that of the therapist, she was trained to use her own finger as an aid in reading. After therapy of more than 6 weeks, progress was observed in reading single-column texts. Two years after stroke, the patient was able to read well single-column texts and newspapers without finger assistance, although some signs of neglect persisted in picture exploration and drawings.

As for the rationale of the Lawson's reeducational enterprise, some points must be stressed. Lawson's approach, especially with his first patient, consisted in using the patient's own awareness that the material she read was incoherent in order to stimulate left-oriented reading behavior. However, as Lawson noted, "this was neither a spontaneous nor a self-learned process for the most impressive feature of the neglect was the patient's own initial unawareness of it." In other words, when the patient, left to herself, was confronted by a meaningless text, she tried spontaneously to extract or construct coherence from the incomplete sample of words she saw rather than to turn to the neglected side for information. Consequently, what Lawson devised was a program that progressed from awareness of incoherence to external verbal "look-left" instructions and then to self-delivered instructions. Furthermore, Lawson rightly noted than "neither was their looking a simultaneous look and move" as in a normal person. One can thus postulate that three steps at least have to be considered at the onset of Lawson's procedure: first, awareness of textual incongruity; second, self-delivered "looking left" instruction; and third, controlled execution of the self-instruction. The presence of the first two steps does not seem guarantee the execution the effective left-oriented scanning (step three).

The single case reported by Seron and Tissot (1973) concerns a 26-

year-old man. When entering the rehabilitation program, one year after his stroke, the patient presented only moderate symptoms of neglect: Simple drawings were normal, but signs of neglect were present in picture exploration, line bisection, reading and writing, as well as in various daily-life activities and during traditional occupational therapy.

A reeducational program was developed for space exploration, line bisection, writing, reading, and various visuospatial activities. The general program rationale was the following. At the first step of each exercise the patient was placed in a complex situation such that he was forced to make an error. The comment about that error by the examiner was intended to provoke awareness of the difficulties. Then the exercises were presented in a simplified form in the right hemifield and with cues, and then progressively translated to the left side. When the patient attain a predefined criterion of correct response in the right side, the cues were progressively eliminated. Progress was manifest in all the activities trained, even though the number of daily sessions were variable according to the activities (only six sessions for line bisection but up to 24 sessions for reading). The authors reported transfer in various daily life activities, such as wheelchair operation, typewriting, and locomotion, but no systematic and independent measures were offered. Finally, in some visuospatial tasks executed 3 months after the end of the therapy (Kohs' design, cube drawing) neglect deficits were still present. The authors noted that their training techniques at the beginning of the therapy, without an initial insistence on awareness of the disorder through specific verbal commands, was not efficacious. They thus concluded that it is necessary to eliminate the anosognosia before effective training procedures can be implemented.

The work of the Diller New York medical team (NYMT) is more extensive, more systematic as regards methodology, and more clearly oriented to a theoretical point of view. They described their general approach to hemineglect treatment in four main stages.

1. Establishment of a pretherapy battery composed of standardized tasks sensitive to the presence of hemineglect.
2. Examination of response styles in order to determine different subgroups of patients.
3. Development of task conditions that influence the importance of hemineglect signs.
4. Construction of a retraining method that, first, helps patients to become aware of their deficit and, second, helps them to overcome their deficit.

The first "diagnosis" step consists of a visual letter cancellation task. Roughly 60% of right brain-damaged patients given this task show either a marked or a moderate neglect deficit. Analysis of response characteristics indicate that hemiinattentive patients produce omission errors, but no commission errors, more frequently on the contralateral side of the page, that some of them explore erratically, and that many perform the task too quickly. Subgroups of patients formed in function of disorder severity (severe or mild) may be distinguished on a large battery of tasks, some of which concern visual external exploration behavior. Qualitative analysis of the parameters that influence patient performance in the cancellation task were systematically examined. The authors observed that the locus of the stimuli play a role: Those situated on the left side were more frequently omitted. Visual and verbal anchorage improved performance: Anchoring from the left was superior to anchoring from the right side, and both types of anchoring were superior to free style performance. Finally, when the distance between stimuli was increased and the patient asked to slow down, the neglect was decreased.

The first step of the therapy was, as in the case of Lawson (1962) and Seron and Tissot (1973), to make the patient aware of his difficulties. This was done through verbal instructions in two task situations: picking up coins and simple copying. The authors stressed that this phase of the therapy is of crucial importance because then "the patient's resistance and suspicions are at a maximum" (Diller & Weinberg, 1977, p. 68).

The treatment began on different tasks, the general logic as summarized by Diller and Weinberg being as follows:

1. Presenting the patient with a task that is sufficiently compelling to cause head turning to the neglected size.
2. Guiding the patient's scanning in a directed, even-paced search of the environment to overcome the "pull" to the right side.
3. Supplying the patient with cues to assist in systematic and orderly scanning and, as the patient improves, gradually reducing cues so that the patient can perform the activity on his own.
4. Providing feedback to the patient as to the correctness of his performance. (Diller & Weinberg, 1977, p. 68)

Tasks, such as light visual scanning, visual cancellations of numbers, and reading paragraphs from newspapers, were systematically administered 1 hour a day for 20 days. After the therapy, patients were encouraged to continue at home with the assistance of their family. The results indicated that the right brain-damaged treated group improved significantly more than a group of control subjects who had received traditional occupational therapy. The therapy used with some individuals is presented in detail. Follow-up indicated that the benefit of the therapies remained stable (Diller & Weinberg, 1977).

Transfer effect were analyzed by a change index on three different levels: tasks close to trained tasks, tasks related to the trained tasks, and tasks unrelated or divergent from the trained tasks. The trained group improved significantly more than the untreated group in each of the three areas, although not on all the tasks. On the whole, the severely impaired patients made more progress than did the others. Finally, the effects of experimental therapy and classic occupational therapy were compared by means of a signal detection technique: The experimental group did better on most of the tasks, but some control subjects also improved.

The authors attribute the efficacy of the treatment to

1. left anchoring being the usual starting point in reading habits and thus being an overlearned skill
2. the importance of awareness of the difficulties combined with elements to overcome it, the rationale being to teach problem solving activities and overcome the "denial reaction."

Even though some transfer was observed to related and less related tasks, the explanation of such transfer effects is far from clear. The selection of the different task areas was empirical and the result of correlational analyses. Thus, the classification of tasks was based on the observation of disorder co-occurrence in various situations rather than on a theoretically motivated approach to the different processing components involved in the tasks.

To generalize the method further, Weinberg et al. (1979) added two new techniques intended for 5 hours of therapy: training in sensory awareness and in spatial organization. The sensory awareness program consisted of training the patient to locate on the back of a manikin the spot corresponding to the point the examiner has touched on the patient's own back. The technique has eight stages in function of the location of the stimulus and whether it is single or double. The spatial organization program focused on training size estimation in three different locations: on the front, on the impaired side, and on the nonimpaired side of the patient. This program was more effective as regards generalization than the original treatment program. Patients with severe impairments still improved more than those with mild impairments. The authors considered that this second study supports the position that a program that incorporates spatial and somatosensory exercises is more powerful than one limited to visual scanning alone.

Finally, a number of other methods based on the same perceptual-cognitive logic are also worthy of mention here. Rao and Bielauskas (1983) presented a case study of a 45-year-old radiologist, the therapy commencing 2.5 months postsurgery. After a 4-month retraining program tailored to the patient's specific neuropsychological deficits, improvements were observed on neuropsychological tests, and transfer was observed by his wife in daily life activities and on work-related task such as scanner interpretation. Young, Collins, and Hien (1983) compared three groups of nine left-hemiplegic patients who received three different kinds of therapy. They observed the superiority of improvement and of transfer of learning in the group who received, along with cancellation and visual scanning training, additional block design therapy. Stanton et al. (1983) used a direct training approach to teach a right hemiplegic patient to operate a wheelchair. This was a stepwise hierarchical program based on verbal self control.

CRITICAL APPRAISAL

Taken together the results of these perceptual-cognitive therapies seem to have been successful, even if it often remains difficult to rule out improvement due to spontaneous recovery or to general stimulation and encouragement. Nevertheless, it seems at least reasonable to accept that the NYMT has presented reliable quantitative data: The results they obtained cannot be explained merely by spontaneous recovery and indicate progress superior to that resulting from unorganized general stimulation therapies.

Nevertheless, it remains that these so-called perceptual-cognitive therapies are in fact atheoretical insofar as they lack any precise cognitive interpretation of the neglect disorders. More specifically, the therapeutic exercises were not selected in function of hypotheses based on precise and well-identified processing component deficits. In fact, the techniques of the NYMT can only be labeled cognitive in that they focused on cognitive functioning, but the selection of the exercises and of the procedures and the progression were determined on the basis of behavioral observations by trial and error. For example, the choice of a left-sided anchorage starting point is justified by the fact that left anchorage activates a classic reading habit and by its better efficiency compared with right anchorage. Such observations are, of course, respectable but not very helpful on the theoretical level, and we do not know why a left anchorage is more efficacious than a right one. In the same vein to pace the visual movements during exploration is considered an efficacious training strategy, but it is far from clear why such a positive effect occurred. One could agree with the authors that such pacing counterbalances a tendency in right-brain-damaged (RBD) patients to move their eyes too quickly to the right side of space, but other interpretations are just as plausible on this mechanistic description: The pacing techniques they used required verbalization, which can activate the left hemisphere and provoke a control on ipsilateral scanning; or the pacing procedure might cause a shift from automatic scanning to controlled orienting eye movements, which Riddoch and Humphreys (1983) consider less defective in neglect patients.

The same general remarks apply to the classification of the NYMT of neglect patients into severe and mild forms. Such a quantitative delimitation is first done through quantitative analyses of the results obtained by RBD patients on various cancellation tasks, whereupon this division is operationalized on a large battery of 21 different tests. Such a classification into two distinct groups in function of only quantitative measurements of the deficits may be of ecological utility, but it does not guarantee that the neglect disorders in both groups are of the same nature nor does it permit the homogeneity of the disorders inside each group that is postulated.

The lack of a precise theoretical interpretation of the neglect disorder combined with the presentation of results of groups of patients only classified according to the degree of gravity of their disorders also makes it impossible to say why some patients improve but others do not. The data from the NYMT indicate clearly that not all the subjects of the mild or of the severe group improve on all the posttest tasks. Such variations, of course, may be due to factors external to the neglect disorders, such as the patient's level of motivation, intraindividual differences in learning abilities, and so on. Yet it may just as well be that these patients had, in fact, different neglect disorders, that is, disorders resulting from the alterations of different processing components, which could explain why some of them reacted to the treatment while others were not. Such grossly qualitative differences have been proposed by Posner, Walker, Friedrich, & Rafal (1984) for parietal and temporal neglect and by Mesulam (1985) and Heilman and Valenstein (1979) for subcortical neglect (disturbances of expectancy), parietal neglect (disorders of spatial template construction), and frontal neglect (motor spatial orientation disturbances).

In summary, whatever their efficiency, the present perceptual-cognitive therapies for neglect were not linked to a clear processing theoretical framework relative to the underlying deficit causing the neglect symptom, nor is it clear why the therapies are efficacious or why there are intraindividual variations in therapy efficiency.

Given these limitations and their generality, present-day therapies are consistent with all the concurrent theoretical interpretation of hemispheric asymmetries of attention. One may either consider, as in Heilman's perspective, that the exercises reestablish the dominance of the right hemisphere on both ipsilateral and contralateral stimulation, or that the left hemisphere (through verbal constraining instructions) progressively develops control on the ipsilateral side, or, as in Kinsbourne's perspective, that repeated stimulation of the left space results in progressively enhanced activation of the right hemisphere that establishes better activation equilibrium between the hemispheres. It may also be that the exercises progressively improve the internal spatial representation (Bisiach, Capitani, Luzzatti, & Perani, 1981) or covert spatial orientation (Riddoch & Humphreys, 1983) considered as higher component deficits of the unilateral attentional disorders. Furthermore, the involvement in the exercises of the sensory, motor, and also attentional-expectancy dimensions is congruent with all the possible variations of neglect syndromes according to the neural network model of Mesulam for the distribution of attention along the frontal (motor space representation), parietal (sensory space representation), and cingulate (motivational space representation) lesions locations.

It is with this criticism in mind that we will now present a patient we treated 7 years ago, before the appearance in neuropsychology of truly cognitive organized therapy. It is in fact the story of a failure, but the interest of such a retrospective analysis of therapy initially conducted in a perceptual-cognitive logic similar to that of the NYMT is that it raises some crucial theoretical questions about the organization of the therapy and its relation to the interpretation of the hemineglect disorder. We are, of course, aware of the intrinsic limitations of retrospective descriptions, as data presently considered theoretically relevant are either lacking or insufficiently detailed. Furthermore, in order not to influence the presentation of the data, the therapy and its evolution will be presented according to the direct reconstructive approaches we used when the therapy was in progress. In the general discussion we will give a tentative reinterpretation of our results in the framework of contemporary theoretical hypotheses on neglect.

CASE DESCRIPTION

The patient was a 50-year-old man who was the director of a small garden business. In January 1973 he presented with a sudden episode of unconsciousness followed by visual disorders consisting of left hemianopsia and dimmed vision. EEG showed right temporal slow waves.

In March 1973, because of the persistence of epileptic signs, the patient was hospitalized in the neurology unit of St. Luc Hospital. At the neurological examination, a left homonymous hemianopsia without macular sparing was observed. A pneumoencephalographic examination showed a hydrocephalus with deviation of the third ventricle to the left, and arteriography indicated a discrete deviation of the cerebral anterior artery. A temporooccipital neoplastic lesion was diagnosed. Surgical intervention on March 28, 1973 permitted the total removal of a tumor (chronic multilobed abscess) located at the temporooccipital junction with an extension toward the cerebellar tentorium. After surgery the patient presented with complete left hemianopsia and significant visual neglect with left asomatognosia and a massive construction apraxia. His motor and sensory functions were normal. Ten days later, neuropsychological examination revealed significant spatial disorientation and signs of neglect in reading, drawing, writing, and locomotion. (Figure 9.1). Language functions were normal apart from difficulties in oral and written spelling.

Five years later (1978), the patient was referred to St. Luc Rehabilitation Center. A more complete neuropsychological evaluation indicated the persistence of a hemineglect syndrome: His bisection of lines was clearly asymmetrical; his drawings of cubes, houses, and flowers were less incomplete in their left part but they were produced on the right side of the paper; and he manifested spatial dysgraphia, inadequate line orientation, and his written productions were limited to the right side of the paper (Figure 9.2).

Reading was difficult because he neglected the beginnings of words or lines, and some neglect behavior appeared in written calculation. The patient was disoriented in space but not in time. There was no visual agnosia, but there was some misinterpretation of pictures not symmetrically scanned. There was discrete unilateral motor aspontaneity but no clear hemiasomatognosia; digital gnosis was normal. There were no language disorders. The patient seemed aware of his trouble but indifferent to it. There was some apathy and depression, and the patient spent long periods sitting in a chair without doing anything. When questioned about his lack of activity, he

FIGURE 9.1. (A) April 1973: copy drawing of a flower. (B) April 1973: spontaneous writing of name and address. (C) April 1973: copy drawing of a bicycle.

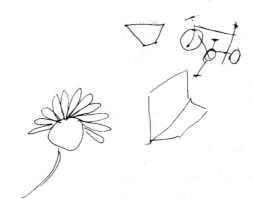

FIGURE 9.2. (A) December 1978: drawing (without model) of a flower, a cube and a bicycle (B) December 1978: writing under dictation.

replied that he could not see well, so he preferred sitting still. Two quantitative evaluations of his neglect were made, one with letter cancellation tasks, another with a square completion task.

The cancellation task was very similar to that of Diller et al. (1974). The patient was asked to cancel letters (C or E) in two conditions of stimulus dimensions. In one case (small letters/high stimulus density), the printed uppercase letters were 2 mm high and separated by a space of 3 mm; in the other case (large letter/low stimulus density), the printed uppercase letters were 3 mm high and separated by a 4 mm interval. In the large letter condition, the subject omitted 6 *E*s out of 27 and 7 Cs out of 27, there being only a discrete tendency of more omissions to the left side (7 letters out of 13 omissions). In the small letter condition, the omissions were 14 of 54 with a marked tendency of more omissions in the left side (10 of 14). The time was 2 minutes 5 seconds in the small-letter condition and 2 minutes 9 seconds in large/low density-letter condition.

The square completion task consisted of asking the patient to fill a gap in the perimeter of 42 small squares (2 x 2 cm) disposed in a 6 x 7 squares matrix. The lacunae (approx 3 mm) were located on any of the four sides, either on the left or on the right side of the square. Some squares, however, were complete. The results (Figure 9.3) indicated that the patient omitted exploring 12 squares situated on the left side of the page and could not repair left-sided lacunae on some squares situated in the part of the page he had explored. Note that this last result is in line with the suggestion of Gainotti, D'Erme, Monteleone, & Silveri (1986) that neglect in right-brain-damaged patients consists of a two-dimensional deficit, one of global scanning exploration and another of local attention.

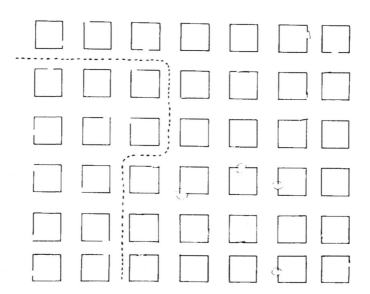

FIGURE 9.3. At the square completion task pretest the patient neglects the square located at the left side of the dotted line, as well as four left lacunae in squares located at the right side.

THERAPY

Our therapy can be divided into four main steps: direct approach therapy (T1), extension to daily life situations (T2), verbal self-instructions (T3), and mental external prosthesis (T4). We will present these four steps in their chronological order of administration.

Therapy 1: Direct Approach Through Conventional Exercises

Content and Rationale

The rationale of the therapy was very close to that of Diller and Weinberg (1977) and similar to that of Seron and Tissot (1973). The exercises focused on scanning behavior, were progressive in nature, and can be divided along the following lines.

From the Well-scanned Hemifield to the Defective. These exercises consisted in starting a visual or visuomanual exploration from an anchor point situated in the nonneglected field of the space and moving the eyes and arm progressively toward a cued point (that is, toward a point verbally signaled and visually underlined) in the neglected part of the space.

In one such exercise, the patient picked up green tokens from a table. At the first level all the tokens were arranged at half-centimeter intervals in line in front of the patient and in parallel with his shoulders. The patient was asked to pick up all the green tokens from the right to the left one after the other until he came to the single red token, which was the last token on the left. Each time the patient stopped before reaching the end of the line, he was verbally reminded that he had to reach the red token. Four different kinds of exercises were presented in this category, such as exercises in visual scanning alone and exercises in visual scanning plus manual exploration (as in the preceding example).

One-step Translation from One Hemifield to the Other. These exercises consisted of moving the eyes in one step from one point in a hemifield to a point located in the other hemifield. A typical example of such a task was an exercise linking the numbers from 1 to 30 in their cardinal order. At the beginning of the program, the numbers were arranged symmetrically equidistant from a central point in a vertical array, alternating between the right and the left hemifields. At the end of the task, the numbers were dispersed randomly over the

304 SERON, DELOCHE, COYETTE

sheet. Three different tasks were constructed in this category, varying according to the eccentricity and the symmetrical/asymmetrical location of the stimuli from the midline.

Shape Analysis. These exercises were intended to teach the patient to consider all the dimensions of an object or an image before acting on or comparing them. Typical tasks consisted of judging the similarity or the dissimilarity of various abstract or meaningful pictures whose right and left halves could differ, completing the square lacunae, and finding the midpoint of a picture. The classic line bisection task was also used. The patient was first asked to cut through the middle of lines that were cued at their left by colored points of different sizes. Each exercise was preceded by verbal instructions reminding the patient to name the color of the cue before cutting the line. There were six different tasks in this category, varying by hypothetical criterion of shape complexity.

Reading Exercises. These exercises were intended to help the patient take account of all the words and lines by having recourse to visual cues, spatial organization of the material, and verbal instructions.

Experimental Procedures

As is customary in relearning approaches, the procedures were designed so that one could manipulate hypothetically relevant variables in the complexity of scanning behavior and measure characteristics of the patient's responses. For example, the sessions devoted to line bisection were constructed so that the following variables could be manipulated:

1. *The dimension of the stimuli* varied progressively in length from 5 to 50 cm (five dimensions used: 5, 10, 20, 30, and 50 cm).
2. *The position of the stimuli* varied by the lines being presented in the right visual field and then being progressively moved to the central part of the field and finally to the leftmost part.
3. *The colored cues* were reduced from a diameter of 1 cm to the no-cue condition (3 steps: 1 cm., 0.5 cm., no cue).

At each step in all the tasks, achievement of 90% correct responses was required to progress in the therapy. As we shall see later, these progressions turned out to be meaningless so further details on the different programs and exercises will not be discussed here.

Results

Before administering the therapy, it was thought that the program would take 3 to 4 months to complete with a schedule of four 45-minute sessions a week and with the selected criterion of response. However, the therapy program was completely finished in only 2 weeks (eight sessions). Such rapidity was surprising: Instead of having a progressive learning curve, the patient immediately gave a nearly perfect performance on each complexity level. For example, in the reading task (the first step being reading aloud simple short words presented in the center of the visual field, the beginning of the words being read, the last step being the reading of a newspaper text without any cue) all the reading exercises were finished in two 45-minute sessions. Indeed, the therapy took only the time required to do the first exercise on each of the proposed levels of difficulty. In each condition a perfect score was almost immediately achieved (Figure 9.4).

Nevertheless, the therapy was clearly not a success in that there were no significant modifications of the neglect behavior in daily life situations. Such a striking dissociation was clearly observed at the end

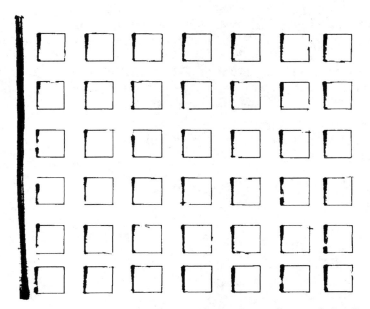

FIGURE 9.4. At the first exercise with colored cues, the completion is perfect.

306 SERON, DELOCHE, COYETTE

of the therapy sessions when the patient would fail to note the therapist's extended hand to shake hands and would frequently bump into the door jamb. His spatial disorientation in the hospital corridors persisted, he could not tell time correctly, and when eating he neglected the food on the left side of his plate. A test of intellectual activity administered during this period (by another examiner and in another room) by means of Raven's Coloured Progressive Matrices indicated low scores, principally due to a systematic neglect of the figures on the left part of the multiple choice responses panels. In fact the patient obtained a score of 24 correct responses out of 36 items. Following Gainotti's suggestion (Gainotti, D'Erme, Mouteleone & Silveri, 1986) we examined the location of the patient's responses: Out of the 12 possible correct responses in each three- panel response location, (left, right, center) there were 4 left-sided correct responses, 11 correct center responses, and 9 right-sided correct responses. There were thus eight errors when the correct response consisted of selecting an item in the left column. Furthermore, as regards the distribution of all the patient's responses (either correct or incorrect), there were 16 right-sided responses, 13 center-middle responses, four left-sided responses, and 3 no-responses. Thus, there seems to be a clear attentional bias in this test.

This durable discrepancy between, on the one hand, adequate behavior during therapeutic sessions and, on the other hand, the persistence of neglect in daily life activities and in not cued evaluation sessions was at that time interpreted as a lack of learning transfer (but note that during therapy no evidence of a learning process at all was observed). Thus we designed another therapeutic program using a more extensive and functional approach to the deficits (Therapy II).

Therapy II. Extension of Exercises to Daily Life Situations

Content and Procedures

Therapy II was planned for a longer period (2 months), and the exercises were less formal. For the most part, the therapy was administered by an occupational therapist while the patient was engaged in ordinary activities (cooking, painting, playing chess, walking, catching a ball, conversing, etc.). During these activities, the therapist intervened each time he observed signs of neglect in the patient behavior. The interventions were verbal and intended to enhance left visual orientation. In addition, as in Therapy I, different spatial cues were used to draw the patient's visual attention to the neglected field.

Results

The changes of scanning behavior during Therapy II were similar to those observed during Therapy I. We observed an important and almost perfect reorganization of scanning behavior as soon as the therapy session commenced. Nevertheless, in some situations, the therapist had to intervene more frequently, especially during activities requiring great attentional resource, such as playing board games and conversations where signs of neglect reappeared episodically.

But, as in Therapy I, no transfer outside the Rehabilitation Center was observed. His family continued to report difficulties at home due to neglect behavior. The tendency to neglect the contralateral space reappeared as soon as the therapeutic environment was left. We then decided to move toward a more verbal or conscious approach to the problem, in order to teach the patient to give himself the attentional instructions to compensate for his hemineglect.

Therapy III. Verbal Self-instructions

Content and Procedures

This therapy, very similar in methodology to autosuggestion, lasted 4 weeks. During the therapeutic sessions, the patient was trained to say repeatedly and in various situations the two following sentences: "The left space does exist," and "I must move my eyes in that direction." The learning of this verbal scanning sequence was done in various situations, the most frequent being the patient sitting at a table engaged in various activities. At the beginning of the therapy, the exercises were intensive: Every 3 minutes the examiner gave a verbal signal to the patient to say aloud the self-instructions and to act, and the examiner checked visually the execution of the scanning behavior. After 2 weeks because of the artificial nature of the technique, the therapist only prompted contingently, that is, when he observed signs of neglect.

Results

As in the preceding therapy, the results were fairly good during the therapy sessions: The patient reacted promptly and adequately to the systematic external signals; and in the second phase of treatment, when the signals were given only when necessary, they soon became rare. In fact, after a week of contingent signals, it was only necessary to give two or three signals during an entire therapy session. Most of the signals were given in the first quarter of the session and almost always during conversation. Nevertheless, there were still no clear signs of transfer outside the therapy setting. The patient's spontaneous comments about these therapeutic effects indicated the limits he perceived in our third technique: "When I am home in quiet surroundings with nothing important to do, sometimes I remember the sentence and move my eyes to the left, but that never happens when I am doing something interesting." During the fourth week of Therapy III, a dramatic event obliged us to reconsider our approach. The patient had an accident while playing with his dog in his garden: He ran headfirst into some barbed wire on his left and seriously injured his face. Consequently, we decided again to modify our reeducational approach to the disorder. Confronted with what we considered to be the impossibility of generating verbal self-instructions to take into account all the space, we decided to construct an automatic attention generator for space orientation independent of the patient's own voluntary attention.

Therapy IV. Use of a Mental Prosthesis

Content and Procedures

To prevent injuries due to neglect behavior in daily life activities, we constructed a device that consisted of a buzzer that delivered a regular high-pitched noise at random intervals of 5 to 20 seconds. The buzzer apparatus was the size of a cigarette package and fit into the patient's left shirt pocket. A button switch was provided to turn off the noise.

Learning sessions were then conducted to familiarize the patient with the apparatus and the procedures. All the learning sessions were given during occupational therapy. The setup of the learning sessions was as follows.

The patient was seated at a table in front of the therapist and occupied with an activity (reading, playing, manual activity, or conversation). As soon as the buzzer sounded, the patient would explore all the space and then turn off the buzzer by pushing the switch. To check the realization of adequate scanning of the left space, a series of tokens was laid out in a half circle in front of the patient. The patient was asked to name in succession the color of the five leftmost tokens before stopping the buzzer. (Between two signals the therapist would change these five tokens.)

9. NEGLECT THERAPY   309

Results

Acquisition of reactive scanning behavior was rapid, although when the ongoing activity was a conversation we were obliged to inhibit a tendency to stop the noise without performing the required scanning behavior. Walking exercises were conducted in the hospital corridor. After 10 complete 45-minute sessions (more or less 300 trials per session), the scanning behavior was immediately elicited by the buzzer.

During the subsequent 2 months, the patient used the apparatus at home and came to the center twice a month. His only complaint was that the noise was pitched too high, so we reduced its intensity. His family reported a significant improvement of his scanning behavior in daily life situations with the aid of the buzzer. The patient seemed to use the alert-attentional gadget regularly and especially when he walked.

DISCUSSION

These four therapeutic trials conducted in succession with the same patient need to be discussed at two different levels: the efficacy of the different strategies used and the theoretical interpretation of the neglect disorder that could be indicated.

As concerns the therapeutic strategies, reservations must be made at the onset regarding the conclusions proposed here. For example, there were no firm indications that continuation of the exercises of Therapy I could not have ultimately lead to progress in daily life activities. It is always possible to argue that more numerous and more intensive exercises sooner or later would have yielded positive results away from the therapeutic setting. In the same way, it must be noted that the verbal self-instruction therapy was stopped and replaced by a prosthesis approach not because there was sufficient evidence of a lack of transfer but because of the serious accident, which urgently called for a more readily efficacious therapeutic solution. What is clear, however, is that in none of the first three therapies did we observe a progressive evolution during therapy sessions indicating the presence of a learning process. Similarly, our preestablished criteria of exercise complexity in relation to the characteristics of the scanning exploration movement never did seem to be relevant. Since there was no learning-like evolution it was, of course, difficult to establish an optimal exercise duration and to determine what the progress should be during the therapy. The only positive argument for continuing a nonevolutive therapy was the rare indications in the literature on animals of beneficial effects of overlearning procedures in cases of brain lesions (Finger, 1978). In a clinical setting, however, it is very difficult to motivate a human subject over long periods of time to continue to do exercises he can do perfectly almost immediately and that seem to produce no improvement in his daily life activities. The difficulty is even greater with neglect patients in that immediate success in therapy may reinforce their anosognosic reaction. Furthermore, as far as therapy strategies are concerned with this single case, we would stress that Therapies I, II, and III were not effective outside the laboratory and that taken together their durations were equivalent or superior to those used by the NYMT.

It may be, however, that some procedural variations could explain why our therapies were not efficacious. For example, the NYMT insisted on the necessity of a left anchorage and left-to-right scanning exercises, whereas in several of our tasks we proposed right anchorage and right-to-left scanning. Although we did not try to control the influence of these parameters, some of our exercises also contained left anchorage and left-to-right scanning, such as our reading exercises, picking up token tasks, and our line bisection tasks. Second, for the direction of scanning, our choice for right-to-left exercises corresponds to the fact that, in reading, what seems difficult for a right-brain-damaged neglect patient is to come back to the beginning of a line after he finishes reading the preceding one. In such situations, what generally occurs is a partial comeback scanning, so the patient does not enter the subsequent line at its beginning. To counterbalance such partial automatic backward scanning, right-to-left direction exercises seem the more reasonable. Furthermore, it must be noted that the superiority of left-to-right over right-to-left scanning has only been established by Diller et al. (1974) in cases of moderate neglect; in cases of severe neglect, left-to-right scanning has proved to be equally efficacious.

Another difference between our therapies and those of the NYMT reside in the pacing instructions issued during scanning tasks. We did not use such a pacing strategy, but this point does not seem to be critical because our patient made no mistakes during the exercises, which indicates that his visual exploration was not too precipitate, or at least that its rapidity had no deleterious effect on the accuracy of his reading or cancelling performance.

Finally, it may also be argued that our patient was totally different from those presented in the rehabilitation literature on neglect. It is indeed evident that our patient differed from those of the NYMT as concerns etiology (multilobe neoplasic tumor) and duration of brain damage (5 years after surgery). Nevertheless, at least from a superficial semiological point of view, the neglect signs of our patient look very similar to those classically described. The fact that he was able to master the different tasks proposed so quickly to him should not necessarily be considered as strange or idiosyncratic. In fact several indications in the literature stress that, under constraining instructions, scanning or covert lateral attention can be promptly reorganized. For example, Riddoch and Humphreys (1983) showed a marked decrease in neglect when the subjects were cued and forced to report stimuli in their neglected field in line bisection tasks. A similar positive cuing effect was also reported in a reaction-time paradigm by Posner et al. (1984) who showed that parietal right-lesioned patients were able to detect stimuli in the space contralateral to the lesion if they had previously been congruently cued. The effect of cuing was also observed by Bisiach in a mental representation task, whereby RBD neglect patients were shown to be able to describe the two sides of the Milano cathedral square when they were explicitly asked to describe each side in succession. Finally, rapid positive effects of anchorage procedures are also implicitly admitted by Diller et al. (1974) who indicated in their pretherapeutic evaluation of cancellation tests that they always present first the noncued cancellation tasks before the anchorage condition, because, as they noted, when the anchorage condition is presented first it may well influence the noncued cancellation task. In other words, these authors recognize that the execution of only one cued cancellation test may modify the immediately following noncued test.

In conclusion, even if the modification of visual exploration under constraining instructions is somewhat sharper in our patient than in other patients, such a difference may be a matter degree rather than of kind.

On the theroretical level, the fact that we never have observed a learning progression curve in our therapy seems to argue against a reestablishment rationale. It seems thus more plausible to suggest that our patient did not learn a new scanning habit but that a shift between two distinct mechanisms of visual orientation occurred during the training exercises: one automatic and defective, the other controlled, and at least partially, preserved. Such a dissociation, clearly in the line of Posner's et al. (1984) and Riddoch and Humphrey's (1983) interpretation of attentional defect in visual neglect, if confirmed in other cases, suggests the need for a reexamination of recovery and reeducation data on neglect. The recovery studies of both Campbell and Oxbury (1976) and Hier, Mondlock, & Caplan

312   SERON, DELOCHE, COYETTE

(1983b) indicate that the neglect signs tend to disappear first on the so-called simple tasks, such as concrete drawing and clinical visual confrontation tasks, but that difficulties still persist with more complex tasks such as block design, Rey-Osterrieth figures, cube counting tests, and so on. A possible interpretation for such a complexity gradient in recovery is that the so-called "complex" tasks are more demanding as regards high-level visual processing, such as orientation discrimination, feature analysis of the stimuli, and so on, so that less processing capacity is allocated to space attentional control, which then proceeds more automatically and thus provokes the reappareance of neglect signs. As far as reeducation is concerned, the results obtained by Young et al. (1983) are also relevant in this regard. These authors compared the effect of three different therapies applied to three groups of comparable neglect patients and showed that the group that obtained the better improvement received along with the cancellation and visual scanning training, additional complex block design treatment. Nevertheless, the superiority of this group appeared not only on tasks very similar to those trained but also on the letter cancellation task, although it had received the same amount of cancellation training as had the others groups. The authors thus suggested that block design training enhances both organizational and cognitive strategies to a greater degree than do the other training exercises. But why was there such a transfer to a simpler task like letter cancellation? We should suggest that by training block design, one trained the patient to take into consideration both sides of space in a more demanding task as regards visual processing and thus that more automatic space exploration mechanisms are trained than in simple cancellation tasks in such a complex situation.

With such a theoretical line, we are now in a better position to interpret why there was such a clear absence of training transfer in our patient. All of our programs (through visual cuing and verbal instructions) were focused on the nondefective or controlled attentional orientation mechanisms, whereas in daily life situations, visual orientation is generally automatically processed, especially as soon as one is engaged in other processing demanding activities. This may, at least partially, explain why, in Therapy II, attentional orientation seemed so difficult to transfer to other contexts even though the exercises focused on self-orientation. As the patient himself explained, he was only able to utter the verbal self-instructions and the associated scanning behavior outside the therapeutic setting when he was not engaged in tasks requiring great attentional resources. This probably indicates a limitation of controlled attentional capacities: As soon as the patient is engaged in tasks consuming controlled cognitive processing, his visual spatial orientation processing shifts to more automatic processing and neglect behavior consequently reappears.

Therefore, if one considers that the distinction between controlled versus automatic visual lateral orientation is pertinent to understand the variations in the neglect disorder of at least some patients, then the rationale for neglect therapy needs to be reconsidered, and different strategies have to be confronted.

One solution, that of the NYMT, is to begin the therapy with explicit scanning exercises that require controlled attentional processing and then, by repetition and progressive fading of cues, to move toward more automatic visual control of space. The results presented by this team indicate that such a strategy could be fruitful, but it is not clear if the improvement is due to a true amelioration of automatic attentional orientation or if the progresses resulted from a more frequent use of controlled space orientation by the patients.

Another strategy could consist of engaging the patient immediately (i.e., at the beginning of the therapy) in relatively complex tasks, that is, in tasks requiring aside visual space control to monitor another demanding task. Such divided attentional exercises requiring the parallel control of two different tasks may be more appropriate for training the patient to control more automatically the allocation of his attentional resources. For example, it is possible by constraining instructions to train the patient to place progressively more and more processing capacities on the nonspatial tasks in order to be sure that spatial attentional control is realized correctly in a more automatic way.

In summary, our neglect patient did not benefit from therapy that focused on his controlled visual orientation, so we had to resort to an external auditory gadget. We do not wish to engage in a debate on the merits of perceptual strategies versus those of prosthetic devices, but we would argue that perceptual remediation activates essentially voluntary attentional mechanisms, whereas visual bilateral orientation is generally automatically processed in daily life situations. We have, therefore, suggested that perceptual remediation of attentional disorders must rely on attentionally divided tasks to activate visual orientation in parallel with other processing activities.

Such a proposal has to be empirically tested, but it has the advantage at the onset of being linked to a theoretical hypothesis, that is, that one aspect of attentional processing deficit is subjacent to disorders.

Finally, it must be stressed that reeducation of hemineglect disorders is still in its infancy and that the recommendation to take into account the possible dissociation between automatic versus con-

314 SERON, DELOCHE, COYETTE

trolled visual attention is only a small part of the whole story. In fact, the main question is now probably the homogeneity of the neglect syndrome. In the few studies that have presented single-case results it seems to be a significant degree of heterogeneity between the patients; a comprehensive analysis of neglect requires the development of single-case methodologies that have proved to be so fruitful with other neuropsychological disorders.

Nowadays, and before a more coherent theoretical framework is offered, the therapeutic interventions must continue to be restricted to the testing of fragmentary hypotheses and to analyzing precisely what occurs with patients.

REFERENCES

Bisiach, E., Capitani, E., Luzzatti, C., & Perani, D. (1981). Brain and conscious representation of outside reality. *Neuropsychologia, 4,* 543–551.

Campbell, D. C., & Oxbury, J. M. (1976). Recovery from unilateral visuo-spatial neglect. *Cortex, 12,* 303–312.

Deloche, G., Seron, X., Coyette, F., Wendling, I., Hirsbrunner, T., & Van Eeckhout, Y. (1983). Micro-computer assistance rehabilitation programs for patients with aphasia or visual neglect. Poster presented at the International Neuropsychological Society, Lisbonne.

Denes, G. F., Semenza, C., Stoppa, E., & Lis A. (1982). Unilateral spatial neglect and recovery from hemiplegia: A follow-up study. *Brain, 105,* 543–552.

Diller, L., Ben-Yishay, Y., Gerstman, L. J., Goodkin, R., Gordon, W., & Weinberg, J. (1974). Studies in cognition and rehabilitation in hemiplegia: study II. Studies in scanning behavior in hemiplegia. *Rehabilitation Monograph 50* (pp. 86–165). Behavioral Science, Institute of Rehabilitation, Medicine, New York University Medical Center.

Diller, L., & Weinberg, J. (1970). Evidence for accident-prone behavior in hemiplegic patients. *Archives of Physical Medicine and Rehabilitation, 51,* 353–363.

Diller, L., & Weinberg, J. (1977). Hemi-attention in rehabilitation: the evolution of a rationale treatment program. In E. A. Weinstein, & R. P. Friedland (Eds.), *Advances in Neurology, Vol. 18.* New York: Raven Press.

Finger, S. (1978). *Recovery from brain damage: Research and theory.* New York: Plenum Press.

Gainotti, G. (1968). Les manifestations de négligence et d'inattention pour l'hémi-space. *Cortex, IV,* 64–91.

Gainotti, G., Caltagirone, C., & Miceli, G. (1977). Poor performance of right brain-damaged patients on Raven's coloured matrices: derangement of general intelligence or of specific abilities? *Neuropsychologia, 15,* 675–680.

Gainotti, G., D'Erme, P., Monteleone, D., & Silveri, M. C. (1986). Mechanisms of unilateral spatial neglect in relation to laterality of cerebral lesions. *Brain, 109,* 599–612.

Gouvier, W. D., Cottam, G., Webster, J. S., Beissel, F. G., & Wofford, J. D. (1984). Behavioral interventions with stroke patients for improving wheelchair navigation. *International Journal of Clinical Neuropsychology, 6,* 186–190.

9. NEGLECT THERAPY 315

Hart, T., Carbonari, J. P., & Sheer, D. E. (1984). *A new single-case methodology for the evaluation of cognitive remediation technique.* Paper presented at the 12th annual meeting of the INS, Houston.

Heilman, K. M., & Valenstein, E. (1979). Mechanisms underlying hemispatial neglect. *Annals of Neurology, 5,* 166–170.

Hier, D. B., Mondlock, J., & Caplan, L. R. (1983a). Behavioral abnormalilities after right hemisphere stroke. *Neurology, 33,* 337–344.

Hier, D. B., Mondlock, J., & Caplan, L. R. (1983b). Recovery of behavioral abnormalities after right hemisphere stroke. *Neurology, 33,* 345–350.

Hurwitz, L. J., & Adams, G. F. (1972). Rehabilitation of hemiplegia: indices of assessment and prognosis. *British Medical Journal, 1,* 94–98.

Larsen, S., Ahrensberg, R. M., Carlsen, O., & Mejding, J. (1984). Processing differences in the right and the left visual half-field. Paper presented at the International Neuropsychological Society, Aachen.

Lawson, I. R. (1962). Visual spatial neglect in lesions of the right cerebral hemisphere, a study in recovery. *Neurology, 12,* 23–33.

Lorenze, E. J., & Cranco, R. (1962). Dysfunction in visual perception with hemiplegia: its relation to activities of daily living. *Archives of Physical Medicine and Rehabilitation, 43,* 514–517.

Marquardsen, J. (1969). Natural history of acute cerebrovascular disease: retrospective study of 769 patients. *Acta Neurologica Scandinavia, 38, (Suppl.),* 1–192.

Mesulam, M. M. (1985). Attentional confusional states, and neglect. In M. M. Mesulam (Eds), *Principles of behavioral neurology* Philadelphia: F. A. Davies.

Posner, M. I., Walker, J. A., Friedrich, F. J., & Rafal, R. D. (1984). Effect of parietal injury on covert orienting attention. *The Journal of Neuroscience, 4,* 1863–1874.

Rao, S. M., & Bieliauskas, L. (1983). Cognitive rehabilitation two and one half years post-right temporal lobectomy. *Journal of Clinical Neuropsychology, 5,* 313–320.

Riddoch, J., & Humphreys, G. W. (1983). The effect of cueing on unilateral neglect. *Neuropsychologia, 21,* 589–599.

Seron, X., & Tissot, R. (1973). Essai de rééducation d'une agnosie spatiale unilatérale gauche. *Acta Psychiatrica Belgica, 73,* 448–457.

Sivak, M., Olson, P. L., Kewman, D. G., Won, D., & Henson, D. L. (1981). Driving and perceptual/cognitive skills: behavioural consequences of brain damage. *Archives of Physical Medicine and Rehabilitation, 62,* 476–483.

Stanton, K., Pepping, M., Brockway, J., Buss, L., Frankel, D., & Waggeners, S. (1983). Wheelchair transfer training for right cerebral dysfunctions: an interdisciplinary approach. *Archives of Physical Medicine and Rehabilitation, 64,* 276–280.

Weinberg, J., Diller, L. (1968). On reading newspapers by hemiplegics-denial of visual disability. Proc. 76th Annu Con Am Psychol Associat 3: 655–656.

Weinberg, J., Diller, L., Gordon, W. A., Gerstmann, L. J. Lieberman, A., Lakin, P., Hodges, G., & Ezrachi, O. (1977). Visual scanning effect on reading-related tasks in acquired right brain damage. *Archives of Physical Medicine and Rehabilitation, 58,* 479–486.

Weinberg, J., Diller, L., Gordon, A., Gerstman, L. J., Lieberman, A., Lakine, P., Hodges, G., & Ezrachi, O. (1979). Training sensory awareness and spatial organization in people with brain damage. *Archives of Physical Medicine and Rehabilitation, 60,* 491–496.

Weisbroth, S., Esibil, N., & Zuger, R. (1971). Factors in the vocational success of hemiplegic patients. *Archives of Physical Medicine and Rehabilitation, 52,* 441–447.

Young, G. C., Collins, D., & Hren, M. (1983). Effect of pairing scanning training with block design training in the remediation of perceptual problems in left hemiplegics. *Journal of Clinical Neuropsychology, 5*, 201–212.

Zarit, S. H., & Kahn, R. L. (1974). Impairment and adaptation in chronic disabilities: spatial inattention. *Journal of Nervous and Mental Diseases, 159*, 63–72.

10 Pragmatics and Cognition in Treatment of Language Disorders

G. Albyn Davis
Department of Communication Disorders,
University of Massachusetts at Amherst

With respect to language function, pragmatics is defined as the study of relationships between language behavior and the contexts in which it normally occurs. Pragmatic treatment strategies are based on assumptions about interactions between the "language processor" and its contexts. Basic investigation of these relationships has expanded considerably since the mid-1970s, corresponding to the relatively recent interest shown by clinical aphsiologists in pragmatic approaches to treatment of aphasia. Although application is usually on a more solid footing when it follows from basic research, the parallel development of basic and applied information about pragmatics leaves clinicians to speculate more than they would like as to the role of pragmatics in rehabilitation (Davis & Wilcox, 1985). Yet, enough basic research has been done to provide clinicians with a continually expanding view as to what pragmatic treatment is supposed to be.

COGNITION AND PRAGMATICS

Some clinicians have thought that pragmatic treatment avoids impaired language and concentrates exclusively on the transformation of contexts. Therefore, it may be useful to begin this chapter with an introduction to pragmatics, especially as it relates to the normal language processor (LP) and, briefly, to cerebral localization. Pragmatics should lead to a complete explanation of natural language

317

behavior that includes the language processor and its surroundings. However, traditional psycholinguistic research and clinical methods have been focused on the processor. Until the mid-1970s, minimal attention had been given to its interactions with the elements of natural contexts. In studies that can be called pragmatic, contexts are not examined in isolation. Instead, they are examined with respect to how they are coordinated with the LP so that natural language behavior is socially appropriate and conveys a speaker's real intentions (Garnham, 1985).

The Language Processor

Because traditional clinical aphasiology has concentrated on assessing and treating an impaired language processor (irrespective of its natural contexts), this processor shall be defined in order to specify the domain of traditional rehabilitation. Psycholinguists and neurolinguists have begun to identify the LP as being one of many components of cognition. Caplan (1984) cited previous designations of the LP as a "language-responsible cognitive structure" (p. 8) or a "mental organ of language," (p. 8) and he went on to characterize the distinctiveness of "this hypothesized autonomous component of the human mind" (p. 8). Aphasia has been investigated as evidence, at least, for the notion that an LP exists (Caramazza, 1984). This research, also, has indicated that this processor resides in the perisylvian region of the left cerebral hemisphere for most people. However, Studdert-Kennedy (1983) warned neurolinguists that the language mechanism operates with some connection to other cognitive mechanisms. He reminded us that the LP, with its own subsystems, is a subsystem of other systems.

The LP is a subsystem of the memory system. The LP's knowledge structures are stored in long-term memory, and its procedures operate within the constraints of duration and capacity that are often designated as short-term memory (or working memory). These basic divisions of memory are probably involved in other modules of cognition, as well, in that long-term memory and short-term memory are needed for visuospatial recognition and construction. On the other hand, knowledge structures and processes have been postulated that may be unique to language behavior. It is possible that syntactical and phonological components may be particularly distinct knowledge structures, whereas lexical knowledge may blend considerably with conceptualization of the world (i.e., semantic knowledge). Certain processes may be necessary for comprehension of language, such as "parsing" an utterance into syntactically defined constituents and "scanning" these constituents leading to interpretation.

Traditional investigation of these processes has consisted of tasks involving on-line recognition of sentences by themselves and tasks involving the comparison of sentences with pictures representing literal meanings of the lexical combinations in these sentences. The LP has been examined with little consideration of who might be speaking these utterances and of where and when they might be spoken. In studies of the normal LP, the crucial parameter has been response time. Assumptions are tested concerning the mental operations that might be contributing to the time it takes a subject to respond in different experimental conditions. This information processing approach to the study of cognition has been applied to the study of interactions between contexts and the LP.

While investigators were focusing on the LP, Olson and Filby (1972) used a typical sentence verification paradigm to study the influence of context on the LP. They asked subjects to compare sentences to pictures of events, and one experimental variable was type of sentence to be comprehended (i.e., active and passive constructions). There was nothing unusual about this manipulation of a language-specific variable, but what was unique at the time was the additional manipulation of the pictured events (i.e., context). Pictures of trucks hitting cars and so on were adjusted so that a subject's attention might be directed either to the agent or object of an action (Olson & Filby 1972). Instead of the usual finding that passive sentences take longer to comprehend than active sentences, Olson and Filby found that, when attention was directed to the object of an action, passives were often easier to comprehend than actives. This study demonstrated that context should become an element in the formula for proposing processes that underlie language behaviors.

Contexts

The contexts surrounding the language processor will be described as consisting of three static components and one dynamic component. The static components include extralinguistic, paralinguistic, and linguistic contexts. The dynamic component is conversation, the most typical natural circumstance in which language is used for the purpose of communication. These contexts determine the interpretation of utterances and determine what people choose to say and how they choose to say it. Therefore, these contexts are processed by the LP; and/or the LP operates in a coordinated fashion with other processors, with the result being the comprehension and production of language in natural situations. With the LP having been physically placed within the perisylvian region of the left hemisphere, processors of elements of context might be placed in other regions of the

320 DAVIS

left hemisphere and in the right hemisphere. Natural communication may entail some activity across the commissural fibers connecting the two hemispheres.

Clinicians usually think of *extralinguistic* contexts as being within the domain of pragmatics. These contexts reside outside of utterances that are heard or spoken by an individual in a conversation. They are external and internal with respect to an individual speaker-listener. *External contexts* include settings, other participants, and movements. The formality of a setting, for example, influences conversational style and lexical choice. Other participants contribute their knowledge of a topic and of other participants, their beliefs and attitudes about a topic and other participants, their roles relative to each other (e.g., mother or daughter, doctor or patient), and their physical distance from each other. Movements include postural stances and shifts as well as differentiated movements such as intentional and unintentional limb and facial gesturing. *Internal contexts* consist of the individual speaker-listener's knowledge of the world and emotional state. Interdependence of contexts is exemplified by the relationship between role and knowledge of a topic (e.g., doctor or mother, discussion of venereal disease). Also, the influence of a variable is relative according to the status of each participant in a conversation; a person can be mother or daughter depending on who the other participant is. The influence of knowledge depends on the degree of overlap of knowledge shared by participants in a conversation.

The need for the LP to join forces with these contexts can be illustrated with meanings that must be created on the spot from proper names that are turned into verb phrases (Clark & Gerrig, 1983). Comprehension of "Please, do a Napoleon" depends on a listener's knowledge of Napoleon (i.e., internal context) and this being a request from a photographer (i.e., external context). Such creative use of vocabulary is common in everyday conversation, requiring a listener to figure out meanings that are not in a standard dictionary or a mental dictionary of word-referent relationships.

Interactions between extralinguistic contexts and the LP have been studied frequently with respect to the conveyance of *speaker meaning* (Morgan, 1979; Searle, 1979). Speaker meaning has been differentiated from utterance meaning as a means of characterizing the common difference between what a speaker means (i.e., nonliteral meaning) and what a speaker says (i.e., literal meaning), respectively. Research has been devoted to an analysis of the processing stages underlying comprehension of indirect requests (Clark & Lucy, 1975) and metaphor (Gildea & Glucksberg, 1983; Ortony,

10. PRAGMATICS AND COGNITION   321

Schallert, Reynolds, & Antos, 1978). Comprehension of indirect requests and metaphor often involves a comparison between the utterance and its context to derive an appropriate interpretation. Nonliteral interpretation, especially of metaphor, may require some involvement of the right hemisphere as indicated in the study of brain-damaged subjects (e.g., Winner & Gardner, 1977). Conversely, the left hemisphere has been described as being a "literal-minded talking robot" (Gardner, 1982).

The second category of context is *paralinguistic* context, which consists of the prosodic trappings of an utterance. Prosodic devices include pitch and intensity variations, syllabic stress, and juncture. They are used to convey the emotional state of a speaker and to convey certain types of semantic and syntactic information. A simple statement of fact, such as "I spoke to my father-in-law last night," may convey a number of different meanings depending on whether it was said with a happy, sad, or angry tone. Furthermore, potential interpretations multiply when extralinguistic contexts are applied, such as a listener's knowledge of the speaker and the topic of conversation. Semantic/syntactic uses of prosody include the following: syllabic stress to identify whether a word is a noun or a verb (e.g., "convict"); stress and juncture cues to resolve the ambiguity of "They are fighting dogs;" or a rising pitch that can turn a statement into a question as in "They really went to the game last night?" The difficulties of right hemisphere damaged persons with emotional prosody indicate that this component of context may be processed in this hemisphere (Foldi, Cicone, & Gardner, 1983), whereas there is some indication that left hemisphere damage impairs the processing of semantic and syntactic prosody (Gandour & Dardarananda, 1983; Heilman, Bowers, Speedie, & Coslett, 1984; Hughes, Chan, & Su, 1983).

Linguistic context is receiving a great deal of attention from linguists. The verbal behavior occurring before and after a linguistic unit has been studied at the intrasentential level (e.g., "Please, do a Napoleon *for the camera*") and at the intersentential level (i.e., discourse). *Discourse* consists of a series of sentences, and linguists are determining the structural rules that are unique to this level of language and that maintain the *coherence* of a discourse. Psycholinguists are learning that coherent discourse is easier to process than incoherent discourse (e.g., Kieras, 1978). Within intersentential discourse, levels of analysis are divided between microstructure and macrostructure (Kintsch & van Dijk, 1978; van Dijk, 1977). *Microstructure* refers to coherence devices between sentences, as in a type of coreference with use of a pronoun to refer to a noun in a previous

322 DAVIS

sentence (e.g., Hirst & Brill, 1980). *Macrostructure* pertains to the global coherence of a discourse as seen in themes and in structural characteristics that make a story different from a description (e.g., Thorndyke, 1977).

In studies of brain-injured persons, the right hemisphere has been implicated further in the coordination of context with the LP for natural language comprehension and production. Processing of discourse may require special integrative capacities of the right hemisphere that capture the theme of a discourse and hold its propositional elements together. Persons with damage to the right hemisphere, although able to comprehend and produce individual sentences, are sometimes unable to interpret the theme or main point of a story (Foldi, et al., 1983; Gardner, Brownell, Wapner, & Michelow, 1983) and tend to wander from the point when telling a story (Gardner, 1982; Myers, 1979; Trupe & Hillis, 1985). They often fail to appreciate coherence among sentences of a paragraph (Delis, Wapner, Gardner, & Moses, 1983). It appears, therefore, that a complete neurolinguistic theory of natural language behavior (i.e., pragmatics) should include some kind of interaction between the two cerebral hemispheres.

The three types of context blend with each other and interact with the LP as an individual uses language to convey ideas in a *conversation*. This dynamic context has been studied with respect to its unique structural characteristics and has been analyzed as to a set of assumptions that each participant brings to this interaction. These assumptions comprise what Grice (1975) called the *cooperative principle* and include the following four "maxims:" (a) be informative, (b) be truthful, (c) be relevant to the topic, and (d) be orderly and clear. Clark and Haviland (1977) considered the cooperative principle to be "a type of social contract" that is inherent to conversation. The maxims are rules by which a participant in any form of communicative interaction (e.g., conversation, a lecture) takes the point of view of the other participant(s) into account when comprehending or when choosing what to say. These are rules for dealing with contextual variables such as shared knowledge of a topic and role relativity. A metaphor can appear to break one of these rules, as when an apparently healthy person says, "She thrust a dagger through my heart." A listener, assuming that the speaker is being truthful and relevant, simply relates the utterance to its context (e.g., topic of ex-lovers) and derives a nonliteral interpretation of the speaker's meaning.

The structural features of conversation revolve around the reciprocal give-and-take of *turn-taking* (Sacks, Schegloff, & Jefferson, 1974). Turn-taking, as well as the assumption of cooperation, introduces elements into language processing that have not been present in traditional laboratory conditions of psycholinguistic study (nor, as shall be seen, in traditional tasks of aphasia assessment and treatment). To facilitate analysis of a conversational *dyad*, the interaction between two people is blocked according to speaker and listener roles and the switching of these roles. Vocal and gestural signal behaviors, called "regulators," are observed to serve housekeeping functions in the management of role-switching (Rosenfeld, 1978; Weiner & Goodenough, 1977). Other behaviors are more directly involved in the communication of messages, especially in dealing with communicative *breakdowns*. A breakdown occurs when a listener has not understood a speaker's message, as indicated by posing a "contingent query" such as "What did you say?" This common situation with an aphasic person was described as leading to "hint-and-guess" cycles, in which the patient produces partial information (i.e., a hint) and the listener responds with a guess (Lubinski, Duchan, & Weitzner-Lin, 1980). An important skill for patients is the ability to recognize the adequacy of the listener's guess and the ability to *revise* a production when the guess is indicative of a breakdown.

Speculations have been offered regarding the roles of each cerebral hemisphere in the turn-taking conventions of conversation. In an article titled "Parliamentary procedure and the brain," Jaffe (1978) suggested that the careful management of speaker and listener roles is dictated by cerebral limitations in the capacity to listen and speak simultaneously: ". . . a common neural substrate is employed for both the production and comprehension of speech. Linguistic machinery functions as a unit. It can be biased toward speaking and listening, but it can't do both at once" (p. 56). In addition, Jaffe proposed that asymmetry of hemisphere function has evolved "under the selective pressure of efficient face-to-face conversation" (p. 61). A division of labor is required; while the left hemisphere is busy switching back and forth between listening and speaking, the right hemisphere is attending to paralinguistic and other cues to the regulation of turn-taking.

A DISORDER OF PRAGMATIC SKILLS?

In the previous section, it was suggested that interaction between the LP and context corresponds to interaction between the left and right cerebral hemispheres, respectively. Although such neat correlations probably are oversimplifications, they may provide a point from which to develop an understanding of differences in communicative behavior between persons with left hemisphere damage and those with right hemisphere damage. Left hemisphere damage (LHD) in the perisylvian region usually results in a primary language disorder, with nonverbal cognition remaining relatively intact. Right hemisphere damage (RHD) reflects a broad double dissociation because of resultant difficulties in nonverbal cognition with the LP appearing to have been spared. Nevertheless, as Gardner (1982) had depicted the intact left hemisphere, some people with RHD seem to be "literal-minded talking robots." The diagnostic problem is one of identifying the presence of communication problems after RHD and, subsequently, of understanding the possible reasons for these communication problems.

Deviations of language behavior seen in many cases of RHD may be best understood as originating in other impairments such as disorientation, muted affect, or inability to carry a tune. Although the common thread of multiple problems seen in aphasia after LHD is the impairment of language, language impairment is not the consistent feature of deficits in a person with RHD. Common threads after RHD include disorientation, indifference, or problems with continuous sounds, any of which may intrude on a normally functioning LP. The primary deficit(s) of RHD do not include aphasia but, instead, include the nonverbal cognitive impairments traditionally attributed to RHD. Unusual verbal behaviors reflect a language disorder that is secondary to these primary impairments. Verbal behaviors after RHD may be manifestations of impairments in the processing of contexts that interact with the LP in natural communicative situations. In a sense, some persons with RHD may be diagnosed as possessing a "pragmatic impairment" of verbal behavior.

A pragmatic disorder of verbal behavior is perceived according to a three-step logic. First, primary impairments after RHD include disruptions of general qualities of RH processing, such as holistic and integrative styles; and they include patterns of deficit among more specific behavioral categories and modalities, such as emotion, music, and visuospatial relationships (Myers, 1984). The occurrence of specific deficits varies with respect to severity and site of lesions. Second, these primary disorders affect the processing of components of context. For example, visuospatial features of external extralinguistic contexts may be misinterpreted (e.g., Wapner & Gardner, 1980), and the internal context of emotional state may become indifferent (Gainotti, 1972; Heilman, Schwartz, & Watson, 1978). Persons with RHD may be indifferent to humor and emotions conveyed in visuospatial representations (Cicone, Wapner, & Gardner, 1980; Gardner, Ling, Flamm, & Silverman, 1975; Morrow, Vrtunski, Kim & Boller, 1981). Other disruptions of context impede verbal behaviors more directly. Failures to recognize and produce paralinguistic contexts are seen through verbal tests involving emotional prosody (e.g., Heilman, et al., 1984; Ross, 1981).

Third, impaired utilization of contexts may interfere with their interactions with the LP, resulting in phonologically and syntactically normal utterances that are disconnected from intentions, situations, and each other. The second and third considerations are inseparable with respect to the previously discussed impairments of linguistic context because impaired holistic and integrative style might be seen most clearly in a patient's missing the point and wandering from the point when dealing with discourse. Literalness in interpretation of metaphor is another example of how the third step might work. Literal interpretation indicates that the statement by itself was understood. It also indicates that the context for the statement was ignored, or it was not processed accurately, or it was not properly linked with the statement.

An assessment of communicative abilities in the person with RHD might be organized around receptive and expressive behaviors that are derived from use of extralinguistic, paralinguistic, and linguistic contexts (Table 10.1). Deficits are not so neatly divisible, however. One cognitive process may contribute to multiple contexts; conversely, one context may benefit from multiple processes. For example, aprosodia could be due to one of two different primary deficits. Muted emotion (i.e., internal context) could result in muted prosody, whereas impaired music processing (i.e., external context) could also result in flat intonation. Treatment of aprosodia would depend on diagnosis of the primary deficit which, in turn, depends on other

TABLE 10.1
Possible Communicative Deficits To Be Assessed in Someone
with Right Hemisphere Damage

	Communicative Deficits	
Contexts	Receptive	Expressive
Extralinguistic	Literalness with meta-	Social inappropriate-
External	phor, proverbs, and	ness of verbal be-
Internal	jokes	havior
	Emotion, in faces and	Muted affect in all
	prosody	expressive modes
Paralinguistic	Aprosodia, for emotion	Aprosodia in speech
Linguistic Macrostructure	Missing the point of	Wandering from the
	discourse and text	point in discourse
	themes, jokes	

326   DAVIS

deficits that would form a pattern indicative of one common thread (i.e., all emotional tasks) or the other (i.e., all musical tasks). Getting the point of a joke may depend on the ability to relate the punch line to knowledge of the world (i.e., internal context) or on an ability to discern links between statements (i.e., linguistic context). One problem with jokes may be related to the more general problem of narrative integration (Brownell, Michel, Powelson, & Gardner, 1983). Certain areas of pragmatics have not been investigated as much as those mentioned in Table 10.1. For example, research should be encouraged concerning the effect of RHD on semantic and syntactic uses of prosody and on the processing of microstructural devices that contribute to coherence between sentences.

GENERAL IMPLICATIONS FOR REHABILITATION OF APHASIA

A pragmatic orientation has been brewing for a long time, originally in the name of a "functional" approach to aphasia rehabilitation. In this section, some general comparisons between cognitive and pragmatic approaches to assessment and treatment are presented. Cognitive approaches follow the traditional lines of focusing on a damaged LP. The pragmatic influence does not obviate cognitive methods, but it does encourage increased incorporation of context as a variable to be manipulated with these methods.

Assessment

Assessment of aphasia is aimed primarily at discovering weaknesses and strengths in linguistic performance for the purpose of planning treatment of a damaged LP. Comprehensive testing of the four language modalities is invariably done before treatment. Repeated assessment of a client is often carried out in an abbreviated form to measure the client's progress. Measurements of progress are reported to physicians, the client, and third-party payment providers. Whether it be for planning treatment or measuring progress, a major concern in assessment revolves around *what* is being measured. The validity of aphasia tests is continually challenged by the natural growth of knowledge about the LP and aphasia. Because of such forces, the American Psychological Association recommends that psychological tests (or, at least, test manuals) be revised periodically. Pragmatics has magnified such challenges to assessment of aphasia.

Comprehensive Evaluation. The content of standard aphasia tests has concentrated on products of the LP without much consideration of contextual variables. In the development of some tests, elimination of contextual influences has been an explicitly stated aim, as in the Token Test (DeRenzi & Vignolo, 1962) and the *Porch Index of Communicative Ability* (Porch, 1967). In his administration manual, Porch (1981) advised scorers of the sentence completion subtest: ". . . the tester should try to listen to each response in as unbiased a manner as possible and not let the knowledge of what the patient is attempting to say affect the scoring. Think of how the word the patient is saying would sound to judges listening to recordings of that word out of context" (pp. 53–54). The influence of extralinguistic (e.g., shared knowledge) and linguistic contexts are to be minimized. This traditional approach to assessment is valid as far as it goes. An acontextual approach is necessary to concentrate on the component of cognition that is impaired in aphasia. It is assessment of the LP per se and can be depicted as evaluation of the *linguistic adequacy* of communicative behavior.

Expansion of assessment from this acontextual focus has been carried out in two directions (Davis, 1983). One direction entailed the measurement of linguistic adequacy in contexts outside of the clinic and for a variety of communicative purposes. The most prominent example of this direction is Sarno's (1969) *Functional Communication Profile* (FCP). The FCP is designed to provide an estimate, from clinical observation, of a patient's comprehension and expression of language at home. The other direction has involved the assessment of something that is more general, namely, a patient's *communicative adequacy*. Holland's (1980) *Communicative Abilities in Daily Living* exemplifies attempts to evaluate ability of a damaged LP, working in conjunction with contexts, to achieve the conveyance of a message. Holland asks, "How well does your client get the message across?" As far as the LP is concerned, linguistic imperfections are ignored as long as the message is conveyed. Also, a client is assessed as to communicative adequacy no matter how a message is conveyed, verbally or nonverbally. With this strategy, context is injected deliberately into assessment of aphasia.

A comprehensive view of pragmatics reveals areas of linguistic performance that have been omitted from supplemental functional measures, as well as from traditional language evaluation. An evaluation should be as complete as possible with respect to how language is used naturally. This "incomplete validity" is illustrated by the exclusive reliance on literal interpretation of linguistic units in traditional subtests of comprehension. Patients are tested with respect to standard meanings of lexicon and, therefore, are not tested in the interpretation of speaker meaning requiring associations with contexts or the creation of meaning on the spot. Also, there are limitations regarding linguistic context, which is understandable because basic research concerning discourse is still fairly new. However, a test could provide controls for microstructural coherence devices and macrostructural differences among types of discourse. This modification may lead to a more systematic assessment of the intersentential level of language, especially for persons with moderate and mild language impairments.

The LP itself could be assessed more completely with respect to demands on linguistic performance outside of the traditional clinic. The real world presents a person with a variety of demands on cognition, particularly for word retrieval. For example, Chapey (1981) has pointed out that assessment and treatment have been focused on convergent processing, namely, the narrow pursuit of a single response. Divergent cognitive style has been neglected. Divergence involves a creative proliferation of several possibilities in a response. Word retrieval is achieved with both styles, but confrontation naming has continued to be the primary source of information about word retrieval ability. A clinician should be careful in generalizing about word retrieval ability from observations only of convergence.

It would be most desirable to obtain observations of linguistic and other communicative behavior in a patient's natural environment outside of the clinic (e.g., Holland, 1982). Clinicians have minimized the practical difficulties by having a family member record behaviors under certain circumstances. However, naturalistic observations can be obtained in the clinic by arranging circumstances that contain contextual variables (see Davis and Wilcox, 1985). These circumstances include conversational interactions and role-playing situations. Data may be gathered with check lists reflecting the occurrence of specific pragmatic behaviors or with rating scales reflecting degrees of accuracy and efficiency in conveying messages. Rating scales can be constructed to measure linguistic or communicative adequacy depending on what the clinician is interested in measuring under the conditions that are established.

In summary, a truly comprehensive assessment of communicative ability would be divided initially into examination of (a) the LP without context, (b) the LP interacting with context, and (c) contexts by themselves. The first portion follows traditional lines with a suggested expansion into more divergent forms of linguistic performance. A model for the second portion is indicated in Table 10.1 with respect to evaluating persons with RHD. That is, pragmatic assessment might be divided into receptive and expressive categories, within which extralinguistic, paralinguistic, and linguistic contexts are evaluated in a manner that follows the basic research in these areas. The dynamic context of conversation should be added to this model, with the structure of Promoting Aphasics Communicative Effectiveness (PACE) therapy as one example of a controlled condition for observing conversational language (see Davis & Wilcox, 1985). Naturalistic observation would complete this portion. Behaviors would be assessed with respect to their linguistic and communicative adequacy. The third section would address components of context per se, receptively, with tests of the agnosias, amusia, and figure and gesture recognition and, expressively, with tests of drawing and gesturing without context.

Although appearing to intrude on neuropsychological evaluation as well as appearing to be overwhelming, this model is simply an outline of comprehensive, pragmatic evaluation of language and communication. Clinical settings and a screening of patients may dictate directions of maximum efficiency for an individual client. Some sections may be important for initial assessment of aphasia; others, for assessing persons with RHD. Others may be more relevant for measuring progress. Furthermore, speech-language pathologists and neuropsychologists may coordinate information gained from their separate assessments according to what is relevant for communicative ability. Future discussions among professionals should determine how these selections and collaborations will be accomplished.

Reporting Progress. Clinical objectives have always had a pragmatic quality. We want our clients to talk better in conversation; we want them to respond more appropriately and quickly at the dinner table at home. We want their progress to be found in real changes in their daily lives that are experienced by their families as well. However, Metter (1985) made the following observation concerning a year of reports on treatment of a patient with Wernicke's aphasia: "The reports quantified marvelous improvements of word recognition, matching, and naming, but on examination I found the patient to have gained no apparent movement in functional communication after this extensive therapy" (p. 43). For a long time, speech-language pathologists have been wary of differences between clinical and functional performance, with Sarno declaring that "improvement which is not reflected in the patient's daily life is not improvement in fact" (Sarno & Levita, 1971, p. 74). The primary problem is that, in some

330   DAVIS

cases, treatment may not be effective in changing functional language ability. Regarding assessment, the problem is found in what is reported as progress.

Measurement often has been aimed at the means of reaching treatment goals rather than reflecting the goals themselves. Measurement of behaviors during treatment drill has been a convenient means of satisfying the press for accountability because it has coincided with principles of programmed instruction. In treatment "programs," transition between steps is based on achieving a percentage of success. Therefore, measurement of matching, imitation, and naming is inherent to programming. In fact, it could be argued that treatment activities have been designed to maximize reliability of measurement at the expense of creating naturalistic conditions in which reliable measurement has proved to be somewhat difficult to achieve. This tendency to make treatment measurable, thereby, measuring everything, has two unfortunate outcomes. It restricts a clinician's and client's behavior during an activity because of demands for reliability. It also results in progress being reported in terms of demands on the LP that are not characteristic of how the LP operates in natural circumstances.

Many clinicians rely on measurement *probes* that satisfy demands for accountability and that free treatment from the shackles of reliability. Probes are regularly administered brief tests designed, at least, to be independent of treatment itself. The idea is to measure "something else," such as performance with items not used in treatment or performance on a different task (Davis, 1986). What is measured is based on goals of specific drills and on overall goals of treatment. For example, imitation drill may be intended to improve a currently weak ability to produce sentences spontaneously. The relevant measure is a probe of spontaneous sentence production, not a measure of the imitation drill. Overall goals pertain to generalization of clinical successes to the use of language outside of the clinic. This brings us back to pragmatics (and the comprehensive model of assessment) as a guide to "what" should be measured.

Regular probing of linguistic performance under conditions of face-to-face conversation and role playing, as described previously, gets closer to the conditions in which family members, neurologists, and other interested parties would be observing the possible effects of treatment. Such probes, conducted in a clinic, are intended to be valid predictors of linguistic and general communicative effectiveness outside of a clinic. In order to reach outside of the clinic, family members can be recruited to obtain regular naturalistic observations that are relevant to objectives of treatment. For example, Beukelman and Yorkston (1980) trained family members to record behaviors with the aid of an audio tape recorder as part of a performance evaluation of persons with motor speech disorders. A family member recorded duration signals for the time it took to receive a message conveyed with an alphabet board or an electric typewriter. Even if a tape recorder were used regularly at the dinner table to obtain transcriptions of conversation, interpretation should be tempered with the reminder that "obtrusive" observation (i.e., when a client is aware of being assessed) may produce a result that differs from unobtrusive measurement (Kazdin, 1982). Although the ideal condition may seem unreachable, careful interpretation of progress is within reach of any clinician.

Treatment

Traditional treatment of aphasia has focused on improving the accuracy and efficiency of the LP. Two principal orientations can be characterized as the cognitive approach (i.e., stimulation of assumed mental processes) and the behavioral approach (i.e., modification of behaviors without assumptions about mental processes). Many clinicians draw from both orientations in a way that has been termed "programmed stimulation" (LaPointe, 1978). These orientations comprise the "direct approach" to treatment of primary language impairment. However, just as pragmatics involves viewing the LP as being bathed in different contexts, pragmatic treatment maintains the traditional direct attack on a damaged LP but also expands this approach with increasing attention to context. Therefore, cognitive and behavioral approaches may be conducted pragmatically (Davis & Wilcox, 1985). The pragmatic influence may be necessary, not so much because it seems to be "practical" or "realistic," but because it may be more tuned in to the way the LP works in real life.

The two orientations to traditional direct treatment are not mutually exclusive approaches that would look different when observed. Each can be depicted as a direction that a clinician might take in conducting an interaction pattern found in both of these directions. This interaction pattern consists of the clinician's presenting a stimulus, the patient's making a response, and the clinician's providing immediate feedback to the response (Brookshire, Nicholas, Krueger, & Redmond, 1978). This pattern is repeated in the several trials of a task. A task may be designed to provide exercise of a level of either comprehension, imitation, or production. One of the differences presented by cognitive or behavioral leans is that the antecedent event (i.e., stimulus) is emphasized in the former orientation so that it might elicit a successful response, whereas the consequent event (i.e., reinforcement schedule) is emphasized in the latter in order to shape responses into the best possible form. With both approaches, programming has been applied so that tasks are planned in steps of gradually increasing difficulty. Such steps are created by changing only one or two variables at a time.

Manipulation of variables is intended to facilitate ease of processing language. Traditional LP-focused variables include utterance length, syntactic complexity, and rate of production. Levels of these variables are used to specify the linguistic stimulus or expected verbal response in a treatment activity. They also define some of the parameters along which a clinician presents feedback as "restimulation" to improve a patient's response (Davis, 1983). With any case it is hoped that success at one step of a program will have lubricated the squeaky LP enough so that it can handle a more difficult step with greater ease than before. We can begin to think of pragmatic variables as possibly achieving the same result in the manner in which Olson and Filby (1972) found that passive sentences become easier than actives in a certain situational context.

Another traditional variable, namely, familiarity of vocabulary, represents overlap between the LP and one component of context, namely, the internal context of world knowledge (i.e., semantic memory). Knowledge of a topic corresponds with knowledge of a specialized lexicon associated with that topic. Much of the lexicon used in standard treatment is not only intended to be familiar to the client, but it is also designed to be familiar to the clinician. This dual familiarity is based on maximizing shared knowledge of topics, especially when clinical interaction turns to conversation.

Weaknesses in the pragmatic quality of such treatment can be defined partly with respect to the omission of context as a variable, in a manner that is similar to the limitations of assessment. Also, treatment has been focused on literal meaning and convergent responding. Behavior programming has fostered training of unnaturally structured utterances by, for example, changing one word at a time between trials in a task (e.g., "want coffee," "want juice," "want toilet," and so on). The cognitive approach has created conditions that maximize the possibility of success, thereby, not exposing a patient to the more likely occurrence of communicative frustration outside of the clinic. Unhappily, these approaches too often do not result in generalization to natural communicative conditions that include impatient stimulators (an external context), anxiety about ability (an internal context), and demands for new information and turn-taking in face-to-face conversation (a dynamic context).

10. PRAGMATICS AND COGNITION   333

PRAGMATIC TREATMENT

Treatment should possess content validity from two sources: one, the accurate identification of a patient's primary deficit(s); the other, an understanding of the cognitive (or behavioral) domain that is being treated. Goals and procedures should be drawn from relevant linkages between these two sources. This is the clinical version of the concern for "ecological validity" (p. 5) in cognitive psychology (Cohen, 1983). Pragmatic research has been expanding our understanding of the LP as it operates under conditions outside of a laboratory. These conditions have been identified as extralinguistic, paralinguistic, and linguistic contexts and the dynamic context of conversation. Goals should be aimed at a patient's primary deficit(s) with direction dictated by our knowledge of the LP in context. Procedures should address an appropriate definition of the disorder and, at some point, should imitate the manner in which the LP will be used by a patient in his or her daily life.

Weak validity of procedures may be one reason for the occasionally weak transfer of treatment successes to the functional use of impaired processes. The "clinic-nature gap," that was identified by Sarno and observed by Metter, is reflected in lack of improvement of an impaired function in natural circumstances, when that function has been shown to operate better than before under conditions arranged in the clinic. Metter (1985) wrote that this problem corresponds to a gap between conditions of language stimulation in the clinic and conditions outside of the clinic. He said that the hospital clinic is sterile, and he recommended that treatment be done in a shopping mall or park. However, a clinic need not be "sterile" with respect to manipulation of environmental influences. Pragmatics enhances traditional procedures by encouraging *more deliberate attention to context as a variable*, in addition to the LP-focused variables of length, syntax, vocabulary, and rate.

Background Information for Planning Treatment

In planning treatment, a clinician obtains information about a client's interests and environment as well as information about the status of his or her damaged LP. For example, Schuell's (1972) test booklet contains space for recording "social history" pertaining to education, occupation, and family. It also reminds a clinician to pay attention to "mental status" such as attitude and emotional state. This information comprises various internal and external extralinguistic contexts. If a patient's contexts are to be manipulated as

334   DAVIS

variables in treatment, it is useful to have identified the nature of these variables for that patient before beginning treatment.

Davis and Wilcox (1985) have sorted extralinguistic contexts into horizontal and vertical categories. As in the example from Schuell's test, most attention has been given to *horizontal contexts* that pertain to a patient's contemporary setting, significant others, knowledge of the world, and emotional state. Clinicians draw from this information in order to color treatment with meanings and lexicon that reflect a client's interests and communicative needs. A clinician will facilitate communication with a client on a foundation of shared knowledge by learning some basic concepts and lexicon pertaining to the client's interests. Emotional state becomes a byproduct of this investigation, when a clinician investigates horizontal contexts that are truly important to a client: What makes a client laugh? What makes him or her happy, hopeful, anxious, or angry?

Less attention has been given to *vertical contexts* that include a client's personal history and plans for the future. These contexts comprise a large portion of a client's internal context for communicative interaction. A typical person with a stroke is of an age that is indicative of five or six decades of accumulated experience and information about the world as it has been in recent history (Davis and Holland, 1981). In this respect, a 30-year-old clinician differs from an elderly client in about 40 years of shared knowledge. This gap is decreased by becoming more knowledgeable about a client's world as it was when the client was 30 years of age. Davis and Wilcox (1985) employed the following procedure:

> This strategy involves determining dates of important milestones such as graduation from school, marriage, birth of children, job starts and changes, divorce, children leaving home, retirement, and so on. Then the occurence of these milestones is associated with a historical 'time-line,' . . . an abbreviated history of key news events and key figures in music, movies, and sports, all of which are found readily in an almanac. (p. 128)

A topic such as the presidential election of 1940, when a client arrived at voting age, can stimulate personal recollections of settings and significant others at that time in the client's life. Such recollections are often energizing for communicative interaction.

Selection of Standard Procedures for Cognitive Deficits

Two basic decisions should be made in the selection of traditional procedures that could be aimed at a primary deficit, whether it be language impairment or a "cognitive disorder," such as impaired visuospatial processing. Both decisions pertain to a sense of pragmatics suggesting that a procedure be relevant.

First, is the procedure relevant to a patient's disorder? If a deficit is defined incorrectly or incompletely, treatment will be incorrect or incomplete. Often a procedure is derived directly from a deficit defined by neuropsychological assessment rather than according to an objective and complete theory of cognition. A patient is said to be impaired in sentence repetition because sentence repetition is tested. A patient is said to be impaired in visuospatial construction because visuospatial construction is tested. The danger of test-bound problem definition was noted by Goldstein (1984) regarding poor performance in copying designs. If a disorder is defined as one of copying designs, then practice in copying designs would seem to be relevant treatment. However, Goldstein noted that an impairment in this task could be due to a visual disorder, a movement disorder, or a coordination disorder. Relevant treatment could proceed in three different directions, and selection of one direction or another should result in treatment that is more efficient in improving the ability to copy designs than if a patient simply practiced copying designs.

Although the first question is basic in that it is independent of approach to treatment, definition of a patient's disorder is somewhat sterile without a clear link between a test observation and a patient's natural functioning. For example, if a link can be established between copying designs and the ability to function in daily life, as in finding one's way around a familiar setting, then perhaps the real disorder is disorientation. Copying designs becomes relegated to the status of just happening to be a traditional means by which some of the cognitive processes of orientation have been measured. In this sense, the first question is related to the second question.

Is the procedure relevant to a patient's functioning in his or her natural environment? With the visuospatial example, a clinician should think about the difference copying designs will make to a patient's life. Treatment goals are related to a client's horizontal contexts. If a patient is an artist, relevance of the procedure is obvious. Following the principle of starting treatment at simple levels, copying designs may help to reorganize processes that are basic for impressionist painting that may be too difficult and discouraging to attempt soon after occurrence of the brain injury. However, what about an average person who never had any interest whatsoever in drawing or copying anything? What does copying designs accomplish for this patient? The answer may lie in a analysis of basic cognitive processes used in this task that are also used in the chores of

336 DAVIS

daily living. Some of these processes may overlap, for example, with visual imagery. Treatment is aimed at these processes, not at the task of copying designs per se.

It is quite common for the first and simplest level of a treatment program to be aimed most directly at a primary deficit and for the final level of a program to reflect the most pragmatic realizations of the process being treated. For example, Grafman (1984) provided a brief description of steps to improve visual imagery in persons with traumatic brain damage. The first step was to ask patients to close their eyes and imagine a familiar living thing, such as a cow. The pragmatic value of this activity by itself might be difficult to imagine. However, the final step of the program included practice in recalling a familiar route with the help of visual imagery. In effect, visual imagery was put to work within a context that might be meaningful to the patient. Perhaps, the aim was to improve recall and the ability to find one's way about a familiar setting. Visual imaging (and even copying designs) might be considered to be simple manifestations of a cognitive capacity that is relevant to orientation. If this is so, then effectiveness of these procedures would be evaluated with respect to whether the patient's ability to find his or her way has improved.

These speculations are intended to illustrate a decision making process that is important for selecting procedures to treat aphasia, as well. For example, a reduction in immediate memory span may be interpreted as being (a) the basis for language comprehension problems and/or (b) an independent problem per se. Procedures would be aimed at increasing short-term memory capacity, and their value would be determined with respect to whether (a) comprehension improves and/or (b) a real life manifestation of memory span improves. Concerning the latter goal, treatment would lead to exercises in recalling a shopping list or names of people who had been introduced at a "party." As another example, spelling practice may be irrelevant to a patient's culture and/or to his or her communicative activities in daily life. It would be relevant to this patient only if it is a means of addressing processes that are basic to something useful. As was indicated previously, practice only in naming as a means of improving word retrieval is incomplete with respect to convergent and divergent manifestations of word retrieval. That is, how often does a person name things in his or her natural language functioning? Therefore, the most efficient use of a treatment session may depend on selectivity of goals and the means for reaching these goals that goes beyond simply dealing with a problem "because it is there."

Enhancement of Standard Language Treatment

This section illustrates deliberate attention to *extralinguistic* contexts in conducting traditional cognitive or behavioral procedures. Contexts include variables that should be incorporated in a strategy of programming generalization across settings, persons, and so on (e.g., Hughes, 1985). Suggestions include standard practices that are consistent with pragmatics as well as enhancements of standard procedures. Many suggestions do not necessarily require proof as to their effectiveness beyond what still needs to be demonstrated with traditional procedures because the procedures remain the same. However, some comparisons of efficacy may be warranted because a pragmatic direction indicates that a clinician may spend more time preparing individualized materials than in traditional clinical practice and may delve into more sensitive areas of semantic content. At least, the following suggestions establish points at which pragmatics may improve the validity of direct treatment procedures as they are designed to maximize LP-context interactions.

Internal Contexts. In a comprehension task, world knowledge (i.e., semantic memory) has been regulated by varying the semantic plausibility of statements presented to aphasic subjects (Deloche & Seron, 1981; Heeschen, 1980; Kudo, 1984; Heilman & Scholes, 1976). Manipulation is in terms of the relationship between a sentence and what a subject already knows about reality. For example, a statement (e.g., *The policeman arrests the thief*) may fit more closely to what is likely to occur in the real world than another statement (e.g., *The thief arrests the policeman*). The variation between plausible and implausible sentences includes a range of probability of occurrence from events that are possible but unlikely to events that are physically impossible (e.g., *The apple eats the boy*). Within this realm of probability lives certain types of metaphor (e.g., *She is suffering from a broken heart*). Semantic plausibility, however, did not affect verbal production in a sentence completion task (Hatfield, Howard, Barber, Jones, & Morton, 1977). Nevertheless, when literal interpretation is tested (ignoring metaphor), aphasic persons usually find it easiest to comprehend sentences that are most consistent with their knowledge of the world, which includes knowledge influenced by subculture-based belief as well as knowledge based on the laws of biology, chemistry, and physics.

Investigations of semantic plausibility indicate that aphasic persons comprehend language with the greatest of ease when content consists of what they know best. This point goes beyond triviality when we consider that what a client knows best is not necessarily what a clinician knows. When a client is someone who had been a delegate to the United Nations, some of the content of treatment should consist of related issues and operations. As indicated in the discussion of vertical contexts, pictures of Presidents, cars, and TV stars from a client's young adulthood are likely to provide stimulation that heightens attention and motivation. Stimulating horizontal contexts, such as a favorite soap opera, provide names to comprehend and retrieve and provide topics for conversation. Clinicians should do enough homework in order to draw from a variety of sources for semantic content and to provide conditions that maximize shared knowledge, thereby enhancing communication with clients.

Semantic content or topics that are emotionally arousing may have a facilitative effect on verbal production processes. It is a common clinical experience to find an aphasic patient being surprisingly verbal when a situation arises that is of utmost importance to that individual. Although anecdotal evidence is indicative of an avenue of stimulation, experimental evidence is merely suggestive of possibilities. "Emotional words" appear to stimulate neurological systems (e.g., right hemisphere) differently from "nonemotional words" in normal adults (Graves, Landis, & Goodglass, 1981). Aphasic individuals respond similarly to normals in that the patients show greater physiological arousal to "emotional" pictures than to neutral pictures (Morrow, et al., 1981). However, there is no direct evidence that this arousal improves naming or other types of word retrieval behavior.

External Contexts. The presentation of external contexts, especially with pictures, is intimately related to stimulation of the internal contexts of semantic memory and emotion. As a means of evoking discrete verbal responses, situational contexts for objects have been studied as to their effect on *object-naming.* Early speculation held that, by putting an object into a meaningful visual context, an aphasic person's nonverbal imagery would be aroused and, therefore, language behavior would be enhanced (e.g., Fitch-West, 1983; Myers, 1980). In one study, a context for objects did not improve naming performance over presenting objects in isolation (Hatfield et al., 1977). The question is difficult to answer with another study because response requirements differed in the object-in-context condition (Williams & Canter, 1982). Subjects were asked to name objects in isolation but were asked to describe in the context condition. Subjects with Wernicke's aphasia retrieved words better when their re-

10. PRAGMATICS AND COGNITION   339

sponses contained the linguistic context of continuous verbalization. Therefore, an object in context has not been shown to facilitate object naming; the effects of situational context on continuous verbal production are unclear.

Manipulation of extralinguistic variables appears to have a greater impact on comprehension, as has been evident in two common treatment drills: following instructions and deblocking. With respect to *following instructions*, comparisons have been made between the use of objects versus the use of abstract "tokens." Clinical training with instructions has included abstract tokens (Holland & Sonderman, 1974) and objects (Flowers & Danforth, 1979). The Token Test was designed to minimize contextual information that would be provided with realistic objects (DeRenzi & Vignolo, 1962). Several comparisons have produced mixed results; either realistic objects are easier than tokens for following instructions, or there is no difference (Kreindler, Gheorghita, & Voinescu, 1971; Lesser, 1979, Lohman & Prescott, 1978; Martino, Pizzamiglio, & Razzano, 1976). It is wise to consider the likelihood that, for many patients, instructions are easier to follow with objects than with tokens. Seron and Deloche refined the study of this dimension by examining the particular combinations of objects that might be used when asking a patient to follow instructions.

Clients practice comprehension of prepositions by placing objects in different spatial relationships to each other. Seron and Deloche (1981) demonstrated that the ease of following instructions, which can be translated into task hierarchies, is related to the congruence between objects and an instruction. Congruence is realized with respect to the usual relationship between objects (e.g., soap on a sink/soap under a sink) or to the physical characteristics of two objects (e.g., ball in a box/box on a ball). The objects create a contextual bias, and persons with Broca's aphasia were found to follow congruent instructions more easily than incongruent instructions. Clinicians usually focus treatment on the LP with comprehension tasks involving unexpected (or unnatural) instructions. A patient's communicative ability may be demonstrated more readily, however, with instructions that are likely to occur in daily life or that, at least, are realistic with respect to the external contextual cues.

Deblocking is a clinical paradigm in which contextual information can be introduced as *prestimulation*. The prestimulation phase of this paradigm consists of presenting a stimulus before the usual stimulus that would be used in a task. A patient is to respond to the second stimulus, not to the first stimulus. Theoretically, prestimulation is analogous to "priming" of semantic memory that has been investi-

340   DAVIS

gated by cognitive psychologists (e.g., Collins & Loftus, 1975). The priming effect has been considered to entail a "prestimulus" that activates (or "primes") an area of semantic memory, thereby, facilitating access to similar information related to subsequent stimuli.

In studies of aphasia, prestimulation has included a picture presented before a paragraph in a comprehension task (Waller & Darley, 1978) and a related word presented before a picture in a confrontation naming task (Pidraza & Darley, 1977). Prestimulation with sentences and pictures was shown to facilitate sentence comprehension in severely impaired aphasic patients (Pierce & Beekman, 1985). This paradigm may become valuable in the practice of metaphor comprehension in that prestimulation may include pictures or sentences leading to different intents conveyed by a sentence. For example, "He lost his shirt" could be preceded by contexts leading either to a literal interpretation or a nonliteral interpretation.

Context Processing Deficits

The intricate integration of circuits among different regions of the brain, including connection between the left and right hemispheres, predicts that different "modules" of cognition are similarly interconnected. Damage to one region (or cognitive function) may upset its interaction with other regions (or functions). Language comprehension deficit, for example, may prohibit the visual imagery that might be induced by questions such as "Which direction does George Washington face on a quarter?" Some aphasic persons possess slight deficits that are outside the realm of purely linguistic processing. These deficits may be a result of damage extending outside the perisylvian language-specific regions, as well as a result of diminished interactive processing. As these deficits occur, abilities to process elements of context may be impaired in some of these patients. Such deficits become a source of treatment objectives that supplement standard language-oriented objectives.

Three elements of context have been shown to be mildly impaired in some aphasic patients: (a) internal context of semantic memory, (b) processing of auditory external context, and (c) processing of paralinguistic contexts. Each of these problems has been found in patients with severe auditory language comprehension deficit (e.g., Wernicke's and global aphasias). Regarding semantic memory, these patients have been found to differ from normals in manner of concept association (Semenza, Denes, Lucchese, & Bisiacchi, 1980). Auditory agnosia can be seen for matching familiar sounds to their source (Cohen, Kelter, & Woll, 1980). Severely impaired patients are deficient in recognizing emotion conveyed by prosody (Schlanger,

10. PRAGMATICS AND COGNITION 341

Schlanger, & Gerstman, 1976) and in interpreting cues to deep structure conveyed with stress and juncture (Baum, Daniloff, Daniloff, & Lewis, 1982). More research needs to be done to determine the significance of these problems for communicative ability.

Dynamic Context: Conversation

Attention to conversation as a treatment mode has provided procedures that supplement standard cognitive/behavioral drills. Depending on which conditions provide the most linguistic success for a client, conversational activities may accompany stimulation drills, may follow a phase of direct stimulation, or may be the preferred condition for stimulating language. Conversational conditions also provide an opportunity to observe whether improved linguistic performance with direct stimulation is generalizing to more natural conditions. Treatment becomes closer to real life demands on the LP with a controlled modeling of face-to-face conversational structure and with less controlled simulated life situations that include role playing. It is a principal strategy for narrowing the "clinic-nature gap."

PACE Therapy. PACE involves some slight adjustments to traditional verbal tasks, and these adjustments conform to certain essential components of face-to-face conversation (see Davis & Wilcox, 1981, 1985). These components are found in four principles for creating a PACE activity, and each principle should be followed when a clinician wishes to provide an activity that models natural conversation.

1. *The clinician and patient participate equally as senders and receivers of messages.* The clinician and patient take turns conveying messages to each other. This alternation of sender and receiver roles allows a variety of feedback operations to occur. While taking turns as sender and receiver, the clinician usually attempts to convey and understand messages as if engaging in a natural conversation with an aphasic person. However, when the clinician wishes to encourage communicative behaviors that are not being pursued by the client, the clinician models these desirable behaviors when carrying out his or her roles in the interaction. Modeling is intended to replace directing the client to behave in certain ways. The client should have opportunities to observe the communicative effectiveness of supplemental gesturing or writing and, then, be able to decide to attempt these behaviors on his or her own, without being told to do so. Direct instruction is reserved for other treatment activities.

342   DAVIS

2. *There is an exchange of new information between the clinician and patient.* The new information condition may be the most powerful feature of this procedure, making it feel different for the clinician from traditional direct stimulation activities. As in confrontation naming or picture description tasks, pictures of objects or events are the usual message stimuli used in PACE. However, instead of being in view of the client and clinician, message stimuli are placed face down; and the participants take turns drawing from the stack of cards, keeping each card hidden from view of the other person. With a card hidden from the receiver, the speaker attempts to convey what is on the card. The receiver attempts to comprehend what the speaker is saying about the content of the card. Instead of already knowing what an aphasic speaker is trying to say, the clinician is in the less secure position of not knowing what the patient is looking at on the card until the client is able to convey this message.

This has been the most difficult of the PACE principles to preserve (Davis, 1980). Because a clinician often knows the content of message stimuli or, at least, knows the general class of stimuli (e.g., all objects, all sports actions), the PACE activity can easily become a matter of trying to recall a known picture that a client probably has chosen, rather than responding to the message conveyed in the client's communicative attempts. The new information condition becomes diluted with repetitive use of the same stimuli. This dilution can be minimized by selecting a subset of message stimuli from an extremely large pool of pictures, changing the pictures from session to session, or having someone else select the stimuli. Also, the clinician should be sensitive to this component of the procedure and, therefore, should respond to the client's message in a manner that is consistent with the principles.

3. *The patient is allowed free choice with respect to selection of communicative channels (modalities) with which to convey messages.* The patient makes an independent choice as to the manner in which a message is to be conveyed. After assessing the patient's abilities in different channels, the clinician provides opportunities to use writing or drawing, for example, by placing paper and a pencil before the patient. However, in the spirit of modeling, described with the first principle, the clinician does not instruct the client to use this or any other channel. Also, perhaps through modeling, the clinician encourages the client to *use modalities in combination.* This strategy differs from traditional tasks that focus a patient on one modality, without the contextual contribution of other modalities. Verbal behavior, in particular, is modeled throughout a session of PACE. Contrary to certain impressions (e.g., Code & Muller, 1983; Tonkovich & Loverso,

1982), this procedure is not "a nonverbal perspective" toward treatment nor is it "formalized gesture training." A silent session of PACE, with clinician and client gesturing, is not the most effective means of promoting "total communication," as verbal ambiguities can be resolved with supplemental communicative channels.

4. *Feedback from the clinician is based on the client's success in communicating a message.* When a message is already known to the clinician and linguistic adequacy is the criterion for success, the clinician's feedback to the client is generally congratulatory (e.g., "good"). Also, the clinician is able to restimulate for a better response by providing a cue to the intended linguistic unit. However, in a genuine new information condition, the clinician does not know if a patient's communicative effort is "good" until the patient confirms the clinician's comprehension, and the clinician should not be able to cue a linguistic unit without knowing the message. Such cues are possible only after the patient has successfully conveyed a message. The client's communication of a message is the basis for the clinician's response as receiver of that message.

When a client attempts to convey what is on a card in PACE, a clinician usually responds with a repeat of what the client said (e.g., "a newspaper") or with a guess or question if the client is ambiguous (e.g., "Newspaper?" or "Is it something you read?"). When the client succeeds in conveying a message, he or she is reinforced with the realization that the clinician understood in a new information condition. Furthermore, the client has an opportunity to practice conversational behaviors that are not typically practiced in standard stimulation drill. The client should respond to the clinician's feedback, either confirming that the clinician understood correctly or, recognizing lack of comprehension, responding with an attempt to revise the first attempt. The interaction becomes a drill in dealing with miscommunication or in functioning within the hint-and-guess cycle described earlier in this chapter. Comprehension skill is used for the purpose of evaluating the clinician's response as receiver, and expressive skills are invoked to revise previously unsuccessful sending behavior.

The following example, from Davis and Wilcox (1985, p. 162), demonstrates several features of PACE interaction. Tom, an aphasic person with limited verbal ability, is interacting with his wife, Virginia. The message stimuli are simple events that could be described with subject-verb-object sentences:

> Tom: (selects a card) "Car . . . uh . . . car . . ."
> Virginia: "Give me . . ."

344 DAVIS

Tom: "Car. It's a car. Water. Girl. Two of them."
Virginia: "What are they doing to the car?"
Tom: "Water . . ."
Virginia: "Wash. Washing the car."
Tom: "Yes."

Although Tom did not say "they are washing the car," he did provide enough information during these "miniturns" to enable Virginia to make a reasonable guess about Tom's message. Tom was able to confirm Virginia's response. Although a spouse would like to have heard a verb to go along with the object-noun, through this carefully structured interaction the spouse may learn to recognize the communicative value of information that comes forth during a hint-and-guess cycle. PACE takes advantage of the contribution made by listeners during a natural conversation. That is, a listener's attention and knowledge determine whether a speaker's message is conveyed, in addition to the speaker's communicative behavior per se. In real life, a speaker's communicative success is a product of a two-way interaction; whereas, traditional drill appears to be based on the assumption that communication is only the speaker's responsibility.

PACE is still some distance from the dynamic conversational context in which the LP operates in real life. However, it does provide a link between standard direct stimulation and natural conversation outside of the clinic. Too often, we have bombarded clients with direct stimulation and then thrust them into real life communicative interactions, hoping that success with the former will lead to success in the latter circumstances. The challenge of pragmatics is to develop steps between these two contrasting demands on language processing. PACE provides one type of transitional step between drill and natural communication. Future development of applied pragmatics should include other types of transitional steps in which more natural stimulus conditions and response expectations are built into treatment programs, extending them further than they have been extended.

Natural Conversation.   One of the final steps of treatment is natural conversation that is conducted in the clinic. Having provided this type of activity, the only types of generalization left to be trained would be generalization of conversational skills to other settings and persons outside of the clinic. Steps in these directions include conducting communicative interactions in settings created in the clinic and with persons other than the clinician in the clinic. Practice with other

10. PRAGMATICS AND COGNITION   345

persons can be achieved with PACE as well as with natural conversation. Practice in varied settings, however, cannot be achieved realistically with PACE. Therefore, if a patient is to practice shopping in a store or ordering in a restaurant, the role playing of relevant interactions is done in the context of relevant props designed to imitate such a setting.

Conversation is a common treatment activity. However, its lack of directiveness leads to wondering about its therapeutic value. It is not clear whether natural conversation contains mechanisms that facilitate change in language or other communicative behavior. Wepman (1976) presented conversation as a content-centered discussion therapy for persons with limited verbal production and no evidence of improvement with standard direct stimulation approaches. Clinician and client discussed vocational topics, which was intended to direct the client's attention away from frustrating verbal effort, thereby, actually facilitating improved verbal production. Reports of this treatment's efficacy were anecdotal, and no follow-up has been reported with respect to replication of the approach. Nevertheless, naturalistic conversation is valuable, at least, as a means of observing generalization of success from stimulation drill and PACE; and generalization may be maximized when a client is able to experience communicative success in this more natural context.

It is difficult to participate in a conversation with an aphasic person. This has been especially true for speech-language pathologists who have seen words retrieved in other activities that are not being retrieved in conversation and who appear to feel compelled to continue stimulating the client for greater linguistic precision during conversational interaction. These urges may be responsible for what Kimbarow (1982) called "therapizing" by clinicians during conversations with patients. Speech acts are often restricted to those found in standard drill, with the clinician questioning and the patient responding (Kimbarow, 1982; Wilcox & Davis, 1977). Instead of responding to the message conveyed by a patient, clinicians often respond with attempts to improve the linguistic adequacy of the means by which messages were conveyed. That is, instead of responding with "You mean you aren't feeling well today?" or with "I'm sorry you aren't feeling well," a clinician, having understood the message, might implore the patient with the following: "No. Say 'I am not feeling well.'" While the urge to improve linguistic precision is compelling, it is also valuable for a patient to experience communicative success in conversation with the other participant (e.g., clinician, spouse) responding to meaning by making comments, rendering opinions, arguing, and engaging in other types of speech acts.

346   DAVIS

Changing Contexts

In this chapter, the implications of pragmatics have focused on changing the communicative abilities of an aphasic patient. Some clinicians have thought that pragmatics entails giving up on improving the patient and turning to modification of settings and people in a patient's environment (e.g., Rosenbek, 1983). Changing the environment is simply one component of pragmatic rehabilitation. It has been addressed as "environmental intervention" for aphasia (Lubinski, 1981a, 1981b) and "environmental education" for dysarthria (Berry & Sanders, 1983).

Lubinski's (1981a) environmental intervention stresses the value of modifying a patient's internal and external extralinguistic contexts. A patient's internal environment consists of attitudes, beliefs, and feelings about his or her communicative crisis that may influence the outcome of language rehabilitation. A clinician can assist the patient in adjusting to the loss of normal language function (Tanner, 1980) and can provide some supportive counseling that may decrease frustration, increase motivation, and foster a realistic approach to the problem (e.g., Webster & Newhoff, 1981). The quickest avenue, however, to decreasing frustration and increasing motivation entails appropriately directed treatment of language deficit. Successful experiences with remaining and improving language abilities and with general communicative abilities breed motivation and foster psychological adjustment. When emotional maladjustments (especially those that stem from premorbid problems) interfere with this process, the clinician should seek assistance from professional counseling services.

Changing the external environment includes assisting significant others and modifying physical settings that Lubinski called "communication-impaired environments." In assisting people in a patient's natural contexts, activities such as counseling are consistent with a pragmatic influence on rehabilitation. Several approaches to family counseling have been described (Luterman, 1984; Porter & Dabul, 1977; Webster & Newhoff, 1981). Most efforts directed toward family members have consisted of assisting them in maximizing communication with the aphasic person. One method has involved family members in PACE interaction (Davis & Wilcox, 1985). A spouse can easily practice communicative options in such dyads with his or her aphasic partner. The spouse, then, may analyze video recordings of these dyads to identify behaviors that should be changed or improved and to increase awareness of behaviors that are a positive influence on an interaction.

EPILOGUE: COORDINATING RESPONSIBILITIES

Pragmatic research should lead to a model for understanding how the language processor operates in relation to the contexts of naturalistic language behavior. Such a model should also refine our understanding of the neuropathologies of language processing and context processing. These impairments have been distinguished in this chapter with respect to focal damage in either the left cerebral hemisphere or the right hemisphere, respectively. For over 40 years, speech-language pathologists have provided comprehensive assessment and treatment of communicative impairments caused by left hemisphere damage. As indicated in this chapter, they have begun to identify communicative deficits associated with more general cognitive disorders. Neuropsychologists have assessed function of both cerebral hemispheres, as well as other psychological dimensions (e.g., emotional state, personality) that form the basis for traditional counseling services. Focusing on the diffuse effects of head injury, they have become involved relatively recently in the treatment of cognitive impairments. Because both professions deal with cognitive impairments, there has been some concern in rehabilitation settings as to who should be responsible for what.

This overlap of territories is striking when considering that primary language impairments interact with nonverbal contexts and, especially, when considering that "pragmatic" secondary language impairments of persons with right hemisphere damage (RHD) may be derived from primary "nonverbal" deficits. Examples from RHD include the meandering discourse production that may be a manifestation of general integration disability and the monotonic intonation that may be secondary to a general tonal production (e.g., singing) problem. In rehabilitation settings, a team approach has characterized the total rehabilitation of persons with multiple disorders. It has been relatively easy to separate ambulation training in physical therapy from speech or language training in communicative disorders clinics. However, it is not as easy to carve out somewhat independent territories of treatment with respect to many cognitive disorders, when treatment of secondary manifestations is directed most efficiently toward the primary disorder. Relying on experience in the treatment of voice and prosody disorders, a speech-language pathologist would naturally be involved with aprosodia by training variable pitch production. It is interesting to consider whether a speech-language pathologist should also be involved with discourse production by treating the integration of block designs.

348 DAVIS

A division of responsibilities may occur with respect to the secondary behavioral manifestations of primary disorders. Speech-language clinicians have been educated in the processes and modalities of communication and have been trained in procedures that stimulate or modify these processes and modalities. Their training and experience are suited for dealing with the symptoms of focal RHD and head injury that pertain to communication. Other specialists in "cognitive retraining" and counseling may focus on areas of other secondary impairments as in basic memory functions, visuospatial processing, personality, stress management, and psychosocial adjustment to crisis. Because some of these communicative and other impairments may originate in a single primary deficit, these different rehabilitation specialists should be coordinating their efforts with respect to a few common objectives defined in terms of the primary deficits.

REFERENCES

Baum, S. R., Daniloff, J. K., Daniloff, R., & Lewis, J. (1982). Sentence comprehension by Broca's aphasics: effects of some suprasegmental variables. *Brain and Language, 17,* 261–271.

Berry, W. R., & Sanders, S. B. (1983). Environmental education: The universal management approach for adults with dysarthria. In W. R. Berry (Ed.), *Clinical dysarthria* (pp. 203–216). San Diego: College-Hill Press.

Beukelman, D. R., & Yorkston, K. M. (1980). Nonvocal communication: performance evaluation. *Archives of Physical Medicine and Rehabilitation, 61,* 272–275.

Brookshire, R. H., Nicholas, L. E., Krueger, K. M., & Redmond K. J. (1978). The clinical interaction analysis system: a system for observational recording of aphasia treatment. *Journal of Speech and Hearing Disorders, 43,* 437–447.

Brownell, H., Michel, D., Powelson, J., & Gardner, H. (1983). Surprise but not coherence: sensitivity to verbal humor in right hemisphere patients. *Brain and Language, 18,* 20–27.

Caplan, D. (1984). The mental organ for language. In D. Caplan, A. R. Lecours, & A. Smith (Eds.), *Biological perspectives on language* (pp. 8–30). Cambridge, MA: MIT Press.

Caramazza, A. (1984). The logic of neuropsychological research and the problem of patient classification in aphasia. *Brain and Language, 21,* 9–20.

Chapey, R. (1981). Divergent semantic intervention. In R. Chapey (Ed.), *Language intervention strategies in adult aphasia* (pp. 155–167). Baltimore: Williams & Wilkins.

Cicone, M., Wapner, W., & Gardner, H. (1980). Sensitivity to emotional expressions and situations in organic patients. *Cortex, 16,* 145–158.

Clark, H. H., & Gerrig, R. J. (1983). Understanding old words with new meanings. *Journal of Verbal Learning and Verbal Behavior, 22,* 591–608.

Clark, H. H., & Lucy, P. (1975). Understanding what is meant from what is said: a study in conversationally conveyed requests. *Journal of Verbal Learning and Verbal Behavior, 14,* 56–72.

Clark, H. H., & Haviland, S. E. (1977). Comprehension and the given-new contract. In

10. PRAGMATICS AND COGNITION 349

R. O. Freedle (Ed.), *Discourse production and comprehension* (pp. 1–40). Norwood, NJ: Ablex.

Code, C., & Muller, D. J. (1983). Perspectives in aphasia therapy: an overview. In C. Code & D. J. Muller (Eds.), *Aphasia therapy* (pp. 3–13). London: Edward Arnold.

Cohen, G. (1983). *The psychology of cognition.* London: Academic Press.

Cohen, R., Kelter, S., & Woll, G. (1980). Analytical competence and language impairment in aphasia. *Brain and Language, 10,* 331–347.

Collins, A. M., & Loftus, E. F. (1975). A spreading activation theory of semantic processing. *Psychological Review, 82,* 407–428.

Davis, G. A. (1986). Questions of efficacy in clinical aphasiology. In R. H. Brookshire (Ed.), *Clinical aphasiology* (pp. 154–162). Minneapolis, MN: BRK Publishers.

Davis, G. A. (1980). A critical look at PACE therapy. in R. H. Brookshire (Ed.), *Clinical aphasiology conference proceedings* (pp. 248–257). Minneapolis, BRK.

Davis, G. A. (1983). *A survey of adult aphasia.* Englewood Cliffs, NJ: Prentice-Hall.

Davis, G. A., & Holland, A. L. (1981). Age in understanding and treating aphasia. In D. S. Beasley & G. A. Davis (Eds.), *Aging: Communication processes and disorders* (pp. 207–228). New York: Grune & Stratton.

Davis, G. A., & Wilcox, M. J. (1981). Incorporating parameters of natural conversation in aphasia treatment. In R. Chapey (Ed.), *Language intervention strategies in adult aphasia* (pp. 169–193). Baltimore: Williams & Wilkins.

Davis, G. A., & Wilcox, M. J. (1985). *Adult aphasia rehabilitation: Applied pragmatics.* San Diego: College-Hill Press.

Delis, D. C., Wapner, W., Gardner, H., & Moses, Jr., J. A. (1983). The contribution of the right hemisphere to the organization of paragraphs. *Cortex, 19,* 43–50.

Deloche, G., & Seron, X. (1981). Sentence understanding and knowledge of the world. Evidences from a sentence-picture matching task performed by aphasic patients. *Brain and Language, 14,* 57–69.

DeRenzi, E., & Vignolo, L. A. (1962). The Token Test: A sensitive test to detect receptive disturbances in aphasics. *Brain, 85,* 665–678.

Fitch-West, J. (1983). Heightening visual imagery: A new approach to aphasia therapy. In E. Perecman (Ed.), *Cognitive processing in the right hemisphere* (pp. 215–228). New York: Academic Press.

Flowers, C. R., & Danforth, L. C. (1979). A step-wise auditory comprehension improvement program administered to aphasic patients by family members. In R. H. Brookshire (Ed.), *Clinical aphasiology conference proceedings* (pp. 196–202). Minneapolis: BRK.

Foldi, N., Cicone, M., & Gardner, H. (1983). Pragmatic aspects of communication in brain damaged patients. In S. Segalowitz (Ed.). *Language functions and brain organization* (pp. 51–86). New York: Academic Press.

Gainotti, G. (1972). Emotional behavior and hemispheric side of lesion. *Cortex, 8,* 41–55.

Gandour, J., & Dardarananda, R. (1983). Identification of tonal contrasts in Thai aphasic patients. *Brain and Language, 18,* 98–114.

Gardner, H. (1982). Missing the point: Language and the right hemisphere. In H. Gardner, *Art, mind, & brain: a cognitive approach to creativity* (pp. 309–317). New York: Basic Books.

Gardner, H., Brownell, H. H., Wapner, W., & Michelow, D. (1983). Missing the point: The role of the right hemisphere in the processing of complex linguistic materials. In E. Perecman (Ed.), *Cognitive processing in the right hemisphere* (pp. 169–191). New York: Academic Press.

Gardner, H., Ling, P. K., Flamm, L., & Silverman, J. (1975). Comprehension and appreciation of humorous material following brain damage. *Brain, 98,* 399–412.

350 DAVIS

Garnham, A. (1985). *Psycholinguistics: central topics.* London: Methuen.

Gildea, P., & Glucksberg, S. (1983). On understanding metaphor: the role of context. *Journal of Verbal Learning and Verbal Behavior, 22,* 577–590.

Goldstein, G. (1984). Methodological and theoretical issues in neuropsychological assessment. In B. A. Edelstein & E. T. Couture (Eds), *Behavioral assessment and rehabilitation of the traumatically brain-damaged* (pp. 1–21. New York: Plenum Press.

Grafman, G. (1984). Memory assessment and remediation in brain-injured patients: from theory to practice. In B. A. Edelstein & E. T. Couture (Eds), *Behavioral assessment and rehabilitation of the traumatically brain-damaged* (pp. 151–189). New York: Plenum Press.

Graves, R., Landis, T., & Goodglass, H. (1981). Laterality and sex differences for visual recognition of emotional and non-emotional words. *Neuropsychologia, 19,* 95–102.

Grice, H. (1975). Logic and conversation. In P. Cole & J. Morgan (Eds.), *Syntax and semantics: Speech acts* (pp. 41–58). New York: Academic Press.

Hatfield, F. M., Howard D., Barber, J., Jones, C., & Morton, J. (1977). Object naming in aphasics—the lack of effect of context or realism. *Neuropsychologia, 15,* 717–727.

Heeschen, C. (1980). Strategies of decoding actor-object relations by aphasic patients. *Cortex, 16,* 5–19.

Heilman, K. M., Bowers, D., Speedie, L., & Coslett, H. B. (1984). Comprehension of affective and nonaffective prosody. *Neurology, 34,* 917–921.

Heilman, K. M. & Scholes, R. J. (1976). The nature of comprehension errors in Broca's conduction and Wernicke's aphasics. *Cortex, 12,* 258–265.

Heilman, K. M., Schwartz, H. D., & Watson, R. T. (1978). Hypoarousal in patients with the neglect syndrome and emotional indifference. *Neurology, 28,* 229–232.

Hirst, W., & Brill, G. (1980). Contextual aspects of pronoun assignment. *Journal of Verbal Learning and Verbal Behavior, 19,* 168–175.

Holland, A. L. (1980). *Communicative abilities in daily living.* Baltimore: University Park Press.

Holland, A. L. (1982). Observing functional communication of aphasic adults. *Journal of Speech and Hearing Disorders, 47,* 50–56.

Holland, A. L., & Sonderman, J. C. (1974). Effects of a program based on the Token Test for teaching comprehension skills to aphasics. *Journal of Speech and Hearing Research, 17,* 589–598.

Hughes, D. L. (1985). *Language treatment and generalization: a clinician's handbook.* San Diego, CA: College-Hill Press.

Hughes, C. P., Chan, J. L., & Su, M. S. (1983). Aprosodia in Chinese patients with right cerebral lesions. *Archives of Neurology, 40,* 732–736.

Jaffe, J. (1978). Parliamentary procedure and the brain. In A. W. Siegman & S. Feldstein (Eds.), *Nonverbal behavior and communication* (pp. 55–66). Hillsdale, NJ: Lawrence Erlbaum Associates.

Kazdin, A. E. (1982). *Single-case research designs: Methods for clinical and applied settings.* New York: Oxford University Press.

Kieras, D. E. (1978). Good and bad structure in simple paragraphs: effects on apparent theme, reading time, and recall. *Journal of Verbal Learning and Verbal Behavior, 17,* 13–28.

Kimbarow, M. L. (1982, November). *Discourse analysis: a look at clinicians' conversational strategies in treatment.* Paper presented at the Annual Meeting of the American Speech-Language-Hearing Association, Toronto.

Kintsch, W., & van Dijk, T. A. (1978). Toward a model of text comprehension and production. *Psychological Review, 85,* 363–394.

Kreindler, A., Gheorghita, N., & Voinescu, I. (1971). Analysis of verbal reception of a complex order with three elements in aphasics. *Brain, 94,* 375–386.

10. PRAGMATICS AND COGNITION   351

Kudo, T. (1984). The effect of semantic plausibility on sentence comprehension in aphasia. *Brain and Language, 21,* 208–218.

LaPointe, L. L. (1978). Aphasia therapy: Some principles and strategies for treatment. In D. F. Johns (Ed.), *Clinical management of neurogenic communicative disorders* (pp. 129–190). Boston: Little, Brown.

Lesser, R. (1979). Turning tokens into things: Linguistic and mnestic aspects of the initial sections of the Token Test. In F. Boller & M. Dennis (Eds.), *Auditory comprehension: Clinical and experimental studies with the Token Test* (pp. 71–85). New York: Academic Press.

Lohmann, L., & Prescott, T. E. (1978). The effects of substituting "objects" for "forms" on the Revised Token Test (RTT) performance of aphasic subjects. In R. H. Brookshire (Ed.), *Clinical aphasiology conference proceedings* (pp. 138–146). Minneapolis, BRK.

Lubinski, R. (1981a). Environmental language intervention. In R. Chapey (Ed.), *Language intervention strategies in adult aphasia* (pp. 223–245). Baltimore: Williams & Wilkins.

Lubinski, R. (1981b). Speech, language, and audiology programs in home health care agencies and nursing homes. In D. S. Beasley & G. A. Davis (Eds.), *Aging: communication processes and disorders* (pp. 339–356). New York: Grune & Stratton.

Lubinski, R., Duchan, J., & Weitzner-Lin, B. (1980). Analysis of breakdowns and repairs in aphasic adult communication. In R. H. Brookshire (Ed.), *Clinical aphasiology conference proceedings* (pp. 111–116). Minneapolis: BRK.

Luterman, D. (1984). *Counseling the communicatively disordered and their families.* Boston: Little, Brown.

Martino, A. A., Pizzamiglio, L., & Razzano, C. (1976). A new version of the "Token Test" for aphasics: a concrete objects form. *Journal of Communication Disorders, 9,* 1–5.

Metter, E. J. (1985). Feature (letter). *Asha, 27,* 43.

Morgan, J. L. (1979). Observations on the pragmatics of metaphor. In Ortony, A. (Ed.), *Metaphor and thought* (pp. 136–147). Cambridge, Eng.: Cambridge University Press.

Morrow, L., Vrtunski, P. B., Kim, Y., & Boller, F. (1981). Arousal responses to emotional stimuli and laterality of lesion. *Neuropsychologia, 19,* 65–71.

Myers, P. S. (1979). Profiles of communication deficits in persons with right cerebral hemisphere damage: Implications for diagnosis and treatment. In R. H. Brookshire (Ed.), *Clinical aphasiology conference proceedings* (pp. 38–46). Minneapolis: BRK.

Myers, P. S. (1980). Visual imagery in aphasia treatment: a new look. In R. H. Brookshire (Ed.), *Clinical aphasiology conference proceedings* (pp. 68–77). Minneapolis: BRK.

Myers, P. S. (1984). Right hemisphere impairment. In A. L. Holland (Ed.), *Language disorders in adults: Recent advances* (pp. 177–208). San Diego, CA: College-Hill Press.

Olson, D. R., & Filby, N. (1972). On comprehension of active and passive sentences. *Cognitive Psychology, 3,* 361–381.

Ortony, A., Schallert, D. L., Reynolds, R. E., & Antos, S. J. (1978). Interpreting metaphors and idioms: some effects of context on comprehension. *Journal of Verbal Learning and Verbal Behavior, 17,* 465–477.

Pierce, R. S., & Beekman, L. (1985). Effects of linguistic and extralinguistic context on semantic and syntactic processing in aphasia. *Journal of Speech and Hearing Research, 28,* 250–254.

Podraza, B. L., & Darley, F. L. (1977). Effect of auditory prestimulation on naming in aphasia. *Journal of Speech and Hearing Research, 20,* 669–683).

Porch, B. E. (1967). *Porch index of communicative ability: Vol. 1. Theory and development.* Palo Alto, CA: Consulting Psychologists Press.

352 DAVIS

Porch, B. E. (1981). Porch index of communicative ability: Vol. II. Administration, scoring, and interpretation (3rd ed.). Palo Alto, CA: Consulting Psychologists Press.

Porter, J. L., & Dabul, B. (1977). The application of transactional analysis to therapy with wives of adult aphasic patients. *Asha, 19*, 244–248.

Rosenbek, J. C. (1983). Some challenges for clinical aphasiologists. In J. Miller, D. E. Yoder, & R. Schiefelbusch (Eds.), *Contemporary issues in language intervention* (pp. 317–325). Rockville, MD: American Speech and Hearing Association.

Rosenfeld, H. M. (1978). Conversational control functions of nonverbal behavior in A. W. Siegman & S. Feldstein (Eds.), *Nonverbal Behavioral and Communication* (pp. 291–328). New York: John Wiley & Sons.

Ross, E. D. (1981). The aprosodias: Functional-anatomic organization of the affective components of language in the right hemisphere. *Archives of Neurology, 38*, 561–569.

Sacks, H., Schegloff, E., & Jefferson, G. (1974). A simplest systematics for the organization of turn-taking for conversation. *Language, 50*, 696–735.

Sarno, M. T. (1969). *The functional communication profile manual of directions.* Rehabilitation Monograph 42, New York University Medical Center.

Sarno, M. T., & Levita, E. (1971). Natural course of recovery in severe aphasia. *Archives of Physical Medicine and Rehabilitation, 52*, 175–178.

Schuell, H. M. (1972). *Minnesota test for differential diagnosis of aphasia* (Rev. ed.). Minneapolis: University of Minnesota Press.

Schlanger, B. B., Schlanger, P., & Gerstman, L. J. (1976). The perception of emotionally toned sentences by right hemisphere-damaged and aphasic subjects. *Brain and Language, 3*, 396–403.

Searle, J. R. (1979). Metaphor. In Ortony, A. (Ed.), *Metaphor and thought.* (pp. 92–124) Cambridge, Eng.: Cambridge University Press.

Semenza, C., Denes, G. F., Lucchese, D., & Bisiacchi, P. (1980). Selective deficit of conceptual structures in aphasia: class versus thematic relations. *Brain and Language, 10*, 243–248.

Seron, X., & DeLoche, G. (1981). Processing of locatives "in," "on," and "under" by aphasic patients: an analysis of the regression hypothesis. *Brain and Language, 14*, 70–80.

Studdert-Kennedy, M. (1983). Introduction. In M. Studdert-Kennedy (Ed.), *Psychobiology of language* (pp. 3–6). Cambridge, MA: MIT Press.

Tanner, D. C. (1980). Loss and grief: implications for the speech-language pathologist and audiologist. *Asha, 22*, 916–928.

Thorndyke, P. W. (1977). Cognitive structures in comprehension and memory of narrative discourse. *Cognitive Psychology, 9*, 77–110.

Tonkovich, J. D., & Loverso, F. (1982). A training matrix approach for gestural acquisition by the agrammatic patient. In R. H. Brookshire (Ed.), *Clinical aphasiology conference proceedings* (pp. 283–288). Minneapolis, BRK.

Trupe, E. H., & Hillis, A. (1985). Paucity vs. verbosity: another analysis of right hemisphere communication deficits. In R. H. Brookshire (Ed.), *Clinical aphasiology.* Minneapolis: BRK.

van Dijk, T. A. (1977). Semantic macro-structures and knowledge frames in discourse comprehension. In M. A. Just & P. A. Carpenter (Eds.), *Cognitive processes in comprehension.* Hillsdale, NJ: Lawrence Erlbaum Associates.

Waller, M. R., & Darley, F. L. (1978). The influence of context on the auditory comprehension of paragraphs by aphasic subjects. *Journal of Speech and Hearing Research, 21*, 732–745.

Wapner, W., & Gardner, H. (1980). Profiles of symbol-reading skills in organic patients. *Brain and Language, 12*, 303–312.

10. PRAGMATICS AND COGNITION 353

Webster, E. J., & Newhoff, M. (1981). Intervention with families of communicatively impaired adults. In D. S. Beasley, & G. A. Davis (Eds.), *Aging: communication processes and disorders* (pp. 229–240). New York: Grune & Stratton.

Weiner, S. L., & Goodenough, D. R. (1977). A move toward a psychology of conversation. In R. O. Freedle (Ed.), *Discourse Production and Comprehension.* Norwood, NJ: Ablex.

Wepman, J. M. (1976). Aphasia: Language without thought or thought without language. *Asha, 18,* 131–136.

Wilcox, M. J., & Davis, G. A. (1977). Speech act analysis of aphasic communication in individual and group settings. In R. H. Brookshire (Ed.), *Clinical aphasiology conference proceedings* (pp. 166–174). Minneapolis: BRK.

Williams, S. E., & Canter, G. J. (1982). The influence of situational context on naming performance in aphasic syndromes. *Brain and Language, 17,* 92–106.

Winner, E., & Gardner, H. (1977). Comprehension of metaphor in brain damaged patients. *Brain, 100,* 717–729.

11 The Emergence of Microcomputer Technology in Neuropsychological Therapies

Larry Fisher
Fargo Clinic, North Dakota

The computer has long served as a model for cognitive processes and has led the way for the new science of cognition. Whether one is working with artificial intelligence, computer models of cognitive functions, computerized testing, or the more mundane use of the computer as a word processor one cannot fail to be impressed with the influence of computers in the theory and practice of neuropsychology. More recently, computers have been emerging as therapeutic tools and cognitive prosthetic devices. To appreciate the potential impact of these changes, consider the following fictional account:

It is 10:00 a.m. at the Advanced Systems Rehabilitation Hospital and John is in his wheelchair. He is thinking about the accident that resulted in his left side paralysis. It is hard for him to remember anything, especially when his mind keeps wandering off the topic. Suddenly the watch on his wrist crackles to life in a high pitched robotic monotone voice . . . "John, it's 10 o'clock and time for you to go to cognition rehabilitation." John's wrist terminal always surprises him when it talks. He prepares to go to his cognition rehabilitation session but he realizes that he has forgotten how to get there. He checks the screen on his wrist terminal and scans the short list of keywords on the screen until he finds the word "lost?" in bold print. He touches the word and the touchscreen immediately responds with "Have you looked left?" He remembers now that his therapist has told him that he neglects his left side. He looks left hoping to see the nursing station and be able to orient himself, but he has wandered too far and he does not

355

356 FISHER

recognize anything. He is beginning to panic but he looks down at the computer screen and sees the words "Still lost?" He presses the "yes" button and the display reads "Anyone around?." He checks the hall, sees a nurse coming and presses the "yes" button again. The computer responds "Ask a question." He asks the nurse if she can help him. She looks puzzled, at first, not understanding John's very slurred speech but a moment later John's wrist terminal recognizes and repeats John's question in perfect robotic speech. The nurse smiles and directs him to the cognition rehabilitation department.

John arrives at the department and goes to his cognitive rehabilitation computer, which is already busy sending a wireless message to his wrist terminal updating the calendar with tomorrow's schedule. This microcomputer with its compact video disc memory is displaying a screen image of the view down the hall from John's hospital room. "Good morning John. Today we are going to continue our lesson in problem solving and cognitive mapping. We will practice using a verbal map to help you get from your room to this department. Because your visuospatial memory is weak we are going to teach you how to use verbal directions and landmarks to get around. What you are seeing on the screen now is the nursing station on your ward. Move the joystick forward now and we will travel down the hall together."

The preceding senario may read like science fiction, but the basic technology for this type of rehabilitation environment is available today. The inexpensive microcomputer or personal computer (PC) has exploded on the public scene in recent years. Rehabilitation therapists have been quick to embrace the new technology, although not without some trepedation (Bracy, 1983; Wilson, 1983; Gummow, Miller, & Dustman, 1983; Katz & Nagy, 1984; Loatsch, 1983; Lynch, 1983; Sena, 1984). Therapists in this area have found the temptation to use this new tool irresistible and the ubiquitous PC has, in short order, become a universal high tech image on hospital brochures. What is computer assisted cognitive rehabilitation? Where is it going? How did it begin? What is available? What does the future hold? It is beyond the scope of this chapter to attempt a definitive history or an exhaustive review of the literature. Even an attempt to characterize the state of the art in this volatile field would be immediately obsolete because of publication lag. Rather, this chapter is designed to step away from the trees somewhat to see the forest of technological change in this field, and to get some perspective on the unique ecosystem created by this revolution.

WHAT IS COMPUTER ASSISTED COGNITIVE REHABILITATION?

Futurists tell us that we are witnessing the birth of the information age where a larger and larger share of our resources and occupations are devoted to the processing of information. They point out that civilization began with the Agricultural Revolution, progressed to the Industrial Revolution, and is now rushing into the Informational Revolution with dizzying speed. This is being felt everywhere, and the rate of change is making some of us uncomfortable and others excited to join right in and take part. The application of computer technology to neuropsychological therapy was a natural outgrowth of the development of an affordable and relatively easy to use PC. The PC has become to the information age what the Model T Ford was to the Industrial Revolution, a widely applicable device that gets us where we are going.

It is usually the case that the first application of computer technology assists us in doing whatever we are already doing. Only later do we realize new and innovative applications. In this regard the computer was first used in cognitive rehabilitation as a very flexible device for stimulus presentation and as a means of storing and processing data regarding response characteristics. That the computer is well suited to this role is evidenced by the rapid popularity of this approach. When the PC emerged on the rehabilitation scene the neuropsychologists, speech pathologists, occupational therapists, and others who were engaged in some form of cognitive remediation were only too happy to put aside their closet full of stimulus presentation devices and replace them all with one small PC and a few diskettes with various programs. In fact, the lure of the computer has helped popularize cognitive rehabilitation as a therapeutic modality, somehow giving the existing methods we were using a new high-tech look that promised more effectiveness and patient acceptance. The blinking lights, along with the appropriate sound effects, certainly are impressive and dress up professional meetings with colorful computerized graphic displays surrounded by crowds of rehabilitation consumers. Nevertheless, many of these early "new" techniques were just paper and pencil procedures in electronic dress and hardly a revolutionary advance.

Whether one is using paper and pencil techniques or computerized techniques, it is important to make a conceptual distinction between cognitive training as an educational activity and cognitive rehabilitation. One can sit any individual, brain damaged or not, in front of a computer terminal and try to teach that person techniques in prob-

358   FISHER

lem solving, memory, or some other cognitive skill. This would be educational, and of course education has its place, but it would not be cognitive rehabilitation. To be therapeutic as opposed to educational, one must have a clear understanding of the patient's cognitive deficits and residual informational processing capacity and have designed a particular approach to cognitive retraining that takes such an analysis into account. This means that the therapist must have a thorough understanding of normal brain function as it applies to a particular patient's unique profile of residual assets and liabilities. It also implies a knowledge and understanding of the overall clinical science of brain rehabilitation, what techniques are appropriate at what time during recovery, what noncognitive problems may contribute to a particular information processing difficulty, and what strategies are effective with what type of problem.

For example, many patients cannot name their relatives or friends. On the surface, it would seem appropriate to consider cognitive training strategies aimed at improving noun storage and recall. However, it is possible that such a patient has a perceptual disorder or face recognition deficit and is unable to put a name to a face because it is poorly perceived. Cognitive rehabilitation requires an understanding of the nature of that particular patient's disorder. This is the basis for the popularity of the process approach to assessment, because it stresses a systematic search for the defective cognitive process rather than taking an impairment at face value. Another example is the patient with a disorder of calculation. One might be tempted to consider remedial arithmetic exercises for such a patient. However, if the deficit is based on a visual field neglect, it would be more appropriate to try to build increased attention to the neglected field than to teach arithmetic. Similarly, a reading disorder based on poor visual perception may require not remedial reading but use of a ruler or other device to keep from skipping lines when reading. More recently, I examined a left-handed patient with a severe disorder in writing. This might appear to warrant a remedial program in writing skills. However, knowing that this patient had a tumor removed via a transcallosal approach (damaging communication pathways between the hemispheres) it was important to examine her for a disconnection syndrome. This is a syndrome where the left brain (which was dominant for language in her case) is cut off from the right brain (which was dominant for handedness in her case). This proved to be true, which suggested that the more appropriate strategy would be to teach her to write with her nondominant right hand, which still had access to the language processing abilities in her left brain.

There is a growing concern about cognitive training being administered by individuals unqualified in brain rehabilitation. I recently received a call from a teacher who had purchased some computerized cognitive training software and was applying it to a brain-damaged child who was required to complete repetitive drills. This teacher was wise enough to realize that this was not appropriate and was asking for help, but how many other individuals are in this situation? Taken to its extreme, one can imagine a shopping mall with a video game center that offered not only amusements but also instant cognitive retraining (for a mere 25¢). Or perhaps brain-damaged patients will be buying their own computerized remedial software to use with their home computers, as a sort of do it yourself brain therapy. Clearly, one must do more than practice cognitive training exercises to accomplish cognitive rehabilitation. The brain is not a muscle that is rebuilt with cognitive exercise. If the patient has a good verbal memory system but a defective visual memory system, one does not just provide practice in visual memory. It would be more reasonable to teach the patient to verbally describe visual information in an effort to store the visual information in the verbal memory system. If that patient is spatially disoriented and cannot develop or remember a visual map, it might help to teach that patient to verbally remember a series of landmarks, thereby translating a visual memory task into a verbal memory task. One can only restructure cognition by a clear understanding of a patient's information processing system. Once that unique system is understood, computerized treatment can proceed by providing cognitive tasks together with instruction in strategies for bypassing the damaged system.

WHY USE A COMPUTER?

What was wrong with the old paper and pencil techniques? Why is everyone switching to microcomputers? First of all, not everyone has switched. Some rehabilitation therapists are computer phobic or just do not feel they have the time to be bothered learning the new technology. Others are satisfied with the existing methods. Craine and Gudeman (1981) describe their comprehensive neurotraining sytem in the framework of noncomputer methods, although their principles are applicable to computerized techniques as well. It might be helpful to consider the advantages and disadvantages of computer-assisted cognitive rehabilitation.

One advantage is that computerized training programs have a high-tech look and, with few exceptions, very high patient acceptance. Tasks can be programmed into a gamelike format and may be highly entertaining, although many programs fail to take advantage of this potential and end up as boring drills. Patients also like to work independently, at their own speed, and take breaks when they wish. They show better tolerance for making mistakes when facing a machine, compared to the humiliation sometimes produced by failing in front of a therapist. Because less therapist time is required to present the tasks, more time is available to provide motivation, or advice as needed. In this way, one therapist can supervise several patients simultaneously and increase the cost effectiveness of the procedure. It also makes the job less tedious for the therapist. The machine improves motivation and learning speed for the patient by giving immediate feedback and at the same time it allows difficulty level to be automatically adjusted to patient performance. The branching capability of the computer allows the task to change according to the type of error made such that each patient's experience with the program is individualized. The computer is also excellent at routine data collection and analysis and helps the therapist keep track of the progress of all patients simultaneously. In one self-contained computer unit the therapist can store both stimulus material and patient records and stay well organized. In fact, the computer tends to blur the distinction between assessment and therapy because ongoing assessments are an intergral part of almost all programs. These can be printed out, in many cases, so that records can be filed, posted, or compared from one time period to another, allowing the patient to strive for a personal best score. Often stimulus parameters are controllable with a precision that would be impossible without a computer. Modality of presentation, type of feedback, delay of feedback, number of cues, size of presentation, speed of presentation, and depth of processing may all be modifiable so as to tailor the program to the patient's needs. The computer is fast, reliable, precise, flexible, and allows tremendous control in both stimulus parameters and data analysis. In short, it is an excellent tool in the hands of a competent rehabilitation professional.

However, the computer is not without its disadvantages. It does require some time to learn and get used to, and there are many things that can go wrong if one is not used to working with computers. Computer tasks may not generalize to practical everyday functions and in general the efficacy of these procedures is unknown. Normative data for the computer tasks may be nonexistent and often there are few guidelines as to the type of patient or condition for which a particular program is appropriate. The reading level required may be unspecified and specific limitations or requirements are seldom indicated. In fact, the documentation manuals are for the

11. MICROCOMPUTER TECHNOLOGY 361

most part inadequate with difficult to understand instructions and limited back up support for consumers who might like to call and ask questions. The more one gets into high-tech procedures the more one can expect to be spending time and money for a technique that may be obsolete in 3 to 5 years. Some software companies give updated programs to their customers at reduced cost but others change their programs without warning so that replacements do not operate as expected. Some companies lock their software to prevent unauthorized copying, but this makes it difficult for consumers to make backup copies for their own use, or to customize programs as needed. Even where programs are unlocked, many are hard to modify without a good background in computer programming. Some provide menus that make it easy for the computer novice to select the features required for a particular patient, but some do not. In some cases a company will provide a set of programs that are not well coordinated and require the patients to learn a completely different response format for each exercise. One exercise might call for a response using the space bar, the next would use the return key, still another would use arrow keys or buttons or joysticks. Stopping a program in the middle can often be a challenge and modifying data that was invalid for some reason may be impossible. Many programs are very concrete and require one exact answer, where other equally correct answers are scored wrong. Some programs are "Goof Proof" and will give a clarification message if the wrong type of response is given, but others just "crash" and refuse to proceed. Also there have been reports that some patients with epilepsy may be vulnerable to sensory evoked seizures from the flickering lights of the computer monitor. The list of advantages and disadvantages can go on indefinitely. It would seem that the advantages outweigh the disadvantages, as measured by the popularity of computerized techniques, but this may not be true for every cognitive therapist.

HOW DID IT BEGIN?

The story of the development of the new computer hardware is interesting in its own right. No other industry has shown such phenomenal growth, with cheaper, more efficient, and smaller computers coming on the market every day. The PC was introduced in 1977 and has only become popular in the 1980s. The original Apple Computer, developed in a garage by Jobs and Wozniak, was a hobbiest's delight because of its low cost, easy expandability, excellent graphics, and flexible input and output features. These characteristics still

362   FISHER

make the PC so popular for cognitive therapies. Oddly enough, the Apple IIe in current use today is based on an obsolete 8-bit microprocessor and yet it has so many diverse applications that it is still used more widely for cognitive rehabilitation than more sphisticated machines such as the Amiga, the Macintosh, or the IBM PC. The value of a computer is based on the software programs available, and Apple IIe software is abundant and varied. In contrast, although the IBM PC has become the industry standard for business it is less popular for educational and rehabilitation purposes (the standard IBM cannot run Apple software programs and vice versa). However, many PCs are compatible with the IBM format and because many organizations already have an IBM type PC there is a demand for therapeutic software in this format. I assume such software will be forthcoming, and that the IBM will become the alternative to Apple for some applications (although because of higher cost I assume it will remain less popular).

Atari and Commodore produce less expensive computers that sell for under $200.00 and are used by some therapists as low cost home training devices. I have been using these machines for rural patients who would not otherwise have access to cognitive rehabilitation procedures. I train the spouse or parent of the patient to act as a surrogate therapist. Periodically we review progress and plan methods of achieving practical and clearly defined goals. This procedure can focus family efforts in a positive direction, which may be therapeutic for all concerned. We are currently studying the effectiveness of this approach for the patient and the family.

When the patient can come into the rehabilitation center, most facilities use an Apple IIe computer, or in some cases an IBM PC. Several patients can work under the direction of a single rehabilitation professional who motivates and monitors the activities. All of these PC computers consist of a microprocessor, monitor or TV, keyboard, and other devices such as a joystick or printer. The advantage of the Apple and IBM PC lies in their ability to be customized or expanded to meet specific needs. For example, one can add voice systhesis for the visually impaired, special customized input devices, voice recognition devices for the handicapped, and a host of other special add on adaptive devices. Additional memory may be added as needed. Special plug-in boards can speed up or slow down the operation of any program to make it harder or easier. Prices at this time for a complete PC system vary, depending on options, but average about $1,500 for the Apple and $2,500 for the IBM PC.

Shortly after the development of the PC, neuropsychologists began applying it to brain-damaged patients. Bracy, Trexler, Lynch, Sbor-

11. MICROCOMPUTER TECHNOLOGY 363

done, and Gianutsos were among the first in the United States and are still leading advocates of the new technology. In 1978, Bracy was writing cognitive rehabilitation programs while Trexler was developing clinical applications. Bracy is now commercially producing cognitive rehabilitation software and also edits a magazine called *Cognitive Rehabilitation*. Other producers of cognitive rehabilitation software include Bob Sbordone, Rosamond Gianutos, Loren Myerlink, and Mark Pendleton.

The encouraging research of early cognitive rehabilitation pioneers set the stage for computerized applications in this field (Diller et al., 1974; Gianutsos, 1980; Miller, 1980). The work of these researchers produced a new optimism regarding the recovery potential of the brain-injured patient. This area was of increasing interest to neuropsychologists who were just becoming computer literate. Attention training, using reaction time tasks, was already being employed in an attempt to speed up the cognitive processing of brain-damaged patients. These attention training procedures were easily adapted to computer presentation (Gummow et al., 1983). They were among the earliest computerized cognitive rehabilitation programs and are still widely used (Trexler, 1982). Perhaps the most interesting attention training programs were the commercial video games, which were first used as recreational activities and later adapted for therapeutic purposes (Lynch, 1983). Theoretical issues with respect to the computerized remediation of attentional disorders have received more consideration than is true for other cognitive disorders. Language remediation procedures have also been computerized (Katz & Nagy, 1984; Rushakoff, 1984) along with perceptual motor, conceptual, and problem solving tasks (Bracy, 1984). Seron, Deloche, Moulard, and Rouselle (1980) have used a computerized program for treating writing impairments in aphasic individuals.

The computer is particularly well suited to memory exercises, an area that has generated a great deal of interest (Kurleycheck & Glang, 1984). Memory retraining is usually proceded by attention training tasks in the more comprehensive cognitive rehabilitation programs, such as the programs by Rosamond Gianutos and Carol Klitzer (Life Science Associates) and by Odie L. Bracy (Psychological Software Services). The memory tasks themselves are varied but generally drawn from experimental psychology procedures, such as paired associates, serial lists, etc. The stimuli vary from verbal to auditory, visual, or spatial; and the memory requirements may include sequenced or nonsequenced recall. These programs represent an improvement over commercial memory games in that they allow for a wide range of task difficulty and are somewhat selective in terms of the cognitive systems required for a particular task. However, many of the programs that are currently available are similar to simplified video games and fail to use the power of the computer as a simulator of life. The tasks are not oriented to the real world and do not promote generalization to real life situations. Many of these programs provide an atheoretical combination of tasks geared more to the programming ability of the author than to the needs of the patient. Often there is little basis for the selection of computerized tasks, or the sequence of tasks presented. More to the point, these programs do not address the fundamental issue as to whether one can improve the capacity for memory by mere practice with a memory task (Miller, 1980).

It has often been suggested that the task of memory rehabilitation should be the alleviation of problems caused by a memory impairment rather than attempting the futile task of restoring impaired memory function (Harris & Sunderland, 1981; Wilson & Moffat, 1984). However, most cognitive rehabilitation programs largely present repetitive memory exercises, rather than instruction in specific problem areas or even in memory strategies. These programs leave the therapist with the task of developing any mediation strategies with little attempt to assess specific needs or individualize the presentation. They often represent little more than electronic flash cards with a built-in scoring system. Such exercises have great face validity for patients and may produce some increase in scores, which serves a motivational or placebo function. A placebo effect may have some therapeutic value (Harris and Sunderland, 1981), but there is little evidence that the exercise itself will restore impaired memory (Ericsson, Chase, & Falcon, 1980; Wilson, 1982).

The concept of retraining basic cognition functions such as memory is very appealing and brings to mind the early work in the area of childhood learning disabilities where attempts to remediate basic functions were largely abandoned in favor of more direct training aimed at getting around a disability (Gaddes, 1985). In the area of cognitive rehabilitation, it is equally unclear that time spent in basic memory remediation is as productive as time devoted to training in specific practical problem areas.

In fairness to the pioneers in this field, I should point out that the authors of these programs do not imply that they represent a complete rehabilitation program. They also stress that these programs do not replace the cognitive rehabilitation therapist. Rather, they present the computer as a tool with which one can teach cognitive strategies to the patient. There is, however, controversy over whether the teaching of cognitive strategies is itself generalizable to practical memory activities. It is clear that no one should be applying these programs in a vacuum, but rather they are intended for use within a comprehensive program including individual and family therapy, physical therapy (PT), occupational therapy (OT), and speech therapy. This does complicate the assessment of the effectiveness of the computerized therapy, but it is in keeping with the prevailing clinical wisdom of cognitive rehabilitation therapy.

Starting at the edge of a new technology, these early programs are easy to criticize but still represent some groundbreaking achievements. It is useful, however, to step back and take a harder look at these procedures, many of which lack any research foundation or theoretical perspective. It is difficult to strike a balance between the desire to encourage innovation and the need to be conservative in the use of this new approach. At this point, caveat emptor describes the attitude regarding the purchase of these programs.

WHAT IS AVAILABLE?

The following examples of available software packages for cognitive rehabilitation are presented for informational purposes only without any implication of endorsement. Some of these programs are being currently marketed to the profession and some are in the process of development. All of them have some provision for storing data regarding patient performance over training sessions and offer various levels of difficulty.

Bracy (1984) produced one of the first of the comprehensive packages of software and it is still widely used. (Psychological Software Services, P.O. Box 29205, Indianapolis, IN 46224, 317/ 291-5809) He uses this software in his own treatment programs as part of an integrated training program including individual and group therapy. He was probably the first to implement a home treatment program using the inexpensive Atari computer. His programs are also available in Apple computer versions. These programs include:

1. Foundation skills (e.g., attention training by reaction time)
2. Visuospatial skill (e.g., maze tasks, paddle ball)
3. Conceptual skills (e.g., number and word concepts)
4. Memory skills (e.g., spatial memory, auditory verbal memory)
5. Auditory skills (e.g., pitch discrimination)
6. Problem solving (e.g., chess type game, cryptograms)

366 FISHER

Gianutos developed her software at Bellevue Hospital/ NYU Medical Center (Life Science Associates, One Fenimore Road, Dept. N., Bayport, NY 11705, 516/472-2111) These programs are unique in that they include provision for training in ocular visual problems. The COGREHAB set consists of the following modules:

1. Pattern recognition
2. Visual field reaction time
3. Free recall
4. Sequence recall
5. Memory span
6. Visual scanning
7. Imperception remediation

Ben-Yishay and Diller (The Institute of Rehabilitation Medicine, 400 East 34th Street, New York, NY 10016) have released a set of software based on the hierarchial training programs developed over the past several years to ameliorate attentional problems. The Orientation Remedial Module is one of the few such programs to be based upon clinically validated techniques (Diller & Gordon, 1981). A custom designed response device is also available. Of course at NYU this module is not used in isolation but is combined with other modules for perceptual-motor speed, visual spatial construction, abstract thinking, and social skills in addition to tailor made applications for personal living and occupational needs. The cognitive remedial training is supplemented by personal counseling, small group interpersonal skill training, and community integration activities, as well as attempts at environmental modifications. All of this may represent several hundred hours of therapy over a 6-month period in a comprehensive program that goes far beyond the cognitive retraining module itself.

Sbordone's software was also an early entry in this field (Robert J. Sbordone, Ph.D., Inc., 8840 Warner Ave. Suite 301, Fountain Valley, CA 92708 714/841-6293) An interesting feature of his programs is that they monitor the patients fatigue level and automatically determine when rest periods or termination of the session is needed. Also task complexity is increased automatically as the patient's performance improves. There is a speech synthesizer option for voice accompaniment to the visual display. The programs include

1. Complex-attention rehabilitation (e.g., visual tracking)
2. Problem solving I (e.g., visual spatial tasks)
3. Problem solving II (e.g., planning tasks)

11. MICROCOMPUTER TECHNOLOGY   367

Meyerink and Pendleton originally introduced their cognitive retraining system for use with the inexpensive VIC-20 computer, which has since become an obsolete machine. However, they have translated their programs recently for the Commodore 64 computer, which is still available (Denver Neuropsychological Associates, 2993 South Peoria, Suite 370, Aurora, CO 80014, 303/337-5659) Their modules can be varied in length, difficulty, feedback, and speed levels. Their programs include

1. Orientation (e.g., attention training by reaction time)
2. Concentration (e.g., vigilance exercises)
3. Memory (e.g., immediate and delayed recall, verbal and visual)
4. Visuospatial (e.g., matching, block design matrix)
5. Special purpose (e.g., tasks to overcome left neglect)

Lynch has not produced any software himself, but he is the leading advocate of the use of commercial computer games and his unpublished guide to the use of these games for the Atari computer is a useful resource (William Lynch, Ph.D., VA Medical Center, Brain Injury Rehabilitation Unit, 3801 Miranda Ave., Palo Alto, CA 94304, 415/493-5000, Ext. 2201). His guide includes information on equipment and software costs, a bibliography, and blank record forms. In addition to the practical information for the Atari, which he has gathered together in this guide, he has recently been including a guide to Apple computer software for language and cognitive skills, which was compiled by Peggy B. Wilson of San Francisco State University. Some other software developers in this field are presented in Appendix 11.1.

It is very difficult to keep abreast of developments in this rapidly proliferating field. How does one describe the state of the art in a field that is changing month by month. Just in terms of hardware alone it is very confusing because even computers from the same manufacturer come in many different models and software is not completely compatible from one model to another. Computers become obsolete quickly and prices change with each new development. At this writing it is very hard to find an Atari 400 or 800 or a VIC-20. The Apple IIc may not run software written on the Apple IIe, which in turn may not run software written for the older Apple II or II+. To make matters more complicated, the Apple company has introduced a new 16-bit Apple IIgs with advanced graphics and sound that may or may not run existing rehabilitation software. Currently the IBM PC is being discounted heavily with the anticipated introduction of the second generation 32-bit IBM with improved speed and memory

368 FISHER

power. Software development is in an even greater state of flux with modifications and additions to old programs and the development of new programs progressing as fast as creative minds can conceive them. Computer hardware becomes obsolete within 2 or 3 years, and software can be obsolete within 18 months. (For this reason few software developers take the time to make their programs user friendly and documentation manuals are frequently inadequate.)

Books and even journals are not published quickly enough to keep pace with these developments. Therefore, it is helpful to have access to newsletters, computer bulletin boards, and workshops. Access to software reviews are helpful and user networks and special interest groups can trade information on consumer satisfaction issues. With this in mind one might consider the resources listed in Appendix 11.2.

To evaluate rehabilitation software consider the following: Is there good documentation and instructions? Does the company have a policy of answering consumer questions? Is the software copy protected or locked? Can the clinician add comments and of servations, modify parameters, and correct data if needed? Is the program flexible and "goof proof" with consistent response requirements? Are there normative and research data to support efficacy and indicate when and how the program is best used? Is the software based on a reasonable theory of brain retraining? Are the cognitive tasks enjoyable and do they have face validity and good patient acceptance (e.g., age appropriate and not childish)? How much supervision is needed; are reading levels specified; what are the response requirements? What about the technical quality, graphics, and sophistication of the program? Is there a print option, save data option, modify instruction option? Is the program easy to use and are there good menus? Are the tasks in the program different from the assessment procedures you intend to use, to prevent contamination of the assessment data? How good is the data analysis and is there easy access to the stored results? These are just some of the features that might make the difference between a useful program and one designed to frustrate and confuse patient and therapist alike. If there are no review articles that evaluate these features of the software you are considering, try to get this information from the seller.

WHAT DOES THE FUTURE HOLD?

The real potential of the microcomputer as a tool for neuropsychological therapy is not in the computerization of existing therapeutic methods but in the unique capacity of the PC to simulate lifelike situations, to interact intelligently and responsively with the patient, and to serve as an adaptive device to replace or augment damaged cognitive functions. This potential has only begun to be realized. The same situation is evident in the field of education where teachers unfamiliar with the true potential of computer technology use it to provide boring repetitive drills and little else. It is unfortunate that so many of us rush into the future looking backwards. But is this the future or just a passing fad?

There is little doubt that the use of computer-assisted cognitive therapy will continue to grow despite the paucity of evidence regarding its efficacy. If nothing else the computer has proven to be effective at increasing the productivity and decreasing the tedium of those who work with it. This is not only true for the office worker but for the cognitive therapist as well. Repetitive cognitive therapy tasks can wear the patience of even the most devoted therapist but the computer never gets bored. Also, with several computers available, a single cognitive therapist can supervise a number of patients simultaneously, keep track of all their progress automatically, and devote more time to the personal and social aspects of the job. Thus, on the basis of increased productivity and decreased therapist burnout the use of the computer in cognitive rehabilitation is here to stay.

It is clear that the efficacy of many of these early computerized cognitive rehabilitation efforts is dependent on the validity of the noncomputerized procedures on which they were based. If the paper and pencil procedure is ineffective or lacks theoretical justification, then there is little reason to believe that the computerized version will be better. Similarly, the value of computer games in therapy should be equivalent to the value of noncomputer games in therapy, at least for the current crop of software. For many of the existing programs, there is already a noncomputerized version currently in use. Thus, much of the criticism of computer therapy is really a reflection of the limitation of the state of the art in this field. This may not always be the case as further theoretical developments in the field allow for a better understanding of normal and abnormal cognition. Also technical developments will offer the opportunity for unique therapies not possible without a computer. We should see realistic simulations of the cognitive requirements common in real life, as only a computer could accomplish. Current developments in artificial intelligence, new laser disc memories, advanced computer video simulation techniques, and the relentless improvements in PC speed and capacity all virtually guarantee a giant wave of unique therapeutic procedures coming our way. If all this technology makes us feel like we are drowning then at least take solice in the fact that there are many other professionals who are also struggling to stay afloat in this sea of change. At the risk of carrying the analogy too far,

370   FISHER

I think we need to anchor our techniques to a more solid theoretical and research foundation if we are to ride the crest of this new technology. This will be the challenge for the future.

As the market for computer-assisted cognitive therapy expands, one can expect more cognitive rehabilitation software in the future to come from large publishing companies with the resources to improve the technical quality of the product. We should see better graphics, improved documentation, and more flexibility for customizing the cognitive tasks and response requirements. Moreover, we can hope that some minimum standards will have been developed for computerized cognitive training. It will no longer be attempted in isolation but be preceded by a complete assessment of neuropsychological function and conducted as part of a comprehensive program of rehabilitation that addresses the multiple handicaps associated with brain injury. It will be performed by rehabilitation professionals who will be well trained in theory and application of cognitive remediation. The computer will be seen as a tool, not as the therapist, and companies will only sell their software to qualified individuals. Generalization will be monitored to avoid situation-specific learning, and research will be available to establish the practical efficacy of the procedures.

The microcomputer applications that have been considered thus far are those devoted to cognitive training. The future will also see a great deal of development in computerized assessment as well, with a blending of the assessment and rehabilitation applications. With the use of artificial intelligence in the form of expert systems, one should see better techniques for monitoring ongoing changes in cognitive function that would lead to modifications in rehabilitation strategies and techniques. Auto mechanics currently use such expert systems to help diagnose and repair cars, and, in the future, cognitive therapists will have access to the knowledge base of experts in the field to assist in understanding a patient's information processing system, plan appropriate cognitive remediation, pick the appropriate software, and establish the parameters that are indicated.

Another application of microcomputers to this field is their use as cognitive prosthetic devices (Fowler, Hart, & Sheehan, 1972; Jones, & Adam, 1979). This is a newly emerging branch of neuropsychological rehabilitation that is quite distinct from assessment and cognitive training applications. It is involved with the use of computer technology to replace or augment impaired cognitive functions. Just as an artificial leg is a physical prosthetic device, so too one can develop a computer device to substitute for a lost cognitive function. Such devices are referred to as cognitive prosthetics. The most common cog-

11. MICROCOMPUTER TECHNOLOGY   371

nitive prosthetic devices are the computerized memory aids. These have been described in detail by Skilbeck (1984) and Harris (1984). Also Vanderheiden (1981) has discussed the application of computers as language processors for aphasic patients. Rushakoff (1984) describes devices now on the market that are designed for patients with language problems. Motor requirements for these devices are minimal, and some of them are equipped with head pointers and "blow controls" or can be activated with eye movements alone.

Many other types of computer adaptive devices are in widespread use at this time (Behrmann, 1984). Devices that read text and give voice output, talking computer terminals, talking typewriters and calculators, text to Braille, and voice to print machines have found uses among the sensory impaired and could be helpful in cognitively-impaired patients with visual and auditory processing deficits. Special input devices, such as light pens, touch-sensitive screens, touch tablets, and the palm sized optical "mouse," can help handicapped individuals gain access to computers. In terms of output devices the old picture communication boards have now been computerized and can use many types of graphic material. In addition, talking typewriters or symbol input devices can produce speech output.

In the area of memory, Harris (1984) describes a wide range of electronic memory aids ranging from desktop units to pocket-sized devices. I have used some of these devices with memory-impaired patients, and they can be helpful for repetitive reminding tasks, such as cuing the patient to take a particular medicine at a particular time. Generally, these devices have an auditory alarm, similar to that found in an alarm watch. However, unlike a simple alarm watch, these devices also display a message such as "time to take your blue pill for your heart." These messages often read out in the form of a dot matrix LCD display that moves across the screen like a Times Square signboard.

Before the advent of these miniature computers, many practitioners, like myself, had used a combination of alarm watch and notepad for head-injured patients. These were helpful but limited in the number of alarms available. Some of these alarm watches also beep on the hour, and I have used this feature by training my patients to use the hourly beep as a reminder to check their notepads while reserving the alarm itself for special appointments. These watches are inexpensive and available, and patients are easily trained in their use. However, they are of less use where multiple medicines are being taken and frequent reminders are needed. In such cases I tried pocket computers designed for busy executives. These are sometimes larger and more complicated to use but have the advantage of multiple

372   FISHER

alarms and the ability to be programed for events months or years ahead. Unfortunately, devices designed for executives are not well suited for brain-damaged individuals, and in some cases this reduces patient acceptance. Also, unlike the alarm watch, these early devices were designed to be carried and could easily be misplaced by a memory-impaired individual. Harris (1984) described a number of different memory cuing devices, which are already obsolete because of the incredibly rapid advance of this technology. He has also outlined the basic requirements for devices of this type. They should be portable; widely applicable; have multiple alarms; and be programmable in months or years, easy to use and inexpensive. He describes a plan for a device that delivers a verbal message via loudspeaker, which might meet these criteria. I have been working on a plan for a similar device that accepts verbal commands to set the alarm and provides verbal output at the appropriate time. Other work in this area is being conducted at the University of Michigan (Levine, Kirsch, Fellon-Kerueger, & Jaros, 1984). Unfortunately, the technology for speech recognition is still in its infancy, and it is difficult to design a small and inexpensive device that will respond to a wide range of commands with acceptable accuracy. At present, the design for such a device would require a piece of hardware that is too big and expensive for practical use. If a smaller and less expensive version were feasible, it would have the advantage of ease of use, but it would still require a good deal of patient training because available speech recognition techniques are limited in vocabulary and reliability.

I have followed with interest the development of wrist terminals led by the Seiko company. These devices look like alarm watches but go far beyond them in data storage and processing. They replace the bulky pocket computers used in the past for multiple alarm applications and are less likely to be lost. Also, they can hold enough data to replace a notepad, telephone book, or calendar. In some cases they are programed through larger PC units that update the calendar daily. For example, the Seiko RC 4000 wrist terminal can memorize 80 alarms up to a year ahead, can display memos, and currently retails for $199.00. This is another step in the right direction, but it is still not sufficiently simple for use by many head-injured patients. One could train a caregiver or spouse in its use and just have the patient wear it, but optimally the patient should be able to operate it independently. In many respects it is easier to train patients to use memory aids that are currently in use by normal individuals. Thus, at this time calendars, note pads, check lists, and alarm watches are more likely to be used than the more advanced high-tech devices. (see also Appendix 11.3).

As the reader should have observed by now, the emergence of the

11. MICROCOMPUTER TECHNOLOGY 373

microcomputer has been sudden, dramatic, and overwhelming to many practitioners in cognitive rehabilitation. This technology holds a great deal of promise for the future but lacks verified clinical utility for the present. The computer is the tool of our time, and it will certainly prove invaluable as we learn to use it properly and apply it to cognitive rehabilitation tasks of known validity.

REFERENCES

Behrmann, M. (1984). *Handbook of microcomputers in special education* (pp. 103–138). San Diego: College-Hill.

Bracy, O. L. (1983). Computer based cognitive rehabilitation. *Cognitive Rehabilitation, 1*, 7–8.

Bracy, O. L. (1984). Using computers in neuropsychology. In Schwartz, M. D. (Ed.), *Using computers in clinical practice* (pp. 257–264). New York: Haworth Press.

Craine, J. F. & Gudeman, H. E. (Eds.). (1981). *The rehabilitation of brain functions: principles, procedures, and techniques of neurotraining.* Springfield, IL: Charles C. Thomas.

Diller, L. et al. (1974). *Studies in cognition and rehabilitation.* (Monograph #50), Institute of Rehabilitation Medicine, University Medical Center, New York.

Diller, L., & Gordon, W. A. (1981). Interventions for cognitive deficits in brain injured adults. *Journal of Consulting and Clinical Psychology, 49*, 822–834.

Ericsson, K. A., Chase, W. G., & Falcon, S. (1980). Acquisition of a memory skill. *Science, 208*, 1181–1182.

Fowler, R., Hart, J., & Sheehan, M. (1972). A prosthetic memory: An application of the prosthetic environment concept. *Rehabilitation Counseling Bulletin, 15*, 80–85.

Gaddes, W. H. (1985). *Learning disabilities and brain function* (pp. 380–383). New York: Springer-Verlag.

Gianutsos, R. (1980). What is rehabilitation? *Journal of Rehabilitation, 46*, 36–40.

Gummow, L., Miller, P., & Dustman, R. E. (1983). Attention and brain injury: a case for cognitive rehabilitation of attentional disorders. *Clinical Psychology Review, 3*, 255–274.

Harris, J. E., & Sunderland, A. (1981). A brief survey of the management of memory disorders in rehabilitation units in Britain. *International Rehabilitation Medicine, 3*, 206–209.

Harris, J. E. (1984). Methods of improving memory. In Wilson, B. A., & Moffat, N. (Eds.), *Clinical management of memory problems* (pp. 46–62). London: Aspen.

Jones, G., & Adam, J. (1979). Towards a prosthetic memory. *Bulletin of the British Psychological Society, 32*, 167–171.

Katz, R., & Nagy, V. T. (1984). CATS: computerized aphasia treatment system. *Cognitive Rehabilitation, 2*, 8–11.

Kurleycheck, R. T., & Glang, A. E. (1984). The use of microcomputers in the cognitive rehabilitation of brain-injured persons. In M. D. Schwartz, (Ed.), *Using computers in clinical practice* (pp. 245–256). New York: Haworth Press.

Loatsch, L. (1983). Development of a memory training program. *Cognitive Rehabilitation, 1*, 15–18.

Levine, S. P., Kirsch, N. L., Fellon-Kerueger, M. & Jaros, L. A. (1984). *The microcomputer as an 'orthotic' device for cognitive disorders.* Paper read at the Second International Conference on Rehabilitation Engineering, Ottawa, Canada.

374 FISHER

Lynch, W. J. (1983). Cognitive retraining using microcomputer games and commercially available software. *Cognitive Rehabilitation, 1,* 19–20.

Miller, E. (1980). Psychological intervention in the management and rehabilitation of neuropsychological impairments. *Behavior Research Therapy, 18,* 527–535.

Rushakoff, G. E. (1984). Clinical applications of communication disorders. In Schwartz, A. H. (Ed.) *Handbook of microcomputer applications in communication disorders* (pp. 148–171). San Diego: College-Hill.

Sena, D. A. (1984). *The effectiveness of cognitive retraining for brain-impaired individuals.* Paper presented at the 92nd Annual Convention of the American Psychological Association, Toronto, Canada.

Seron, X., Deloche, G., Moulard, J., & Rouselle, M. (1980. A computer based therapy for the treatment of aphasic subjects with writing disorders. *Journal of Speech and Hearing Disorders, 45,* 45–58.

Skilbeck, C. (1984). Computer assistance in the management of memory and cognitive impairment. In Wilson, B., & Moffatt, N. (Eds.), *Clinical management of memory problems* (pp. 112–131). London: Aspen.

Trexler, L. (Ed.). (1982). *Cognitive rehabilitation.* New York: Plenum Press.

Vanderheiden, G. (1981). Practical application of microcomputers to aid the handicapped. *IEEE Computer, 14,* 54–61.

Wilson, B. (1982). Success and failure in memory training following a cerebral vascular accident, *Cortex, 18,* 581–594.

Wilson, P. B. (1983). Software selection and use in language and cognitive rehabilitation. *Cognitive Rehabilitation, 1,* 9–10.

Wilson, B., & Moffat, N. (1984). Rehabilitation of memory for everyday life. In Harris, J. E. & Morris, P. E. (Eds.), *Everyday memory: actions and absent mindedness* (pp. 207–233). London: Academic Press.

APPENDIX 11.1

Volin, R. A. and Groher, M., Language Stimulation Software Series, (Aspen Systems Corp., 1600 Research Boulevard, Rockville, MD, 20850, (301) 251-5000). Writing, naming and reading remediation for aphasics. (Apple II+, Apple IIe, Apple IIc, IBM PC).

Major, B. J. and Wilson, K. J., Computerized Reading for Aphasics. (College-Hill Press, Microcomputer Software Division, 4284 41st Street, San Diego, CA, 92105, (619) 563-8899, (800) 854-2541). Nine programs for aphasic adults to remediate reading and comprehension. (Apple II+, Apple IIe).

Eugene Sunday, Ph.D., Clinical Software Group, Dept. of Psychological Services. St. Michael's Hospital, 38 Shuter Street, Fourth Floor, Toronto, Ontario, Canada M5B 1A6 (Commodore 64 computer)

Richard J. Browne, and Joseph Stadford have developed CAP-TAIN: Cognitive Training Series, a set of 21 programs that include exercises in conceptual skill as well as attention and visual motor abilities. The software is designed for both evaluation and training of basic cognitive functions and uses a mouse device for input. A mouse is a small device on a roller that makes it easier to communicate with a computer because you just move and click the device instead of typing (thereby reducing the motor requirements for the patient). A new version using a track-ball input device, such as those seen in video game centers, is being developed. Contact Network Services, Huguenot Professional Center, 1915 Huguenot Road, Richmond, VA, 23235, (804) 379-2253. (Apple II+, Apple IIe computer).

Marvin Brooke (Emory University), Leonore DeKroes (Georgia Tech), Louisa Branscomb (Georgia State University), and several others have teamed together to develop a set of cognitive rehabilitation programs that are currently being tested at the Rehabilitation Research and Training Center at Emory; (404) 329-4810.

Jacqueline Smith (William Beaumont Hospital, Speech and Language Pathology, 3601 West 13 Mile Road, Royal Oak, MI 48092 (313) 288-8085) has developed a series of rehabilitation exercises for the remediation of cognitive, language, and reading deficits. (Apple II series computers and IBM PC) Available from Hartley Courseware, Inc., 123 Bridge, Dimondale, MI 48821 (517/646-6458).

Parrot Software, 190 Sandy Ridge Road, State College, PA, 16803, (814) 237-7282. Aphasia retraining software (Apple series computers).

The Greentree Group, Inc., P.O. Box 28, Mohnton, PA, 19540 (Apple II+, IIe).

Vaughn, G. W. et al., Remote Machine-assisted Treatment and Evaluation System (REMATE). This system is unique in that it communicates over the telephone lines to deliver assessment and treatment services for language-impaired individuals with a terminal in their homes. Training tasks include reading and writing exercises, as well as speaking and listening drills. This is public domain software available to aphasic vererans (Contact Gwenyth R., Vaughn, Project Director for REMATE, Audiology-speech Pathology Service, Birmingham Veterans Administration Medical Center, Birmingham, AL, 35233).

Katz, R. C. Programs for language impairments including keyboard skills, comprehension of questions, sentences, and stories. Sun-

376 FISHER

set Software, 11750 Sunset Blvd., Suite 414, Los Angeles, CA, 90049 (Apple II+, Apple IIe).

Katz, R. C. and Nagy, V. T., Computerized Aphasia Treatment System (CATS). Public Domain software for assessment and treatment of aphasic problems including paragraph comprehension, arithmetic problems, letter matching, and five reading tasks. Write to Communications Laboratory, Audiology and Speech Pathology Service, Veterans Administration Outpatient Clinic, Attention: R. C. Katz, 425 South Hill Street, Los Angles, CA, 90013.

Create, P.O. Box 8896, Green Bay, WI 54308.

Designware, 185 Berry Street, San Francisco, CA, 94107.

Sunburst Communications, 39 Washington Avenue, Pleasantville, NY, 10570.

University Park Press, 300 North Charles Street, Baltimore, MD 21201.

Brain Link Software, 317 Montgomery, Ann Arbor, MI 48103. Exercises for language remediation (Apple II+ or IIe).

Computations, Inc., P.O. Box 502, Troy, MI 48009.

Computer-Advanced Ideas, Inc., 1442 A, Walnut Street, Suite 341, Berkeley, CA 94709.

Edu-ware Services, Inc., 22222 Sherman Way, Canoga Park, CA 91303.

Laureate Learning Systems, Nill Street, Burlington, VT 05401.

Program Design, Inc., 11 Idar Street, Greenwich, CT 06830.

Davidson and Associates, 6069 Grove Oak Place, #12, Rancho Palos Verdes, CA 90274.

Stachowiak, F. J. Rheinische Landesklinik Bonn. Kaiser-Karl-Ring, 20 5300 Bonn 1. West Germany (microcomputer-assisted rehabilitation of language disorders in aphasic patients).

11. MICROCOMPUTER TECHNOLOGY   377

Beaumont, J. G. Department of Psychology. University of Leicester Leicester LE1 7RH, Great Britain. D.H.S.S. Project: Microcomputer aided assessment of neurological states.

Skilbeck, C. Neurological/Stroke Rehabilitation Unit. Frenchay Hospital Bristol, Great Britain. (microcomputer-based assessment and rehabilitation of memory and cognitive impairments).

Robertson, I. Astley Ainslie Hospital. Grange Loan. Edinburgh EH9 2HL Great Britain. (microcomputer-based rehabilitation for visual perceptual impairments and attention/concentration difficulties).

Larsen, S. Department of Education and Psychology. The Royal Danish School of Education Studies. 101 Emdrupvej. 2400 Copenhagen. Denmark (Visual hemifield asymmetries assessment).

Deloche, G. Hôpital de la Salpêtrière, 47 Boulevard de l'Hôpital, 75651 Paris Cedex 13. France. Seron, X., & F. Coyette, Cliniques St.Luc Avenue Hippocrate, 10 . 1200 Bruxelles. Belgique. Van der Linden, M. Hôpital de Bavière, 66 Boulevard de la Constitution. 4020 Liege Belgique: ZORGLUB GROUP: Microcomputer-based assessment and rehabilitation of language, attentional, and memory disorders. (Apple IIe).

Coltheart, M. Department of Psychology, Birbeck College, Malet Street London WCI E 7HX. Great Britain. The MRC psycholinguistic database (for selection of items to be used in testing or training batteries and satisfying predetermined psycholinguistic constraints).

APPENDIX 11.2

Resources

Models and Techniques of Cognitive Rehabilitation, Educational Service Department, Community Hospital, 1500 North Ritter Ave., Indianapolis, IN 46219, (317)-353-5661. (annual conference)

Odie Bracy, (317)-291-5809. (inservice workshops)

Cognitive Rehabilitation, 6555 Carrollton Avenue, Indianapolis, IN 46220. (magazine)

378   FISHER

Computers in Psychiatry and Psychology, 26 Trumbull St., New Haven, CT 06511, (203)-562-9873 (newsletter)

Micropsych Network, Professional Resource Exchange, Inc., P.O. Box 15560, Sarasota, FL 32277-1560, (813)-366-7913. (newsletter)

Computers in Human Behavior, Pergamon Press, Inc., Maxwell House Fairview Park, Elmsford NY 10523. (journal)

Bulletins on Science and Technology for the Handicapped, AAAS, 1515 Massachusetts Ave. NW, Washington, DC 20005. (newsletter).

Regarding the development of a Division of Computers in Psychology of the APA. Contact Amirah Elwork, Ph.D. Dept. of Mental Health, MSS403, Hahnemann University, 230 N. Broad St., Philadelphia, PA 19102 (APA division)

Bob Klepac, Ph.D., Academic applications, modem (904)-893-9621 (Computer Bulletin Board)

Ivon Goldberg, M.D., Psychomnet, voice (212)-876-7800. (Computer Bulletin Board)

Marvin Miller, M.D., voice (317)-846-5688, modem (317)- 846-8917 (Computer Bulletin Board)

Psycho-Info Exchange, modem (212)-662-7171 (enter 'guest' for first and last name and '123' for password. (Computer Bulletin Board)

Directory of Psychologists Using Apples, Academic Apple-cation, 2815 Kilkierane Dr., Tallahassee, FL 32308, voice (904)-893-3706 (directory)

For a directory of rehabilitation facilities involved in cognitive rehabilitation see Cognitive Rehabilitation, Vol. 2, No. 6, Nov. 1984, p. 14–15. (directory)

For directory of Apple commercial software that has been categorized by cognitive skill areas see Kreutzer, J. and Morrison, C. (1986). A Guide to Cognitive Rehabilitation Software for the Apple IIe/IIc Computer, Cognitive Rehabilitation, Vol. 4 (1), 6–17 (directory)

For a database of rehabilitation aids see Abledata System, National Rehabilitation Information Center, 4407 Eighth Street, NE, The Catholic University of America, Washington, DC 20017, (202)-635-6090 (directory)

For a list of software for aphasia and cognitive rehabilitation with clinical application notes see the Compilation of Clinical Software for Aphasia Rehabilitation and Cognitive Retraining, Clinical Software Resources, 2850 Windemere, Birmingham, MI 48008 (directory)

For a directory of aphasia remediation software see the Software Registry Number Three, James Fitch, Editor, Department of Speech Pathology and Audiology, University of South Alabama, Mobile, AL 36688. (directory)

For a list of language retraining programs see Trace Software Registry, Trace Center, 314 Waisman Center, 1500 Highland Avenue, Madison, WI 53706. (directory)

Books of Interest

Grossfeld, M. L., and Grossfeld, C. A., Microcomputer Applications in Rehabilitation of Communications Disorders, 1986, Aspen Publishers, Inc., Rockville, Maryland. (ISBN: 0-87-189-287-1)

Adamovich, B. B., Henderson, J. A., and Auerbach, S., Cognitive Rehabilitation of Closed Head Injured Patients, A Dynamic Approach, 1985, College-Hill Press, Inc., San Diego, CA (ISBN 0-933014-67-8)

Schwartz, A. H. (Editor), Handbook of Microcomputer Applications in Communication Disorders, 1984, College-Hill Press, Inc., San Diego, CA (ISBN 0-9333013-13-9)

Golden, C. J. (Editor), Current Topics in Rehabilitation Psychology, 1984, Grune and Stratton, Inc., New York, NY. (ISBN 0-8089-1641-6)

Schwartz, M. D. (Editor), Using Computers in Clinical Practice, Psychotherapy and Mental Health Applications, 1984, The Haworth Press, New York, NY. (ISBN 0-86656-208-7)

Wilson, B. A. and Moffat, N. (Editors), Clinical Management of Memory Problems, 1984, Aspen Systems Corp., Rockville, MD (ISBN 0-89443-308-3)

Rosenthal, M., Griffith, E., Bond, M. R. and Miller, J. D., Rehabilitation of the Head Injured Adult, 1983, F. A. Davis Company, Philadelphia, PA. (ISBN 0-8036-7625-5)

APPENDIX 11.3

Robots and Rehabilitation

Despite my hope for the future of cognitive prosthetic devices, my clinical experience thus far shows some patient resistance to these high-tech marvels. The same is bound to be true for the ultimate prosthetic device, the personal robot. I have always contended that an unimpaired companion is the best memory aid of all, but now the age of the electronic companion is upon us. The personal robot can keep track of wandering patients, assist in their reality orientation, provide mental stimulation, and operate as walking cognitive prosthetic devices. Self-navigating robotic companions are similar in some ways to a human companion but have some advantages and disadvantages. They are less intelligent at present and less flexible. Also, they obviously lack human warmth and social skills, although some of them are charming in an R2D2 sort of way. There is no end to the list of ways in which humans currently outdo robots; however, there are some possible advantages to robots. For example, a "people walker" robot can act as the legs of paralyzed patients and help provide locomotion that can even climb stairs or traverse difficult terrain. Such devices can be made to respond to voice command and have built-in navigational ability to avoid obstacles and find specified locations. Add robotic arms and such a device might aid in feeding and grooming. Add robotic intelligence and the device might help with everyday decision making and memory tasks.

The robot might also provide automated control over household appliances and security devices, turning them on and off as needed and thereby reducing the memory demands placed on the patient. Such a device could possibly help digest complex information and feed back a simplified version to the cognitively impaired patient. For example, the robot might record speech input from the phone or radio and play this back to the patient at a reduced speed so as to increase intelligibility. Or it might recognize and repeat instructions two or three times so that with repetition the information might be better absorbed. It might be capable of "natural language" comprehension and be able to translate complex messages into simple phrases for the patient with receptive problems. It might also transform verbal material into nonverbal pictorial or symbolic messages. The reverse type of translation could be accomplished for patients with expressive difficulty. Such a device might recognize dysarthric or aphasic speech and decode the message, taking into account the context of the conversation via artificial intelligence programs. This formerly unintelligible message would then be repeated in clear robotic sythesized speech. Many such devices are either currently on the drawing board or are being discussed at professional meetings. I would hope that within the next 10 years we will see many commercially available cognitive prosthetic devices of this type.

12 Cognitive Neuropsychology and Rehabilitation: An Unfulfilled Promise?

Alfonso Caramazza
The Johns Hopkins University

In this paper I consider some of the principal problems faced by cognitive neuropsychology, especially as they arise in the context of the rehabilitation of acquired cognitive disorders. This analysis will necessarily be theoretical as I have no particular competence in the areas of clinical neuropsychology or therapeutic intervention. My remarks will be restricted, therefore, to the analysis of the *possible* relationship between theoretical advances in cognitive neuropsychology and therapeutic intervention. In what follows I first describe briefly the goals and scope of cognitive neuropsychology. I then consider whether features of this approach may warrant the claim that cognitive neuropsychology provides the basis for a specific form of therapeutic practice. Given my limited understanding of clinical neuropsychological practice, especially in the area of rehabilitation, this latter analysis will be informed by a reading of the chapters that comprise this volume. My conclusion will be that despite the impressive progress documented in this volume in the application of cognitive neuropsychological analyses for remediation practice, there remain major issues to be addressed in future work.

---

¹The research reported here and the preparation of this paper were supported by NIH grant NS22201, and grants from the Seaver Institute and the Lounsbery Foundation.

COGNITIVE NEUROPSYCHOLOGY

Cognitive neuropsychology is strategically located at the boundary of the cognitive and neural sciences. Like other subdisciplines of cognitive science its objective is to provide a formal characterization of the mental structures and operations that subserve human cognitive capacity (e.g., linguistic ability, perception, reasoning, and so forth). Unlike other subdisciplines of cognitive science, however, it relies on the analysis of acquired cognitive disorders—patterns of impaired cognitive performance consequent to brain damage—to infer the structure of normal cognitive mechanisms. Because the observations used by cognitive neuropsychology can be related, albeit indirectly, to local brain structures, such pairings may serve as the basis for mapping cognitive mechanisms onto brain structures and, therefore, provide the basis for a neural theory of human cognitive processes. However, despite its favorable position on the cognitive science/neuroscience continuum, cognitive neuropsychology has failed to exploit successfully this opportunity to develop nontrivial neural models of human cognitive capacities. This failure reflects in large measure intrinsic limitations of the interpretive burden that cognitive neuropsychological observations may carry—the pairing of neural lesions with functional disorders can support little more than a modern "phrenology." However, as I have argued elsewhere (Caramazza, 1988) the present state of affairs within cognitive neuropsychology also reflects, at least in part, incorrect methodological choices by its practitioners. I will return to the issue of brain-cognition relationships in the concluding section of these remarks where I briefly consider the role that such relationships may play in the development of a theory of cognitive rehabilitation.

Over the past two decades we have witnessed a major growth in experimental research with brain-damaged patients, which has had as its explicit goal that of informing theories of normal cognitive functioning. That is, research on the nature of cognitive dysfunctions in brain-damaged patients has increasingly been used to constrain claims about the structure of the representations and processes that characterize cognitive abilities. Stated differently, this type of research has sought to explain patterns of acquired cognitive disorders in terms of specific deformations (functional lesions) of a hypothesized model of normal cognitive functioning. It is this emphasis on the explicit characterization of the normal cognitive system as a procondition for the formulation of an explanatory account of particular forms of cognitive dysfunction that distinguishes cognitive from classical neuropsychology,[2] the latter, medical approach having as its primary objective that of relating clinically specified clusters of symptoms to site of brain damage.[3]

The shift in focus in neuropsychological research from a concern with relating syndrome types to locus of brain damage to a concern with the implications that particular forms of cognitively impaired performance may have for theories of cognitive functioning has had a major methodological consequence. The conceptual and methodological framework for inferring the structure of normal cognitive mechanisms from patterns of cognitively impaired performance and, for the related objective of explicating cognitive disorders by reference to particular deformations of hypothesized models of cognitive processing, is quite distinct from that used in classical neuropsychology. The distinction hinges on the realization that impaired performance is a function of the structure of the normal cognitive system that subserves the performance in question *and* specific transformations (due to brain damage) of this system. In other words, the relationship between cognitively impaired performance and the cognitive mechanisms presumed to support the relevant performance is mediated by a hypothesized functional lesion to the system. However, because functional lesions must themselves be inferred from a patient's performance, no subset of this performance, no matter how arbitrarily large (short of *all* the theoretically relevant performance), can be used for the a priori classification of patients. A crucial implication from this line of reasoning is that only single-patient research allows valid inferences about cognitive mechanisms from the analysis of cog-

---

[2]We should note that the distinction between cognitive and classical neuropsychology is not categorical but one of degree. Classical neuropsychology was also concerned with the formulation of models of normal cognitive functioning. However, this concern was secondary to that of identifying syndrome types by reference to locus and form of brain damage. In this approach the articulation of the structure of cognitive mechanisms received scant attention with the consequence that the details of cognitive processing were left mostly implicit.

[3]It must be emphasized that cognitive neuropsychologists are no less concerned with relating cognitive mechanisms to neural processes than those researchers who continue to work within the classical neuropsychology approach. The distinction between the two approaches is that cognitive neuropsychology assumes that meaningful statements about brain-cognition relations can only be made for well-articulated claims about cognitive processes. On this view, claims about brain-cognition mapping involves relating hypothesized cognitive mechanisms to brain structures (or neural processes) and not merely constellations of symptoms to locus of brain damage (see Caramazza, 1988, for further discussion).

386 CARAMAZZA

nitively impaired performance (see Caramazza, 1986, for detailed discussion).

Important as this specifically methodological conclusion is for neuropsychological research, an even more important general implication follows from the emphasis on the development of detailed cognitive models as the basis for explicating patterns of cognitively impaired performance. This concerns the style of research that is appropriate for the goals of cognitive neuropsychologists. Specifically, and very briefly, the type of observations needed for meaningful claims about the structure of cognitive mechanisms require ever more detailed analyses of patient's performance. To distinguish among alternative hypotheses about the "locus" of functional lesions in a model of cognitive functioning or about the representations and processing structure supported by a cognitive mechanism we need fine-grained analyses of patient's impaired performance. However, no amount of detail in the experimental observations can replace the theoretical effort needed to elaborate in explicit terms the models that are supposed to provide the explanatory framework for understanding cognitive disorders. To illustrate this point, consider the following problem that has arisen in the course of research by my colleagues and myself on the issue of one of the hypothesized components of processing in the spelling system.

The spelling process is very complex. It recruits a number of different cognitive, linguistic, perceptual, and motor mechanisms in its ordinary functioning. Damage to any one of these mechanisms will result in some form of dysgraphia, each form presumably reflecting the locus of functional damage to the system. Research of dysgraphia has provided empirical support for a functional architecture of the spelling system that includes each of the major components schematically depicted (as a visual summary) in Figure 12.1.

Despite (or perhaps because of) the increasingly intense research effort directed at understanding the bases for dysgraphia, many important theoretical and empirical issues must be addressed. These issues concern the very basic question of which type of cognitive architecture most appropriately characterizes the spelling process, as well as matters specific to each of the postulated components of the system. It is not possible to consider all or even several of these difficulties here. I have chosen, therefore, to consider only one *representative*, if restricted, set of issues in some detail—issues that arise in the context of considerations about the processing role of the graphemic buffer and the interactions of this mechanism with other processing components. With appropriate modification, similar analyses

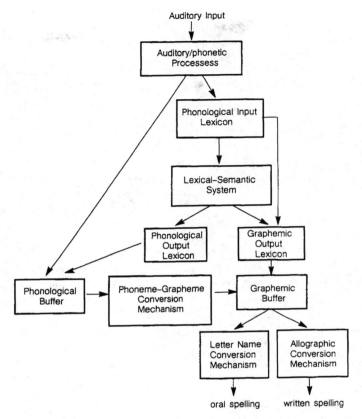

FIGURE 12.1. Schematic diagram of the spelling process.

could have been undertaken for other components of the spelling system.

A number of investigators have proposed that one of the mechanisms engaged in the spelling process is a working memory component that temporarily stores the graphemic representation of a word during execution of appropriate output processes (Caramazza, Miceli, Villa, & Romani, 1987; Ellis, 1982; Newcombe & Marshall, 1980; Wing & Baddeley, 1980). Empirical support for this proposal has been obtained both in research with normal (Wing & Baddeley, 1980) and brain-damaged subjects (Caramazza et al., 1987; Hillis & Carmazza, in press; Miceli, Silveri, & Caramazza, 1985).

We have proposed a set of criteria for identifying selective damage to the graphemic buffer within the functional architecture of the spelling system discussed earlier (Caramazza et al., 1987). The proposed criteria are the following: (a) A similar pattern of spelling errors should be obtained for unfamiliar (nonwords) and for familiar words, across all output modalities (oral and written spelling and typing) and all input modalities (spontaneous writing, written naming, writing to dictation, and delayed copying) because the graphemic buffer is equally implicated in each of these spelling tasks; (b) spelling accuracy should not be affected by lexical factors such as word frequency, grammatical word class or concreteness because by hypothesis lexical components of the system are intact; (c) spelling accuracy should not be affected by orthophonological factors such as phonology-to-orthography probability mappings because p-g mapping processes are hypothesized to be intact; (d) lexical paragraphias (semantic, morphological, or phonological) should not occur for the same reason as in (b); and (e) spelling errors should occur with increased frequency as a function of word length because each grapheme to be stored introduces a potential error. In addition, errors should reflect the degradation of the spatially encoded, graphemic representation of the target word. The expected types of spelling errors are deletions, substitutions, insertions and transposition of letters, which lead to the production of phonemically implausible nonwords (at least some of which would include orthographic violations; e.g., rpiest). We have reported a number of patients whose spelling performance conforms with expectations derived from the hypothesis of selective damage to the graphemic buffer: patient L.B. (Caramazza et al., 1987); patients D.H. and M.L. (Hillis & Caramazza, in press); and (possibly) patient F.V. (Miceli, Silveri, & Caramazza, 1985). Despite the apparent strength of the empirical evidence favoring this hypothesis, the notion "graphemic buffer" remains woefully underspecified.

Our present understanding of the graphemic buffer is that it is a fast-decaying, capacity-limited component for the temporary storage of graphemic representations. However, we have neither estimates of the time course of information decay nor of the capacity of the proposed working memory system. Worse still, we have very little understanding of the type of information stored in the buffer. The assumption that the representations held in the graphemic buffer consist of spatially-coded strings of graphemes (Caramazza et al., 1987) leaves unspecified both the nature of the "strings"—words, morphemes, graphemic clusters corresponding to syllables, or just frequently occurring clusters of graphemes—and the nature of information beside graphemes that is needed in the process of spelling (e.g., capitalization, letter doubling). Nor does this conception of the graphemic buffer say anything about how attentional mechanisms may interact with the buffer in spelling performance. Without a more detailed characterization of the buffer, a number of empirical facts presumably related to the functioning of this component of processing cannot be properly evaluated. Thus, we have recently obtained evidence from patients with putative functional lesions to the graphemic buffer that the morphological structure of a word affects processing in the buffer (Badecker, Hillis, & Caramazza, unpublished), that letter substitution errors are almost always substitutions of consonant for consonant and vowel for vowel (Caramazza & Miceli, in press), and that there are indications that attentional deficits may affect processing at the level of the graphemic buffer (Hillis & Caramazza, in press; unpublished). However, nothing in our present conception of the structure of the graphemic buffer would predict the observed effects. Does this mean that our hypothesis of a functional lesion at the level of the graphemic buffer is false? Although this may indeed be the case we cannot say at this time. Unless we articulate in greater detail our claims about the graphemic buffer we will not be able to provide motivated accounts for important aspects of dysgraphic patients' performance, nor, of course, will we be able to adequately evaluate alternative claims about the nature of the graphemic buffer or, indeed, even whether the proposed functional architecture containing a graphemic buffer constitutes an appropriate characterization of the spelling process.

Obviously, we are confronting not only empirical issues that may be resolved directly by further experimentation and analysis, but also theoretical ones. To address the issues that have arisen from our research a detailed articulation of the structure of the graphemic buffer is needed. Thus, we must decide on a decay function and a capacity parameter for the buffer, as well as on the type of information we assume to be represented in the hypothesized buffer. Short of adequate theoretical developments the experimental results we have obtained remain uninterpretable.

From the preceding discussion it should be obvious that even in the narrow context of a relatively simple component of processing, such as the graphemic buffer, the theoretical and empirical problems to be resolved are anything but trivial (consider by contrast the far greater problems that must be faced in dealing with a more complex component such as the phonological lexicon). Here I am trying to draw the reader's attention to the fact that the theoretical and empirical issues confronting us are articulated in terms of highly detailed patterns of performance in the context of claims about cognitive mechanisms. There has been no mention, and indeed none can be justified, of clinical types such as surface dysgraphia, phonological

390 CARAMAZZA

dysgraphia, and the like. The reason for this should be quite apparent. The articulation of the theoretical machinery assumed to support the spelling ability and the patterns of impaired performance to be accounted for far outstrip the gross partitionings provided by clinical classification. All that is obtained by patient classification is a theoretically arbitrary, behavioral grouping. This is true whether the classification scheme used is the classical one (Broca's aphasia, Wernicke's aphasia, etc.) or its modern incarnation in the areas of reading and spelling disorders (deep dyslexia, surface dyslexia, phonological dysgraphia, etc.). In short, a coherent cognitive neuropsychology cannot be carried out within the framework of classification-based research. And, yet, many of the chapters in this volume rely on a strategy of patient classification in their purportedly cognitive neuropsychological approach to the rehabilitation of cognitively-impaired patients.

What is Cognitive Neuropsychology's Specific Contribution to an Informed Rehabilitation Strategy?

I have argued that the principal feature that characterizes cognitive neuropsychology (and distinguishes it from classical neuropsychology) is its avowedly cognitivist stance (with its methodological consequences). That is, the position that impaired cognitive performance is to be explicated by appeal to specific transformations of a postulated model of cognitive functioning. This stance has allowed neuropsychologists to make considerable progress in understanding various aspects of the structure of cognitive mechanisms. In particular, and important in the present context, this cognitivist stance has forced us to reevaluate our characterization of acquired cognitive disorders. We now are much more aware of the need to carry out detailed analyses of patient's performance if we are to understand the underlying causes for a particular form of disorder. We are no longer content with the superficial characterization of a patient's deficit as alexia, agrammatism, anomia, etc. We now seek to characterize the impairment in a patient by reference to some hypothesized component(s) of a cognitive system. This stance entails an analytic approach that has served us well, as is amply apparent from the chapters in this volume, at least with respect to the kind of characterizations that are given of patient's cognitive disorders. The crucial issue, however, is whether there is a specificity to this approach, which if adopted would have transparent consequences for therapeutic practice. On this issue, like Basso (this volume), I remain skeptical.

Lest my skepticism be misunderstood as general pessimism about the whole enterprise, let me point out at the outset one aspect of the cognitive neuropsychological approach to rehabilitation that is an uncontestably welcome addition to the repertoire of the therapist. I have in mind the obvious advantages for rehabilitation that accrue from a theoretically informed, detailed analysis of a patient's impaired performance. Indeed, without such an analysis it is not even clear that there could be an informed therapeutic practice: One must have a relatively clear idea of the nature of the disorder before trying to devise an appropriate therapeutic strategy. Cognitive neuropsychology has contributed importantly in this regard. Granted this obviously positive development, we should go on to ask ourselves how the cognitive neuropsychological approach has concretely affected therapeutic practice (the chapters in this volume) and, more generally, how it could do so in principle. That is, we should ask ouselves what might be the implications for therapeutic practice of having a cognitive analysis of patients' impaired performance.

A cognitive neuropsychological analysis of a patient's performance presumably provides a hypothesis about the nature of the transformation a cognitive system has undergone as a consequence of brain damage. The nature of the hypothesized transformation (functional lesion) may be more or less detailed depending on the level of theoretical development for a specific domain of human cognition. For example, we have a deeper understanding of the machinery that subserves sentence comprehension than that that subserves conscious awareness of the world around us. Consequently, our hypotheses about the nature of sentence comprehension deficits are likely to be better articulated than those about the nature of disorders of consciousness. A fair assessment of the potential contribution of cognitive neuropsychology for therapeutic practice should consider those domains of cognition where presumably we have made some progress in understanding the structure of the cognitive mechanisms assumed to subserve the relevant cognitive abilities. Language processing is supposed to be one such area. I will focus, therefore, on examples from this cognitive domain in the following analysis.

Grant me for the moment, although nothing hinges on this for what follows (substitute your preferred example for the one I have chosen), that our analysis of patients with putative damage to the graphemic buffer is indeed correct. Note that the hypothesis of a functional lesion at the level of the graphemic buffer rests on a highly constraining, not-obviously-related set of observations, ranging from performance on familiar and unfamiliar words to spelling performance across modalities of input and output to highly detailed levels and types of errors. Were this hypothesis to be correct it would have the potential (with the caveats raised earlier) of representing a truly explanatory (and not merely descriptive) account of the patients' performance. And yet it is not apparent to me that this knowledge provides interesting constraints for an informed therapeutic strategy. To be sure, we may be able to come up with some obvious therapeutic strategies to use with patients with putative deficit to the graphemic buffer (assuming for the moment that the deficit to the buffer always takes the form of a reduction in processing efficiency, defined either as a capacity limitation or abnormally fast decay). Thus, one might propose to "teach" the patient a spelling strategy to circumvent the reduced processing efficiency. For example, we could teach the patient to spell words a syllable at a time (indeed there is some indication that one of our patients, L.B., spontaneously began to use this strategy, unfortunately only with modest success). This strategy may even prove to be of some help. Note, however, that this strategic choice could just as easily have been informed by the mere observation that the patient spelled very short words almost flawlessly. Crucially for present purposes, the point I am trying to make is that there is nothing *specifically* about our theory of the structure of the spelling system (or the reading system, the naming system, the sentence comprehension system, and so forth) which serves to constrain our choice of therapeutic strategy. Merely "knowing" that the probable locus of deficit is at the level of the graphemic buffer does not, on its own, allow us to specify a therapeutic strategy. To do so requires not just a theory of the structure of the spelling system, but also, and more important, a theory of therapeutic intervention—a theory of the ways in which a damaged system may be modified as a consequence of particular forms of intervention. Of course, this latter theory must, in the end, be compatible with our theories of cognitive mechanisms, but it is *not* determined in any obvious, direct way by cognitive theory.

Consider a second example. Suppose we have a patient whose performance in sentence comprehension tasks is explicable by hypothesizing a functional lesion to a particular processing component within a theory of sentence processing, specifically, a deficit in a mechanism that assigns thematic structure to sentence constituents. Of what use is this information? Can we, merely in virtue of the stated claim, specify a therapeutic strategy? It does not seem to me that the information provided by the cognitive neuropsychologist has much to say for therapeutic practice *qua* theoretically driven approach to the remediation of the hypothesized deficit. The hypothesized functional lesion represents a hypothesis about the nature of the transformation the cognitive system has undergone as a function of brain damage. It does not inform us about the steps that could be most efficacious for overcoming the sustained damage; the hypothesized transformation does not constrain the range of therapeutic procedures that would be most effective in overcoming the observed deficit. Of course, this is not to say that the specific information about the nature of the patient's disorder may not guide the cognitive functions one focuses on for therapy, as was elegantly demonstrated by Byng and Coltheart (1986).

An important distinction should be drawn at this point. We should distinguish between the impact for therapeutic practice that may be expected from (a) the methods used by cognitive neuropsychologists to arrive at some hypothesis about the nature of the functional lesion(s) in a patient and (b) the *content* of the cognitive theories that guide our investigations of brain-damaged patients. I have suggested that the application of methods of cognitive neuropsychology as a step in the process of devising rehabilitative strategies has obvious advantages; it permits a sophisticated diagnosis of the nature of the difficulties a patient experiences in cognitive processing. By contrast, however, even when we may be confident that our hypothesis about the nature of the functional lesion(s) in a patient is correct, this information is of limited use in specifying an informed therapeutic strategy because the content of our cognitive theories does not specify the modifications that a damaged system undergoes as a function of the different types of experiences with which a patient may be presented. This limitation can only be corrected by the development of theories specifically designed to deal with the problem of rehabilitation. The content of current cognitive theories does not constrain in any obvious way the nature of possible therapy-determined modifications of a system: A cognitive theory is *not* a theory of cognitive rehabilitation. We should not confuse the attested benefits that accrue from the careful use of diagnostic procedures (considerably advanced by the introduction of cognitive neuropsychological methods) with the hoped-for-benefits from a strictly cognitive analysis of impaired performance in brain-damaged patients. And, most important, we should not confuse theories of cognitive processing with theories of rehabilitation.

In my remarks thus far I have argued that if there is a specificity to the relationship between cognitive neuropsychology and rehabilitation, this is to be found more at the level of the methodology used for diagnosis of cognitive disorders (and the role that such diagnoses may play in determining rehabilitation strategy) than in anything concerning the content of cognitive theories. In some respects I have merely stated the obvious: One cannot take exception with the obvious merits of a detailed analysis of patients' performance for an informed therapeutic practice (especially so in light of the excellent use to which such analyses may be put, as amply demonstrated by the chapters in this volume). In another sense, however, the stated claim need not be trivially true: There need not necessarily be a positive connection between just *any* type of detailed analysis of patients' performance and efficacious therapeutic intervention. In other words, it need not merely be detailed analysis *qua* detailed analysis that is useful for therapy, but that type of detailed analysis that is motivated by adopting a cognitive perspective on the nature of impaired performance in brain-damaged patients. On this view, a highly detailed analysis of patients' performance uninformed by cognitive theory would not necessarily be useful for guiding therapeutic intervention. Thus, one of the motivations for distinguishing between a cognitive neuropsychological approach to therapy and other possible approaches is that cognitive neuropsychology provides especially useful analyses of the nature of the deficits that underlie patients' performance, analyses that may be especially well suited to guide therapeutic intervention.

As I have already indicated I would like to be partisan to this view. However, the force of this conviction is not based on the empirically demonstrated superiority of the cognitive neuropsychological approach to therapy but on intuition alone. Specifically, my conviction (and probably that of most other cognitive neuropsychologists) is supported by the realization that a coherent analysis of a patient's performance—one that is not merely a consideration of the patient's performance on a random subset of the indefinitely large number of possible tasks—must be informed by some theory or other, explicit or implicit. Were this not the case we would just as likely find reason to consider, say, whether a patient can read, better or worse, words that contain the letter "a" as opposed to the letter "e" or whether the patient can read, better or worse, words that contain an odd as opposed to an even number of letters, and so forth. This observation allows us to conclude that the analysis of patients' performance guided by cognitive theory may offer the basis for a theoretically motivated explanation of these patients' performance. Such analyses may even lead to the development of cognitively-based theories of rehabilitation, but they do not imply such theories. Thus, although I would like to believe that the analysis of a patient's performance informed by cognitive theory provides a *more* useful basis for guiding therapeutic intervention than one not so informed, this belief remains empirically unsupported. The chapters in this volume clearly show that the detailed analysis of patients' impairments may successfully be used to decide on the type of therapeutic intervention to use with a patient. They do not show, however, that the analysis must be guided by cognitive theory. Perhaps, though not auspiciously, *any* detailed analysis would do as well.

I have suggested that we do not have empirical reasons for believing that it is the specifically cognitive nature of the theories that inform the detailed analyses of patients' performance that played the determining role in the successful therapeutic interventions reported in this volume. There is equally little reason for believing that it is the specific content of the cognitive theories themselves that played the determining role. Thus, consider the case where we have analyzed a patient's performance as reflecting a deficit in thematic mapping, a difficulty presumably tied to some processing deficit of the thematic structure of verbs. Suppose further that the therapeutic procedure used in this case turns out to be quite effective in remediating the comprehension impairment with which the patient originally presented. At this point we should ask ourselves whether we would have used a different therapeutic strategy had we had a different hypothesis about the functional lesion in the patient. Thus, suppose that we had instead hypothesized that the patient's comprehension impairment was the result of a deficit in processing traces, phonologically null anaphoric elements that mark the phrasal position of moved elements in a sentence, which presumably results in comprehension failure similar to that reported for the patient under consideration in this example (Grodzinsky, 1986). Would this alternative hypothesis, as the basis for the observed sentence comprehension impairment, have led us to adopt a different therapeutic strategy for the patient? If so, we would then be able to assert that the content of the cognitive theory we adopted played a role in determining therapeutic intervention. However, it is not apparent to me, and the chapters in this volume do not help out in this regard, that the content of the theories adopted had such a determining effect on the choice of therapeutic strategy.

CONCLUSION

The promise of cognitive neuropsychology for therapeutic practice is that the detailed functional analysis of cognitive disorders will provide a basis for the informed choice of therapeutic intervention. This position has been clearly articulated by Mitchum and Berndt (in press). They state: "To the extent that a model of the processes normally involved in a particular language behavior can be defined, therapies can be developed that focus on individual components that are believed to give rise to the pattern of symptoms found in a patient" (p. 4). They go on to suggest for the case of sentence production, the focus of their paper, that "Much of the difficulty in determining the best means of intervention for these (sentence production) deficits is the lack of well-articulated models to describe how sentences are produced by normal speakers. It is possible to overcome this problem, to some extent, by generating an explicit conceptual model of the functional components necessary to accomplish a specific cognitive task" (p. 30). Once we are in possession of such models, these can serve as the basis for the "Extensive and theoretically-motivated analysis of the patients' symptoms (which) helps to distinguish among (the) various possible underlying causes of sentence formulation deficits" (p. 31). The outcome of such an analysis can then serve to plan appropriate intervention strategies to improve the patient's processing at the identified level of difficulty.

I share with Mitchum and Berndt and the authors of the chapters in this volume the conviction that a mature cognitive neuropsychology will constitute an essential ingredient for the development of a theoretically informed therapeutic practice. Unlike these authors, however, I find that the promise of cognitive neuropsychology as a guide for the choice of intervention strategies is still largely unfulfilled. In part this may be due to the fact that our analyses of cognitive disorders remain woefully underspecified, as exemplified by my analysis of those disorders of spelling that are supposed to result from damage to the graphemic buffer. The situation is considerably worse in those cases where the putatively cognitive analysis goes no further than the mere classification of patients into clinical categories, such as surface dyslexia, agrammatism, phonological dysgraphia, etc. This brand of "cognitive" analysis consists of little more than the mere relabeling of patterns of performance without theoretical motivation (e.g., classification of patients as deep or surface dyslexic where it is clearly the case that these classifications subsume patients with deficits to different cognitive mechanisms).

A more important reason for my skepticism is the one I have discussed at length in this paper; namely, that no convincing evidence has been presented in support of the view that it is the specifically cognitive character of the analyses of patients' performance that is to be credited for the putative successes in remediation reported in this volume.

Finally, there is the problem, raised earlier in this chapter, of the unsupported (and overly simple) assumption that all one needs for motivating therapeutic intervention is a theory of normal cognitive processing and a procedure for uncovering, from patterns of impaired performance, the locus of functional lesion to the normal system. Undoubtedly, the identification of the underlying cause of an impairment is an important step in deciding on an intervention strategy. However, an informed choice cannot be made in the absence of an equally rich theory of the modifications that a damaged cognitive system may undergo as a function of different forms of intervention. This latter aspect of the rehabilitation process remained unexplored in those papers purportedly directed at demonstrating the usefulness of cognitive neuropsychology for remediation. It is difficult from such a limited focus to evaluate how a mature cognitive neuropsychology might contribute to the development of remediation theories.

In concluding I would like to raise the issue of the neural dimension of cognitive neuropsychology, an issue that was ignored in the chapters in this volume but which I believe is crucial for the development of an informed therapeutic practice. As already noted, cognitive neuropsychology is principally concerned with the development of theories of normal cognitive mechanisms through the analysis of impaired performance in brain-damaged patients. This enterprise may proceed independently of neural considerations. That is, a cognitive theory may be developed by considering *only* the behavioral manifestations of a disorder. There is no need for such an enterprise to be concerned with the nature of neural damage—its locus and extent. This does not mean, however, that issues concerning the nature of brain pathology *qua* physical system are not germane to the problem of determining appropriate therapeutic strategies. On the contrary, for this latter purpose questions about the particular form of brain damage in a patient may play a fundamental role in devising intervention strategies. For example, diffuse and focal damage may require different forms of intervention. It is to be hoped that future work will consider the contribution made by the form of neural pathology to the remediation process. The development of a coherent theoretical foundation for therapeutic practice will benefit not only from progress in cognitive neuropsychology but also from a deeper appreciation of the neural bases for cognitive mechanisms and the relationship between cognitive and neural pathology.

ACKNOWLEDGMENT

I thank Kathy Yantis for her help in the preparation of this paper.

REFERENCES

Badecker, W., Hillis, A., & Caramazza, A. (1988). Lexical morphology and its role in the writing process: Evidence from a case of acquired dysgraphia. Unpublished manuscript.

Byng, S., & Coltheart, M. (1986). Aphasia therapy research: methodological requirements and illustrative results. In E. Hjelmquist, & L. G. Nilsson (Eds.), *Communication and handicap: Aspects of psychological compensation and technical aids.* North Holland: Elsevier Science Publishers.

Caramazza, A. (1988). Some aspects of language processing revealed through the analysis of acquired aphasia: the lexical system. *Annual Review of Neuroscience, 11*, 395–421.

Caramazza, A. (1986). On drawing inferences about the structure of normal cognitive systems from the analysis of patterns of impaired performance: the case for single-patient studies. *Brain and Cognition, 5*, 41–66.

Caramazza, A., & Miceli, G. (in press). Orthographic structure, the graphemic buffer and the spelling process. To appear in C. von Euler (Ed.), *Brain and Reading.* Mac-Millan/Wenner-Gren International Symposium Series.

Caramazza, A., Miceli, G., Villa, G., & Romani, C. (1987). The role of the Graphemic Buffer in Spelling: Evidence from a case of acquired dysgraphia. *Cognition, 26*, 59–85.

Ellis, A. W. (1982). Spelling and writing (and reading and speaking). In A. W. Ellis (Ed.), *Normality and pathology in cognitive functions.* London: Academic Press.

Grodzinsky, Y. (1986). Language deficits and the theory of syntax. *Brain and Language, 27*, 135–159.

Hillis, A., & Caramazza, A. (1988). The effects of attentional deficits on reading and spelling. Unpublished manuscript.

Hillis, A., & Caramazza, A. (in press). The Graphemic Buffer and mechanisms of unilateral spatial neglect. *Brain and Language.*

Miceli, G., Silveri, M. C., & Caramazza, A. (1985). Cognitive analysis of a case of pure dysgraphia. *Brain and Language, 25*, 187–212.

Mitchum, C. C., & Berndt, R. S. (in press). Aphasia Rehabilitation: an approach to diagnosis and treatment of disorders of lanuage production. In M. G. Eisenberg (Ed.), *Advances in clinical rehabilitation, II.* NY: Springer Publishing Company.

Newcombe, F., & Marshall, J. C. (1980). Transcoding and lexical stabilization in deep dyslexia. In M. Coltheart, K. E. Patterson, & J. C. Marshall (Eds.), *Deep dyslexia.* London: Routledge & Kegan Paul.

Wing, A. M., & Baddeley, A. D. (1980). Spelling errors in handwriting: a corpus and a distributional analysis. In U. Frith (Ed.), *Cognitive processes in spelling.* London: Academic Press.

Author Index

A

Adam, J., 370, *373*
Adams, G.F., 289, *315*
Ahrensberg, R.M., 291, *315*
Alajouanine, T., 21, *34*
Albert, M., 31, *36*, 67, *103*, 108, 116, *151*, *157*, 222, 245
Allport, D.A., 41, *61*, 76, 79, *99*, 117, *150*
Anderson, J.A., 171, *174*
Anderson, J.R., 109, *150*
Anderson, T.P., 21, *34*
Andreewsky, E., 183, 185, *204*, 236, *245*, 250, *286*
Annett, J., 141, *150*
Antos, S.J., 321, *351*
Arenberg, D., 130, *155*
Atkinson, R.C., 107–108, *150*

B

Babul, B., *352*
Bachy, N., 6, 8, 45
Baddeley, A., 11, *13*, 108, 113, 117–120, 124–125, 130, 132, 141, 143–144, 147, 148, 150, *156–158*, 387, *398*
Badecker, W., 389, *398*
Bailey, S., 19, 31, *34*
Bainton, D., 5, *14*, 23, *35*
Barber, J., 337–338, *350*

Barlow, D.H., 148, *153*
Barnard, P., 40, *61*
Barrera, M., Jr., 130, 136, *152*
Barrett, J., 123–124, *152*
Barry, C., 118, *155*
Basso, A., 5, 18–21, 23, 32, *34*, 108, *151*, *175*, *204*, 390
Bastard, V., 53, *64*, 95, *104*
Baum, S.R., 341, *348*
Bayles, K.A., 117, *151*
Beaumont, J.G., 12, *14*
Beauvois, M.F., 6, 9, *14*, 25, 30, *34*, 51, *61*, 71, 74–75, 97, *99–100*, 117, *151*, 160, *173*, 176, 181, 186, 189, 200, *204*, 220, *245*, 282, *286*
Becker, J., 116, *154*
Beekman, L., 340, *351*
Behrman, M., 51, *61*, 97, *100*
Behrmann, M., 371, *373*
Beissel, F.G., 291, *314*
Ben-Yishay, Y., 8, *14*, 291, 301, 310–311, *314*
Benenson, M., 5, *15*, 22, *36*
Benson, D.F., 211, *245*
Bermudez, A., 75, *103*
Berndt, R.S., 77–78, *101*, 164, *173*, 395, *398*
Berry, W.R., 346, *348*
Besner, D., 162, *173*

400 AUTHOR INDEX

Beukelman, D.R., 330, *348*
Bielauska, L., *315*
Binder, L.M., 126, *151*
Binks, M.G., 132, 141, 145, *152*
Bishop, D.V.M., 47, *61*, 229, *245*
Bisiacchi, P., 340, *352*
Bisiach, E., 298, *314*
Bjork, R.Z., 143, *154*
Blumstein, S.E., 78–79, *100, 102*
Boies, S.W., 8, *15*
Boller, F., 324, 338, *351*
Bolton, L.S., 142, *151*
Boureston, N., 21, *34*
Bower, G.H., 109, 110, 142, *150, 151*
Bowers, D., 321, *350*
Bracy, O.L., 356, 363, 365, *373*
Branle, P., 127, *151*
Brewer, W.S., 110, *151*
Briards, D.J., 249, *286*
Brill, G., 322, *350*
Britton, P., 134, *155*
Brockway, J., 296, *315*
Brody, B., 117, *151*
Brookshire, R., 25, *34*, 138, *151*, 331, *348*
Brouwers, P., 117, *154*
Brown, J., 76, *101*, 211, *245*
Brown, J.W., 66, *100*
Brownell, H., 87, *100*, 322, 326, *348, 349*
Bruce, C., 51, 52, *61*
Brunner, R.J., 20–21, *34*
Bruyer, R., 148, *151*
Bub, D., 84, *100*, 162, *173*, 176, 181, 200, *204*, 214, 227, *245*
Buenning, W., 131, 137, *152*
Buffery, A., 32, *34*, 96, *100*
Buongiorno, G.C., 182, 200, 202, *204*
Burton, A., 32, *34*, 96, *100*
Buschke, H., 147, *151*
Buss, L., 296, *315*
Butters, N., 112, 116–117, 147, *151, 154, 156*
Butterworth, B., 76, 79, 81, *100*
Buttler, J., 5, *15*, 22, *36*
Byng, S., 6, 8, *14*, 46–49, 57, 59–60, *62*, 160, *173*, 229, *245*, 393, *398*
Byrne, R.W., 135, *156*

C

Caltagirone, C., 181, *204, 205, 314*
Campbell, D.C., 290–291, 311, *314*

Cancelliere, A., 162, *173*
Canter, G.J., 66, 87, *104*, 338, *353*
Capitani, E., 18, 20–21, 23, 32, *34*, 298, *314*
Caplan, D., 317, *348*
Caplan, L.R., 290–291, 311, *315*, 316
Caramazza, A., 3, *14*, 27, *34*, 68, 77–78, 84, *100–103*, 164, *174*, 249–250, 285, *287*, 318, *348*, 387–390, *398*
Carbonari, J.P., 291, *315*
Carlomagno, S., 6, 8, 183, 200, 202, *204*
Carlsen, R.M., 291, *315*
Castaigne, P., 21, *34*
Cermak, L.S., 112–117, 125–126, 132, *151, 152*
Chan, J.L., 321, *350*
Chapey, R., 24, *34*, 328, *348*
Chase, W.G., 364, *373*
Chassin, G., 53, *64*, 95, *104*
Christinaz, D., 12, *14*, 89, *100*
Cicciarelli, A.W., 18, *35*
Cicone, M., 87, *100*, 321–322, 324, *348, 349*
Clark, E., 19, *34*
Clark, H.H., 320, 322, *348*
Coates, R., 20, *36*
Cockburn, J., 120, 148, *158*
Code, C., 32, *34*, 96–97, *100*, 342, *349*
Cohen, G., 333, *349*
Cohen, N.J., 114, *152*
Cohen, R., 93, *100*, 340, *349*
Colby, K.M., 12, *14*, 89, *100*
Collins, A.M., 340, *349*
Collins, D., 296, 312, *316*
Collins, M., 23, *35*
Colombo, A., 182, 200, 202, *204*
Coltheart, M., 4, 6, 8, 9, 12, *14, 15*, 40, 46–49, 56–60, *62*, 70, 72, 83, 88, *99, 100–103*, 159–163, 166, 170, *173–174*, 181, 183, 185, *204, 214* 221, *245*, 249, *286*, 393, *398*
Coslett, H.B., 321, *350*
Cottam, G., 291, *314*
Cox, C., 117, *154*
Coyette, F., 6, *314*
Craik, F.I.N., 108, 114, 127, 133, *152*
Craine, J.F., 359, *373*
Cranco, R., 289, *315*
Crosson, B., 131, 137, *152*
Crovitz, H.F., 118, 126–127, 133, *152, 156*
Cubelli, R., 23, *35*

AUTHOR INDEX 401

Culton, G.L., 54, *62*
Cutting, J., 126, *152*
Czopf, G., 29, *35*

D

D'Erme, P., 302, 306, *314*
Dabul, B., 346, *352*
Damasio, A.R., 115, *152*
Damasio, H., 115, *152*
Danaher, G.G., 124, *154*
Danforth, L.C., 339, *349*
Daniloff, J.K., 341, *348*
Daniloff, R., 341, *348*
Dardarananda, R., 321, *349*
Darley, F.L., 92, *103*, 340, 351, *352*
Davelaar, E., 162, *173*
David, R., 5, *14*, 19, 22, *35*
Davies, A.D., 132, 141, 145, *152*
Davies, K.R., *36*
Davis, G.A., 9, 11, 45, *62*, 98, *100*, 214,
    245, 317, 327–332, 334, 341–343,
    345–346, *349*, *353*
de Partz, M.P., 6, 8, *14*, 45, 46, *62*, 181,
    202, *204*, *246*
De Renzi, E., 20, *35*, 117, *152*, 182, *204*,
    327, 339, *349*
Delis, D.C., 328, *349*
Deloche, G., 6, 8, 12, *15*, 53, *64*, 95, *104*,
    142, *157*, 178, 183, 185, 203, *204*,
    205, 236, *245*, 249–250, 256, 258,
    284, *286*, *287*, 291, *314*, 337, 339,
    349, 352, 363, *374*
Denes, G.F., 289, *314*, 340, *352*
Derouesne, J., 6, 9, *14*, 25, 30, *34*, 51, *61*,
    74–75, 97, *99*, 160, *173*, 176, 181,
    186, 189, 200, *204*, 220, *245*, 282,
    286
Desi, M., 183, 185, *204*, 236, *245*
Diamond, R., 144, *152*
Diller, L., 289, 291, 293–295, 301, 303,
    310–311, *314*, *315*, 363, 366, *373*
Drummond, S.S., 92, *101*
Dubois-Charlier, 211, *245*
Ducarne, B., 2, *14*, 21, *34*, 267, *286*
Duchan, J., 322, *351*
Duncan, G.W., *36*
Dustman, R.E., 356, 363, *373*

E

Ebbinghaus, H., 106, *152*

Ehrlichman, H., 123–124, *152*
Eisenson, J., 21, *35*
Ellis, A.W., 41, *62*, 76, 80, *101*, 176, 179,
    204, 214, *245*, *246*, 387, *398*
Enderby, P., 5, *14*, 23, *35*
Engel, D., 93, *100*
Ericsson, K.A., 364, *373*
Escourolle, R., 21, *34*
Esibil, N., 289, *315*
Ezrachi, O., 289, 295, *315*

F

Faglioni, P., 20, 23, *34*, *35*, 182, *204*
Falcon, S., 364, *373*
Fedio, P., 117, *154*, *156*
Fellon-Kerueger, M., *373*
Ferrand, I., 6, 8
Feyereisen, P., 77, *101*
Filby, N., 319, 332, *351*
Finger, S., 310, *314*
Finkelstein, S., *36*
Fisher, R.P., 114, *152*
Fitch-West, J., 95–96, *101*, 338, *349*
Flamm, L., 324, *349*
Flowers, C.R., 339, *349*
Fodor, J.A., 41, *62*
Foldi, N., 321–322, *349*
Fowler, R., 370, *373*
Francis, W.N., 168, *174*
Frankel, D., 296, *315*
Franklin, S., 33, *35*, 42, 46, 52–55, 57–
    59, *62*, *63*, 90, 93–94, 97, *101*
Freedman-Stern, R., 138, *157*
Friedrich, F.J., 311, *315*
Fukusako, Y., 81–82, *102*
Funkestein, H.H., *36*
Funnel, E., 160, 163, *173*, 232, *246*
Furst, C., 120, *152*
Fuson, K.C., 249, *286*

G

Gaddes, W.H., 364, *373*
Gainotti, G., 182, *205* 289, 302, 306,
    314, 324, *349*
Gallistel, C.R., 247, *286*
Gandour, J., 321, *349*
Gardner, H., 50, *62*, 77, 87, *100–101*,
    142, 222, *245*, 321–322, 324, 326,
    348, *349*, *352*, *353*
Garnham, A., 318, *350*

402 AUTHOR INDEX

Gasparrini, B., 124, 129, *152*
Gelman, R., 249, *286*
Gerrig, R.J., 320, *348*
Gerstman, L.J., 289, 291, 295, 301, 310–311, *314, 315,* 341, *352*
Geschwind, N., 65, *101*
Gheorghita, N., 339, *350*
Gianutsos, J., 133, *152*
Gianutsos, R., 133–134, 137, *152,* 363, *373*
Gildea, P., 320, *350*
Glang, A.E., 363, *373*
Glasgow, R.E., 130, 136, *152*
Glisky, E.L., 12, *14,* 144–145, *152, 153, 156*
Gloning, K., 22, *35*
Glucksberg, S., 320, *350*
Golden, A.M., 24, *35*
Goldfarb, R., 25, *35*
Goldmeier, E., 131, *154*
Goldstein, G., 335, *350*
Goodenough, D.R., 323, *353*
Goodglass, H., 44, *62,* 69, 90, *103,* 117, *151,* 338, *350*
Goodkin, R., 290, 301, 310–311, *314*
Gordon, W., 289, 291, 295, 301, 310–311, *314, 315,* 366, *373*
Gouvier, W.D., 291, *314*
Graf, P., 114, 144, *153*
Grafman, J., 127, 136, *153,* 336, *350*
Graham, S., 12, *14,* 89, *100*
Granholm, E., 116, *151*
Graves, R., 338, *350*
Green, G., 98, *101*
Greenberg, F.R., 21, *34*
Grewel, G., 249, *287*
Grice, H., 322, *350*
Grober, E., 76, *101,* 117, *153*
Grodzinsky, Y., 395, *398*
Grossberg, S., 131, *153*
Grossman, J.L., 130, *153*
Gruneberg, M.M., 135, *153*
Gudeman, H.E., 359, *373*
Guinto, F.C., 73, *102*
Guleac, J., 82–83, *102*
Gummow, L., 356, 363, *373*

H

Hadar, U., 67, 80, *101*
Hagen, C., 18, 23, *35*
Hankey, A.I., 23, *36*

Hanson, W.R., 18, *35*
Harlock, W., 20, *36*
Harnish, R., 125, *157*
Harris, J.E., 119, 120, *153,* 364, 371, 372, *373*
Harris, T., 118, 146–147, *150, 153, 156*
Hart, J., 77–78, *101,* 370, *373*
Hart, T., 291, *315*
Harvey, M.T., 126–127, *152*
Hasher, L., 111, *153*
Hatfield, F.M., 6, *14,* 25, 30, *35,* 50, *62,* 175–179, 181–182, 189, 200–203, *204,* 232–233, *246,* 337–338, *350*
Hausman, C.P., 130, *155*
Haviland, S.E., 322, *348*
Head, H., 58, *62*
Hecaen, H., 211, *246*
Heeschen, C., 336, *350*
Heilman, K.M., 190, 201, *205,* 297, *315,* 321, 324–325, 337, *350*
Heiss, W.D., 22, *35*
Helm, N., 31, *36,* 67, *101*
Helmick, J.W., 55, *62*
Henderson, L., 68, *101,* 233, *246*
Henschen, S.E., 249, *287*
Henson, D.L., 291, *315*
Hermand, N., 53, *64,* 95, *104*
Hersen, M., 148, *153*
Hien, M., 296, 312, *316*
Hier, D.B., 214, 226, *246,* 290, 311, *315*
Hillis, A., 387–389, *398*
Hilton, C.R., 23, *36*
Hinton, G.E., 171–*173, 174*
Hirsbrunner, T., 291, *314*
Hirst, W., 117, *153,* 322, *350*
Hitch, G.J., 108, *150*
Hodges, G., 289, 295, *315*
Hogenraad, R., *246*
Holland, A., 25, *35,* 327–328, 339, *349, 350*
Holmes, J.M., 55, *63*
Honeygosky, R., 92, *101*
Horn, L.C., 116, *155*
Horn, R.W., 126–127, *152*
Howard, D., 4, 6, 8, 9, 33, *35,* 42, 46, 50–55, 57–59, *61–63,* 76–77, 80, 90, 92–94, 97–*101,* 337–338, *350*
Howes, J.L., 126, 130, *153,* 222, *245*
Huber, W., 55, *64*
Huff, F.J., 73, *102*
Hughes, C.P., 321, *350*
Hughes, D.L., 337, *350*

AUTHOR INDEX 403

Huijbers, P., 80, *102*
Hulicka, I.M., 130, *153*
Humphreys, G.W., 73, *101*, 297–298, 310–311, *315*
Huppert, F.A., 113, *153*
Hurford, J.R., 249, *287*
Hurwitz, L.J., 289, *315*

I

Iavarone, A., 182, 200, 202, *204*
Itoh, M., 81–82, *102*

J

Jackendoff, R.S., 47, *63*
Jaffe, J., 323, *350*
Jaffe, P.G., 132, 134, *153*
Jaros, L.A., *373*
Jefferson, G., 322, *352*
Jenkins, J., 24–25, *36*, 53, 56, *64*, 94, *103*
Jimenez-Pabon, E., 24–25, *36*, 53, 56, *64*, 94, *103*
Joanette, Y., 230, *247*
Job, R., *173*, 183, *204*
John, E.R., 79, 88, *101*
Johnson, M.G., 23–24, *35*
Johnston, J.C., 170, *174*
Jonasson, J.T., *173*
Jones, A.L., 5, *14*, 23, *36*, 60, *63*
Jones, C., 67, 80, *101*, 337–338, *350*
Jones, E.V., 47–49, 60, *63*
Jones, G., 370, *373*
Jones, M.K., 123, *153*
Jones-Gotman, M., 123–124, *153*
Jusczyk, P., 4, *15*

K

Kahn, R.L., 290, *316*
Kaplan, E., 44, *62*
Kapur, N., 125, *153*
Karpf, C., 12, *14*, 89, *100*
Katz, A.N., 132, 134, *153*
Katz, R., 356, 363, *373*
Katz, R.C., 12, *14*
Kay, J., 80, 99, *101*, 183, 185, *205*
Kay, M.C., 73, *102*
Kazdin, A.E., 331, 350
Kearns, K.P., 55–56, *63*
Keith, R.L., 95, *102*
Kellar, L., 76, *101*

Kelter, S., 93, *100*, 340, *349*
Kemp, R., 96, *100*
Kempen, G., 80, *102*
Kenin, M., 18, *35*
Kertesz, A., 18–21, *36*, 54, *63*, 84, 87, *100*, *102*, 162, *173*, 176, 181, 200, *204*, 214, 227, *245*
Kewman, D.G., 291, *315*
Kieras, D.E., 321, *350*
Kikel, S., 124, *154*
Kim, Y., 324, 338, *351*
Kimbarow, M.L., 345, *350*
Kinsbourne, M., 114, *158*
Kintsch, W., 109, 110, 139, *153*, 321, *350*
Kirsch, N.L., *373*
Koenigsknecht, R.A., 53, *64*, 95, *104*
Kohn, S.E., 69, 82, *102*
Kopelman, M.D., 113, *154*
Kornhuber, H.H., 20–21, *34*
Koskas, E., 222, *246*
Kovner, R., 131, *153*
Kreindler, A., 339, *350*
Kremin, H., 222, 236, *246*
Krueger, K.M., 331, *348*
Kugera, H., 168, *174*
Kudo, T., 337, *351*
Kuhlenbeck, H., 86, *102*
Kurleycheck, R.T., 363, *373*

L

Laiacona, M., 20, *34*
Lakine, P., 289, 295, *315*
Lambert, J.L., 144, 148, *156*
Landauer, T.K., 143, *154*
Landis, T., 74, 88, *102*, *103*, 338, *350*
Lapointe, L.L., 9, *14*, 59, *63*, 197, 201, *205*, 331, *351*
Larrabee, G.J., 73, *102*
Larsen, S., 291, *315*
Laudanna, A., 68, *100*
Lawson, I.R., 291–292, 294, *315*
Lecoq, P., 110, 115, *156*
Lecours, A.R., 225, 230, *246*
Leiman, B., 119, *154*
Lendrem, W., 5, *14*, 23, 36, 60, *64*
Lepoivre, H., 148, *151*
Lesser, R., 8, 65, 68, 73, *99*, *101–102*, 183, 185, *205*, 339, *351*
Levin, H.S., 73, *102*
Levine, S.P., *373*
Levita, E., 54, *64*, 329, *352*

404 AUTHOR INDEX

Lewinsohn, P.M., 124, 130, 136, *152*
Lewis, J., *314, 348*
Lewis, K., 60, *64*
Lhermitte, F., 21, *34*, 117, *151*, 225, 230, 246
Lichtheim, L., 43, *63*
Lieberman, A., 289, 295, *315*
Lincoln, N.B., 5, *14*, 23, *36*, 60, *63*
Lindsay, P.H., 141, *154*
Linebarger, M.C., 47, *63*
Ling, P.K., 324, *349*
Lis, A., 289, *314*
List, G., 93, *100*
Loatsch, L., 356, *373*
Lockhart, R.S., 108, 127, *152*
Loftus, E.F., 340, *349*
Lohmann, L., 339, *351*
Lomas, J., 18, *36*
Longman, D.J.A., 143, *150*
Longuet-Higgins, H.C., 249–250, *287*
Lorenze, E.J., 289, *315*
Loverso, F., 342, *352*
Lubinski, R., 322, 346, *351*
Lucas, D., 85, 86, *103*
Lucchese, D., 340, *352*
Lucy, P., 320, *348*
Luria, A.R., 1, 8, *14*, 18, 22, 30, *36*, 50, 54, *63*, 121, *154*, 175, 177–179, 200, *205*, 282, *287*
Luterman, D., 346, *351*
Luzzatti, C., 20, *34*, 298, *314*
Lynch, W.J., 356, 363, *374*

M

Macaluso-Haynes, S., 138, *157*
MacCarthy, R., *102*
Maly, J., 95, *102*
Mammucari, A., 21, *36*
Mandler, G., 111, 114, 144, *153, 154*
Marcel, T., 183, 185, 189, *205*, 217, 233, 236, *246, 247*
Margolin, D.I., 84, *102*, 176, 179, *204*
Marin, O.S.M., 47, *64*, 217, *247*
Markowitsch, H.J., 112, *154*
Marquardsen, J., 289, *315*
Marshall, J.C., 3–4, *15*, 46, 55, *62, 63*, 70, 83, 91, *100, 102–103*, 134, *154*, 161, *174*, 181, 183, *204–205*, 211, 214, 234, 236, 245, *246*, 250, 286, 387, *398*

Marshall, R.C., *14*, 21, 23, *36*
Martin, A., 117, *154*
Martin, D.C., 116, *155*
Martin, R.C., 68, *102*
Martino, A.A., 339, *351*
Martone, M., 116, 151, *154*
Masterson, J., 160, *173*, 183, *204*
Masullo, C., 182, *204, 205*
Mate-Kole, C., 67, 80, *101*
Mattis, S., 131, *153*
Mayes, A.R., 112–115, 117, *154*
Mazaux, J.M., 256, *287*
McAndrews, M.P., 85, *103*
McCabe, P., 19, 21, *36*, 54, *63*
McCarthy, R., 71, 77–78, *104*, 117, *157*, 162, *174*, 185, *205*
McCarty, D.L., 122, *154*
McClelland, J.L., 41, *63*, 170–172, *174*
McCloskey, M., 249–250, 285, *287*
McGlone, J., 22, *36*
McGuirk, E., 5, *14*, 23, *36*, 60, *63*
McLaughlin, P., 76, *100*
McLeod, P., 60, *64*
McReynolds, L.V., 55–56, *63*
Meacham, J.A., 119, *154*
Mehler, J., 4, *15*
Meikle, M., 5, *15*, 22, *36*
Mejding, J., 291, *315*
Messerli, P., 19, *36*
Mesulam, M.M., 297, *315*
Metter, E.J., 329, 333, *351*
Meudell, P.R., 112–115, *154*
Miceli, G., 68, 78, *100*, 164, *174*, 182, *204, 205, 314*, 387–389, *398*
Michel, D., 326, *348*
Michelow, D., 87, *100*, 322, *349*
Milberg, W., 78–79, *100, 102*
Miliotis, P., 116, *151*
Miller, E., 89, *102*, 134, 145, *154, 155*, 363–364, *374*
Miller, P., 356, 363, *373*
Milner, B., 108, 123, *153, 154*
Milton, S.B., 145–146, *155*
Mitchell, J.R.A., 5, *14*, 23, *36*, 60, *63*
Mitchum, C.C., 395, *398*
Moerman, C., 82–83, *102*
Moffat, N., 131, 140–141, *155, 158*, 364, *374*
Monteleone, D., 302, 306, *314*
Moore, W.H., 29, *36*
Moraschini, S., 21, *34*

AUTHOR INDEX

Moreines, J., 117, *151*
Morgan, J.L., 320, *351*
Morris, P.E., 119, 122, 139, *155*
Morris, R., 134, *155*
Morrow, L., 324, 338, *351*
Morton, J., 4, 33, *35*, *36*, 42, 50, 52–55, 57–59, *62*, *63*, 70–72, 83, 90–91, 93–94, 97, *101*, *103*, 115–116, 142, *155*, 170, *174*, 179, *205*, 212, 229, *246* 337–338, *350*
Moscovitch, M., 85, *103*, *155*
Moses, J.A., Jr., 322, *349*
Moulard, G., 12, *15*, 178, 203, *205*, 363, *374*
Mohr, J.P., 20, *36*, 214, 226, *246*
Mondlock, J., 290–291, 311, *315*
Monks, J., 135, *153*
Monoi, H., 81–82, *102*
Monroe, P., 20, *37*
Muley, G.P., *36*
Mulhall, D., 5, *15*, 22, *36*
Muller, D.J., 342, 349
Mulley, G.P., 5, *14*, 23, *36*, 60, *63*
Myers, P.S., 322, 324, 338, *351*

N

Nagode, J., 116, *151*
Nagy, V.T., 356, 363, *373*
Naydin, V.L., 30, *36*, 177–179, 200, *205*
Neary, D., 114, *154*
Nebes, R.D., 116, *155*
Nespoulous, J.L., 230, *247*
Neumann, O., 86, *103*
Newcombe, F., 55, *63*, 70, 73, *103*, 161, *174*, 183, *205*, 211, 234, 236, *246*, 387, *398*
Newhoff, M., 346, *353*
Nichelli, P., 117, *152*
Nicholas, M., 67, 10, 138, *151*, 331, *348*
Niliotis, P., *151*
Nolan, K.A., 84, *103*
Noll, J.D., 29, *36*
Norman, D.A., 141, *154*
North, A.J., 138, *157*

O

Obler, L.K., 67, *103*
Ogrezeanou, V., 94, *103*
Olson, D.R., 319, 332, *351*

Olson, P.L., 291, *315*
Orchard-Lisle, V., 33, *35*, 42, 52–55, 57–59, *62*, *63*, 77, 80, 90, 92–94, 97, *101*
Orgogozzo, J., 256, *287*
Orianne, E., *246*
Ortony, A., 320, *351*
Oxbury, J.M., 290–291, 311, *314*

PQ

Paivio, A., 109, *155*
Pajurkova, E.M., 120, *155*
Parisi, D., 67, *103*, 118, *155*, 164, *174*
Parkin, A.J., 112, 114, *155*
Parkinson, R.C., 12, *14*, 89, *100*
Parlato, 6, 8, 182, 200, 202, *204*
Pass, R., 131, *154*
Patten, B.M., 123, *155*
Patterson, K.E., 4, 6, 8, 9, *14*, *15*, 33, *35*, *36*, 42, 46, 50, 52–55, 57–60, *62*, *63*, 70, 80, 90–91, 93–94, 97, *100*, *101*, *103*, 159–161, 163, 170, *174*, 179, 181, *204*, 214, 217–218, 222, *245*, *246*, *247*, 250, *286*
Payne, M., 116, *154*
Pearlstone, Z., 43, *64*
Pease, D.M., 90, *103*
Peelle, L.M., 51, *61*, 97, *100*
Peeters, A., 227, *247*
Pena-Casanova, J., 75, *103*
Pepping, M., 296, *315*
Perani, D., 298, *314*
Perecman, E., 76, *101*
Pessin, M.S., *36*
Peterson, L.R., 133, *155*
Peterson, M.J., 133, *155*
Pettit, J.M., 29, *36*
Philippe, C., 138, *155*
Phillips, D.S., 21, 23, *36*
Piatsetky, E.B., 8, *14*
Pickergill, M.J., 23, *36*
Pickering, A., 113, *154*
Pierce, R.S., 340, *351*
Piercy, M., 113, 115, *153*, *155*
Pillon, B., 142, *157*
Pizzamiglio, L., 21, *36*, 177–178, *205*, 339, *351*
Podraza, B.L., 92, *103*, 340, *351*
Poeck, K., 55, *64*, 73, 75, *103*
Porch, B.E., 327, 351, *352*
Porter, J.L., 346, *352*

AUTHOR INDEX

Posner, M.I., 8, *15*, 311, *315*
Potter, H., 87, *100*
Powell, G., 19, *34*
Powell, G.E., 141, *155*
Powelson, 326, *348*
Power, R.J.D., 249–250, *287*
Prescott, T.E., 339, *351*
Pring, T.R., 55, *63*
Prins, R.S., 18, *36*
Prior, M., 160, *173*
Purell, C., 33, *36*, 52, *63*, 91, *103*
Pwelson, J., *348*
Quatember, R., 22, *35*

R

Rabin, P., *157*
Rafal, R.D., 311, *315*
Rao, S.M., *315*
Ratcliffe,G., 70, 73, *103*
Rattock, J., 8, *14*
Razzano, C., 21, *36*, 339, *351*
Reason, J.T., 10, *15*, 85–86, *103*, 111, 119, *155*
Rectem, D., 148, *151*
Redmond, K.J., 331, 348
Regard, M., 74, 88, *102*, *103*
Rentschler, G.J., 92, *101*
Reynolds, R.E., 321, *351*
Rich, S.A., 130, 142–144, *155*
Richards, J., 249, *286*
Richardson, J.T.E., 118, *155*
Riddoch, M.J., 73, *101*, 160, *173*, 297–298, 311, *315*
Roberts, M., 177–178, *205*
Robertson-Tchabo, E.A., 130, *155*
Rodriguez, R., 19, *36*
Roediger, III, H.L., 122, *156*
Roeltgen, D.P., 190, 201, *205*
Roig-Rovira, T., 75, *103*
Rosenbek, J.C., 346, *352*
Rosenfeld, H.M., 323, *352*
Ross, E.D., 325, *352*
Rousselle, M., 12, *15*, 178, 203, *205*, 363, *374*
Rozin, P., 144, *152*
Rumelhart, D.E., 41, *63*, 110, *156*, 171–172, *174*
Rushakoff, G.E., 363, 371, *374*

S

Sacks, H., 322, *352*

Saerens, J., 82–83, *102*
Saffran, E.M., 39, 47, *63*, *64*, 217, *247*
Saillant, B., 71, 74, *100*
Samuels, I., 117, *151*, *156*
Sanders, S.B., 346, *348*
Sands, E., 21, *36*, 60, *64*
Sarno, M.T., 21, *36*, 44, 54, 60, *64*, 327, 329, *352*
Sartori, G., *173*, 183, *204*
Sasanuma, S., 81–82, *102*, 176, *205*
Satz, P., 124, 129, *152*
Sax, D.S., 116, *151*, *154*
Schacter, D.L., 12, *14*, 85, *103*, 114, 118, 130, 142–145, *152*, *153*, *156*
Schallert, D.L., 321, *351*
Schegloff, E., 322, *352*
Schlanger, B.B., 340, *352*
Schlanger, P., 341, *352*
Schneider, W., 111, *156*
Scholes, R.J., 337, *350*
Schreiber, V., 126, *151*
Schrier, R., 78, *100*
Schuell, H., 2, 5, *15*, 24–25, *36*, 52–53, 56, *64*, 94, *103*, 333–334, *352*
Schwartz, H.D., 324–325, *350*
Schwartz, M.F., 47, *63*, *64*
Searle, J.R., 320, *352*
Seemueller, E., 20–21, *34*
Semenza, C., 289, *314*, 340, *352*
Semenza, C., *352*
Sena, D.A., 356, *374*
Seron, X., 2, 6, 8, 9, 12, *15*, 53, *64*, 65, 77, 88–89, 95, *103–104*, 106, 121, 136, 142, 144, 148–149, *151*, *156*, *157*, 178, 200–201, 203, *205*, 249–250, 256, 258, 284, *286*, *287*, 291–292, 294, 303, *314*, *315*, 337, 339, 349, 352, 363, *374*
Serrat, A., 74, *102*
Shallice, T., 7, *15*, 41, 43, 52, 60, *64*, 76, 79, *104*, 108, 117, *156*, *157*, 162, *174*, 176, 181, 183, 185, 200, *205*, 247
Shankweiler, D., 21, *36*
Sheehan, M., 370, *373*
Sheer, D.E., 291, *315*
Shewell, C., 30, *35*, 159, 163, *174*
Shiffrin, R.M., 107–108, 111, *150*, *156*
Shore, D.L., 124, 130, *156*
Signoret, J.L., 142, *157*
Silveri, M.C., 68, 78, *100*, *102*, 302, 306, *314*, 387–388, *398*
Silverman, J., 324, *349*
Silverman, M., 60, *64*

AUTHOR INDEX 407

Sivak, M., 291, *315*
Skilbeck, C., 371, *374*
Skilbeck, C.E., 19, *35*
Skinner, B.F., 144, *156*
Slater, P.C., 114, *156*
Snape, W., 118, *155*
Snow, C.E., 18, *36*
Sobel, L., 20, *37*
Sonderman, J., 25, *35*, 339, *350*
Sparks, R., 31, *36*
Speedie, L., 321, *350*
Spinnler, H., 108, *151*
Squire, L.R., 114, 144, *152, 153, 158*
Stachowiak, F.J., 55, *64*
Stampp, M.S., 130, 142–144, *156*
Stanton, K., 296, *315*
Stemberger, J.P., 68, 72, *104*
Stern, G., 5, *15*, 22, *36*
Stern, L.D., 112, *156*
Sterste, A., 116, *151*
Stiassny, D., 117, *152*
Stoppa, E., 289, *314*
Studdert-Kennedy, M., 318, *352*
Su, M.S., 321, *350*
Subirana, A., 22, *36*
Suger, G., 20–21, *34*
Sunderland, A., 118, 147, *150, 156*, 364, *373*
Swisher, L.P., 18, *35*
Sykes, R.N., 135, *153*

TU

Taborelli, A., 175, *204*
Tanner, D.C., 346, *352*
Thomson, D.M., 109, 132, *156*
Thorndyke, P.W., 322, *352*
Tiberghien, G., 106, 110, 115, 141, *156*
Tissot, R., 19, *36*, 291–292, 294, 303, *315*
Tolosa-Sarno, E., 75, *103*
Tomlinson, 211, *245*
Tompkins, C.A., 21, 23, *36*
Tonkovich, J.D., 342, *352*
Trappl, R., 22, *35*
Trexler, L., 363, *374*
Treyens, J.C., 110, *151*
Trupe, E.H., 322, *352*
Tsvetkova, L.S., 30, *36*, 177–179, 200, *205*
Tulving, E., 12, *14*, 43, *64*, 109–110, 122, 132, 144, *152–153*
Tupper, A.M., 5, *15*, 22, *36*
Tzortzis, C., 108, *157*

Uhly, B., 117, *152*
Ulatowska, H.K., 138, *157*

V

Valdois, S., 230, *247*
Valenstein, E., 297, *315*
Vallar, G., 108, 117, *151, 157*
Van Der Borght, F., 77, *101*
Van Der Kaa, M.A., 8, 9, 11
Van Der Linden, 8, 9, 11, 136, 144, 147–148, *156, 157*
Van Dijck, T.A., 139, *153*, 321, *352*
Van Eeckout, Ph., 142, *157*
Van Hoesen, G.W., 115, *152*
Vanderheiden, G., 371, *373*
Vignolo, L.A., 21, 23, *34*, 60, *64*, 175, *204*, 327, 339, *349*
Vikis-Freiberg, V., 223, *247*
Villa, G., 78, *102*, 387, 388, 398
Vinarskaya, E.N., 30, *36*, 177–179, 200, *205*
Voinescu, I., 94, *103*, 339, *350*
Vrtunski, P.B., 324, 338, *351*

W

Wagenaar, E., 18, *36*
Waggeners, S., 296, *315*
Walker, J.A., 311, *315*
Wallace, G.L., 87, *104*
Waller, M.R., 340, *349*
Wallesch, C.W., 20–21, *34*
Wapner, W., 87, *100*, 322, 324, *348, 349, 352*
Warrington, E.K., 71, 75, 77–78, *102, 104*, 108, 113–114, 117, 124–125, 132, 144, *150, 156, 157*, 162, *174*, 183, 185, *205, 247, 249*, 287
Watkins, M.J., 133, *152*
Watson, R.T., 324–325, *350*
Watter, K.P., 118, *150*
Watts, M.T., 91, *102*
Way, G., 126, *157*
Weber, R.J., 125, *157*
Webster, E.J., 346, *353*
Webster, J.S., 291, *314*
Wechsler, E., 5, *15*, 22, *36*
Weddel, R., 175, 177–178, 189, 202, *204*
Weidner, W.E., 29, *36*
Weigl, E., 53, *64*, 92, *104*
Weinberg, J., 289, 291, 294–295, 301, 303, 310–311, *314, 315*

AUTHOR INDEX

Weiner, S.L., 323, *353*
Weisbroth, S., 289, *315*
Weiskrantz, L., 113–114, 132, 144, *157,
158*
Weiss-Doyel, A., 138, *157*
Weitzner-Lin, B., 323, *351*
Wendling, I., 291, *314*
Weniger, D., 55, *64*
Wepman, J., 2, 5, *15*, 21, 24, *37*, 52, 94,
104, 353
Wetzel, C.D., 114, *156, 158*
Wheatley, J., 134, *155*
Wickens, D.D., 113, *158*
Wiegel-Crump, C.A., 53, *64*, 95, *104*
Wikus, B., 95, *102*
Wilcox, M.J., 45, *62*, 98, *100*, 214, *245*,
317, 328–329, 331, 334, 341, 343,
345–346, *349, 353*
Wilkins, A., 11, *13*, 119–120, 147, *150,
155, 158*
Williams, M., 113, *158*, 338, *353*
Williams, S.E., 66, *104*, 222, *247*
Wilson, B., 118, 120, 130, 135, 137, 141,
146, 148, *150, 158*, 364, *374*

Wilson, P.B., 356, 364, *374*
Wing, A.M., 387, *398*
Winner, E., 321, *353*
Winocur, G., 114, *158*
Wipplinger, M., 55, *62*
Wofford, J.D., 291, *314*
Wolfe, J., 116, *151*
Woll, G., 340, *349*
Won, D., 291, *315*

YZ

Yamadori, A., 222, *245*
Yarnell, P., 20, *37*
Yates, F.A., 121, *158*
Yorkston, K.M., 331, *348*
Young, G.C., 296, 312, *316*
Zacks, R.T., 111, *153*
Zaidel, E., 227, *247*
Zanobio, M.E., 18, 32, *34*, 108, *151*
Zarit, S.H., 290, *316*
Zeiss, R.A., 130, 136, *152*
Zuger, R., 289, *315*
Zurif, E.B., 50, *62*

Subject Index

A

Acalculia, 32, 249–250
Activation and elaboration processes in memory, 111
Agrammatism
treatment of, 47–49
Alexia without agraphia, 74
Amnesia (interpretation of)
encoding deficit, 112–113
retrieval deficit, 114
storage deficit, 113
Amnesic syndrome deficits, 112
in Alzheimer's disease, 116–117
in aphasia, 117–118, 128–129
in closed head injury, 118
in Hungtington's disease, 116
in Korsakoff syndrome, 115, 116
with cortical lesion, 117
Anatomical reorganization, 29–30
Anomia
evaluation of, 222–231
modality specific, 65
optic, 73, 75
treatment of, 65–104, 238–242
Aphasia
optic, 74
Aphasic syndromes, 18–19, 44
Attentional disorders, 8
reeducation of, with microcomputers, 363

Automatic vs. controlled process
in memory encoding, 111
in visual orientation, 311–313
Automatic-volontary dissociation
in naming, 84–87

BC

Behavior therapy, 2, 8, 25
Bilateral tactile anomia, 9
Blissymbolics, 31
Category specific naming impairment, 77–79
Communication abilities in daily-living, 327
Context in language, 319–323
external context, 338–339
extralinguistic context, 320
internal context, 338–339
linguistic context, 322
paralinguistic context, 321
Conversation, 321–323, 341–347

D

Deblocking effect, 92
Depth of encoding (memory), 108–109
Distributed representation model (in reading), 170–173
Divergent cognitive style in language, 327
Dual coding theory, 107–108, 109

410 SUBJECT INDEX

Dysgraphia
  deep, 50–51
  lexical, 181
  phonological, 181
  surface, 181
Dyslexia (alexia)
  agnosic, 74
  deep, 4, 46–47, 51, 215–222
  phonological, 4
  surface, 4, 45–46, 163–166

EF

Ecological validity of therapy, 10–11
Encoding specificity, 109, 130
Evaluation of numerical abilities, 253–256
Facilitation therapies, 7, 8, 52–54, 90
Functional Communication Profile (FCP), 327

GH

Gesture cuing, 92
Hemineglect
  reeducation of, 291–315

IK

Imagery in memory, 109, 113
Information (semantic)
  defective access to, 7, 25, 30, 43–44, 52, 78–79
  loss of, 7, 25, 30, 43–44, 77–78
Intelligence and aphasia, 19
Korsakoff syndrome, 115

L

Language self-monitoring, 81
Localisation of function, 4
Long-term maintenance of treatment effect, 131, 148, 195, 267, 281–282

M

Melodic Intonation Therapy, 31, 95, 142
Memory therapy, 11
Mental external prosthesis in therapy, 89, 120, 146, 308–309, 371–372, 380–381
Microcomputer, 11–13
  assessment with, 12, 370

in reeducation, 355–373
  simulation with, 12
  software package for cognitive rehabilitation, 366–368
  training with, 12
Model of spelling, 380–386

N

Naming
  in conversation, 66–67
  model of, 69–72, 212–214
  phonemic processes in, 67
  semantic processes in, 67
  syntactic processes in, 68
  treatment of, 69–72, 212–214
  written words, 83
Neuropsychological syndromes, 2, 3, 44
Number lexicon, 250–251
Number transcoding
  models of, 249–253
  reeducation of, 258

O

Operativity
  in naming, 77
Organization of long-term memory
  componential model, 109–110
  contextual model, 110, 113, 114
  network model, 110

P

Phonemic cuing, 33, 42, 51–52, 80, 91
Porch Index of Communication Ability (PICA), 327
Pragmatic approaches in aphasia
  assessment, 326–331
  theory, 317–326
  treatment, 333–348
Pre-therapeutic diagnosis, 2–7
Pre-therapeutic evaluation, 41–44, 58–59
Promoting Aphasics Communication Effectiveness Therapy (PACE), 98, 329
Prospective memory, 119–120

R

Reading
  dual route, 159, 211–212

SUBJECT INDEX 411

lexical route, 159, 211–212, 217–222
non-lexical route, 160, 211–212
reeducation of, 231–238
Recovery
etiology, 21
for aphasia, 17–37
influence of age on, 21
in general, 6
in neglect, 289–291
lesion parameters in, 20
pattern of, 18–19
right hemisphere contribution in, 29
theory of, 28–31
Reconstruction therapies, 50–52, 282, 303
Reorganization therapies, 89, 90, 121–140, 182-203, 211–247
Restoration therapies, 45–52, 88–90
Right hemisphere
and emotion, 87
and language, 322, 324–325
and therapy, 95–96
Rivermead Behavioral Test, 148

S

Semantic cuing, 93–94, 96–97
Semantic vs episodic memory, 110, 114
Single-case studies vs group studies, 1, 2, 44, 59
Slips of action, 119
Stimulation therapy, 2, 24–25, 88, 94–95

T

Technical methods of memory reeducation
a method of "vanishing cues," 144–145
face name method, 122, 124
letter cuing, 134, 135, 136
link method, 121–122, 124–125

loci-method, 121–122, 130
melodic-song cuing, 142
peg-method, 121–122, 123, 128
PQRST method, 136–137
reconstruction-of-context method, 141–142
semantic cuing, 132–133
story line cuing, 133, 136
story schema method, 138–140
with microcomputers, 363–364, 371–372
Therapy
efficacy, 5, 9–11, 23, 54–59, 60, 329–331
intensity, 8, 60
rationale of, 23–28, 39–64, 390–395
Tip of the tongue, 81–82, 85–86, 97
Token test, 19–22, 32
Transfer of learning to
daily-life situations, 98, 129–131, 148, 306–307
other modalities, 55–57, 295
other tasks, 55–57, 197, 295
Treatment
hierarchies, 45

VW

Verbal strategies in memory reeducation, 132–140
Visual agnosia
apperceptive, 73
associative, 73
Visual imagery in therapy
naming, 95–96, 121–132, 239
Visuo-gestural disconnection, 75
Working memory, 108
Writing
cognitive approach in rehabilitation of, 181, 189–203
technique of rehabilitation in, 176–182
visuo-kinesthetic method, 189